Elisa Mattiello
Analogy in Word-formation

Trends in Linguistics
Studies and Monographs

Editor
Volker Gast

Editorial Board
Walter Bisang
Jan Terje Faarlund
Hans Henrich Hock
Natalia Levshina
Heiko Narrog
Matthias Schlesewsky
Amir Zeldes
Niina Ning Zhang

Editor responsible for this volume
Volker Gast

Volume 309

Elisa Mattiello

Analogy in Word-formation

A Study of English Neologisms and Occasionalisms

DE GRUYTER
MOUTON

ISBN 978-3-11-063717-5
e-ISBN (PDF) 978-3-11-055141-9
e-ISBN (EPUB) 978-3-11-054973-7
ISSN 1861-4302

Library of Congress Cataloging-in-Publication Data
A CIP catalog record for this book has been applied for at the Library of Congress.

Bibliographic information published by the Deutsche Nationalbibliothek
The Deutsche Nationalbibliothek lists this publication in the Deutsche Nationalbibliografie;
detailed bibliographic data are available on the Internet at http://dnb.dnb.de.

© 2018 Walter de Gruyter GmbH, Berlin/Boston
This volume is text- and page-identical with the hardback published in 2017.
Printing and binding: CPI books GmbH, Leck

♾ Printed on acid-free paper
Printed in Germany

www.degruyter.com

Preface

The goal of this book is to fill a gap in lexical morphology, especially with reference to analogy in English word-formation. Hitherto, many studies have focused their interest on the role played by analogy within English inflectional morphology, chiefly as a means of extension of patterns across paradigms. However, the analogical mechanism also deserves attention and investigation in word-formation, in particular, on account of its relevance to neology in English. It is in the latter realm that this book is meant to provide in-depth qualitative analyses and stimulating quantitative findings.

The book conciliates the generative, rule-based morphological approach with the connectionist analogical approach of computational models. It discusses morphological processes that necessitate an analysis in terms of paradigmatic structure, and which therefore belong to what Bauer, Lieber, and Plag (2013) have termed 'paradigmatic morphology'. These processes, as the three scholars admit, are so numerous in English that they cannot be dismissed as isolated exceptions in a rule-governed system. The book regards instances of such processes as paradigmatic substitutions of the variable part in analogical proportions, but also proves that some instances of analogy additionally conform to rule patterns.

The book gathers the research and results of a NetWordS (European Network on Word Structure) project on analogy in English neologisms. The project proposal was submitted in February 2014 to the European Science Foundation and accepted for a short-visit grant covering a brief stay at the University of Vienna in September of the same year. The grant gave me the opportunity to discuss the topic of my project work with the host institution research leader, Wolfgang Ulrich Dressler, as an eminent scholar in the field of morphology in general, and with other partners and experts in word-formation (especially, Franz Rainer), and in the diachronic evolution of the English language (Nikolaus Ritt). To these scholars I express my deepest gratitude, as well as to the ESF Members of the Steering Committee, whose belief in the value of this project allowed me to fulfil it.

Since my stay in Vienna, Wolfgang Dressler has become my mentor and the person who patiently read the whole manuscript and generously made detailed comments and invaluable remarks on it. During his numerous stays in Viareggio and Pisa, as well as in our exchanges via e-mail, he provided exemplary support and constant feedback on earlier drafts of the book. Learning from his experience and expertise is an honour and an enormous privilege that one cannot but hope to be offered, and I am hugely indebted to him for allowing me to be one of the privileged.

I am also extremely grateful to Marianne Kilani-Schoch and Klaus-Michael Köpcke for their precious comments both on the theoretical part and on the actual examples discussed. Their detailed remarks and bibliographical suggestions have been fundamental in refining an earlier version of my work.

I am also greatly indebted to my 'slang colleagues and friends', especially to Jonathon Green, who explored the whole database and offered me remarks and additional examples from his stupendous dictionary of slang, and to Julie Coleman, who suggested up-to-date sources and extensive archives to search for new English words.

Many other people contributed, to a greater and lesser extent, to the realisation of this book, offering me support, help, advice, and actual material. I warmly thank Belinda Blanche Crawford Camiciottoli, Matej Durco, Karlheinz Mörth, and Vito Pirrelli for their precious assistance on corpus linguistics tools and existing English corpora. I also owe thanks to Antonio Bertacca and Giovanni Iamartino for their feedback as lexicologists and historical linguists, especially at the earliest stages of the work. Moreover, I am immensely thankful to Pier Marco Bertinetto, Mark Aronoff, and Michele Loporcaro for their encouragement and support in the completion of this project.

I also warmly thank the statisticians of the Department of Economics and Management of the University of Pisa, especially Caterina Giusti and Monica Pratesi, for their support in preparing the tests and interpreting the results.

Thanks also go to the native English speakers who participated in the experiment, for their generous gift of help and time, and to one of them in particular, Steven David Smith, for his patient revision of the whole manuscript and suggestions for improvement.

Nor can such a project be undertaken without the resources of libraries and the assistance of their staff, especially the librarians of the ex-Department of English Studies and of the Language Centre of the University of Pisa, Anna Bonechi, Pina Deffenu, and Laura Matteoli, who have always accommodated my requests rapidly and efficiently.

In addition, the topic of this book was presented at several international conferences, whose audiences deserve thanks for their insightful observations and comments.

Finally, this book could not appear without the support and endless encouragement of Marcella Bertuccelli Papi, Paolo Maria Mancarella, Lavinia Merlini Barbaresi, Mauro Tulli, and of many colleagues and friends at the University of Pisa, to whom I wish to express my words of authentic gratitude.

It is in stressful and difficult times that some fruitful work can come out, and this work definitely had its birth in the hardest time of my life. However, my husband taught me strength in the face of adversity, and our daughter taught us how strong our trio could be. I wish to dedicate this book to them – Luca and Matilde – who have accompanied me in this arduous journey, helping me, day by day, not to lose determination and enthusiasm.

Pistoia, November 2015

Contents

1	**Introduction —— 1**	
1.1	An overview of the term 'analogy' in linguistics —— 1	
1.2	Aims of the book and its contribution to word-formation theory —— 4	
1.3	Definition and operationalisation of the concept of analogy —— 12	
1.4	Relevant literature —— 13	
1.5	Organisation of the work —— 16	
2	**New words, neologisms, and nonce words —— 23**	
2.1	Terminological distinction —— 24	
2.2	New words in diachrony —— 26	
2.3	Criteria for new word-formation —— 28	
2.4	The database of new English words and the methodology —— 29	
2.5	Further remarks on the new words in this work —— 33	
2.6	Quantitative data on the new words in this work —— 35	
3	**Analogy in English word-formation —— 36**	
3.1	The diachronic relevance of analogy to language change —— 37	
3.2	Key concepts for the investigation of analogy in word-formation —— 47	
3.3	A working model of analogy —— 64	
3.4	Psycholinguistic aspects of analogical word-formation —— 100	
4	**Analogy in specialised language —— 112**	
4.1	Types of analogical formation in specialised language —— 113	
4.2	Types of target and their relationships with the models —— 117	
4.3	The functions of analogical specialised words —— 120	
4.4	Distribution of analogical specialised words —— 122	
4.5	Final remarks on analogy in specialised words —— 128	
5	**Analogy in juvenile language —— 132**	
5.1	Types of analogical formation in juvenile language —— 134	
5.2	Types of target and their relationships with the models —— 141	
5.3	The functions of analogical slanguage words —— 143	
5.4	Distribution of analogical juvenile words —— 146	
5.5	Final remarks on analogy in juvenile words —— 152	

6 Analogy in journalistic language —— 154
6.1   Types of analogical formation in journalistic language —— 155
6.2   Types of target and their relationships with the models —— 159
6.3   The functions and effects of analogical journalistic words —— 162
6.4   Distribution of analogical journalistic words —— 165
6.5   Final remarks on analogy in journalistic words —— 169

7 Analogy in literary works —— 171
7.1   Analogy in Gerald Manley Hopkins —— 172
7.2   Analogy in James Joyce —— 180
7.3   Quantitative data on literary analogies —— 189
7.4   Final remarks on analogy in literary works —— 191

8 Acceptability of new analogical words —— 193
8.1   Method —— 194
8.2   Problems and hypotheses after pilot tests —— 198
8.3   Results and discussion —— 201

9 Conclusions —— 213

References —— 220

Lexical index —— 232

Subject index —— 243

1 Introduction

1.1 An overview of the term 'analogy' in linguistics

Analogy is a very old concept in linguistics, and one that has attracted a plethora of interpretations and definitions. Originally, the Greek term αναλογία (*analogía*) denoted a real mathematical proportion, which was used by Greek grammarians, from Aristophanes of Byzantium and Aristarchus of Samothrace onwards, in order to categorise morphological forms (Schironi 2007). Then analogy was introduced into Latin grammar and became a basic criterion for working out grammatical rules. Hermann Paul (1846–1921), the nineteenth-century Neogrammarians' leading theorist, as well as the structuralist Ferdinand de Saussure (1857–1913) inherited the word in this sense. Interestingly, the term 'analogy' was either kept as *analogia*, or translated into Latin as *proportio, comparatio, secundum rationem*, or even as *regula*. In addition, Latin grammarians adopted the Greek proportional descriptive technique, especially used for morphological inflection, according to which A : B = A' : X (X = B'). In other words, if one knows that the plural of *shoe* is *shoes*, one may reasonably deduce that the plural of *tie* is *ties* in line with the following analogical reasoning: *shoe* : *shoes* = *tie* : X (X = *ties*).

The concept of proportion and its correlated notion of substitution were pervasive in the varied literature which took analogy into consideration. Bloomfield (1933), for instance, claimed that "[t]he utterance of a form on the analogy of other forms is like the solving of a proportional equation" (p. 276), as in his example *Charlestoner* [1927] 'one who performs the dance called Charleston' (OED2),[1] coined after *dancer* [c1440], *waltzer* [1811], *two-stepper* [n.d.] (see *two-step* [1900] OED2, s.v. *two*), and so on. Bloomfield (1933) viewed regular analogies of this type as "habits of substitution" (p. 276), i.e. as paradigmatic substitutions of the variable part in the analogical proportion (e.g. *Charleston* in *Charlestoner* substitutes *waltz* in *waltzer*).

In the 1960s and 1970s, however, analogy became a rather illegitimate topic in linguistics, expressly banned – especially in the United States – by generative grammarians such as Noam Chomsky (1957) and, later, Paul Kiparsky (1974) and Mark Aronoff (1976), and replaced by other more adequate notions. According to

---

[1] Henceforth, the abbreviation OED will be used for the *Oxford English Dictionary Online*, which is continuously being updated from the second (OED2) to the third edition (OED3). The year in square brackets represents the first attestation in the OED, unless otherwise specified. Needless to say, the first attested date of the words in print may not correspond to their first use. When 'no date' is available, the words are followed by [n.d.].

Kiparsky (1974: 259), for instance, the general concept of analogy should be refuted because, although it allows the following proportion: *ear* : *hear* = *eye* : **heye*, there is no verb **to heye* (meaning 'to see') in English. Unlike Bloomfield (1933), generativists analysed words such as *Charlestoner* as formed via rules – i.e. the syntagmatic concatenation of the morphemes *Charleston* and *-er* – rather than on the model of words such as *waltzer*.

Nonetheless, the neogrammarian notion of analogical formation ("Analogiebildung" in Paul 1880) had not disappeared and, against the Chomskyan generative tradition and American structuralism, it came back as a legitimate area of enquiry. Charles Hockett, in particular, was the first to defend Bloomfield's (1933) concept of analogy:

> An individual's language, at a given moment, is a set of habits – that is, of analogies. Where different analogies are in conflict, one may appear as a constraint on the working of another.
>
> (Hockett 1968: 93)

Thus, we do not form **swimmed* as the past tense of *swim*, on the analogy represented by *sigh* : *sighed* (and similar weak verbs), because the regular pattern here meets a constraint in the form of the subregularity represented by *sing* : *sang*.[2] Anttila (1977) was another unequivocal defender of analogy, which he also called "pattern" or "structure" (p. 25).

The end of the twentieth century was characterised by an increased interest in the concept of analogy, especially connected to the psycholinguistic studies of the 1980s (see Bybee 1988), or to computational models where analogy is the only morphological mechanism available. In such models, analogical algorithms are developed which can be used to predict, generate, or select new forms on the basis of the similarity of a given base with existing forms in the lexicon. Three well-known such algorithms are Skousen's Analogical Modeling (AM, Skousen 1989, 1992; Skousen, Lonsdale, and Parkinson 2002; Skousen and Stanford 2007), the Tilburg Memory Based Learner (TiMBL, Daelemans and van den Bosch 2005; Daelemans et al. 2007), and the Generalized Context Model (Nosofsky 1986, 1990).

Exemplar-based models suggest that exemplars that are stored in our memory can help predictions on language behaviour and the analogical algorithm capitalises on the multiple relationships that words in the lexicon may

---

[2] Cf. "blocking by rule" in Rainer (2012: 179–180; see also Rainer 1988). A different case is provided by "blocking by word" (Rainer 2012: 179), as in the case of **stealer*, whose formation is blocked by the existence of the simplex word *thief*.

have. In these models, analogies are based on sets of words of varying sizes, where a set may consist of a single word or thousands of words. In this approach, analogical algorithms can model both rule-like behaviour (with very large analogical sets) and local analogies (with a single item as model) (see Chapman and Skousen 2005 and Arndt-Lappe 2014 for applications of Analogical Modeling within the realm of derivational morphology).

In the same years, Becker (1990) reopened the debate on the notion of proportional analogy as developed by Paul (1880), thus attracting the attention of prominent morphologists, such as Plag (1999) and Bauer (2001). In the present century, Itkonen (2005) has additionally explored analogy from a cognitive-philosophical perspective. Hill (2007) has discussed the subject of proportional analogy from a historical perspective. Recently, van den Bosch and Daelemans (2013) have elaborated a computational approach called Memory-based Language Processing (MBLP), which can be viewed as an implementation of the analogical, exemplar-based strand of linguistic theories developed throughout the twentieth century.[3]

In the pertinent modern literature, analogy is considered one of the main mechanisms or guiding principles in language learning and change (Hock [1938] 1991; Anttila 2003; Hopper and Traugott [1993] 2003; Fischer 2007; Bybee 2010; Aronoff and Fudeman [2005] 2011; Fertig 2013; cf. Amiot 2008 for French), and a key notion in inflectional morphology and its diachronic evolution. For instance, many English strong verbs have been regularised by analogy with weak forms: regular *help–helped–helped*, from the previous irregular paradigm *help–holp–holpen*, is a case in point (Fertig 2013: 8). Instead, an example of a verb which has resisted analogical change is *bring–brought* (Fertig 2013: 9). Finally, a countertrend to morphological regularisation is the change from *dive–dived* to American English *dive–dove*, which is formed by analogy with *drive–drove* (*Online Etymology Dictionary*).

Another relevant realm for analogy concerns psycholinguistic studies and experiments on first language acquisition and speech errors. For example, the impact of types of analogy on L1 acquisition has recently been studied by Dressler and Laaha (2012) for German. Indeed, unconscious analogies are often the source of children's overgeneralisations according to fully productive, partially productive, and even unproductive rules. For English, various studies by Eve Clark (e.g. Clark 1981, [2003] 2009) have demonstrated the role of analogy in the formation of novel

---

[3] For a more detailed account of the historical development of the term 'analogy' in linguistics, see Rainer (2013: 141–149).

compounds by young children, such as *garden-man* or *plant-man* (vs. less transparent *gardener*), coined by analogy with well-known forms ending in *-man* (e.g. *dustman, fireman*, etc.).

Moreover, Victoria Fromkin's works on speech errors (Fromkin 1973, 1980) have shown that many errors are caused by phonological (and semantic) similarity between two items: for instance, when *ambitious* is pronounced in the place of *ambiguous* (Fromkin 1980: 3), or when two similar words are blended (e.g. **shaddy* ← *shabby* and *shoddy*) (Fromkin 1973: 36). Interestingly, the latter example is analogical with attested lexical blends, such as slang *fantabulous* [1959] ← *fantastic* and *fabulous*, 'of almost incredible excellence' (OED2), or *ginormous* [1948] ← *gigantic* and *enormous*, 'very large, simply enormous' (OED2) (see analogy in speech errors in 3.4.4). Studies on second language acquisition, by contrast, seem to disregard analogy as a relevant mechanism in language learning, with very few exceptions (e.g. Lyster and Sato 2013), which integrate an analytic rule-based system with a memory-driven exemplar-based system (Skehan 1998), but still on the learning of English inflection.

1.2 Aims of the book and its contribution to word-formation theory

Despite its versatile character, the common (mis-)conception that most scholars still have of analogy as a rare or unimportant process largely departs from its original meaning and current relevance. This book aims to disprove the myths that: a) analogy is inconsequential in English word-formation (Bauer 1983; Plag 2003), and b) it is devoid of relations to morphological rules (Dressler and Merlini Barbaresi 1994; cf. Dressler and Laaha 2012; Mattiello 2016).

In word-formation, different schools of thought consider analogy, and its correlated notion of creativity, either as an exceptional process that stands in contrast to the productive formation of novel words using rules (Plag 1999), or as the most important means of derivation including both productive and unproductive patterns (Zemskaja 1992). The notion of schema with various degrees of abstraction and productivity, which was introduced by Bybee (1988) and refined by Köpcke (1993, 1998), makes this already complex picture even more complicated. Although Köpcke (1993) developed his model of schemas (vs. rules) for inflectional morphology, this concept is also applicable to word-formation (see also Arndt-Lappe 2015 for an overview of analogy in contemporary word-formation theories, and its relation to other mechanisms in synchronic morphology, such as rules or schemas).

In general, traditional generative approaches to word-formation, such as Aronoff's (1976) and Spencer's (1991), tend to think of rules as the basis of broad generalisations, reserving analogy for local, lexically restricted patterns. Generativists have recently recognised the importance of analogy in inflectional morphology, as a means of generalisation/extension of a morphological pattern across paradigms (Aronoff and Fudeman [2005] 2011: 92), but they do not confer any regularity on analogical word-formation. In such a rule-based approach to morphology, analogy is conceived as a surface means to produce neologisms or occasionalisms (see 2.1 for a distinction) via particular defaults of individual (complex) words, rather than productive rules. A clear expression of this view, which is frequently found in the generative literature, is, for example, in Bauer (1983):

> If instances of word-formation arise by analogy then there is in principle no regularity involved, and each new word is produced without reference to generalizations provided by sets of other words with similar bases or the same affixes: a single existing word can provide a pattern, but there is no generalization.
>
> Bauer (1983: 294)

This definition, however, is too restrictive and inadequate to cover all the possible facets of the concept of analogy. It excludes, for instance, analogical compounds such as the well-known *ear-witness* [1539] 'a person who testifies to something on the evidence of his own hearing' (OED2), after *eyewitness* [1539],[4] and *software* [1960] 'the programs and procedures required to enable a computer to perform a specific task' (OED2), after *hardware* [1947], which at the same time conform to rules.

A theoretical approach which deals with the analogical mechanism is Booij (2010), who develops a model known under the name of Construction Morphology. Constructionist theories address the interesting question of how analogy is related to schemas, which are regarded as the central mechanism in word-formation. In Booij (2010), it is claimed that schemas and subschemas may operate on symbolic features, and that the crucial difference between analogical formations and schema-based formations lies in their making reference to different degrees of abstraction. Analogy in this model is defined as a strictly local mechanism, which is complementary to schemas and may constitute an initial stage of

---

4 The first quote in the OED for the two terms is the same – "One *eye wytnesse*, is of more value, then tenne *eare wytnesses*" (R. Taverner, tr. Erasmus, 1539, *Prouerbes*, OED3) – but the latter is certainly modelled on the former.

the development of a schema (Booij 2010: 88–93; cf. 3.2.2 for a pertinent discussion). Similarly, in my approach (Mattiello 2016), analogy as a local mechanism is identified with the concept of 'surface analogy' (defined below and in 1.3), whereas 'analogy via schema' can be viewed as an extension of the former, from a single model to a group of prototype words that share the same model (see a clearer distinction in 1.3).

Therefore, the flexibility of schemas and subschemas gives Construction Morphology a conceptual advantage over many other morphological models. However, as observed by Bauer, Lieber, and Plag (2013):

> [I]n addition to schemas and subschemas, analogy is needed as an additional and quite separate mechanism in order to account for the manifold isolated analogical formations that seem to be quite common in English (and other languages).
>
> Bauer, Lieber, and Plag (2013: 633)

This brings us to the family of performance-orientated connectionist approaches, in which analogy is the only morphological mechanism available. In computational analogical theories, we observe that analogy is conceptualised as a predictive mechanism, where predictability emerges from the fact that models are selected by algorithms.

A crucial property of computational analogical models that is particularly relevant for morphological theory is that they have been claimed to be able to account for both local analogy and rule-governed behaviour. For instance, in their approach, Derwing and Skousen (1989) claim that a description based on analogy may become a real alternative to a description based on (productive) rules. Therefore, they propose an analogy-based account that excludes the notion of rule, or subordinates it to the superordinate analogical principle. In this regard, Bauer (2001: 75) argues that "[t]here are a number of reasons for believing that morphology is basically a matter of rule-governed behaviour, and a number of reasons for believing that it works basically by analogy" (see his arguments and counter-arguments for taking a rule-governed vs. an analogical approach to morphology) (Bauer 2001: 76–84). The two concepts, therefore, are not inconsistent with one another (Mattiello 2013).

In a similar attempt to attribute a prominent role to analogy, Becker (1990) – widely criticised by Plag (1999: 17) – argues in favour of the extension of the notion of analogy to productive processes by equating it with the notion of rule. Becker (1990, 1993) discusses analogy in terms of productive replacive word-formation patterns, i.e. patterns where new words are coined from existing complex words via affix replacement (see also Arndt-Lappe 2015). Krott (2009: 136) has recently adopted a similar line of thought, by assuming that "analogy underlies regularities that appear to be governed by rules".

In fact, the two notions of analogy and rule neither exclude one another, as in the former (connectionist) approach, nor do they overlap, as in the latter approach. They are two distinct processes that act autonomously, but may combine in the formation of new words, as when surface analogies are modelled on precise actual words, but also belong to grammatical morphology. Thus, from the viewpoint of analogy, the above-mentioned example *ear-witness* can be analysed according to the proportion *eye* : *eyewitness* = *ear* : X (X = *ear-witness*), but from the viewpoint of grammatical rules it can be analysed as a regular compound noun obtained through the combination of two noun bases: i.e., [[*ear*]$_N$ + [*witness*]$_N$]$_N$.

Hence, Dressler and Merlini Barbaresi's (1994: 39) claim that analogical formations "lie outside morphological grammar" because they do not involve morphological rules applies only to a restricted number of analogies, but not to the process as a whole. I certainly agree with the two authors that analogy is a particularly relevant notion within extra-grammatical morphology. The latter is a cover term provided by Natural Morphology (Dressler 2000) that applies to a set of heterogeneous formations "which do not belong to morphological grammar, in that the processes through which they are obtained are not clearly identifiable and their input does not allow a prediction of a regular output" (Mattiello 2013: 1). For instance, the acronym *FLOTUS* [1983], coined after *POTUS* [1895] for the 'First Lady of the United States' (OED3, s.v. *first lady*), and the blend *Bremain* [2016] ← (*Great*) *Britain/British* and *remain* (*The Guardian*), created on the model of *Brexit* [2012] ← (*Great*) *Britain/British* and *exit* (*Wordspy*), are analogical extra-grammatical words.

Yet many analogies occur that perfectly comply with rules (Dressler and Laaha 2012) and can be accounted for within grammatical morphology, as stressed by Bat-El (2000):

> The point is that not only is analogy found in what is commonly considered grammatical morphology, but also that it can be accounted for within a grammatical theory (correspondence theory), the same theory that accounts for grammatical morphology …
>
> Bat-El (2000: 63)[5]

---

5 By "correspondence theory", Bat-El (2000: 62) means the theory developed in Optimality Theory by scholars who view analogy as "correspondence between two surface forms", e.g. forms that have the same prosodic template.

In addition, analogy often gives birth to productive series (cf. Bauer 1983: 96), as with the bound morpheme *-licious* (often preceded by vowel), which was originally a "splinter" (Lehrer 1996, 2003) from *delicious* used in new blends. Yet, this splinter has recently been labelled "combining form" in OED3 and "suffix implying excellence, appeal" in Green (2010), given its regularity in the formation of new words, such as *babelicious* [1991] or *bootylicious* [1994] 'sexually attractive' (OED3), and Lehrer's (2007) jocular *blendalicious*. *-Licious* words constitute a series, i.e. a homogeneous set of prototype actual words sharing the same formation and functioning as model or "schema" to new analogical words (see Köpcke 1993, 1998; Booij 2010). Therefore, like regular derivatives and compounds, *-licious* words do not lie outside morphological grammar, but rather within that part of morphology which is defined "marginal" (Dressler 2000: 1), in this case, transitional between derivation and compounding.

A still different type of analogy occurs in back-formation, i.e. the creation of a morphologically simplex form from a word which is (erroneously) analysed as morphologically complex on the basis of analogy with derivational or inflectional patterns. According to Bauer, Lieber, and Plag (2013: 520), "back-formation is at least partially paradigmatic in nature and can even be viewed as a special kind of analogy". For instance, the verb *lase* [1962] 'to operate as a laser' (OED2) has been coined from the acronym *laser* [1960], by analogy with the pairs *mix–mixer*, *print–printer*, etc., although the deleted part *-er* is not an actual suffix, but the shortening of *Emission of Radiation*. Similarly, the verb *baby-sit* [1946] is back-formed from *baby-sitter* [1937], from the same abstract pattern of *-er* formations. Yet, this case is different from the surface analogy obtaining the noun *dog-sitter* [1942] from the same base. A comparison between the two cases shows a different proportion, namely: *baby* : *baby-sitter* = *dog* : X (X = *dog-sitter*) vs. *play, read, write* ... : *player, reader, writer* ... = X : *baby-sitter* (X = *baby-sit*). In the first case, the model is a precise actual word (i.e. *baby-sitter*), whereas, in the second case, it is the abstract derivational pattern forming agentive nouns from verbs that functions as model. Thus, the first analogical process forming a new word is progressive, whereas back-formation is a regressive process based on the deletion of a (supposed or pseudo-) suffix.

This book clarifies the relationship between analogy and creativity, on the one hand, and rule and productivity, on the other hand, but also considers the whole gamut of interpretations of analogy and of analogical word-formation types. It accommodates analogy within the tripartite Viennese model elaborated and developed by Dressler and his colleagues (see, e.g., Dressler and Ladányi 1998; for L1 acquisition, see Laaha et al. 2006; Korecky-Kröll et al. 2012). This model includes, besides the above-mentioned surface analogy (as in *FLOTUS*), analogy via schema (the *babelicious* type), to which I have added analogy obtained in combination with productive rules (the *ear-witness* type) (see types and subtypes of analogy in 3.3.1). As van Marle (1990: 268) stresses, "analogy, even within the realm of derivational morphology, is no homogeneous concept". This book, therefore, intends to bring clarity to a field rife with terminological and conceptual complexity.

The book principally focuses on cases of surface analogy (see Motsch's 1981: 101 "Oberflächenanalogie"), which can be defined as the word-formation process whereby a new word (called 'target') is coined that is clearly modelled on a precise actual model word (hence 'model', 'base', 'analogue', 'source', or 'trigger'). In surface analogy, the target can be associated with the model as far as it shares with it similarity in some (or more) trait(s). In general, the more evident the similarity to the model, the more straightforward the association. Wanner (2006: 121) calls this type of association "analogical assimilation", that is, the process that connects the target to its model on the basis of shared similarity features. Therefore, surface analogy differs from rule productivity, in that the creation of a new analogical word depends on the similarity with an existing model word, rather than with an abstract pattern, or template, describable in a rule format (see similarity in 3.2.5).

In this book, it is claimed that, in analogical word-formation, similarities can be identified at different language levels (phonological, morphotactic, and/or semantic), and categorised along different parameters and scales, as investigated in Mattiello (2016) for neologisms in existing collections. For instance, the exocentric compound *beefcake* [1949] '(a display of) sturdy masculine physique' (OED2, s.v. *beef*), from the *Rice University Neologisms Database*, is analogous with slang *cheesecake* [1934] 'display of the female form in the interest of sex-appeal' (OED2). Indeed, *beefcake* resembles its model semantically (*beef* and *cheese* are co-hyponyms of 'food'), morphotactically (same compound head *cake*), and phonologically (phonological identity of the second syllable and similarity of the first stressed syllable, with identical nucleus /iː/). Similarity at various levels, as in this case, facilitates the recoverability of the model word *cheesecake*.

Against Dressler and Karpf (1995: 101), who argue that, for language acquisition, "surface analogies ... do not manipulate meaning and form in a regular, i.e. predictable way (as grammatical rules do)", in this book it is argued that surface analogies may allow output prediction. For instance, the analogical formation *mouse potato* [1994] 'a person who spends large amounts of leisure time using a computer, esp. surfing the Internet' (OED3, s.v. *mouse*), from slang *couch potato* [1979] 'a person who spends leisure time passively or idly sitting around, esp. watching television or videotapes' (OED2, s.v. *couch*), is fully predictable. Indeed, its creation is anchored in the proportion that substitutes the first element of the model (the Variable Part *couch*) with *mouse*, and leaves the second element *potato* invariable (see Variable vs. Invariable Part in 3.2.5). Meaning is also predictable from the invariable element *potato*,⁶ which metaphorically likens a person to a tuber, suggesting inactivity, idleness, and uneventful or monotonous life. Moreover, just as *couch* in the model suggests the place where the *potato* spends most of his/her leisure time, *mouse* in the target metonymically stands for the computer, i.e. the instrument used by the *potato* in his/her free time. Analogical formations from the same model word with an invariable left element are *couch rat* [1988] 'one who spends time watching television' and *couch tomato* [1988] 'a female couch potato' (Algeo 1991: 35). Their form and meaning are equally predictable from the model (Mattiello 2015).

In general, the research questions that are posed in the present work include:
1. What is the overall role played by analogy in English word-formation?
2. How can we associate newly coined analogical formations with their models? How is the model recoverable? Are some models preferred or dispreferred for analogical formation?
3. To what extent is the coinage of a new analogical word predictable and to what extent is it not? Are some types of target word more possible, probable, or acceptable than others?
4. What are the contexts and textual genres which favour and motivate analogical word-formation? Why do speakers choose to coin a new word which bears a resemblance to another particular item rather than using only word-formation rules?

This work aims to shed more light on the way the analogical mechanism works. It provides evidence for Klégr and Čermák's (2010: 237–238) statement that "analogical coinage is not an independent and separate process, but instead a motivated exploitation of all types of word-formation processes, whether rule-governed or not". In particular, it supports the claim that analogy acts as a fundamental principle in word-formation, in that it is transversely relevant both to grammatical and to extra-grammatical morphology, and even to marginal morphology, as illustrated by secreted combining forms (e.g. -(*a*)*holic*, from *alcoholic*, with respelling,⁷ as in

---

6 Cf. the colloquial meaning of *potato* [1815] offered in OED3: 'a person or character, esp. of a specified sort (usually with negative or derogatory connotations)'.
7 The alternative spelling -*oholic* is attested in several formations, but the vowel pronunciation is the same as in -*aholic*, i.e. schwa.

newsaholic [1979], coined after *workaholic* [1947] 'a person addicted to working' OED3).

Furthermore, in the work it is claimed that analogy greatly benefits from the institutionalisation and lexicalisation processes (Brinton and Traugott 2005: 45–48), in that institutionalised and lexicalised words (i.e. words established as the norm and whose morphological boundaries are erased or opacified) become potential candidates for the attraction of new words formed by analogy. For instance, the initialisms *mRNA*, *rRNA*, and *tRNA* [1961–1962] 'messenger, ribosomal, transfer RNA' (OED3) have been coined on the analogy with institutionalised *RNA* and *DNA* [1942] '(desoxy)ribonucleic acid' (OED2–3) (see surface analogy with enlargement in 3.3.1), and the blend *brinner* [2008] ← *breakfast* and *dinner* (*Rice University Neologisms Database*) is created on lexicalised *brunch* [1896] ← *breakfast* and *lunch* (5.1).

Another prediction concerns the linguistic motivation of words (see "motivation" vs. "arbitrariness" in Saussure [1916] 1995). Indeed, if we start from the assumption that motivated words are more probable than arbitrary (i.e. unmotivated) ones, we can assume that new words that are both rule-governed and motivated by analogy are the most probable (and acceptable) ones. By contrast, new words that are created on the model of exact words, by surface analogy, but are ungrammatical, are likely to be less probable. Experiments on native English speakers can help corroborate these assumptions and rate existing (attested) analogical neologisms as well as non-existing (yet conceivable) analogical formations as either acceptable/very likely or unacceptable/very unlikely. Empirical scales showing the average degree of acceptability of analogies in isolation and in context are elaborated and discussed in chapter 8.

In this work, it is also claimed that, in analogical word-formation, the process of association of the target with the model word plays a central role in vocabulary understanding and language learning. This association helps native and non-native English speakers to access, memorise, and learn newly coined words using their prior knowledge of model items. In addition, this association may be favoured by either the exophoric (situational) context or the endophoric (intratextual) context of the novel word. In particular, the co-occurrence of model and target in the same text (context) or even the same sentence (micro-context) can significantly help disambiguate new analogical words, especially poetic occasionalisms (Dressler 1993) and journalistic nonce words that humorously evoke or allude to their models (Mattiello 2014). From a textual perspective, analogies can be distinguished into anaphoric, i.e. referring back to a previously mentioned model word, and cataphoric, i.e. anticipating the model. The distance between model and target within the text is another variable which determines both the recognisability of the target word (Mattiello 2014) and the recoverability of the model word (see 8.1.3). Therefore, the textual neighbourhood between target and model words is not a 'striking' fact (cf. the quote below), but an intentional and well-motivated fact:

> From the point of view of paradigmatic relatedness, it is quite striking that new words of a particular morphological category are often coined in the textual neighbourhood of morphologically related forms with the same base, but a different suffix.
>
> Bauer, Lieber, and Plag (2013: 524)

Lastly, this work regards analogy as a promising area of investigation in lexical innovation. Analogy indeed allows us to elucidate the coinage of many new words in English, and to make some predictions on the possible directions in which the English lexicon tends to expand. The investigation of new English words and their privileged contexts of creation provide a further rationale for the present work. Quantitative studies conducted on corpora of British and American English will help corroborate the role of analogy in English grammatical and extra-grammatical word-formation and substantiate the hypothesis that, at present, English vocabulary expansion is also partially governed by analogy.

1.3 Definition and operationalisation of the concept of analogy

In this work, analogy is defined as the word-formation process whereby a new word is coined that is either based on a precise actual model word, or obtained after a set of concrete prototype words which share the same formation (i.e. series) or some of their bases/stems (i.e. word family). The former is called 'surface analogy' (see 1.2), whereas the latter is termed 'analogy via schema' (see 1.2 for the notion of schema, 3.3.1 for types and subtypes of analogy).

Thus, analogy does not exhibit the same level of abstraction as rules, although a schema may represent the first stage towards the development of a more regular pattern, or even of a rule (see 3.2.2 for analogy vis-à-vis rules, 3.1 for analogy and language change). Furthermore, although analogical words are not obtained by abstract rules, they may be regular (derived or compound) words conforming to rule patterns (see surface analogy combined with rule in 3.3.1). By contrast, instances of pure surface analogy (3.3.1) are often extra-grammatical words. More precisely, the concept of analogy is transversely relevant to grammatical, extra-grammatical, marginal, and even ungrammatical morphology (see

3.3.6 for a more detailed morphological categorisation, also 3.3.3 for types of target words).

In my approach to analogy, an essential prerequisite for considering a word to be 'analogical' is that it can be explained by a proportional equation in which the target equals its model (3.2.4). Occasionally, a proportion is made possible only by reanalysing the model as complex, or resegmenting it at a different morphological boundary (3.2.6). In analogy via schema, the proportion is between a target word and a series or a family of words. This is the reason why analogy with a schema model represents a higher level of abstraction than surface analogy, with a unique item as model. However, unlike rules, schemas are identifiable with concrete sets of words called 'analogical sets'.

Another prerequisite for an analogical word is that it exhibits some form of similarity with its model, be it phonological, morphotactic, semantic similarity, or, more often, a combination of these (see 3.2.5 for similarity features). If the target resembles its model at the phonological level, it can be described in terms of Variable and Invariable Part. The latter (shared) portion can correspond to a word, a word part, or a series of letters, and be either the word beginning or the word end, more rarely the middle part or scattered letters. By contrast, if the target does not resemble its model from the phonological viewpoint, its morphotactics and semantics can help the association with the model. Thus, the presence of an Invariable Part is not a precondition for analogical formations (see surface analogy with no Invariable Part in 3.3.1), only for prototypical cases. A distinct semantic link between target and model is instead very important for the association of the former with the latter, especially a semantic link in the Variable Part (see 3.3.4 for types of similarity relationships), more evidently in the Invariable Part.

In addition to the model–target similarity at various levels, what facilitates the identification of the model and/or the acceptability of the target is their co-occurrence in the same text or discourse. From this textual perspective, anaphoric analogies, i.e. following the model, can be discriminated from cataphoric analogies, i.e. preceding it (see 3.3.5 for target–model distance).

1.4 Relevant literature

Before delineating the structure of the work, I would like to mention the most recent and relevant literature on the topic of analogy.

The literature on analogy is rich and varied, with works differing in terms of approach to the topic, language studied, and school of thought. A lexicological approach is in Schironi (2007), who studies the etymology and early uses of the

Greek term *analogía*. A historical approach is in Anttila (1977), Hock [1938] (1991), Wanner (2006), and Hill (2007), who explore the potential of proportional analogy, particularly, in relation to language change, with numerous examples from the history of Romance languages. Adopting the same perspective, McMahon (1994) helps understand the function of analogical extension and levelling in morphological change. More recently, Fischer (2007) explores the crucial role (also theorising the concept) of analogy in morphosyntactic change. Both Lahiri (2000) and Blevins and Blevins (2009) provide helpful introductory overviews of the concept of analogy in different disciplines, including mathematics, logic and philosophy, Natural History, and grammar. Semantic analogies, a subject discussed by Blevins and Blevins (2009: 7–8) and usually illustrated by metaphors – i.e. relations between aspects of meaning of the analogue mapped to those of the target – are not dealt with in the present work.

Two contemporary works related to the topic of analogy include David Fertig's book *Analogy and Morphological Change* (2013) and Gary Miller's book *English Lexicogenesis* (2014). The former focuses on the role of analogy in language (especially morphological) change, and explains the concept of analogy in historical linguistics and vis-à-vis other notions (reanalysis) and mechanisms (back-formation, contamination, blending). The latter devotes an entire chapter to "novel word crafting" (Miller 2014: 83–100), discussing analogical creations, puns, language plays, Homer Simpson's *-ma-* infixation, and expletive insertion. Some of Miller's (2014) notions, such as those of "lexicogenesis" (p. 83) and "lexical diffusion" (p. 88), deserve consideration in this book.

Eminent books elaborated within the Generative Grammar framework, such as Aronoff (1976) and Scalise (1984), and later authors, such as Spencer (1991) and Haspelmath (2002), treat analogy as peripheral to English morphology, and therefore unimportant. Similarly, authors of standard descriptions of present-day English word-formation, such as Bauer (1983, [1988] 2003), Plag (2003), and Bauer, Lieber, and Plag (2013), mention only in passing the role of analogy in English vocabulary expansion (cf. Szymanek 2005; Klégr and Čermák 2010), especially relating it to back-formation (Bauer, Lieber, and Plag 2013: 20). Both Plag (1999) and Bauer (2001) contrast analogy (and creativity) with more stable notions, namely, productivity, regularity, and rules. Bauer, Lieber, and Plag (2013: 518–530) also discuss analogy in a chapter devoted to paradigmatic processes, as part of what they call "paradigmatic morphology" (p. 519). The concept of paradigmatic morphology is particularly useful to describe the process of paradigmatic substitution which occurs in analogical formation (see 3.2.4).

On the other hand, analogy-based accounts, such as Derwing and Skousen (1989), Skousen (1989, 2009), and Becker (1990), assign a central role to the notion of analogy. Skousen (1989) even elaborates his "analogical modeling of language". Against input-orientated rule models, Bybee and Eddington (2006) elaborate output-orientated schema models. The most sophisticated schema model is Köpcke's (1993, 1998) for inflectional morphology. Computational approaches related to analogical modelling are illustrated in a special issue of *Language and Speech* (see Wiechmann et al. 2013; van den Bosch and Daelemans 2013). The notion of schema (and subschema) and its relationship with analogy are the objects of study of Booij's (2010) Construction Grammar.

In contrast to analogical models, in Motsch (1981) the notion of analogy is restricted to surface analogy, i.e. analogy formed after precise actual words and word forms. Zemskaja (1992), as a prominent example of the Russian tradition of word-formation, and Ladányi (2000) discuss the concept of analogy in relation to general word-formation, the former in order to re-evaluate analogy, and the latter in order to elaborate a productivity–creativity scale, and to show its relation to analogy in derivation. Similar terminological distinctions between recurring dichotomies in morphological accounts (e.g. productivity vs. creativity; rule vs. analogy) are given in van Marle (1990) and in the theoretical chapter of Mattiello (2013), as well as in Rundblad and Kronenfeld (2000) (folk-etymology vs. analogy), and De Smet (2013) (blending vs. analogy). Munat (2016: 93–95) provides a recent account of the discussion on the productivity–creativity distinction, where analogy is not viewed as representative of creativity, but rather as a "re-creation" process (Munat 2016: 96).

Psycholinguistic works concerning analogy include three blocks of studies. The first block is on first language acquisition (for English, see Clark 1981, [2003] 2009; for German, see Dressler 2003; Kilani-Schoch and Dressler 2002, 2005; Laaha et al. 2006; Dressler and Laaha 2012; Korecky-Kröll et al. 2012; for Italian, see Lo Duca 1990). The second block of studies deals with speech errors (Fromkin 1973, 1980). The third block instead concerns experiments on association in analogical change (Thumb and Marbe 1901), and on the production, representation, and processing of analogical compounds (Gagné and Shoben 1997; Libben 1998, 2006, 2008; Gagné 2001; De Jong et al. 2002; Gagné and Spalding 2006; Libben and Jarema 2006; Krott 2009; Smith, Barratt, and Zlatev 2014).

Finally and most importantly, Dressler and Ladányi (1998) is a key paper for the approach to analogy adopted in the present book. Although the authors concentrate on the grammatical productivity of word-formation rules, in their paper they accurately distinguish rule productivity from analogy. More precisely, the model elaborated at the University of Vienna within the framework of Natural

Morphology discriminates among: a) surface analogy vs. b) analogy via schema (cf. "local" vs. "extended analogy" in Klégr and Čermák 2010: 235) vs. c) rule productivity (see also Ladányi 2000; Gardani 2013). This model is a turning point in the interpretation and analysis of the new words that occur in English, in that it allows us to accommodate neologisms in the three categories. While my focus in this work – and in three previous studies on the subject (Mattiello 2014, 2015, 2016) – is on the first (and partially the second) category, the latter category (rule productivity) is only discussed when combined with surface analogy.

Analogy in word-formation is an area of enquiry still open to heated debate and the present work contributes to this debate a) by clarifying the concept of analogy in general and in English morphology in particular, and b) by elucidating its connection and interface with other related topics.

The studies mentioned above have dealt with analogy only incompletely or in areas different from the word-formation morphological module. The present work, by contrast, supports and develops a model of analogy in word-formation and confers a prominent role on this concept. In this work, I claim that analogy does not exclude productivity, and is connected to an array of other relevant concepts, namely lexicalisation (Brinton and Traugott 2005), reanalysis (Hock [1938] 1991), overgeneralisation in acquisition models (Dressler and Laaha 2012), and classification in computational models (Wanner 2006). I partly embrace Skousen's (2009) approach, according to which "Analogical Modeling" is included in a general theory of language prediction. Similarly, I claim that analogy can help output prediction as well as the identification of new word-formation patterns, e.g., when recurrent splinters in blends become productive combining forms (see 3.1.2; cf. McMahon 1994: 76). However, our approaches are basically different, insofar as Skousen (1989, 2009) neither assumes that there has to be one single model for analogy to occur, nor that the model must always be highly similar to the target.

Lastly, in the present work the acceptability of established analogical formations and the potentiality of novel analogies are tested via experiments, and empirical data is provided showing the degree of acceptability vs. unacceptability of analogies (or felicitous vs. infelicitous analogy; cf. Austin's 1962 pragmatic concept of "felicity (conditions)" in Speech Act Theory).

1.5 Organisation of the work

The work is divided into eight main chapters. Chapter 2 makes a terminological distinction between the cover term 'new' or 'novel word' and the subcategories of 'neologism' vs. 'occasionalism'. In this chapter, new words are also discussed and distinguished from the diachronic viewpoint, and from the viewpoint of their structural/formal properties. Specifically, criteria for new word-formation are identified which meet the principles of well-formedness discussed in the literature. This chapter finally enumerates the various heterogeneous sources of the novel words included in the present work, explaining the methodology for database selection, and provides quantitative data of neologisms vs. occasionalisms, also showing their chronological distribution in past and present centuries.

Chapter 3 takes into account the theoretical framework of linguistic research and investigates the role of analogy in this framework. In particular, it shows the peripheral role that analogy plays in Generative Grammar (Aronoff 1976; Scalise 1984; Spencer 1991), in contrast to the much more important role that it plays within analogy-based approaches, especially neostructuralist computational models (Skousen 1975, 1989, 2009). In this chapter, a theoretical model of analogy in word-formation is offered which represents an elaboration of the tripartite model developed by Dressler and Ladányi (1998, 2000), later applied by Ladányi (2000) to Hungarian poetic language, and by Dressler (2007) to German poetic occasionalisms. Yet poetry is not expected to be the only preferential context for analogical creation.

This chapter offers an overview of the complex architecture of analogy in the synchronic formation of new English words. The model proposed distinguishes pure surface analogies (Motsch 1981; cf. isolated paradigms) vs. schemas (cf. families of paradigms) vs. (major–minor) rules. The model is gradual rather than a true continuum, and assumes combinations of one with another category, or shifts from one to another (sub-)type, as a consequence of language evolution and lexical innovation. Hence, the chapter also discusses the diachronic relevance of analogical word-formation, since most studies on language change (Kiparsky 1968; Hock [1938] 1991; McMahon 1994; Brinton and Traugott 2005) and more specifically on morphological change (Lahiri 2000; Fertig 2013) discuss analogical levelling and morphological regularisation in inflection, but overlook the importance of analogy in lexical development and word-formation.

In the third chapter, such concepts as "four-part analogy" (from Neogrammarians, see, e.g., Hock [1938] 1991; also in Aronoff and Fudeman [2005] 2011), "systematic" vs. "sporadic analogy" (McMahon 1994), "paradigm" (Anttila 1977; Blevins and Blevins 2009), "analogical levelling" and "proportional analogy" (earliest in Paul 1880; Hermann 1931; but see also Hock [1938] 1991) are taken into consideration and critically discussed. Conscious analogies (i.e. as in word play) are also differentiated from unconscious analogies (i.e. those unconsciously produced in speech errors or as a subclass of spontaneous innovations). Other topics that deserve discussion in this theoretical chapter are full–partial productivity vs. creativity (Plag 1999; Dressler and Ladányi 2000; Ladányi 2000; Bauer 2001;

Dressler 2003); token vs. type frequency and institutionalisation (Fischer 1998; Brinton and Traugott 2005); and analogical modelling and language prediction (Skousen 2009). Lastly, the process of classification/categorisation (Wanner 2006: 120–121) is used to develop the concept of similarity, or resemblance, between the newly coined word (the target) and its model. The similarity features elaborated on hitherto (Mattiello 2016) are presented and a hypothesis for their generalisation and extension to all analogical neologisms in English is formulated. The chapter concludes with some suggestions for the exploration of analogical word-formation in psycholinguistic studies. In particular, analogy is briefly treated in relation to first language acquisition (3.4.1), psycholinguistic experiments (3.4.2–3.4.3), and speech errors (3.4.4).

The four successive chapters deal with analogy in four different domains and provide both qualitative and quantitative corpus-based analyses of novel surface analogies and of analogies via schemas. Chapter 4 explores specialised analogies, i.e. new analogical formations used in specialised terminology by economists, politicians, jurists, or doctors with their colleagues. Most of the texts used for illustration are taken from the *British National Corpus* (BNC) and the *Corpus of Contemporary American English* (COCA). In this chapter, it is shown how neologisms can become stable within a restricted speech community whose members share professional knowledge and vocabulary. The role of context in the interpretation of specialised surface analogies is less central, in that experts share a precise, transparent, and unambiguous (i.e. monoreferential) terminology that may help analyse new coinages and recognise their origin. New specialised words, therefore, may aid or reinforce professional closeness among experts.

However, this chapter also stresses the importance of neologising in scientific and technical contexts for naming reasons. As Algeo (1991: 14) claims, "when there are new things to talk about, we need new words to name them". In various fields, new inventions, discoveries, technical and social changes require new words (or new meanings as in neosemanticisms) to express concepts or refer to things. Interestingly, new words often rely on words that are already present in the lexicon, and are coined by analogy with them. The medical term *ZIFT* [1986] 'zygote intra-fallopian transfer' (OED2), coined after the acronym *GIFT* [1984] 'gamete intra-fallopian transfer' (OED2), is a case in point. These analogical neologisms with a denomination function often become established, and can be (re)used at both national and international levels, especially within élite groups.

Chapter 5 examines juvenile analogies in existing collections on the web and similar online sources. The online databases explored include the *Rice University Neologisms Database* and *Neologisms*. These databases cover an overall period of eleven years, from 2003 to 2014, providing examples of both stable neologisms, also attested in dictionaries, and *ad hoc* nonce words used by adolescents with their peers. For each entry, compilers have provided information about the word's part of speech, the morphological or semantic process obtaining it, its description, its etymology, its use in context, and the source from which it has been taken. Another source of data is the *Urban Dictionary*, whose primary compilers – i.e. teenagers and young people – provide their own explanations, etymologies, and contexts of occurrence of the words added.

This chapter shows that juvenile analogies are mainly created either to produce a jocular/playful effect or to show off. Another reason for creating new words is the reinforcement of social closeness and in-group vocabulary. Most of the new words analysed are only used by students, so the accessibility to this language is restricted to small speech communities. However, it is found that, although teenagers are commonly innovative in their slanguage (Mattiello 2008a), many analogies that they produce are grammatical (see the *beefcake* example, 1.2), and therefore comparable to the phenomena of morphological regularisation which occur in first language acquisition (3.4.1).

Chapter 6 investigates journalistic analogies in the collection *Neologisms – New Words in Journalistic Text* (1997–2012), in the *TIME Magazine Corpus*, and in online newspapers. The newspapers investigated include the archives of *The Guardian*, *The Observer*, and *The Independent*, which illustrate creative analogies in use. This chapter demonstrates that the pragmatic motivations for neologising in the case of newspaper analogies range from the creation of social closeness with the reading public to the attraction of their attention. These functions motivate the colourful nature of some journalistic analogies in the above-mentioned *Neologisms – New Words in Journalistic Text* collection. They indeed include, besides grammatical neologisms (e.g. *bird cafeteria* [2011] 'a small box provided for wild birds to feed themselves', after *bird-house* [1855], OED3), creative formations, such as the blend *adultescent* [1996] 'an adult who has retained the interests, behaviour, or lifestyle of adolescence' (OED3), which has been coined after *kidult* [1960] 'an adult with juvenile tastes' (OED2). The (micro-)context is especially relevant in this case for the disambiguation of the novel terms, in that the targets often require their models to be analysed and understood.

Chapter 7 analyses literary and poetic analogies and is based on the concept of "poetic licence" (Dressler 1981, 1993, 2007; Dressler and Panagl 2007; Rainer 2007), i.e. the writer's licence that allows him/her to deviate from linguistic norms. In particular, the chapter shows how two well-known authors – the Irish writer James Joyce and the British poet Gerard Manley Hopkins – deviate, with their work, from the norms of word-formation. Many of the neologisms coined by Hopkins are poetic compounds in the sense of Boase-Beier (1987) and Salmon

(1987), resulting from an interaction of standard grammar with poetic principles. Although they have not become stable words, and mainly remain occasionalisms in the traditional sense of words used for unique occasions, their status is accepted by a large speech community, on account of the poet's authority. The same licence is conferred on the writer when (s)he coins new words in his/her novels. James Joyce's novel *Finnegans Wake* emblematically provides examples of analogical formations that depart from the norm. In general, the more audacious the writer the more audacious (i.e. ungrammatical) the occasionalisms that (s)he forms may be.

This chapter examines both grammatical compounds (e.g. James Joyce's *riverrun* [1927] 'the course which a river shapes and follows through the landscape' OED3, probably coined after *riverbed* [1781]),[8] and extra-grammatical formations, such as the exotic reduplicatives created again by Joyce (also in Dressler 1993: 5028), and other derivations that infringe principles of universal grammar (cf. "derivational innovations" in Ladányi 2000: 1). From the pragmatic viewpoint, the chapter shows that literary/poetic analogies are principally used for artistic and aesthetic reasons, their context being particularly relevant, both semantically and phonologically, for production and interpretation (Dressler 1981; Zemskaja, Kitajgorodskaja, and Širjaev 1981; Brinton and Traugott 2005). In this chapter, a distinction is also made between "surface analogy in context", i.e. structural parallelism according to the syntagmatic axis of language, and "surface analogy without context", i.e. structural parallelism according to the paradigmatic axis of language (Ladányi 2000: 18).

I agree with Ladányi (2000) that in poetic occasionalisms analogy usually works via defaults of individual (complex) words (i.e. surface analogy). However, against her classification of poetic analogies, I do not consider contaminations as "a special type of surface analogy working via two default words" (Ladányi 2000: 20; cf. Zemskaja's 1992: 191 "play on words"). Contaminations, or blends, differ from analogy: e.g., we cannot consider *absotively* [1914] or *posilutely* [1914] 'emphatically; without a doubt' (OED3) analogical words with both *absolutely* and *positively*, but they are rather blends of the two adverbs (see also De Smet 2013).

Finally, chapter 8 describes and discusses the results of an experiment conducted on native English speakers to test the felicitousness (i.e. acceptability) of both attested analogical formations and conceivable analogical nonce words. In

---

8 The first attestation of *riverrun* in the OED is in Joyce's *Work in Progress* (1927), but the term has later been reused by other authors, namely W. Everson (1954), P. Such (1973), and G. Williams (2002).

the tests, the informants were asked to rate a series of analogies which are heterogeneous in terms of word-formation pattern involved and grammaticality vs. ungrammaticality of the novel word. The analogical target words were presented before in isolation and then with their contexts, as well as with the model word(s) which triggered them.

Although results are not statistically significant due to the small number of informants, quantitative findings show that the mean degree of acceptability of analogies mainly depends on the type of motivation that forms the analogy. If the formation is purely analogical with a grammatical model word, but the target is ungrammatical, it is judged as less acceptable than a rule-motivated target. A scale of analogy is provided from the most likely or acceptable case to the least likely one, and even those which a native speaker judges as unacceptable in his/her language. This part of the work shows that Aronoff's (1983) concept of "potential word" (vs. "actual" and "virtual word" in Rainer 2012) is applicable to the assessment of novel analogical formations, and that it is a gradual concept, since some new words obtained via analogy are considered more probable than others.

The conclusive chapter discusses the findings of this study on analogy in four different domains, namely: 1) specialised language, 2) teenagers' slang, 3) journalism, and 4) literary works. On the horizontal axis, this chapter discusses the array of morphological categories that are affected by analogical formation. On the vertical axis, the chapter discusses the heterogeneity of functions that analogical words may perform in separate, often divergent, contexts. Quantitative analyses on the position of the Invariable Part in all formations, as well as on the frequency of neologisms (vs. occasionalisms) and of anaphoric (vs. cataphoric) neoformations in each domain are also discussed in this conclusive chapter.

Let me conclude this Introduction with a quote from McMahon (1994):

> [W]e cannot know with any certainty whether analogy will be triggered by a particular set of circumstances or not, but there are certain characteristics it will tend to exhibit once it starts to work.
>
> McMahon (1994: 76)

McMahon (1994) adopts a non-predictive approach to analogical change, focusing her analysis on the synchronic and diachronic integration of morphological change with other components of grammar, i.e. phonology and syntax. Yet she admits that, in spite of the "sporadic nature of analogy" (McMahon 1994: 76), some attempts can be made to suggest constraints on this concept, or to discern some tendencies and generalisations indicating the directions in which analogical processes move.

The present work proposes such constraints on analogy, showing when it typically occurs, how it usually works, and what pathways it follows when it operates. The ultimate goal of this work is to help understand and model analogy in English word-formation.

2 New words, neologisms, and nonce words

New English words are coined on a daily basis (Lehrer 2006) and lexicographers often find it very difficult to encompass such a range of new vocabulary within their dictionaries. For instance, Jonathon Green's *Neologisms. New Words since 1960* (1991) is a dictionary of nearly 2,700 new words and phrases that entered the English language in the thirty years between 1960 and 1990. Green (1991: viii) also declares in the Introduction to his dictionary that there are thousands of new coinages that he has chosen to ignore, either because he uses British, rather than American English as a benchmark, or because they belong to the plethora of endlessly generated technical terms which have not made the leap from specific to general use. Yet, as he himself admits, Science and Computing are two linguistic gushers that deserve attention for their proliferation of new terms, and this claim is even more pertinent to the current century.

The American parallel compendium of new words entitled *Fifty Years among the New Words, 1941–1991* was edited by John Algeo in 1991. For fifty years, a column on new words named "Among the new words", firstly edited by Dwight L. Bolinger and later by Willis Russel, appeared in 113 instalments of the well-known journal *American Speech*, and is still published in the twenty-first century (see, e.g., Glowka et al. 2000; Glowka and Melançon 2002). As Algeo (1991: 1) comments, this is "the longest-running documentary record of new English words", and therefore the motive behind the inclusion in his book. Needless to say, although analogy is not mentioned as one of the etymological sources for some of the new words recorded, the origin of words such as *narrowcast* [1978] 'to transmit programs over subscription radio or cable television' or *telecast* [1940] is certainly analogical, based on *broadcast* [1921] (Algeo 1991: 6). Another interesting case commented on in Algeo's (1991) Introduction concerns the word *sandwich* [1762], named after John Montagu, 4th Earl of Sandwich, who used to eat slices of cold beef placed between slices of toast. The reanalysis of such a word as a compound (see 3.2.6) – although it has neither semantic nor morphological connection with *sand* – has given birth to similar new words, such as *duckwich* [1943] and *turkeywich* [1943], by substitution of the first syllable (Algeo 1991: 6).

Another testimony of the relevance of analogy to English novel vocabulary is the latest twelfth edition of the *Concise Oxford English Dictionary* (2011). This dictionary contains over 240,000 words and phrases, four hundred of which are totally new entries including analogical words. For instance, the noun *mankini* [21st cent.] 'brief one-piece bathing garment for men' has been created after *bikini* [1947] (see 3.2.6). Similarly, the verb *upcycle* [1994] 'to reuse (waste material) to create a product of higher quality or value than the original' has an analogical origin, as a play on the verb *recycle* [1925].

Speakers may choose to create new analogical formations on account of their attractiveness, humorousness, or because they allude to their models and are therefore easier to be memorised. Examples of new analogical formations appertain to diverse domains. They include: a) specialised terms designed to name new discoveries, alliances, and illnesses; b) adolescents' creative vocabulary items coined as cryptic in-group slang; c) journalistic occasionalisms meant to play on words and jocularly attract the readers' attention; and d) audacious neologisms or nonce words invented by poets and novelists for stylistic reasons. Since different terms can be used to refer to new words – namely 'neologism', 'nonce word', and 'occasionalism' – a terminological clarification seems to be in order at this stage, before I illustrate the sources of the database used in this work.

2.1 Terminological distinction

From the terminological viewpoint, new words represent a confused and often controversial field of study, with lexicographers and linguists having different views and providing divergent definitions of what should be considered a 'new word', a 'neologism', or a 'nonce word'.

In OED3, for instance, 'neologism' is concisely defined as "a word or phrase which is new to the language; one which is newly coined". Lexicographers, indeed, tend to use the labels 'neologism' and 'new word' interchangeably in the titles of their dictionaries (see, e.g., Algeo 1991; Green 1991). Among linguists, however, 'new word' is viewed as a cover term for any newly coined word, whereas 'neologism' is reserved for "new words which are meant to enrich the lexical stock of a language (or which are already accepted as such)" (Dressler 1993: 5028). Szymanek (2005) more accurately distinguishes between 'derivational neologisms' – i.e. new complex words "coined according to some well-established and productive patterns" (p. 430) – and other new words "created *ex-nihilo*, with no activation of any morphological process", hence called 'root-creations' (Szymanek 2005: 430). Brinton and Traugott (2005: 43) instead claim that root creation (or coinage) "involves the invention of a new root morpheme", while they define neologism in general as "a new word of the language". Schmid (2011: 71–81) discusses neologisms in terms of "establishment", which in its turn includes three processes (lexicalisation, institutionalisation, and entrenchment) (see "institutionalization" in Brinton and Traugott 2005: 45) and three stages (creation, consolidation, and establishment).

On the other hand, lexicographers and linguists seem to agree that a 'nonce word' (also called 'occasionalism', see Christofidou's 1994 "Okkasionalismen") is coined for a particular use and unlikely to become a permanent part of the vocabulary (Algeo 1991: 3; Bauer 2001: 39). OED3 specifies that the term was coined by James Murray to refer to "a word apparently used only 'for the nonce', i.e. on one specific occasion or in one specific text or writer's works".[1] As specified by Green (1991: vii), nonce words are "one-off coinages that when newly minted seemed apparently bound to enter the general vocabulary, but soon vanished, lost amid the linguistic ephemera".

Therefore, nonce words or occasionalisms can primarily be distinguished from neologisms because of their different (permanent vs. temporary) functions: on the one hand, stable neologisms are meant to enrich a language lexicon (Dressler 1981; see Koefoed and van Marle 2000: 306 for "lexical enrichment"), while, on the other hand, nonce words merely have a stylistic (more provisional) function.

Unlike neologisms, nonce formations are not commonly viewed as part of the lexicographer's brief, although some humorous nonce words are reported in the OED: e.g., Tennyson's †*achage* [1875] (after *breakage* [1775]) in "O, the Pope could dispense with his Cardinalate, and his *achage*, and his breakage" (*Queen Mary*, OED3). As far as their function is concerned, Fischer (1998: 5) claims that nonce formations are spontaneously coined, in general, to cover some immediate communicative need, such as economising, filling in a conceptual/lexical gap, or creating a stylistic effect. As far as their formation is concerned, Brinton and Traugott (2005: 45) stress that they are "formed by applying regular word formation rules", whereas according to Ladányi (2000: 2) they are often the product of surface analogy.

In this study, 'new word' is used as an umbrella term covering both 'neologism' (i.e. a new word that is accepted by the speech community and meant to enrich the language lexicon) and 'nonce word' (or 'occasionalism') (i.e. a new word coined for a particular occasion and not institutionalised yet). Therefore, unlike most lexicographers, I do not use 'neologism' interchangeably with 'new word' and 'newly coined word', but include the former in the latter (more general) category, whereas I use 'nonce word' as a synonym of 'occasionalism'. However, I consider the status of nonce words often transitory or transitional, in that they often evolve into institutionalised neologisms (Fischer 1998: 3). I agree with Bauer, Lieber, and Plag's (2013: 30) claim that both neologisms and nonce words

---

[1] Cf. the psycholinguistic meaning of 'nonce word' as unmotivated word with a possible phonological structure.

"deal with the creation of a new word using the available resources of the language of the community; the difference is merely a matter of whether speakers pick up the new word".

We must also admit that some novel words remain borderline cases between nonce formations and true neologisms. For example, poetic compounds (Boase-Beier 1987) and other *ad hoc* formations occurring in poetic language represent instances of words attested only once and for the most part not recorded in lexicographic works, but they are part of the literary heritage of a language and thus deserve the same attention as neologisms. Furthermore, although some occasionalisms are used only once, those coined by famous writers tend to be reused by other authors, either as parodies or as plagiarisms, or else as new words authorised by poetic licence (see "Poetische Lizenzen" in Dressler and Panagl 2007). The present study analyses both neologisms and nonce words, as far as they can illustrate analogy in English word-formation.

2.2 New words in diachrony

New words should also be considered from a diachronic perspective. Indeed, like nonce words, neologisms are also inherently transitional (Schmid 2008: 1), in that a word may be a neologism for one language user and familiar to another. The concept of novelty *per se* has diachronic relevance. A word is truly new only at the time when it enters the lexicon of a language. By contrast, when a word is attested in prominent dictionaries for decades and becomes part of the common vocabulary, it is no longer felt as a proper neologism.

In diachrony, new words can be classified into:

Past neologisms: Several new words were introduced into the English lexicon during the Early Modern English period (late fifteenth century–late seventeenth century), when the greatest vocabulary expansion of English was recorded. Words coming from Latin (e.g. *agenda* [a1623], *data* [1645], †*instruct* [1529], *nucleus* [1668], *propaganda* [1668]) or French (e.g. *brigade* [a1649], *civilisation* [1656], *elegant* [c1475], *regime* [c1475]) contributed to this expansion (Mazzaferro 2009: 39). However, they represent neologisms only from a historical viewpoint, in that synchronically they are no longer considered 'new words'.

Recent neologisms: A great number of novel words have entered the English vocabulary since the last century, especially in the 1980s–1990s, with the advent of new technologies and new media, such as the Internet. They include words like *blog* [1999] ← *web* + *log* (OED3), *e-reader* [1999] 'a hand-held electronic device used for reading e-books' (OED3), *netizen* [1984] ← *net + citizen* (OED3), and *vapourware* [1993], used humorously for 'a piece of software which, despite being publicized or marketed, does not exist' (OED2), which have become part of the institutionalised language and are, therefore, codified in dictionaries.

Present-day neologisms/occasionalisms: Newly coined words enrich the English vocabulary every day, with analogy playing a fundamental role in their coinage. Most of them originate from the news, tabloids, TV shows, sit-coms, blogs, social network sites, and other state-of-the-art genres. Some are occasionalisms in the traditional sense, because they have expressly been coined for a single occasion and tend to vanish as rapidly as they have been created. A case in point is the ephemeral verb *prooflisten* [2000] 'to listen to a recording of words or music to check for errors' (after *proofread* [1845]), which occurred in Christine Webb's letter of 4th March 2000 in *The Guardian*, and was later recorded in *Wordspy*. Other words, instead, seem more stable. The word *advertainment* [1999], for instance, occurs eleven times in *The Guardian* complete archive and once in *The Independent* and in COCA ("They believe disclaimers will ruin the beauty of '*advertainment*'", 2004). Therefore, like its attested analogues *docutainment* [1978] 'a film or other presentation which includes documentary materials, and seeks both to inform and entertain' (OED2), *infotainment* [1980] 'broadcast material which seeks to inform and entertain simultaneously' (OED3), and *edutainment* [1983] 'an activity or product intended to be educational as well as enjoyable' (OED2), it is expected to become an institutionalised neologism. The truncation of the first part in the attested neologisms (i.e. *docu*(*mentary*), *info*(*rmation*), *edu*(*cation*)) indeed suggests that all these formations were once blends, until the second part became a productive combining form *-tainment* (see 3.1.2). In *advertainment*, the first part is a recognised back-clipping from *advert*(*isement*).

This study mainly focuses on recent and present-day neologisms (or nonce formations) obtained through analogy.[2] This part of the English lexicon can aptly illustrate the procedure whereby analogy obtains target words from distinct items or schemas. Crosschecks of present-day neologisms with the online version of the OED have been useful to establish the early attestations of the items examined. They have also been helpful in verifying if the items are isolated cases of surface analogy, or can be associated with other comparable examples of the same series

---

2 Some past neologisms may be mentioned, especially in the descriptive part of chapter 3, where some instances from past centuries may be used to provide a sample of all possible types of analogy. However, both targets and models have been accurately dated.

or word family. Corpus analysis in BNC, COCA, *TIME Magazine Corpus*, or online archives has given an idea of the representativeness, frequency, distribution, and use of neologisms.

2.3 Criteria for new word-formation

A clarification concerning the well-formedness of neologisms and the psycholinguistic aspects of new word-formation (Aitchison [1987] 2003: 174–187; Booij 2005: 231–254) is in order in this chapter. In general, the following criteria can be established for new word-formation (for a psycholinguistic account, see Schmid 2008: 15–19):

1. *Transparency*: Speakers producing novel forms favour new formations that are phonologically, morphologically, and semantically transparent (Aitchison [1987] 2003: 181). Hence, morphologically opaque items are not likely to be produced, unless the speaker is trying to be amusing or deliberately decides to create an eye-/ear-catching form (as in journalistic vocabulary or young speech) (cf. Lipka 2000).
2. *Regularity*: Adult speakers show a strong tendency in their production of nonce formations to obey the regular patterns of word-formation rules (and restrictions on them), word-formation types, schemas (Aitchison [1987] 2003: 174–180). The major forces behind this conformist behaviour are paradigm pressure and coercion by analogy (cf. Bauer 2001: 71–97; for analogy, see "Family Size effect" in De Jong, Schreuder, and Baayen 2000: 329). Illegal formations may be conscious acts of creativity (cf. Bauer 2001: 62–71). Irregular forms are less likely to become institutionalised in large sections of the speech community (cf. Aitchison [1987] 2003: 182–184).
3. *Productivity*: Speakers rarely produce new forms on the basis of no longer productive patterns. Although they have no difficulty in segmenting and analysing established products of no longer productive word-formation types, for instance suffixation with -*th* (as in *grow-th*, *tru-th*), they hardly ever use the patterns to form new words (cf. Bauer 2001: 54, 151; see Lindsay and Aronoff 2013 for rivalries between productive suffixes). Moreover, speakers of Italian could be more prone to producing a novel compound following the productive V–N pattern than speakers of English, whereas N–N will be the commonest pattern for English novel compounds (cf. Italian *salvadanaio*, lit. 'save money', vs. English *moneybox*) (Schmid 2008: 19).
4. *Decodification*: If speakers decide that decoding of a new form could be difficult, they tend to provide sufficient contextual material for the disambigua-

tion. As a universal preference, the new word is more often anaphoric of previous contextual material than cataphoric of what follows. For ease of decodification, speakers may also select one or several strategies to mark the newness of the word. Metalinguistic markers include explicit assertions of the newness of the word, such as *so-called*, the use of definitions or explanations of the meanings, inverted commas (in writing ' '/ " " or gesturing), and, in computer-mediated communication, hyperlinks to definitions found elsewhere on the net (cf. Hohenhaus 1996: 139–142).

5. *Informativity*: Speakers producing a novel word are invariably forced to reduce the wealth of information they want to convey because, at least in English, they tend to restrict themselves to a small number of constituents. This is especially true for compounding. For instance, multiple-word compounds such as Joyce's *upturnpikepointandplace* [1939] (*Finnegans Wake*, p. 5) are generally avoided, unless for occasionalisms with an anaphoric function.

6. *Mnemonic effect*: Speakers who coin creative compounds are influenced by their positive "mnemonic" effect (Bauer 1983: 142). For instance, a metaphor-based compound is a more successful strategy for word-formation than borrowing, because the motivation and imagery that such a compound evokes will make it easier to memorise (Bauer 1983: 142). Similarly, creative compounds that exhibit alliteration or rhyme, such as *knee-mail* [2000] 'a prayer, especially one said while kneeling' (*Wordspy*) rhyming with *e-mail* [1979], are not accidental. Indeed, both alliteration and rhyme in novel words "aid memorability" (Benczes 2006: 187), thus strengthening the positive mnemonic effect alluded to by Bauer (1983: 142).

7. *Analogy*: A further influencing factor with regard to the emergence of creative compounds in particular is analogy. According to Lamb (1998), speakers make extensive use of already existing forms when creating new ones – that is, their creative ability is also based on analogy: "The analogical principle can account for much of the ability of people to interpret and form new combinations; they simply make appropriate substitutions in previously learned combinations used as exemplars" (Lamb 1998: 265). Thus, *e-mail* motivates *knee-mail*. This analogy-based substitution process is natural and "appears to be innate and universal" (Lamb 1998: 265).

2.4 The database of new English words and the methodology

Given the heterogeneity of contexts in which new analogical formations are created in English, the database constructed for this study gathers data drawn from varied sources:

- Newspaper databases, in particular, the online archives of three British English newspapers, namely, *The Guardian*, *The Observer*, and *The Independent*. Online newspapers are chronologically consistent, generically varied, and carefully dated. Besides allowing word/phrase searches, they can also provide overall information about the words' token frequency in the archives surveyed. Moreover, they show the new words in their context of use, so acting as corpora of British English.
- Existing collections of new words, namely *Neologisms – New Words in Journalistic Text* (1997–2012), which provides 819 neologisms taken from newspapers and catalogued by year at Birmingham City University, and Suzanne Kemmer's *Rice University Neologisms Database* (2004–2014), with currently 9,016 entries collected over the years by English Linguistics students at Rice University (see also *Neologisms*). In the latter collection, the sources are various and range from spontaneous conversation to book titles, magazines, comics, web pages, e-mail, Facebook, TV shows, and similar popularising texts.
- Literary works, including some of Gerard Manley Hopkins' Victorian poems (1967) and James Joyce's novel *Finnegans Wake* (1939). The two authors are respectively representative of late nineteenth-century English poetry and early twentieth-century Irish fiction. Reference is also made to Boase-Beier (1987) for poetic compounds in Modern English poetry and to Neuhaus (1989) for Shakespeare's neologisms (see also Salmon 1987 and Garner 1987).
- Previous literature on the topic of creative neologisms and nonce formations, more significantly, for English, Adams (1973, 2001), Hohenhaus (1996, 2007), Fischer (1998), Baldi and Dawar (2000), Glowka et al. (2000), Glowka and Melançon (2002), Lehrer (2003, 2006, 2007), Szymanek (2005), Küpper (2007), Munat (2007), Krott (2009), some parts of Bauer, Lieber, and Plag (2013), and Miller (2014). Three lexicographic works on this topic are Algeo's (1991) *Fifty Years among the New Words: A Dictionary of Neologisms, 1941–1991*, Jonathon Green's (1991) synchronous *Neologisms. New Words since 1960*, and his more recent *Green's Dictionary of Slang* (2010). Furthermore, many extra-grammatical formations included and analysed in Mattiello (2013), as well as some of the slang words in Mattiello (2008a) are relevant examples to illustrate neology. For Dutch neologisms, see van Marle (1990); for Italian neologisms in literary texts, see Iamartino (1999) and Merlini Barbaresi (2011); for derivational innovations in Hungarian, see Ladányi (2000).
- Searches in various online sources and websites, more precisely: *Wordspy – The Word Lover's Guide to New Words*, the site created by Paul McFedries to keep track of emerging vocabulary in the English language, and Aaron

Peckham's *Urban Dictionary*, with thousands of new slang words being submitted every day by ordinary (normally young) people.
- Advanced searches in the OED, especially restricted to analogical words, which are generally indicated as being created 'after the word X' in the dictionary etymology.
- Advanced searches by using a corpus query system – i.e. Adam Kilgarriff's *Sketch Engine*. This corpus linguistics tool allows us to find concordances for any word, phrase, or string, in one of the corpora that they provide, or in a corpus of our own. The two corpora of English that I have explored include the *British National Corpus* (96,048,950 words) and *enTenTen12* 'English Ten-Ten web corpus' (11,191,860,036 words). The former consists of texts of various types and genres, including literary texts, periodicals, miscellanies, specialised books, collections, recorded speeches, whereas the latter contains texts drawn from the World Wide Web.
- Advanced searches by using corpus-based resources and investigating the corpora on the website created by Mark Davies, Professor of Linguistics at Brigham Young University (BYU). The corpora that have been selected for quantitative analyses include:
    1. *Corpus of Contemporary American English* (COCA 1990–2012, 440 million words), with 190,000 texts equally divided (88 million words each) among spoken, fiction, popular magazines, newspapers, and academic texts, and different sub-genres, such as movie scripts, sports magazines, newspaper editorial, or scientific journals;
    2. *TIME Magazine Corpus* (1923–2006, 100 million words); and
    3. *Global Web-Based English* (GloWbE 2012–2013, 1.9 billion words), with texts from 1.8 million web pages in twenty different English-speaking countries.

The interface of these corpora allows us to search for exact words or phrases, wild cards, lemmas, part of speech, or any combinations of these. On the BYU website, we can search for collocates within a ten-word window, which often gives us good insight into the meaning and use of a word, and we can also download large amounts of corpus-based data, including word, phrase, or collocate frequency. Collocates also give us the possibility to look for the models of new analogical words.

As this list of main sources shows, the database comprises both stable items, attested in corpora, archives, dictionaries, or literary works, and more ephemeral creations, attested only in the web sources consulted and therefore less stable, but nonetheless significant for the evolution of the language and the impact of the Internet on contemporary vocabulary.

The methodology used for data collection was also varied, combining advanced search with manual selection.

For the database's construction, the online edition of the OED was firstly explored, since it offers an advanced search option whereby words created 'after' other words can be selected. Close reading of each entry was then necessary to determine whether these were actually pertinent to my database of analogical words, according to the criteria explained in 1.3.

Besides the words' definitions, the OED also provided additional information about the words' origin and diachronic development, their earliest written attestation, their usage, and, for specialised terminology, the field to which they belong. Etymological information was essential to establishing the type of analogy involved and the model word or schema triggering it.

This basic database was then expanded by means of corpus linguistics tools (*Sketch Engine*), which were particularly useful for identifying new words created after a schema model, especially using an asterisk (*) in a character string to substitute the Variable Part.

Existing corpora, such as BNC or COCA, were also used to examine contextualised examples of those entries that the OED's *Thesaurus* labelled as belonging to specialised categories, such as sciences (medicine, anatomy), technology (electronics, computing), economics, military, politics, etc. Data crosscheck provided authentic contexts where specialised analogies were created or are currently used. This data is specifically dealt with in chapter 4.

Advanced search tools were also used for the selection of juvenile analogies in online resources. For instance, the *Rice University Neologisms Database* offers an advanced search option which allows us to specify the word's grammatical category, word-formation type, and where the submitted word should be found ('anywhere', 'in definition', or 'in source'). The *Urban Dictionary* allows for search by entry, but also provides cross-references to formally or semantically related words, which may be either the model or the target of analogical formation depending on their earliest attestation. Close reading of the entries' descriptions and contexts provided by the young compilers was finally crucial to discriminating between relevant and irrelevant cases. Relevant cases are the object of study in chapter 5.

New vocabulary added to the *Wordspy* website was also monitored for miscellaneous examples belonging to different domains. Like the *Urban Dictionary*, *Wordspy* offers both a manual search option, by providing an alphabetically ordered list of the entries, and, under each entry, a 'Some Related Words' link, which allows users to compare the currently explored entry with other related ones. Information about the words' etymology and contextualised examples are additionally provided under the entries. Many of the instances in *Wordspy* were found to belong to the journalistic domain.

An exclusively manual search was instead necessary for paper dictionaries (Algeo 1991; Green 1991) and the collection *Neologisms – New Words in Journalistic Text*, this latter for further instances of journalistic neologisms/occasionalisms, which are investigated in chapter 6.

Previous literature on the topic of creative neologisms in English was also read for additional data. Lastly, the works selected for literary analogies (see chapter 7) were carefully inspected, although many of the instances identified (especially Hopkins' neologisms) were also found in the OED's main quotations.

Therefore, in chapters 4–7, each domain where analogy is at work is exemplified by a sample of analogies, which is not meant to be exhaustive, but representative enough of the types and morphological categories involved.

2.5 Further remarks on the new words in this work

Another clarification to be made here concerns the difference among novel compounds/affixed words vs. novel abbreviations/blends vs. multi-lexical words vs. phrases/clauses/sentences (Lieber 2005).[3] The new words analysed in this work include novel compounds (e.g. *air-rage* [1996] 'extreme anger or frustration felt during a flight', OED3, s.v. *air*, after *road rage* [1988]) as well as new affixed words, such as *Clintonism* [1992] 'the policies or principles advocated by President Clinton' (OED2), coined after *Bushism* [1980] (see also 8.3.1). These are clearly morphological neologisms.

As for compounds, Scalise (1992: 180–181) also makes a key distinction between "loose compounds" and "strict compounds", assuming that in Italian the former 1) do not allow phonological amalgamation, but 2) have compositional meaning. For instance, in *spartiacque* 'watershed', vowel deletion (a form of phonological amalgamation) is blocked by a strong boundary between the words *sparti* and *acque* (vs. **spartacque*). However, the meaning of this loose compound is compositional. On the other hand, in *quintessenza* 'quintessence', the strong boundary between *quinta* and *essenza* weakens to become a strict compound.

---

[3] Cf. Algeo (1991: 2), who includes among the new words in his dictionary not only single words and compounds, but also idiomatic phrases.

In English, the most frequently cited criterion for distinguishing compounds from phrases is stress (Lieber 1992: 83). Indeed, English compounds are typically stressed on the left-hand element (e.g. *bláckbird*). However, the stress pattern of *apple píe* is on the rightmost stem, i.e. is typical of phrases. Another more reliable criterion is inseparability (Lieber 1992: 84, 2005: 377). That is, the elements of a compound in English may not be separated by an intervening modifier, as in **bláck heavy board*. Therefore, although *black márket* and *black móney* are stressed on the rightmost element, I consider them compounds in English, at least loose compounds which cannot be separated by any modifier. In the present work, both *black market* and *black money* will be taken into consideration as possible models for new analogical compound words (see, e.g., 3.3.2).

Moreover, the new words in this work also include blends, such as *Clintonomics* [1992] ← *Clinton + economics*, 'the economic policies of President Clinton' (OED2), based on *Nixonomics* [1969], *Reaganomics* [1970], and other *-nomics* words,[4] as well as abbreviations originating from multi-lexical words, phrases, or even clauses. For instance, the Internet slang alphabetisms *FOFL* [2011] 'fall on the floor laughing' and *ROFC* [2011] 'roll(ing) on the floor crying' are both attested in the Rice collection as new words from *ROFL* [2008] 'roll(ing) on (the) floor laughing'.[5] A comparable case from the same collection is *VTD* [2008] 'verbally transmitted disease', humorously coined after *STD* [1974] 'sexually transmitted disease' (OED2, s.v. *S*). Although these examples originate from multi-lexical words or phrases, they are used as words in netspeak, especially by students, as in "I'm *FOFL*ing". Hence, they are considered relevant examples to the present work on analogy in word-formation, i.e. still morphological neologisms.

By contrast, the humorous expression *on all fives* [1793] 'on hands, knees (or feet), and another part of the body' (OED3), coined after the phrase *on all fours* [a1375], is a syntactic (vs. morphological) neologism not included in the analysis. For similar reasons, the analogy *carpe noctem* [2013] 'enjoy the night' (*Rice University Neologisms Database*), created after Horace's Latin aphorism *carpe diem* 'enjoy the day', is considered irrelevant to the present work.

---

4 Algeo (1991: 6) notices that the splinter *-(o)nomics* is generally blended with words that end in *n*.
5 In the *Urban Dictionary*, *ROFL* is pronounced as one word (i.e. /rɒfl/) by various native speakers, and alternatively spelt in lower case letters (*rofl*) or with dots (*R.O.F.L.*).

2.6 Quantitative data on the new words in this work

The novel words included in the present work amount to 874 examples. Among them, 471 are neologisms and 403 are occasionalisms. To discriminate between the two categories, both available lexicographic material (e.g. OED2/3) and corpora, such as COCA or BNC, have been explored. After the exploration, I decided to include words with more than one attestation, either in the OED or in the investigated corpora or in both, among recognised neologisms, and words occurring only once, in corpora, texts, or dictionaries, among occasionalisms. Sometimes the OED describes entries as 'nonce words'/'nonce formations'. The words having such a label were included in the occasionalisms category.

From the diachronic viewpoint (see 2.2), some of the new words included in the book (18.64%) are past neologisms, or obsolete words which were new only when they were firstly used, e.g., by authors in literary texts. Others (51.71%) are recent neologisms that have acquired a status and recognition in the last century. They account for the highest percentage of the word list in the book. Still others (23.91%) are present-day neologisms or occasionalisms that are waiting for recognition and inclusion in dictionaries. A small group of words (5.72%) mainly consists of 'no date' nonce words taken from the previous literature on English neology or word-formation, whose earliest attestation is not precisely indicated by the scholars.

The numbers and percentages of the new words discussed in this book (no-date words omitted) are summarised in Table 1.

Tab. 1: Numbers and percentages of the new words in this book across time

Century	XIV	XV	XVI	XVII	XVIII	XIX	XX	XXI
Word Number	8	2	12	26	8	104	454	210
Word Percentage	0.9%	0.2%	1.4%	3.1%	0.9%	12.6%	55%	25.4%

3 Analogy in English word-formation

> If instances of word-formation are not produced by rules, then there must be some other process which allows them to be coined. This process is probably analogy ...
>
> Bauer (1983: 294)

> [M]orphological processes that seem to necessitate an analysis in terms of paradigmatic structure and analogy ... are too numerous to be dismissed as isolated exceptions in an otherwise well-behaved system.
>
> Bauer, Lieber, and Plag (2013: 530)

As the brief historical account given in the Introduction shows, analogy has been the object of interest of many scholars, who have either supported this concept due to its effect on morphological regularisation, or called into question its regularity and predictability. However, the examples adduced in the literature to illustrate the analogical process and demonstrate (or question) its significance mostly belong to inflectional morphology, and rarely pertain to the area of word-formation.

Bauer, Lieber, and Plag (2013: 518–530) have identified this gap in morphological description and offered an analysis of inflection, but also derivation and compounding processes in terms of paradigmatic structure and analogy. In their seminal work, they extend the term 'paradigm' from sets of inflectionally related word forms of the same lexeme to the morphological relatedness of derived words and compounds. They even offer the label "paradigmatic morphology" (Bauer, Lieber, and Plag 2013: 519) for cases that cannot be analysed in terms of concatenation, but have to be considered in terms of a grid of related words. To account for such relatedness or similarity between words in the lexicon, they thus invoke the notion of analogy. It is the core aim of the present chapter to investigate analogy in English word-formation, and to show that there are a number of phenomena and processes in English morphology which strongly suggest an analysis in terms of paradigmatic structure or analogy.

The first part of the chapter explores the diachronic relevance of analogy to language change. It offers an overview of the branches of linguistics which have been affected by analogical change, but especially concentrates on morphological change and on the role of analogy in the development of word forms. Two case studies which belong to word-formation (-*napping* and -*sitter*) are examined in this part in order to support the role of analogy in both morphological and lexical development and, specifically, in the evolution of the English lexicon.

The second (more substantial) part investigates analogy from the synchronic perspective. It elaborates a model where different types of analogy can be accommodated, and provides classifications of the various types of model words, target words, and similarity relationships occurring between them. This part aims to restore analogy to the magnitude it had with Paul (1880) and Neogrammarians, and to re-establish the value of proportional equations for the analysis of analogical formations.

The third part of the chapter concentrates on the psycholinguistic relevance of analogy. Although psycholinguistic purposes are far from the interests of this work, this part offers some starting points for the discussion of analogy in three pertinent domains of application, namely, first language acquisition, psycholinguistic experiments on analogical change and word recognition, and speech errors. These are realms in which analogy is currently under examination by experts (see, e.g., Clark [2003] 2009 and Dressler and Laaha 2012 for first language acquisition), but still needs more in-depth investigation for the word-formation component of morphology.

3.1 The diachronic relevance of analogy to language change

The first scholar who discussed analogy and its influence on language change was Hermann Paul. In the fifth chapter of his *Prinzipien der Sprachgeschichte*, Paul (1880: 107) introduced the concept of 'analogical proportions' ("analoge Proportionen") in order to explain, for instance, the formation of the plural Latin noun *senati*, after the proportion *animus* : *animi* = *senatus* : X. About fifty years later, Eduard Hermann (1931) employed Paul's proportional reasoning to explain German cases of phonological change in his work *Lautgesetz und Analogie*.

For English, a masterpiece on morphonological change is Hock ([1938] 1991: 168), in which the writer used the notion of "four-part analogy" to describe the generalisation or extension of a morphological pattern across paradigms. For instance, it is because of four-part analogy that the plural of *cow* is *cow-s* replacing the earlier form *kyne/kine*. The new plural *cows* generalises the plural formation familiar from other words, such as *arm* : *arm-s*, *car* : *car-s*, and so on. Sometimes the older form that existed before the analogical levelling remains as a relic, used for special meanings. For instance, the old plural of *brother*, i.e. *brethren*,[1] is now

---

1 Cf. the variant Middle English plural *sistren* [c1507] found as a correspondent to the male *brethren*: e.g., "I recommend me to you, and to all my *brethren* and *sistren*" (T. Stapleton, c1507, *Plumpton Correspondence*, OED2).

used only to refer to fellow-members of a church or social organisation, not to *brother-s* in the literal sense of the term.

The importance of analogy in morphological (especially inflectional) change has mainly been dealt with by McMahon (1994), whereas Roswitha Fischer (1998) has focused on lexical change, and Olga Fischer (2007) on morphosyntactic change. Moreover, analogy has diachronically been investigated for its ties with the processes of grammaticalisation (Traugott and Heine 1991; Hopper and Traugott [1993] 2003) and lexicalisation (Brinton and Traugott 2005).

3.1.1 Analogy and morphological (word-formation) change

In word-formation, analogy has also played a part in the development of the English lexicon. A case in point is the noun *belief* [c1175]. According to the *Online Etymology Dictionary*, in the twelfth century this noun replaced Old English *geléafa* 'belief, faith' (OED2), originating from West Germanic *ga-laubon* ← *ga-* + *leubh-*, 'to hold dear, esteem, trust'. In this case, analogy altered the intensive prefix *ga-* on the analogy of the prefix *ga-* in the Proto-Germanic verb *ga-laubjan* (Old English *belyfan*, Modern English *believe*).

The noun *wealth* [a1300] – from Old English *wela* 'well-being', Middle English *welþe* – is another case in point. Indeed, the unproductive suffix *-th* was added to *weal* in the mid-thirteenth century, on the analogy of *health* [c1000] (OED2).

Similarly, the English word *morpheme* [1896] used in linguistics appears to have an analogical origin. According to the OED, it was coined from ancient Greek μορφή (*morphe* 'form, shape'; cf. the combining form *morph-/-morph*, both initial and final), after German *Morphem* (J. Baudouin de Courtenay, 1895). Then the suffix *-eme* was added in English on the analogy of *phoneme* [1879], later also in *grapheme* [1935], *lexeme* [1940], and similar words used in linguistics.

In compounding, a germane example is *spokesman* [1519]. The OED describes it as an irregular formation from *spoke(n)*, the past participle of the verb *speak*, and *man* (cf. earlier *speakman*). Morphological analogy has here inserted a linking element *-s-* on the analogy of *craft-s-man* [1362], later reused in *hunt-s-man* [1567], *state-s-man* [1592], *sport-s-man* [1651], etc. Apropos, Krott and colleagues (Krott, Baayen, and Schreuder 2001; Krott, Hagoort, and Baayen 2004; Krott et al. 2004, 2007) have shown that the notorious variability in the use of linking morphemes in Dutch and German compounds can be accounted for by analogy.

Another interesting example is the compound *grandmother* [1483] (from French *grand-mère*), which replaced earlier *grandame* (*Online Etymology Dictionary*), probably by analogy with *grandfather* [1424] (from French *grand-père*), which in the early fifteenth century superseded the form *grandsire*. The fact that *grandfather* is a lexicalised word, i.e. a word whose morphological boundaries have been erased over time, may have encouraged the analogical formation of its female counterpart.

Similarly, many extra-grammatical formations which are adduced as cases of lexicalisation in Brinton and Traugott (2005: 40–42) act as models for analogous formations. The link between the blend *blog* [1999] ← *web* + *log* (OED3) and its target *vlog* [2005] ← *video* + *blog*, which is recorded in the *Urban Dictionary* for 'a journalistic video documentation on the web of a person's life', is clearly analogical.

Another instance of analogy from a lexicalised word is the clipped compound *wi-fi* [1999]. Indeed, according to OED3, it has been reinterpreted as a shortening of *wireless fidelity* on the model of *hi-fi* [1935] ← *high fidelity*. In both the model and the target, the pronunciation of the second element -*fi* has been altered (/faɪ/ vs. /fɪ/), so that it rhymes with the first element.

The acronym *dinkie/-y* [1986] ← *double/dual income no kids* + -*ie/-y*, 'either partner of a usually professional working couple who have no children' (OED2) and its sister formation *nilky* [n.d.] ← *no income lots of kids* + -*y*, cited by Fischer (1998: 185), also illustrate the relationship between lexicalisation and analogy, in that both targets are coined on the model of lexicalised *yuppie* [1984]. *Yuppie* is also the model for *guppie* [1984] ← *gay*, 'a homosexual yuppie' (OED2), and a large number of similar terms recorded in Algeo (1991: 9). According to Green (1991: 7), *AIDS* [1982], a lexicalised acronym for 'acquired immune deficiency syndrome', has set the pattern for *GRID* [n.d.] ← *Gay-Related Immune Deficiency* and *ACIDS* [n.d.] ← *Acquired Community Immune Deficiency Syndrome*.

These instances show the diachronic importance of lexicalisation for the evolution of the lexicon, and the contribution of analogy for the stabilisation of the word-formation process involved, be it infixation, blending, clipping, or acronym formation (Mattiello 2013).

3.1.2 The case of combining forms

Further evidence of the diachronic relevance of analogy to morphological change is provided by the development of combining forms, especially the type labelled "abbreviated" (e.g. *eco-* in *eco-art* [1970] 'artistic works having an ecological or environmentalist theme' OED3) and the type called "secreted" (e.g. -(*a*)*holic* in *foodaholic* [1965] 'a person who has an obsession with food' OED3). The difference between the former and the latter type is in the fact that, whereas the meaning of *ecological* is entirely retained in the abbreviated combining form *eco-*, in -(*a*)*holic* only the semantic elements 'person addicted to' are kept from the meaning of *alcoholic*, but the semantic element 'alcohol' is not.² The origin of combining forms of both types is a long-lasting process, which depends on the productivity of the combining forms and their profitability (see 3.2.3) for the creation of new forms.

As discussed by Fradin (2000: 35–47), forms such as -*(a)holic* or -*gate* (from *Watergate*), as in *Irangate* [1986], can be considered as "affixes – or affix-like – constituents" (Fradin 2000: 37). This statement is based on two ideas, namely: 1) these forms have a stable meaning and a fixed phonological representation, and 2) semantically, they are functions. The existence of productive series for these forms substantiates the fact that they have a stable (suffix-like) status. However, new words formed using units such as -*(a)holic* or -*gate* rely on concrete words (e.g. *workaholic*, *Irangate*) and not on abstract patterns, like suffixed words. The label "secreted affixes" finally proposed by Fradin (2000: 46–47) is therefore a good compromise allowing us to distinguish this type of combining forms from proper affixes, or from blends. Indeed, unlike learned derivation (i.e. derivation concerning knowledge domains, such as medicine or chemistry), the range of meanings shown by secreted affixing is wider and more unexpected, and, unlike blends, secreted affixes involve predicate dropping and a partial abstraction/generalisation (see Fradin 2000: 46–47 for a discussion on these differences). It is undeniable, though, that the origin of combining forms (or secreted affixes) is a diachronic fact of language evolution.

In order to explain the diachronic development of combining forms, let us consider two case studies, namely, the complex nouns *dognapping* [1921] and *dog-sitter* [1942] (OED3). Instinctively, I would consider these two nouns as analogical formations from, respectively, *kidnapping* [1682] and, as already said (see 1.2), *baby-sitter* [1937]. From the viewpoint of similarity, the two word pairs exhibit resemblance at the morphotactic level. Indeed, *dog-nap(p)-ing* exactly reproduces the structure of the synthetic compound *kid-nap(p)-ing*, and, in the same way, *dog-sit(t)-er* replicates *baby-sit(t)-er* in form. The fact that the second compound members (*nap*, *sit*) and the suffixes (-*ing*, -*er*) are shared between the target and the model also entails similarity at the phonological level. Lastly, at the semantic level, we can predict the meanings of the two new words from the models' meanings, i.e.: 'the stealing of a *dog*' (OED3) and 'a person who takes care of a *dog* in the absence of its owner' (OED3, s.v. *dog*).

However, taking into account these two cases of analogy, one may reasonably raise the following questions:

---

2 See also Warren (1990: 119) for the distinction between "secretion" and "abbreviation" in combining forms. More examples on this distinction are in Mattiello (2008b: 181–185).

1. Do *dognapping* and *dog-sitter* belong to surface analogy or to analogy via schema? What is the delimitation between the two types?
2. Do they give rise to productive series? Or, at least, can we predict other similar analogical formations?
3. When (and how) have the second elements *-napping* and *-sitter* acquired the status of combining forms?

The etymology of the two words is comparable, in that both seem to have been created from the concatenation of *dog* and a combining form (i.e. *-napping* or *-sitter*). However, this is the *a posteriori* etymological description offered by the OED. The etymology of the two words is actually: *dog* has substituted *kid* in the proportion *kid* : *kidnapping* = *dog* : *dognapping*, and it has substituted *baby* in the proportion *baby* : *baby-sitter* = *dog* : *dog-sitter*. In other words, in both cases, it is not a matter of concatenation, but a matter of substitution.

The origin of the two combining forms *-napping* and *-sitter* is comparable as well. According to OED3, the earliest formation coined after *kidnapping* is *dognapping*, and *dog-sitter* is recorded as the earliest formation created after *baby-sitter* in the mid-twentieth century. This suggests that, initially, *dognapping* and *dog-sitter* were surface analogies on precise model words, rather than on series of prototype words.

Then other formations have followed the same patterns, conferring productivity and regularity on the second elements *-napping* (*petnapping* [1967], *art-napping* [1978], *ship-napping* [1988], *corpsenapping* [1991] OED3), and *-sitter* (*cat sitter* [1948], *house-sitter* [1949], *pet sitter* [1976], *granny-sitter* [1985] OED3; cf. University slang *bed-sitter* [1927] ← *bedroom* + *sitting-room*, following a different pattern, OED2). Yet it is difficult to determine exactly when these two elements became productive enough to deserve the label of 'combining forms'. What can be asserted with certainty is that they have originated productive series. However, it is worth noting that series are often time-restricted. In other words, when a series starts to exist, its expansion is generally rapid at the beginning and may gradually become slower as time goes by. The combining form *-licious*, for instance, has become productive in the twenty-first century (see 1.2), especially among young speakers, whereas *-gate* (see 3.3.1) was much more productive in the newspapers of the 1970s–1980s, to denote scandals comparable with the Watergate scandal of 1972. However, the fact that series are time-restricted is not specific to combining forms, and may be explained in terms of profitability (3.2.3).

As can be deduced from the above discussion, I reject the general statement that analogy lacks predictability (cf. Dressler and Karpf 1995; Plag 1999). This statement is clearly disconfirmed by the above-mentioned examples, in which the outputs *petnapping* and *pet sitter* are straightforwardly predictable because of the existence of the pattern forming *dognapping* and *dog-sitter*. In Bauer's (2001: 76) terms, the analogical principle establishes that "any new form can be created as long as there is a suitable pattern for it to be formed on".

Other similar formations are attested in *The Guardian* (*catnapping* [1999], *foxnapping* [2001], *birdnapping* [2011]) and still others can be predicted which follow the patterns *X-napping* and *X-sitter*, where *X* stands for a noun denoting a human being, an animal, or a thing.

Table 2 and Table 3 respectively show the occurrence of *-napping* and *-sitter* in new words (column 1), their frequency both in COCA and in the *TIME Magazine Corpus* (columns 2–3), and their context of use (column 4). Given the different size of the two corpora (440 vs. 100 million words), frequencies have been normalised per million words (pmw):

Tab. 2: *-Napping* words and their frequency and use in COCA and TIME

-napping words	Frequency in COCA	Frequency in TIME	Context
catnapping	19/0.04 pmw (1991–2004)	8/0.08 pmw (1939–1984)	Do you suppose he had anything to do with the **catnapping**? (*McNally's Luck* 1992)
dognapping	7/0.01 pmw (1990–2004)	2/0.02 pmw (1960–1965)	We spotted the **dognapping** suspects, corner of 1st and 49th. (*New York Minute* 2004)
baby-napping	2/0.004 pmw (1992–1993)	–	The city's been noticeably quiet since the thwarted **baby-napping** … yet still you patrol. (*Batman Returns* 1992)
biznapping	1/0.002 pmw (1993)	–	A decade ago, California and its cities engaged in some **biznapping** themselves, actively canvassing the rest of the nation and persuading many businesses to relocate here. (*San Francisco Chronicle* 1993)
chicknapping	1/0.002 pmw (1995)	–	Of the fourteen "**chicknapping**" cases I was aware of, six young disappeared from their new group without a trace, three returned (escaped?) to their original group within a week, and five were alive and with their new group the last

-napping words	Frequency in COCA	Frequency in TIME	Context
			time the group was located. (*Natural History* 1995)
dessert-napping	1/0.002 pmw (1996)	–	Not only was Sam's eagle eye now upon them all, but that sort of thing ended when Sam ended her **dessert-napping**. (*Christian Science Monitor* 1996)
golfnapping	1/0.002 pmw (1998)	–	The victim of this **golfnapping** identified himself as Christer Andersson, an 11 handicap from Halmstad, in southern Sweden. (*Sports Illustrated* 1998)
gosling-napping	1/0.002 pmw (2008)	–	Looks like we have a serial **gosling-napping** pair. (*Chicago Sun-Times* 2008)
groundhog-napping	1/0.002 pmw (1993)	–	Rita witnesses the **groundhog-napping** and runs back toward the knob. (*Groundhog Day* 1993)
sitter-napping	1/0.002 pmw (2007)	–	There's a lot of **sitter-napping** and stealing top sitters from friends. (*Where did all the baby sitters go?* 2007)
bike-napping	–	1/0.01 pmw (2003)	There's a dog, some **bike-napping** mafiosi and three old chanteuses whose diet consists entirely of frogs they catch by tossing hand grenades into a nearby stream. (*Time Magazine* 2003)
boatnapping	–	1/0.01 pmw (1981)	What made the **boatnapping** particularly odd was the fact that the warships were armed with cannons and could easily have blown the attacking tug out of the water if their crews had wished. (*Time Magazine* 1981)
boxcar-napping	–	1/0.01 pmw (1963)	They charge that Eastern **boxcar-napping** has produced a shortage of cars for moving grain and lumber. (*Time Magazine* 1963)
dolphin-napping	–	1/0.01 pmw (2001)	"These dolphins are overworked and in horrible conditions," says Homero Aridjis, a poet who is the

-napping words	Frequency in COCA	Frequency in TIME	Context
			organization's president. "This is **dolphin-napping**." (*Time Magazine* 2001)
oxnapping	–	1/0.01 pmw (1952)	Since he has promised the Canadian government that no adult musk ox will be killed in the process, the job of **oxnapping** promises rich yields in exercise and excitement. (*Time Magazine* 1952)
pupnapping	–	1/0.01 pmw (1934)	Thus did the snatching of a famed dog call attention to **pupnapping**. (*Time Magazine* 1934)

Tab. 3: *-Sitter* words and their frequency and use in COCA and TIME

-sitter words	Frequency in COCA	Frequency in TIME	Context
housesitter	17/0.03 pmw (1991–2003)	4/0.04 pmw (1992)	So I added, During the week, I have a **housesitter**. (*The Antioch Review* 2001)
tree-sitter	6/0.01 pmw (2000–2009)	1/0.01 pmw (1989)	Last April, news came from Oregon that a 22-year-old **tree-sitter** had fallen 150 feet to her death. (*Associated Press* 2003)
pet-sitter	6/0.01 pmw (1993–2012)	–	She's trying to get her business going. She's a **pet-sitter**. (*Washington Post* 1995)
cat-sitter	1/0.002 pmw (1992)	–	I had a cat once. It was a long time ago, but I'm in great demand as a **cat-sitter** for my friends. (*Vanish with the Rose* 1992)
dog-sitter	–	1/0.01 pmw (2003)	That's when you have to either limit your travels to places that accept canines or pack Fido off to a kennel or **dog-sitter** until the party is over. (*Time Magazine* 2003)

The existence of these analogical words has originated a schema, with prototype words which function as model for the analogy. Therefore, the line of demarcation between the type called surface analogy and that called analogy via schema is at times difficult to establish, at least, diachronically speaking. Synchronically, as a minimum, two target words obeying the same pattern should be attested to develop a schema.

This argument concerning the diachronic relevance of analogy to lexical evolution and morphological change could be generalised to other combining forms. For instance, Lehrer (2007) observes that:

> When a splinter becomes so common that people start using it frequently, it may lose its connection with the source word and can be considered as a morpheme in its own right. Of course, since there is a scale from a completely novel splinter to a completely conventional morpheme, the transition from splinter to independent morphemehood is a diachronic process.
>
> Lehrer (2007: 121)

In particular, a candidate that she mentions for this transition is -*umentary*. According to the OED, it is a splinter (from *documentary*) found in numerous blends: e.g., *mockumentary* [1965] 'satirical play or film in the form of a documentary' (OED3), *rockumentary* [1969] 'a documentary on the subject of rock music' (OED3), and *shockumentary* [1970] 'a documentary film with shocking subject matter' (OED3) (see also *soapumentary* [n.d.] 'soap opera documentary' in Lehrer 2007: 123). In other words, the OED does not mention its status as an independent morpheme, nor does it attest -*umentary* as a separate entry. However, the frequency, productivity, and regularity of these formations make us imagine that a transition from splinter to combining form is under way.

Table 4 shows the relevance and token/normalised frequency of -*umentary* in new blends attested in COCA and in the *TIME Magazine Corpus*:

Tab. 4: -*Umentary* words and their frequency and use in COCA and TIME

-umentary words	Frequency in COCA	Frequency in TIME	Context
mockumentary	28/0.06 pmw (1994–2012)	–	Let me start here by confessing that I don't have a clue which parts of this movie are real documentary and which parts are more like **mockumentary**. (*NPR_FreshAir* 2006)
rockumentary	10/0.02 pmw (1991–2009)	–	The ultimate **rockumentary** about Presley's career. (*Chicago Sun-Times* 2002)
copumentary	1/0.002 pmw (2008)	–	The police then quickly cut together the surveillance shots that made the Tibetans look most vicious – beating

-umentary words	Frequency in COCA	Frequency in TIME	Context
			Chinese bystanders, torching shops, ripping metal sheeting off banks – and created a kind of **copumentary**: Tibetans Gone Wild. (*Rolling Stone* 2008)
dogumentary	1/0.002 pmw (2006)	–	And Athens filmmaker Erica McCarthy, inventor of the "Uga-cam," made an Uga **"dogumentary"** film, "Damn Good Dog," that was released last year. (*Atlanta Journal Constitution* 2006)
schlockumen- tary	1/0.002 pmw (2005)	–	Although Lehner calls it a **"schlockumentary,"** the film helped attract private funding to join Hawass in a shared dream: a full stratigraphic dig for the lost city of the pyramid makers. (*Smithsonian* 2005)

The similarity among the above words – including the fact that the first component is a monosyllabic word and, in most cases, the syllable exhibits the rime /ɒk/ or the nucleus /ɒ/ – is symptomatic of their analogical origin and of the gradual evolution of a schema.

The role of diachronic language development is therefore crucial for the model of analogy adopted in the present work. For instance, the above-mentioned case of *-umentary* words shows how a word end (i.e. a splinter) merging with other words (or word parts) to form new blends has become frequent in use, regular, productive, and has therefore developed into a final combining form. Fradin (2000: 37) would even include *-umentary* in the category of "secreted affixes" (e.g. *-gate* or *-holic*), which exhibit a certain level of abstraction and allow generalisations. However, unlike suffixed words, new *-umentary* words are not coined after an abstract pattern, but still depend on concrete forms. In Natural Morphology, combining forms, such as *-umentary*, *-gate*, etc., can be accommodated within that part of "marginal morphology" (Dressler 2000: 7) concerning the internal boundaries, in particular, among phenomena that are transitional between derivation and compounding.

A counterargument against the role of analogy in diachronic language development is the existence of word sets which do not evolve into established schemas. For instance, the set comprising *billion* [1690], *trillion* [a1690], *quadrillion* [a1690] (modelled on *million* [c1390]), and the fanciful formations *jillion* [1942], *squillion* [1943], and *zillion* [1944] referring to 'a very large but indefinite number' (OED2), has produced no affix/combining form *-illion* yet (cf. Klégr and Čermák 2010: 236). However, *jillion, squillion,* and *zillion* may be mere arbitrary alterations of the word *million*, which is at times used, hyperbolically, to indicate 'an enormous number' (OED3). I would then exclude these nonce formations from the realm of analogy (cf., instead, *squillionaire* [1979], OED2, created on the model of *zillionaire* [1946] in 3.3.4).

3.2 Key concepts for the investigation of analogy in word-formation

The following subsections aim to discuss some key concepts that are necessary to frame and model analogy in word-formation. These concepts include productivity vs. creativity (3.2.1), analogy vis-à-vis rules (3.2.2), and frequency, profitability, and recoverability of the model (3.2.3). Other concepts on which this section intends to shed more light are proportion (3.2.4), similarity (3.2.5), and reanalysis (3.2.6). With reference to reanalysis, the phenomena of folk-etymology, word play, and back-formation will also be discussed.

3.2.1 Analogy: productivity or creativity?

Bauer (1983: 295) raises the question of whether it is possible to distinguish between a theory based on rule-governed productivity and one based on analogy, rejecting the hypothesis that these two concepts are equivalent. Indeed, at the end of a chapter entitled "Productivity", Bauer (1983) claims that analogical formations are either unique forms or extremely limited in productivity. He defines an analogical formation as:

> [A] new formation clearly modelled on one already existing lexeme, and not giving rise to a productive series.
>
> Bauer (1983: 96)

However, in the same chapter, Bauer (1983) does not preclude the option that an analogical formation may provide the impetus for a series of formations, as in the case of words in *-scape* (e.g. *seascape* [1799], *dreamscape* [1858], *cloudscape* [1868], after *landscape* [1605]; cf. Mattiello 2007), which, he admits, are closely related to the concept of productivity. Nonetheless, he claims that cases of "genuine analogical formations", such as *ambisextrous* [1929] 'ambisexual' (OED2) and *wargasm* [2004] 'the act of getting off on violence' (*Urban Dictionary*, but already in Bauer 1983), "cannot be accounted for by any kind of rule" (Bauer 1983: 96), in that, unlike rules, they are coined because of a phonological similarity with the words *ambidextrous* and *orgasm*. Actually, in *ambisextrous*, the word *sex* has been intercalated within *ambidextrous*, and in *wargasm* the two words *war* and *orgasm* merge where they overlap. Hence, the morphological operation behind the formation of these words is not analogy, but blending.[3]

In particular, the above-mentioned types of blend, *ambisextrous* and *wargasm*, share with model words such as *entreporneur* [n.d.] 'entrepreneur + porn' (Mattiello 2013: 120) and *slanguage* [1879] 'slang + language' (OED2) the same morphotactic structure involving overlapping constituents. In other words, they are "overlapping blends" (Mattiello 2013: 121–123), i.e. blends which exhibit a phonological overlap of vowels, consonants, or syllables between the constituents, with or without a proper shortening. In *wargasm*, for instance, neither *war* nor *orgasm* have been shortened in the new formation, at least from the phonological viewpoint. Indeed, one of the criteria of well-formedness for blends is "recoverability", that is, they must preserve as many segments from the source words as possible (Mattiello 2013: 140), as happens with *wargasm* and its model *slanguage*, although the two do not share any Invariable Part, only morphotactic similarity (3.3.1).

In a similar vein, Plag (1999: 20) claims that "analogical formations should be distinguished from instantiations of productive word formation rules". His conception of local analogy is close to Bauer's (1983) and seems to be restricted to cases of surface analogy. Indeed, at the end of a chapter where he discusses word-formation rules, Plag (2003) argues that "sometimes new complex words are derived without an existing word-formation rule, but formed on the basis of a single (or very few) model words" (p. 37), i.e. via analogy. The examples of analogy that he provides illustrate this process as a proportional relation between corresponding words (e.g. *sea* : *sea-sick* = *air* : *air-sick*; *ham* : *hamburger* = *cheese* : *cheeseburger*).

Although I agree with Plag (2003) that the primary mechanism operating in the formation of *airsick* [1785] 'sick from the motion of an aircraft' (OED3; see also *carsick* [1908]) is surface analogy with *sea-sick* [a1566], we cannot deny the regularity of this formation, or of similar compounds mentioned in the literature. For instance, the compound noun *whitelist* [1842] 'a list of people or things considered acceptable' (OED3), cited by Adams (2001: 84) as the analogically coined

---

3 Cf., however, the development of -*gasm* as a recurrent splinter in the *Urban Dictionary* (chapter 5).

antonym of *blacklist* [1624], or the compound verb *chaindrink* [n.d.], which according to Kastovsky (1986a: 419) is modelled on *chainsmoke*,[4] entirely conform to productive word-formation rules (see 3.2.2 for analogy vs. rules; see Benczes 2006 and Crawford Camiciottoli 2015 for creative compounds).

A different case is provided by the proportion obtaining *cheeseburger* [1938] (OED2), after *hamburger* [1889]. Indeed, *Hamburger* was originally coined from the name of the German city of Hamburg, for 'a native or inhabitant of Hamburg' [1617] (OED2). Yet, the derived word (with a different meaning) was later reanalysed as *ham* + *burger* (although there is no *ham* in a *hamburger*), thus giving rise to the series which includes *chickenburger* [1936], *beefburger* [1940], *vegeburger* [1945],[5] *eggburger* [1960], and similar -*burger* words (OED2; cf. the free form *burger* [1939] which OED2 gives as a shortening of *hamburger*). Therefore, *cheeseburger* originates from a productive schema (see 3.1.2 for a variety of examples showing the development from surface analogy to series and then to combining form). As Plag (2003: 38) himself admits, "[i]n such cases, the dividing line between analogical patterns and word-formation rules is hard to draw".

Word creation is another concept that is relevant to the production of analogical words. Ronneberger-Sibold (2000, 2008), for instance, has opposed regular (productive) word-formation to word creation, i.e. the production of new lexemes via intentional extra-grammatical operations, such as shortening, extra-grammatical derivation, and blending, in domains such as humorous literary texts and brand names. She also distinguishes between extra-grammatical "creative techniques" and regular rules or models of word-formation (Ronneberger-Sibold 2008: 203–205).

Another tendency among scholars is to discuss analogy in relation to, not productivity, but creativity. For instance, Hohenhaus (1996: 323) discusses 'direct analogy' ("direkte Analogie") as one of the mechanisms of '*Ad hoc* word-formation' ("*Ad-hoc*-Wortbildung"), defined by him as 'the creative formation of new words' ("das kreative Bilden neuer Wörter").

Creativity is commonly viewed as the native speaker's ability to create new complex words in an unpredictable (i.e. non-rule-governed) way. However, this

---

[4] The verb *chaindrink* 'to have drink after drink without pause' is not attested in the OED, but its model *chainsmoke* has been attested since 1934 (e.g. in "I've *chain-smoked* for nearly five years"), as a back-formation from *chain-smoker* (Olsen 2014: 45). Cf. *chainsmoker* [1890] from German *Kettenraucher*.

[5] The first part of *vegeburger* is a recurrent splinter *vege*- from *vegetable*, also occurring in *vegelate* [1985] ← *vegetable* + *chocolate*, 'chocolate that contains a certain proportion of vegetable fat' (OED3) and *Vegemite* [1923] ← *vegetable* + *Marmite*, 'a proprietary name for: a type of savoury spread made from yeast extract and vegetable extract' (OED3).

position is revised by van Marle (1990), who conceives of analogy as the synchronic process which governs "rule-creating creativity":

> [T]he speakers of a language have the capacity to construct rules on the basis of the existing words, a capacity we called 'rule-creating creativity'. This ability, then, directly bears upon analogy as a synchronic morphological force.
>
> van Marle (1990: 267)

Although the term 'creativity' is often associated with unconventionality and sometimes with expressivity (Baldi and Dawar 2000; see "expressive morphology" in Zwicky and Pullum 1987), or with rule deviation (cf. Ladányi 2000) and unpredictability (Plag 2003; Ronneberger-Sibold 2008), when applied to the creation of rules – as the term 'rule-creating creativity' implies – it is not understood as the opposite of productivity. Ladányi (2000) indeed suggests that the two concepts of productivity and creativity represent a continuum that forms the basis of her productivity-creativity scale. Productivity, indeed, is not an absolute but a gradual concept, that is, we can distinguish between fully productive and partially (or un-)productive rules.

A less strong position on the regularity and productivity of analogy is in Klégr and Čermák (2010):

> Analogy is the backbone of creativity, i.e. the native speaker's ability to extend the language system in a motivated but unpredictable (non-rule governed) way which may or may not subsequently become rule-governed, predictable and productive.
>
> Klégr and Čermák (2010: 235)

This definition suggests that analogy is neither a static nor a homogeneous concept. Accordingly, instances of analogical formations 'may or may not' ultimately result in predictable and productive rules.

In support of the latter claim, I would like to mention the case of *-erati* formations. Miller (2014: 90) observes that blends like *glitterati* [1956] 'the celebrities or 'glittering' stars of fashionable society' (OED2) and *digerati* [1992] ← *dig(ital)*, 'those people having professional involvement or (exceptional) expertise in information technology' (OED3) are modelled on *literati* [1620]. Actually, *-erati* (and earlier *-ati*) is a recently recognised combining form originated from *literati*, and used to form nouns 'designating elite or prominent groups of people who are associated with what is specified by the stem word' (OED3). Many nonce formations are indeed coined after this pattern: e.g., *niggerati* [1932] (Green 2010), *rockerati* [1900], *chatterati* [1990], *jazzerati* [2000], and *numerati* [n.d.], *soccerati* [n.d.] cited by Klégr and Čermák (2010: 231) and Miller (2014: 90). The occurrence and frequency of some of these words in COCA is an index of the productivity of this element: e.g., *glitterati* (78), *digerati* (25), *Niggerati* (5), *Twitterati* (5), *arterati* (1), *Blazerati* (1), *chatterati* (1), *designerati* (1), *jazzerati* (1), and *politerati* (1). Therefore, although originally *-erati* was sporadically used as a creative splinter in blends, when its use became more regular and its formatives more predictable, it acquired the status of productive combining form (see 3.1.2).

Hence, it seems not unreasonable to distinguish cases of surface analogy that can be classified as creative, because of their irregularity, non-rule-governedness, and only partial predictability, from cases that are fully predictable, regular, and productive.

Furthermore, it seems that, like productivity, the concept of creativity is also scalar. Indeed, different degrees of creativity can be envisaged according to two hierarchies:

1. a) Use of unproductive rules (e.g. *-th* in *sloth* [c1175] ← *slow*, 'physical or mental inactivity' OED2) <
   b) Violation of a rule (e.g. *-ise/-ize* added to a person name in *Shakespearised* [2003])[6] <
   c) More violations of a rule (e.g. in James Joyce's *endlessnessnessness* [1922], *Ulysses*, cited by Dressler 1993: 5028, *-ness* is added twice to a noun) <
   d) No reference to any rule (e.g. the word *gas* [1662] was invented, apparently *ex nihilo*, by the Flemish chemist J. B. van Helmont).
2. a) Use of analogy and productive rule (e.g. *battle-worthy* [1889] 'fit for use in battle' OED2, after *seaworthy* [1807], conforms to a compounding rule) <
   b) Use of analogy and unproductive rule (e.g. *coolth* [1547] 'coolness' OED3, after *warm-th* [c1175]) <
   c) Use of analogy without any rule (e.g. *half-caf* [1990] 'a drink of coffee made using caffeinated and decaffeinated coffee mixed in equal parts' OED3 is coined after *decaf* [1956], a shortening from *decaffeinated*).

Of the two hierarchies in (1a)–(1d) and (2a)–(2c), only the latter involves creativity and analogy.

---

6 From *Neologisms – New Words in Journalistic Text*: "It was apparently first used in 1836 by the American transcendentalist Ralph Waldo Emerson, who complained that the English dramatic poets have *Shakespearised* now for two hundred years".

3.2.2 Analogy vis-à-vis rules

In the literature, two opposite tendencies can be delineated. On the one hand, we find, especially generative, approaches that appeal to analogy exactly in those cases in which linguistic behaviour is not rule-governed, but exceptional, unproductive, unpredictable, or irregular (cf. e.g. Prasada and Pinker 1993). On the other hand, we find approaches that claim that analogy is the basis of any rule-based, productive behaviour in morphology (cf. Blevins and Blevins 2009 and Arndt-Lappe 2015 for an overview).

In particular, some authors have regarded analogy with a unique model and fully productive rules as the two opposite poles of a continuum. Bloomfield (1933: 275), for instance, establishes a tripartition among 1) "unique analogy", 2) "irregular analogy" (that is, unproductive and limited to a very few forms), and 3) "regular analogy". Dressler (1977) instead specifies:

> [W]e must differentiate between 1) the productive application of a WFR [Word-Formation Rule] where existing words might only trigger or favor the occurrence of the neologism, without being its direct cause, and 2) surface analogy ...
>
> Dressler (1977: 20)

Fertig (2013) likewise distinguishes analogy from rules on the basis of the concrete model of the former vs. the abstraction of the latter:

> [R]ules are usually understood to be explicit and abstract, in the sense of being dissociated from any words that instantiate them, whereas analogy is based on relations among mental representations of words in something like an associative network ...
>
> Fertig (2013: 130)

In this book, analogy and rules are not viewed as mutually exclusive concepts, although they differ in various respects. First, as observed by Fertig (2013), analogy is based on concrete models of precise similar forms, rather than on abstract templates describable in rule format. Hence, the formation of French *alun-ir* 'to land on the moon', *amerr-ir* 'to land on the sea', cited by Kilani-Schoch and Dressler (2002: 298), and the recent *amars-ir* 'to land on Mars' (W. U. Dressler, personal communication) is not based on the abstract rule forming French verbs in *-ir*, but on the exact model of *atterr-ir* 'to land'. An English equivalent example is offered by Philip Dick (*The Simulacra*, cited by Munat 2007: 172), who formed the creative analogy *unmarsed* [1964] on the concrete model of *unearthed* [1513].

Similarly, the Spanish noun *andinismo* (from *andino* 'Andean') 'climbing high mountains in the Andes' is clearly modelled on *alpinismo* 'alpinism, the sport of climbing high mountains, esp. in the Alps' (from *alpino* 'Alpine') rather than on the suffix *-ismo*, although the latter is very productive in Spanish (Rainer 2013: 109).

In English, another relevant example is *adulthood* [1850] 'the condition or state of being adult' (OED3), which is not coined after the productive pattern of *-hood* suffixation, but after the specific model of *childhood* [OE], as the following quote suggests: "We know of no lovelier trait in *childhood* or *adulthood* than openness of character" (J. Brookes, *Manliness*, 1875, OED3). Instead, in *Adamhood* [1828] 'humanity' (OED3), the exact model is no longer *childhood*, but *manhood* [c1225], although the word-formation rule involved is again *-hood* suffixation.

The second aspect distinguishing analogy from rules is that the former is output-orientated, whereas rules are also input-orientated (Dressler and Laaha 2012: 108). In other words, in rules, both the input and the output need to be explicitly defined, whereas in analogy only the output needs to be, since there is no abstraction in the input.

The third aspect involves the distinction between potential/possible and actual words. Haspelmath (2002: 273) defines a potential/possible word as "a lexeme that could be formed according to the word-formation rules" (see also Aronoff 1983). Therefore, a potential word is one that is well-formed and grammatical, but not attested. Rainer (2012: 179) adds to the above-mentioned dichotomy a third type of word which he calls "virtual", because it cannot be a possible base of word-formation. While this trichotomy may be useful for a rule-based morphological approach, in an analogical approach to word-formation, there is no concept of 'potential word', because all words are potentially created, or possible, as long as there is an existing word that can act as model. Nor is there a concept of 'virtual word', in that all analogical words are possible bases of analogical word-formation. In terms of "availability" (Bauer 2001: 211; also in Plag 1999: 34; see 3.2.3), not all rule patterns are available and can be used in rule-governed morphological coining, whereas, in theory, all words can be used as available patterns for analogical coining.

The fourth aspect involves the notion of constraint. This concept is especially relevant in Optimality Theory, in which rules are rejected, and constraints are considered as violable and ranked, that is "lower-ranked constraints can be violated in an optimal output form to secure success on higher-ranked constraints" (McCarthy and Prince 1993: 6). The term 'constraint', therefore, suggests that restrictions are not necessarily absolute (Bauer 2001: 126), and some of them are more central than others. Thus, while in the application of a morphological rule a high number of (compatible or interrelated) constraints intervene (see, e.g., Aronoff's 1976 "unitary base constraint" and "word-based word-formation", or Scalise's 1988 "unitary output constraint"), in analogical formations constraints are limited in number or even absent, and this reduces the possibility to predict the output.

As a consequence, analogy is less predictable than rules. In particular, in analogy the output is neither fully predictable, as with rules, nor fully unpredictable, but partially predictable on the basis of the availability of a certain word (or word set) and of its potential to become the model for the creation of new words.

It is also worth noting that the existence of a regular model word may confer more regularity on the target word. Indeed, analogical formations are not necessarily devoid of rules. The above-mentioned *adulthood*, for instance, is both modelled on a precise lexical item (*childhood*) and on the derivational pattern of -*hood* suffixation.

Moreover, analogical formations can become bases of word-formation rules. For instance, the formation *malware* [1990], from *mal*- in *malicious*, 'programs written with the intent of being disruptive or damaging to a computer' (OED3), modelled on *hardware*, *software*, and similar words (see 3.2.3), acts as a regular base in *anti-malware* [n.d.] 'anti-viruses' (*WWW*). The concept of analogy that I develop in this book does not overlap, but may combine with rules (see 3.3.1).

3.2.3 Frequency, profitability, and recoverability of the model

Other concepts that are connected with analogy and deserve clarification are frequency, profitability, and recoverability. Frequency, for instance, is a fundamental notion in the determination of productivity. Indeed, some scholars affirm that processes are productive if they create large numbers of words (Fleischer 1975; Kastovsky 1986b). Frequency is also strongly correlated to Bauer's (2001: 211) concept of "profitability", i.e. the extent to which the availability of a process is exploited in language use. In other words, profitability is a consequence of frequency of types, namely, the number of items in the language that contain the process or item under consideration (cf. frequency of tokens, i.e. the actual occurrences of the item in the language or in a specific corpus).

In analogical formation, both type frequency and token frequency can be considered relevant concepts, especially when referred to the model word. Wanner (2006), for instance, claims that analogy is favoured both if the analogical model has high token frequency, and if it recurs with high type frequency, and thus possesses "social weight" (p. 122).

In particular, as for token frequency, lexicalised and highly frequent words in the language are likely candidates as model words for the analogical process. The lexicalised blend *motel* [1925], for instance, serves as model for the coinage of *apartotel* [1965] ← *apartment* + *hotel*, 'a type of hotel which offers private suites for self-catering' (OED3), *boatel* [1956] ← *boat* + *hotel*, 'a ship with the facilities of a hotel' (OED2), and *skytel* [n.d.] 'a hotel near the airport', cited by Lehrer (2007: 123).[7] By contrast, items with low token frequency, such as Lewis Carroll's occasionalism *frumious* [1871], explained by him as a blend of *fuming* and *furious* (OED2), are less probable candidates as model words in analogical word-formation.

As for the type frequency of the potential model word, those words that recur with high type frequency in linguistic practice encourage the profitability of a morphological pattern, for what is called "Family Size effect" (De Jong, Schreuder, and Baayen 2000: 329). A frequently used pattern, for instance, is in *hardware*, which provides the model for *software*, and, later, both are models for *firmware* [1968] 'a permanent form of software built into certain kinds of computer' (OED2), *spyware* [1983] 'software that enables information to be gathered covertly about a person's computer activities' (OED2, s.v. *spy*), and *vapourware* [1993] (OED2, see 2.2). Additional terms belonging to this family include *adware* [1983] 'software that automatically displays advertising material on a computer' (OED3), *bloatware* [1991] 'software that requires an excessive amount of disk space or memory' (OED3), and the above-mentioned *malware* (OED3, see 3.2.2). In particular, this is a case of analogy via schema, i.e. with a set of prototype words, with *hardware* and *software* being the archetypes. With regard to the morpheme *ware*, Bauer, Lieber, and Plag (2013: 528) observe that, although it is a free form and can be found in many compounds (e.g. *glassware*, *tableware*, etc.), for words such as *spyware*, *freeware*, *netware*, etc., a compound analysis is not convincing. Indeed, in these words, *-ware* is more plausibly a bound splinter with a distinct meaning 'software' than a free compound component. However, in *hardware*, the meaning of 'software' is only partially present (see also *-aware* in Green 1991: 16).

Furthermore, high token/type frequency also helps the recoverability of the model. 'Recoverability' is used here to mean the capability that a hearer has to identify the model of an analogical formation which a speaker has produced. For instance, the hearer's capability to identify the model *hardware/software* when (s)he encounters a novel target, such as *adware* or *firmware*, clearly depends on the frequency with which the model occurs. In 3.2.5, it will be shown that the

---

7 In memory-based language processing, van den Bosch and Daelemans (2013: 319) represent token frequencies as "exemplar weights". In particular, they claim that the distance between a new exemplar (the target) and a memory exemplar (a model stored in memory) is divided by the weight (or token frequency) of the memory exemplar. In other words, they claim that "more frequent exemplars are drawn closer in distance to new exemplars" (van den Bosch and Daelemans 2013: 319; see also Daelemans and van den Bosch 2005).

similarity features [f$_n$] which the target and the model share, as well as the part of the model which remains invariable in the target constitute two further elements on which the recoverability of the model depends.

3.2.4 Analogy as proportion

The interpretation of analogy as a proportional equation derives from classical antiquity and has survived until our days, thanks to Paul (1880), Saussure [1916] (1995), and Bloomfield (1933). Rainer (2013) is a successful recent attempt to revive the traditional proportional model and elaborate Paul's (1880) dichotomy between 'ideal analogy' ("ideelle Analogie") and 'individual analogy' ("individuelle Analogie"). In his classification of analogy in Spanish, Rainer (2013: 151) distinguishes between 1) 'proportional' vs. 'non-proportional analogy' ("analogía proporcional" vs. "no proporcional"), and between 2) 'concrete' vs. 'abstract model' ("modelo concreto" vs. "abstracto").

The type of proportional analogy with a concrete (i.e. unique) model corresponds to the concept of surface analogy: e.g., Spanish *durmienda* (lit. 'place where one sleeps, one's bedroom') is a proportional analogy with the unique model of *vivienda* (lit. 'place where one lives, one's home'). On the other hand, Rainer (2013) suggests that the model of Spanish *afganización* (← *afgano* 'Afghan' + *-ización* '-ization') is not a precise word, but an abstract model.

The type of non-proportional analogy is instead illustrated by the Spanish words *taxicomanía* and *mieditis*, which are respectively coined on a concrete and abstract model (Rainer 2013: 151). As for *taxicomanía* (← *taxi* 'taxi' + *toxicomanía* 'toxicomania'), the similarity is clearly with the second blend component. Yet, it is not possible to formulate a proportional equation which links *taxicomanía* to *toxicomanía*, because the two words are solely connected by a phonological similarity, not by a morphotactic one. This type of formation can be considered analogical only in Bauer's (1983: 96) broader conception of analogy (see *wargasm* in 3.2.1), that is, as formation based on a concrete model identifiable as one word, in this case, *toxicomanía*.

The case of *mieditis* (← *miedo* 'fear' + *-itis* '-itis') is rarer. Indeed, although the suffix *-itis* is used in medical Spanish – as well as in medical English – to refer to words which denote an 'inflammation' (e.g. Spanish *amigdalitis* 'tonsillitis'), the meaning associated with *mieditis* (colloquial for *miedo*) seems to depart from the original meaning of the suffix and is instead connected with '(metaphorical) infirmity'. Rainer (2013: 166) explains that in Spanish two independent suffixes *-itis* have developed that correspond to the two meanings of 'inflammation' vs.

'figurative infirmity, exaggerated affection', with differences in register, use, and type of base. Thus, the formation of *mieditis* is non-proportional with the abstract pattern forming *amigdalitis* and similar inflammations.

In English, colloquial words comparable to Spanish *mieditis* have recently been coined. For instance, neither *nettitis* [1999] 'imaginary condition of illness caused by the Net' (*Neologisms – New Words in Journalistic Text*) nor *end-of-the-semesteritis* [2008] 'lack of motivation to work hard near the end of the semester' (humorous, *Rice University Neologisms Database*) are proportional with the pattern of standard *tonsillitis* [1801]. In line with Olsen (2014: 36) "when *-itis* appears with a native English lexeme, its meaning shifts to 'addiction, abnormal excess of'" (e.g. *computeritis, facebookitis, junk-fooditis*, etc.). According to Green (2010), this suffix is used humorously to create imagined 'diseases', as in *danceitis* [n.d.], *workitis* [n.d.], etc.

There are also several English examples that are comparable to Spanish *taxicomanía*. For instance, like *taxicomanía*, the blend *gayborhood* [2008] ← *gay + neighborhood*, 'gathering of homosexual males' (*Rice University Neologisms Database*) differs from its longer component for only one phoneme. Yet, this formation is analogical neither with the second component, nor with both components (cf. Hockett 1968: 62).

In the present work, I embrace a narrower view of analogy, which excludes non-proportional cases such as *gayborhood*. Here I keep the concept of blending distinct from that of analogy (see De Smet 2013). In particular, whereas some blends can be formed on the model of others, i.e. by surface analogy, not all blends are analogical in nature. Only those that are analysable according to a proportional equation are.

For instance, analogy can explain the formation of the recent journalistic blend *Merkozy* [2011] ← *(Angela) Merkel + (Nicolas) Sarkozy*, 'the unified position of France and Germany during the early twenty-first century European sovereign debt crisis' (*Wiktionary*), created on the pattern of the nicknames *Bennifer* [2008] ← *Ben (Affleck) + Jennifer (Lopez)* and *Brangelina* [2011] ← *Brad (Pitt) + Angelina (Jolie)*.[8] In this case, the following proportion can be envisaged: *Ben ^ Jennifer : Bennifer = Merkel ^ Sarkozy : X (X = Merkozy)*.

As this proportion shows, both morphotactic affinity and semantic resemblance inspire the association of the target *Merkozy* with its model *Bennifer*, in that they share the same structural pattern (overlap blending) and semantic components, i.e. members of famous couples (either in life or in politics), although the model blends first names and the target last names.

---

8 Both target and model(s) are attested in the *Rice University Neologisms Database*.

Moreover, proportion can explain the coinage of the following neoformations recorded in Algeo (1991: 10–11): *hit lady* [1980] 'a woman who commits murder for hire' ← *hit man* [1970], *middlebrow* [1924] 'a person who is only moderately intellectual' ← *highbrow* [1898]/*lowbrow* [1901], and *moonquake* [1906] 'a seismic tremor of the moon's surface' ← *earthquake* [c1325]. Some of Algeo's novel words are discussed in more depth in the subsections indicated in round brackets: *beefcake* [1949] ← *cheesecake* [1934] (1.2), *build-down* [1983] 'a systematic reduction of nuclear armaments' ← *build-up* [1943] (3.3.4), *cartnapping* [1964] 'the act of stealing a grocery cart' ← *kidnapping* [1682] (*-napping* in 3.1.2), *gray market* [1934] ← *black market* [1727] (3.3.2), and *grayout* [1942] ← *blackout* [1929] (3.3.2). Two are contextualised in 3.3.5: namely, *hot war* [1947] 'a military conflict' ← *cold war* [1945] and *inner space* [1958] 'the part of one's mind or personality that is not normally experienced' ← *outer space* [1842].

Algeo (1991: 10) classifies all the above-mentioned words as cases of "blending". In actual fact, they are merely new compound words whose right or left component replaces a similar element of the model. Resemblance or similarity is, therefore, another concept which deserves attention for the investigation of analogy.

3.2.5 Analogy as similarity

As Anttila (1977: 16) affirms, "[e]ver since antiquity an analogy has been a relation of similarity". In particular, analogy expresses a "similarity in relationships which are proportional" (Lahiri 2000: 1). Similarity, therefore, is the relationship of partial formal and semantic affinity that can be established between a source word/word set, i.e. the model, and a target word, the analogous formation. As Olsen (2014) puts it:

> The process of analogy allows a new word to be created by analyzing a base as a formal and semantic complex A + B. If one of the elements, A or B, is exchanged for an element C, perceived as more appropriate for the desired meaning of the new word, either C + B or A + C arises.
>
> Olsen (2014: 45)

The relationships characterising surface analogy and analogy via schema are basically relationships of morphotactic similarity, that is morphological properties between words, series, or word families added to phonological properties (cf. Dressler 2003 for families of paradigms in inflectional morphology). In addition, there are relationships of semantic affinity, as when the model and the target share synonymous or, more frequently, antonymous components.

Similarity (or partial sameness) can be identified from two different perspectives. From the speaker's perspective, similarity is the relationship that allows the coinage of a new complex word – the target (T) – modelled on an existing word – the model (M) – which shares one or more trait(s) with the target. For instance, this similarity is identified when a model word, such as *black market* [1727], is analysed as complex. Then its phonological, morphological, and semantic structure is reproduced in a potential word, such as *white market* [1943] 'authorized dealing in things that are rationed or of which the supply is otherwise restricted' (OED2, s.v. *white*), which resembles its model for some shared trait.

From the hearer's perspective, however, similarity is the relationship that allows the model's recoverability. In this case, the relationship of partial similarity allows the hearer to analyse the new word *white market* according to the existing pattern of *black market*, and to classify the former under this latter pattern (see "classification" or "categorization" in Wanner 2006: 121).[9]

In analogical formation, the target T is normally analysable in terms of Invariable Part (IP) and Variable Part (VP). The former is the part that is shared by T and M, whereas the latter is the part that varies in T and replaces a different component of M. The Invariable Part may be either the first or the second component of the new analogical formation, and can be identified with various elements, namely, a word (base) (e.g. in compounds or derived words), an affix (in prefixed or suffixed words), a combining form, a word part (in clippings), a splinter (in blends), or a series of letters (in acronyms).

The Invariable Part, however, should not be confused with the similarity features [f_n] which are owned by both the target T and the model M, and which allow the new coinage (from the speaker's perspective) and the model's recoverability (from the hearer's perspective). The formula below expresses the relationship between T and M:

T is analogous to M (T ← M) iff both T and M are analysable as Variable Part (VP) + Invariable Part (IP) or Invariable Part (IP) + Variable Part (VP). In terms of association with the model, T is associated with M (T → M) for the similarity feature(s) [f_n] iff both T and M exhibit [f_n]

---

[9] Wanner (2006: 121) defines analogy as "a process that marks items of partial or full local identity by assimilation or classification (categorization)". Yet the term 'assimilation' that he uses may be confused with the term used in linguistics to refer to the phonological process by which one sound becomes more like a nearby sound. Hence, terms such as 'association' or 'classification' have been preferred in the present work and elsewhere (cf. Mattiello 2016).

The similarity features [f$_n$] consist of an array of affinities at various language levels, namely, phonological, morphotactic, and semantic (partly taken from Mattiello 2016):
- *Phonological features*: The phonological features shared by T and M include segmental and suprasegmental features. Segmental features consist of:
    1. Structure of the stressed syllable (onset, nucleus, coda; body, rime);
    2. Segments of the stressed syllable (consonant, vowel, semi-consonant);
    3. Phonemes.

    Suprasegmental features involve prosodic aspects such as:
    4. Word length (monosyllabic, disyllabic, polysyllabic word);
    5. Word stress (primary and, in case, secondary stress).
- *Morphotactic features*: The morphotactic features shared by T and M include:
    1. Type of morphology (grammatical vs. marginal vs. extra-grammatical);
    2. Morphological category (compounding, derivation, clipping, etc.);
    3. Syntactic category of the base(s) (noun, verb, adjective, etc.).
- *Semantic features*: The semantic relationships that link T to M comprise:
    1. Near identity with small motivation: synonymy (denotational synonym vs. denotational and connotational synonym);
    2. Massive semantic overlap: paronymy;
    3. Contradictory opposition: antonymy;
    4. Other contrasts: especially, co-hyponymy, hyperonymy–hyponymy;
    5. Small semantic overlap.

By way of illustration, let us now analyse the target *white market* and its model *black market* in terms of Variable and Invariable Part and similarity features [f$_n$]:
- [*white*]$_{VP}$ + [*market*]$_{IP}$ ← [*black*]$_{VP}$ + [*market*]$_{IP}$;
- *Phonological features*:

    1–2. Structure/Segments of the stressed syllable /ɑː/: same body, that is, Consonant (onset) + Vowel (nucleus);
    3. Phonemes: shared phonemes /mɑːkɪt/;
    4. Word length: trisyllabic words;
    5. Word stress: primary stress on the second syllable and secondary stress on the first syllable (/ˌwaɪtˈmɑːkɪt/ → /ˌblækˈmɑːkɪt/).
- *Morphotactic features*:
    1. Type of morphology: grammatical;
    2. Morphological category: compounding, esp. loose compounds (2.3);
    3. Syntactic category of the bases: Adj. + Noun.
- *Semantic features*:
    3. Contradictory opposition: antonymy between *white* and *black*.

The list of similarity features [f_n] varies according to the greater (vs. smaller) resemblance between the target and the model word. In general, the greater the similarity between T and M, the higher the number of features that they share, the easier 1) the analogical coinage and 2) the model's recoverability. As Wanner (2006: 122) suggests, analogy preferentially takes place between "locally contiguous items", that is between items that share all features under current focus of relevance minus one. For instance, there is contiguity (phonological neighbourhood) between the target words *rock-/shock-umentary* mentioned in 3.1.2 and their model *mock-umentary*. Locally contiguous items of this kind also facilitate the model's recoverability. More on similarity relationships in 3.3.4.

3.2.6 Analogy vs. reanalysis

According to Hock ([1938] 1991: 176), the use of proportional analogy "is often preceded and triggered by morphological reinterpretation", or reanalysis. For instance, in the oft-quoted example of *hamburger*, reanalysed as *ham + burger* (see 3.2.1), a morphological resegmentation of the word *Hamburg-er* has triggered the analogised forms *cheeseburger* [1938], *beefburger* [1940], etc. Booij (2005: 262) similarly views reanalysis – i.e. when "the existing word combination is given another structural interpretation" – as the first step of the two mechanisms involved in morphological change, the second step being analogy.

However, as appropriately observed by Hopper and Traugott ([1993] 2003: 56), analogy and reanalysis involve innovation along different axes. While reanalysis operates along the syntagmatic axis, by developing new out of old structures, analogy operates on the paradigmatic axis, by modelling new forms on already existing constructions (or words, as in the case of word-formation).

Klégr and Čermák (2010: 236) even consider "*ad hoc* ... reanalysis" as one of the characterising features of analogical formations. According to them, for instance, the ending part *-illion* in *million* has been reinterpreted as an affix or combining form, and this has allowed the coinage of *zillion* (cf. 3.1.2). I do not share this view, in that not all analogical formations are triggered by reanalysis. Therefore, considering the latter a defining characteristic of analogy is in some cases incorrect. Reanalysis only occurs when the model of the analogical formation is either a simplex word reinterpreted as complex or has a different segmentation. Hence, some linguists have considered reanalysis as a "false analogy" (see Rainer 2013: 155).

More commonly, when the model word is simplex, it may be reanalysed as complex in order to allow the analogy to occur. For instance, the origin of the word *bikini* [1947] is actually from the name of the atoll *Bikini*, in the Marshall Islands, but the *bi-* element has been reinterpreted as a combining form from the Latin prefix meaning 'two'. Hence, this reanalysis has triggered the formation of *monokini* [1964] 'a one-piece beach garment or swimming costume' (OED3) and *trikini* [1967] 'any of various designs of ladies' swimsuit which consist of three main areas of fabric' (OED2), by substituting *bi-* respectively with *mono-* 'alone, single' and *tri-* 'three' (cf. *facekini* and *burkini* in *The Observer*, 2014). A parallel reanalysis involves the formation of *trialogue* [1532] 'a dialogue or colloquy between three persons' (OED2), after *dialogue* [c1450], the first syllable of this being mistaken for the prefix *di-* 'two' (see also *monologue* [c1550], *quadrilogue* [c1475], and the combining form *-logue*).

By contrast, when the model is complex, no reanalysis is involved, with very few exceptions of complex words that are resegmented, such as the above-mentioned *hamburger*.

Further evidence of the independence of the two mechanisms of analogy and reanalysis is provided by folk-etymology. McMahon (1994: 74) discusses folk-etymology under the heading "sporadic analogy" (cf. Rundblad and Kronenfeld 2000), specifying that it is produced when words of foreign origin are reinterpreted in one's native language, or have their morphological boundaries shifted to obtain a more transparent word. However, not all cases of folk-etymology involve analogy.

For instance, in the dialect form *sparrowgrass* [1664], the original Medieval Latin word *sparagus* 'asparagus' has been reanalysed as a complex word (from *sparrow* and *grass*) whose elements already exist in English. Yet, this is not a case in which proportional analogy intervenes, in that *sparrowgrass* is not modelled on one specific lexical item (cf. *grass-sparrow* [1883] 'grass-finch, a common American sparrow' OED2). A comparable case is the word *cockroach* [1624] 'a well-known large dark-brown beetle-like insect' (OED2), whose origin is from Spanish *cucaracha*, reinterpreted as *cock* and *roach*, with no analogy.

A different case is the folk-etymology *Godzilla* [1965] 'the name of a very large dinosaur-like monster from the 1956 U.S. film *Godzilla, King of the Monsters*' (OED3). The name of the monster is actually an alteration – by folk-etymology – of Japanese *Gojira*, the title of the film from which the American version was adapted. This alteration was clearly influenced by the existence of English *gorilla*, but also by the name *God*. Indeed, *Godzilla* was later resegmented as *God* and *-zilla*. Then the latter became a combining form used, for instance, to coin *Bridezilla* [1995] 'a woman thought to have become intolerably obsessive or overbearing in planning the details of her wedding' (OED3) and other nonce words referring to 'a particularly imposing person (or thing)' (e.g. *Bosszilla* [1988], *groomzilla* [2003], *mom-zilla* [2005] OED3). In this example, folk-etymology originated the model *Godzilla*, but analogy only occurs – after reanalysis – in the formation of *-zilla* target words.

Another phenomenon which is often connected with analogy and may (or may not) involve reanalysis is word play or puns, i.e. words which are intentionally formed by altering or distorting existing words, generally with the intention of playfulness, mockery, or parody. For example, the word *herstory* [1970] 'in feminist use: history emphasizing the role of women or told from a woman's point of view' (OED2) is described by the OED as a punning alteration of *history* [OE]. However, it could be analysed as a proportional analogy in which reanalysis intervenes. Indeed, first, the model has fancifully been reinterpreted as *his story*. Then, the supposed possessive adjective *his* has been replaced by the female counterpart *her* in the analogical formation.

A comparable example is the verb *girlcott* [1884] 'of a woman or group of women: to boycott' (OED3). Here the model *boycott* [1880] 'to refuse to handle or buy (goods) as a protest' (OED3), whose origin is actually from the name of Captain Charles C. Boycott, has humorously been reanalysed as complex, although *boycott* is neither semantically nor morphotactically a compound. Yet, the homophony between the first syllable in *boy-cott* and the noun *boy* has encouraged both the reanalysis and the subsequent playful substitution in the analogical formation *girl-cott*.

However, analogical word play is not necessarily preceded by reanalysis. For instance, the formation *copyleft* [1976] is a play on the word *copyright* [1735] used as a parody in the slogan "*Copyleft* – all rights reversed" and referring to 'the practice of using copyright law to offer the right to distribute copies and modified versions of a work' (*Wikipedia*). In this case, the substitution of *right* with *left* in the analogical formation occurs at a morphological boundary, with no reanalysis.

By contrast, back-formation is generally correlated with both reanalysis and analogy (see McMahon 1994; Plag 2003). Indeed, in back-formation, words are formed by deleting a (normally supposed) suffix by analogy with other pairs. For instance, the verb *rotavate* [1950] 'to break up (soil, etc.) with a Rotavator' (OED3) has been back-formed by subtracting *-or* from the noun *Rotavator* [1936] ← *rotary + cultivator*, 'a machine with rotating blades for breaking up or tilling the soil' (OED3), on the basis of a proportional analogy with word pairs such as *act–actor*. Thus, analogy is here connected with reanalysis, in that *-or* was originally part of the second blend component, and has only later been reanalysed as a suffix added to the verb *rotavate* in *Rotavator*.¹⁰

3.3 A working model of analogy

3.3.1 Types of analogy

The model of analogy that I propose distinguishes among different types and subtypes of analogy:

Surface analogy: This is the type of analogy that corresponds to Motsch's (1981: 101) "Oberflächenanalogie", i.e. the word-formation process whereby a new word is coined that is clearly modelled on an actual model word.

This type of analogy represents the traditional idea of analogy as a local mechanism (see "local analogy" in Klégr and Čermák 2010: 235 and in Booij 2010: 88–93; cf. Miller 2014: 88, who claims that "all analogy is local"). According to Arndt-Lappe (2015), local (or surface) analogy can be defined on the basis of three prerequisites: a) the model is restricted to one particular lexeme, b) a very high degree of similarity between target and model is involved, and c) the productivity of the process is very limited, in the extreme case producing only one new word.

A further distinction within this type is among:

Pure surface analogy: In pure surface analogy, the crucial motivation is pure similarity with a concrete model and not with an abstract pattern. An example of pure surface analogy is the noun *extrapolation* [1872] used in mathematics to indicate 'the action or method of finding by a calculation based on the known terms of a series, other terms outside of them' (OED2), and modelled on *interpolation* [1763] used in the same domain. Similarly, the adjective *Galwegian* [1870] 'belonging to Galloway' (OED2) is coined on the concrete model of *Norwegian* [1607], and the noun *outro* [1967] 'a concluding section' (OED3) is clearly obtained from the model *intro* [1923] ← *introduction*, also in Miller (2014: 89), reinterpreting *in* as an adverb opposite to *out*. Another case of pure surface analogy is the noun *octant*

---

10 Cases of back-formation (and folk-etymology) which involve reanalysis and/or analogy can also be observed in the acquisition of Italian inflection. For instance, an Italian child (Anastasia, 3;2) has back-formed the singular noun *occo (instead of *occhio* 'eye') from the plural *occhi* 'eyes', by analogy with the pair *fiocco–fiocchi* 'flake-s'. Another small Italian girl (Matilde, 2;7) has reinterpreted the final /ɪ/ sound of English *pony* as an Italian plural marker, thus back-forming the singular *pono* according to Italian nominal inflection in masculine nouns.

[1672] 'an instrument in the form of a graduated eighth of a circle' (OED3), which originates from the combining form *octo-* 'eight', after the concrete model of *quadrant* [?c1400], but not after an abstract (rule-format) model. More recently, the proprietary name *Aerobie* [1985] 'a thin plastic ring which is spun through the air in a catching game' (OED3) owes its origin to *Frisbee* [1957] – originally from the 'Frisbie' bakery in Bridgeport – whose final part was changed to avoid legal problems. Another example of pure surface analogy is *doubleton* [1906], used in Whist and Bridge for 'two cards only of one suit, in a player's hand' (OED2), and created after the model *singleton* [1876]. *Wordspy* also records the acronym *YIMBY* [1988] ← *yes in my back yard*, 'a person who favors a project that would add a dangerous or unpleasant feature to his or her neighborhood', a pure surface analogy on *NIMBY* [1980] ← *not in my back yard* (OED3).

All the above-mentioned examples can be analysed only in terms of substitution of part of a model word (the Variable Part) in the target.

Surface analogy with enlargement/reduction: Another subtype of surface analogy entails an enlargement or reduction of the model word. For instance, acronyms or initialisms, such as slang *BFF* [1987] ← *Best Friend(s) Forever* (OED2, s.v. *B*) or *OMG* [1917] 'Oh my God!' (OED3), act as model words for the targets *BFFL* [2010] ← *Best Friend(s) For Life* and *NOMG* [2013] 'No, oh my God!' (*Rice University Neologisms Database*). A comparable case from the same collection is *VPOTUS* [2008] 'Vice-President of the United States', enlarged from *POTUS* [1895]. But this subtype is not confined to extra-grammatical formations. For instance, in *Disorient Express* [2008] humorously coined after *Orient Express* [1883] for 'a state of confusion' (*Rice University Neologisms Database*), the enlargement involves the prefix *dis-*.

The opposite process of reduction is rarer and is illustrated, for example, by the formation *IMO* [1989] 'in my opinion', after the model of *IMHO*, attested slightly earlier [1984] for 'in my humble/honest opinion' (both OED2, s.v. *I*). Another comparable case is *IMBY* [1989] 'a person who wants his or her neighborhood to have some feature that other people consider dangerous or unpleasant' (*Wordspy*), after the above-mentioned *NIMBY* [1980].

I admit that these are rather atypical cases of surface analogy, but their analysis as proportional equations – e.g., *Best Friends Forever* : *BFF* = *Best Friends For Life* : *BFFL*, or *orient* : *Orient Express* = *disorient* : *Disorient Express* – confirms their analogical nature.

Surface analogy with no Invariable Part: A non-prototypical subtype of pure surface analogy exhibits no invariable part, but only similarity at the morphotactic and/or semantic level. This subtype is more frequent in extra-grammatical than in grammatical formations. For instance, the blend *linner* [2010] 'a meal between lunch and dinner' (*Rice University Neologisms Database*) is based on *brunch* [1896] (cf. 1.2), although target and model do not share any word part. A comparable case is the back-clipping *mill* [1786] 'one-thousandth of a dollar' (OED3), which was shortened from classical Latin *millēsimum*, on the analogy of *cent* [1782] ← *centesimum*, 'in the American monetary system, the hundredth part of a dollar' (OED3). In both cases, a proportional description is possible, in that targets are obtained via the same operation as their models (i.e. blending, clipping) and the words' meaning helps the association (i.e. *breakfast*, *lunch*, and *dinner* are co-hyponyms of 'meals', while *mill* and *cent* are 'units of measurement').

In spite of its non-prototypicality, this subtype of analogy shows that the analysis as proportion and the semantic/morphotactic similarity criteria are essential for analogical formations (1.3), whereas the presence of an Invariable Part is not crucial. In *linner* and *brunch*, different parts of the word *lunch* have been retained (cf. *l*- vs. -*unch*). In *mill* ← *cent*, the Invariable Part -*esimum* has even been deleted.

Surface analogy combined with rule: When analogy combines with rules, the motivation is twofold. The primary motivation is analogy, i.e. similarity with a precise lexical item, but the target also obeys word-formation rules, hence the additional motivation is conformity to rule patterns. For instance, the target *fluorescence* [1852] 'the distinctive luminosity shown by some substances when illuminated with light' (OED3) is coined after the concrete model of *opalescence* [1805], but also exhibits a regular nominal suffix -*escence* found in other formations (e.g. *effervescence*, *iridescence*, etc.). Similarly, *minification* [1894] 'diminution or reduction in size' (OED3) has its model in *magnification* [1672], and both obey the rule which obtains abstract nouns by adding the suffix -*ation* to verbs ending in -*ify* (e.g. *magnify*, *minify*). Furthermore, in both cases, the base is from classical Latin (*magnificus*, *minor*).

The compounds *laughing post* [1810] and obsolete †*laughing stake* [1630] were both coined by analogy with their synonym *laughing stock* [?1518] 'an object of derisive laughter or general ridicule' (OED3), but also in conformity with productive compounding rules. According to the *Online Etymology Dictionary*, the compound *whipping-stock* [1615] 'a person who is frequently whipped' (OED2, s.v. *whipping*) is coined after the same model, but similarity here is with the second constituent of the compound (i.e. *stock*).

On the other hand, the nautical term *oldster* [1818] 'a midshipman who has served for over four years' (OED3) is coined after *youngster* [1608] 'a boy or junior seaman on board ship' (OED2), with an unproductive suffix -*ster* (only productive in Old and Middle English; cf. Adams 1973: 172–175).

Moreover, the spelling of the adverb *gaily* [a1375] 'cheerfully, joyously' (OED3), regularly derived from *gay* + *-ly*, is currently preferred over *gayly* because of the analogy with the concrete model *daily* [OE adj., 1416 adv.]. Hence, here analogy is orthographic, combined with the *-ly* adverb formation rule.

Other comparable examples reported in the OED include *ageism* [1969] 'age discrimination' (OED3; also in Green 1991: 5), on the pattern of *sexism* [1866] and *racism* [1903], and *hands-on* [1905] 'designating an attitude characterized by involvement' (OED3), based on *hands-off* [1860]. Less recent examples are *whiteboard* [1883] 'a white surface for use like a blackboard' (OED2), which is regularly created after *blackboard* [1739], and obsolete †*waste-time* [1609] 'a means of wasting time' (OED2), after *pastime* [1490]. According to the OED, *airhead* [1943] 'an airbase close to an area of active operations where troops can be evacuated by air' (OED3) has been created after the military terms *beachhead* [1940] 'a fortified position of troops landed on a beach' (OED2, s.v. *beach*) and former *bridge-head* [1812] 'a fortification protecting the end of a bridge' (OED2, s.v. *bridge*; cf. French *tête de pont*). An additional case is the adjective *writerly* [1957] 'characteristic of a professional writer or literary man' (OED2), which has its model in *painterly* [a1586]. Both have been created after the abstract pattern of an agentive noun ending in *-er*, to which the *-ly* adjectival suffix is added.

Miller (2014: 85–89) mentions further surface analogies that can also be analysed in terms of derivation or compounding rules. For instance, *underwhelm* [1956] 'to leave unimpressed' (OED2), after *overwhelm* [?a1400] (also *underwhelmed* on *overwhelmed*), is a regular derived word. Similarly, *try-hard* [1922] 'a person who tries very hard' (OED3) and *work-hard* [1922] (OED3, s.v. *work*) are regular compounds created after *die-hard* [1844] 'one that dies hard', as shown by the following quote: "The country did not want *cryhards* or *diehards*: it wanted *tryhards* and *workhards*" (*Times*, 1922, 21 January, OED3). By contrast, the humorous colloquial noun *coolth* [1966] 'the quality of being relaxed' (OED3) cited by Miller (2014: 89, see also 3.2.1) has been formed after *warmth* [1600] 'an excited or fervent state of the feelings', after an unproductive *-th* rule pattern.[11] Another unproductive suffix (*-eer*) occurs in the formation of *orienteer* [1965] 'a person who takes part in orienteering' (OED3), after the model *mountaineer* [1599] (or *volunteer* [a1618] according to Bauer 1983: 290).

---

11 Kubozono (1990: 4) interprets *coolth* as a blend of *cool* and (*warm*)*th*, but this is clearly not the case, in that the former's meaning does not include the latter's meaning.

All the above-mentioned examples can be analysed both in terms of a paradigmatic substitution of the Variable Part, and in terms of a syntagmatic concatenation of Variable + Invariable/Invariable + Variable Part. These are not cases of analogy by rule (cf. Gardani 2013), since, in my model, analogy does not involve the same level of abstraction as rules and it is instead based on concrete words (3.2.2), but surface analogies which also comply with (un-)productive rules.

Analogy via schema: This is the type of analogy that is related to Köpcke's (1993, 1998) schema model elaborated for inflectional morphology, and which corresponds to Klégr and Čermák's (2010: 235) "extended analogy" (i.e. providing a pattern for a series of formations). Therefore, the difference between surface analogy and analogy via schema is mainly diachronic, as shown in 3.1.2 (cf. also Bybee 2010 on analogy being the first step towards the development of a schema).

A schema is a concrete model identifiable as two or (preferably) more target words. The words that serve as schema constitute: 1) a series of words sharing the same formation, or 2) a word family, i.e. a group of words sharing the same base(s). Cf. Wittgenstein's notion of "family" cited in Kilani-Schoch and Dressler (2005: 178), also "analogical set" in Wanner (2006: 123). The case of the series *firmware*, *spyware*, etc. (from *hard-/soft-ware*) has already been discussed (see 3.2.3).

Combining forms: Other cases that I classify as analogy via schema are combining forms. For instance, the neoclassical combining form *-phaty* (forming nouns with the sense 'method of cure, curative treatment') has originated words such as *homœopathy* [1826] and *hydropathy* [1843], which act as interfixed model (see *-o-*) for the new word *naturopathy* [1901] 'a theory of disease and system of therapy based on the supposition that diseases can be cured by natural agencies' (OED3).

Another frequent combining form is *-culture*, from classical Latin *-cultūra* (as in *agricultūra* 'agriculture'), mostly added to Latin bases and found in internationalisms relating to 'farming and cultivation' (OED3). Here the words *agriculture* [?1440] and *horticulture* [1678] have established the interfixed pattern (see the linking element *-i-*) for *pisciculture* [1807] 'fish farming', *pomiculture* [1852] 'fruit growing', *apiculture* [1864] 'bee-keeping', *mariculture* [1867] 'the cultivation of the living resources of the sea', *viticulture* [1872] 'vine-growing', and *animaliculture* [1879] 'the rearing of animals', all attested in the OED.

An established final combining form discussed in Mattiello (2007) and earlier in Marchand ([1960] 1969: 211) is *-scape* (from *landscape* [1605]), forming nouns denoting 'a view, picture of' (OED3). The earliest formations are from the eighteenth century: i.e., *offscape* [1711] 'a distant view or prospect' (OED3), *rockscape* [1754] 'a pictorial representation of rocky scenery' (OED3), *prisonscape* [1796] 'a view or picture dominated by a prison' (OED3), and *sea-scape* [1799] (OED2). They acted as model for new words which were mainly coined in the nineteenth century: i.e., *skyscape* [1817], *waterscape* [1826], *riverscape* [1854], *city-scape* [1856], *townscape* [1867], *cloudscape* [1868], *roofscape* [1891], *moonscape* [1907], *urbanscape* [1958], and *lunarscape* [1965] (OED2-3, more examples in Mattiello 2007: 106).[12]

Another series is formed after George Orwell's *Newspeak* and *Oldspeak* [1949], which have recently inspired the creation of *doublespeak* [1957] 'deliberately ambiguous or imprecise language' (OED2, s.v. *double*),[13] *spacespeak* [1963] 'the jargon associated with workers in the space industry' (OED3, s.v. *space*), and *computerspeak* [1968] 'computer jargon' (also *computerese*, OED3). They all contain the combining form *-speak* – or the "suffix" according to OED2 (see "secreted affix" in Fradin 2000: 37) – used to denote 'a particular variety of language or characteristic mode of speaking'. Other neologisms from Lehrer (2007: 124) are *sportspeak* [1968] 'the language or jargon typically used to describe sport' (OED3, s.v. *sport*), *blandspeak* [n.d.], *blogspeak* [n.d.], and *nounspeak* [n.d.].

The combining form *-(a)thon* (from *marathon* [1896]), as in *walkathon* [1930] 'a long-distance or protracted walk' (OED3) and *telethon* [1949] 'an especially prolonged television programme used to raise money for a charity' (OED2), has been reused in the targets *moviethon* [1954], *pianothon*, *poolathon*, and *rockerthon*, all attested in a [1963] quote of the OED. Other nonce formations are reported in Lehrer (2007: 122): e.g., *bikathon* [n.d.], *dancethon* [n.d.], *jogathon* [n.d.], *performancethon* [n.d.], and *swimathon* [n.d.].

Also the German *fest* 'festival', as in *Oktoberfest* [1810], has paved the way for American English *gabfest* [1897] 'a gathering for talk' (OED2) and *talk fest* [1910] 'a session of lengthy discussion or conversation' (OED2), and later for *liquor-fest* [1952], *hen fest* [1963], *filmfest* [1970], all showing the combining form *-fest*.[14]

---

12 It is worth noting that the base for *-scape* formations can be either a noun (*moon*), or an adjective (*lunar*), or even an adverb (*off*).
13 Cf. its synonym *double-talk* [1938] and the compound *double-think* [1949] 'the mental capacity to accept as equally valid two entirely contrary opinions' coined by Orwell (OED2), with which *doublespeak* exhibits similarity of the first component *double*.
14 According to the OED, *fest* is a free morpheme used, with qualifying words, to denote 'a festival or special occasion'. Given its etymology (from *festival*) and its frequency as a second element in complex words, it seems to be more a combining form than a freestanding noun. Indeed, in OED2, only its use in combination is attested in English. See also Green (2010), who describes *-fest* as a slang suffix indicating 'a gathering or get-together'.

The word *panorama* [1791] has similarly inspired the formation of the combining form *-orama*, added to initial elements of ancient Greek origin to form nouns designating scenic exhibits. The model word set includes *cosmorama* 'a peep-show of the world' (OED2), *cyclorama* 'a picture of a scene arranged on the inside of a cylindrical surface' (OED2), *diorama* 'a mode of scenic representation' (OED2), *georama* 'a terrestrial globe' (OED3), and *myriorama* 'a picture consisting of a number of separate sections which form different scenes' (OED3). Most of them – except *cyclorama* [1840] – are earliest attested in 1823. From the mid-twentieth century onwards, this combining form was used to create several analogical words, also with English initial elements, as in *Motorama* [1947] 'an exhibition of General Motors motor vehicles' (OED3) and the nonce words *audiorama* [1954] 'a display of acoustic instruments', *striporama* [1954] 'a burlesque movie', and humorous *donutorama* [1992], all attested in the OED. In the variant *-rama* the interfix *-o-* is omitted, as in *Cinerama* [1951] 'the proprietary name of a form of cinema film projected on a wide curved screen by three cameras' (OED3).

A very productive combining form is *-gate* (from *Watergate* [1972]), used to designate 'actual or alleged (political) scandals involving corruption', as in *Dallasgate* [1975], *Koreagate* [1976], *Hollywoodgate* [1978], *Irangate* [1986], etc., with the first element designating the name of the place where such a scandal occurred. This combining form has also been added to the proper name or nickname of a person or organisation implicated in the scandal, as in *Floodgate* [1978], *Billygate* [1980], and the recent *Monicagate* [1998] and *Beyoncégate* [2013] mentioned by Miller (2014: 89). Kemmer (2003: 91) describes the process forming *-gate* as "a substitution blend giving rise to a new family of words", whereas Miller (2014: 89) includes these formations under the heading "puns", admitting that some of them clearly belong to language play: e.g., Oliver North's *Gategate* [1987] and Clinton's *Whitewatergate* [1993]. More examples are found in Baldi and Dawar (2000: 968) and Lehrer (2007: 121).

Other scholars (e.g. Fradin 2000) discuss the degree of abstraction of such combining forms as *-gate* and *-holic*, which have a stable meaning and a fixed phonological representation, and, therefore, may be considered to be "affixes" or "affix-like" constituents (Fradin 2000: 37). Actually, although generalisations are possible for these constituents – e.g., *-gate* denotes 'a scandal involving a cover-up X' and *-holic* 'a person addicted to X' – the level of abstraction that we have in these formatives is not the same as we have in affixes. In other words, they create productive series, but their models are still concrete forms, namely, *Dallasgate*, *Koreagate*, *Hollywoodgate*, etc. for the former and *workaholic* [1947], *milkaholic* [1955], *sugar-holic* [1955], etc. for the latter (for *-(a)holic*, see also 3.1.2).

The OED also cites more recent combining forms. The formations ending in -*licious* (e.g. *groovalicious* [2002]) and -*tainment* (e.g. *irritainment* [1993] 'irritating entertainment' OED3) have already been mentioned (1.2, 2.2). In addition, OED3 reports some nonce formations that exhibit the combining form -*tastic* (← *fantastic*), such as *poptastic* [1992] 'designating or relating to a very good performance of pop music' (OED3), and other puns which are phonologically similar to *fantastic*: i.e. *fun-tastic* [1939], *fad-tastic* [1962] (in the advertisement "*fad-tastic* discounts"), and *van-tastic* [1975] (in the headline "Trucks: *Van-tastic*").

Two initial combining forms include *Franken-* and *yester-*. The former, from *Frankenstein* [1838], has obtained *Frankenfood* [1992] 'genetically modified food' (OED3) and similar nonce words relating to genetic modification (e.g. *Frankenfruit* [1992], *Frankenplant* [1998], *Frankenscience* [1999] OED3). The latter, from the cranberry words *yesterday* [*c*950] and *yesternight* [OE], has originated a series including words with the sense 'immediately preceding the present' (OED3). Some examples are *yestereve* [1604], *yestermorning* [1654–5], *yester-afternoon* [1806], *yester-week* [1839], *yester-year* [1870], and *yesterclass* [2008] 'the class session prior to this one' (*Rice University Neologisms Database*) (cf. *yestermorrow* [2011] ← *yesterday* + *tomorrow*, 'when you can't remember what day something happened', *Urban Dictionary*).

Combining forms, in spite of their marginality between derivation and compounding (see "marginal morphology" in Dressler 2000), are instances of both rule productivity and analogy via schema. However, before becoming productive, most of the above-mentioned combining forms were recurrent splinters in blends, as the abbreviation of the first component in *irritainment* (and other -*tainment* words) may suggest. Lehrer (2007: 120) indeed observes that "[o]nce a blend is created, the splinter may be reused".

Frequent splinters: Like combining forms, frequent splinters create series, by analogy.[15] For instance, the splinter -*ercise* ← *exercise* has become productive in English, so much so that Baldi and Dawar (2000: 968) have assigned it the label of "unconventional suffix". Hence, after *sexercise* [1942] 'sexual activity regarded as exercise' (OED3), some new analogical words have been formed which refer to 'physical activity': e.g., *dancercise* [1967] 'dancing performed as an exercise' (OED2) and *boxercise* [1985] 'a form of aerobic fitness routine incorporating moves and exercises from boxing training' (OED3) (cf. the verb *aerobicise* [1982] in 3.3.3). Other novel words refer to 'non-physical (but strenuous) activity', such as the creative formations *commutercize* [n.d.] and *computercize* [n.d.] cited by Baldi and Dawar (2000: 968), or *deskercise* [n.d.] found in Lehrer (2007: 117).

---

15 See Bauer, Lieber, and Plag (2013: 525–530) for a discussion and illustration of splinters.

Another splinter discussed in Lehrer (2007: 121) is -(l)ish (← English). For instance, by analogy with the blend *Spanglish* [1954] ← *Spanish* + *English* (OED2), *Japlish* [1960] ← *Japanese* + *English* (OED2) has been created. Other blends have also been coined – namely, *Chinglish* [1957] ← *Chinese* + *English* (OED3), *Hinglish* [1967] ← *Hindi* + *English* (OED3), and *Singlish* [1972/1984] ← *Sinhalese/Singaporean* + *English* (OED3). However, in these cases, the right element is retained in full, at least phonologically, because graphically the initial *e* is deleted.

Adams (2001: 139) also highlights the splinter *-ar* (← *star* or *stellar*), which is first found in *quasar* [1964] 'quasi-stellar' (OED3), and later in *pulsar* [1968] 'pulsating star' (OED3), *collapsar* [n.d.] 'collapsing star', and *spinnar* [n.d.] 'spinning star'. Another recurrent splinter is *-arian*, which, according to Adams (1973: 170), is a suffix that occurs in a subgroup of words "inspired by *vegetarian* [1842] and having to do with 'beliefs about diet'".[16] They include *dietarian* [1880] 'one who lives in accordance with prescribed rules for diet' (OED2), *fruitarian* [1893] 'one who lives on fruit' (OED2), and, in the twentieth century, *nutarian* [1909] 'a vegetarian whose diet is based on or confined to nut products' (also in James Joyce's *Ulysses*, 1922, OED3), *meatarian* [n.d.] (also *meatitarian* in Lehrer 2007: 126), and *sea-foodetarian* [n.d.] (Adams 1973: 170). With the exception of the latter, in which a bigger portion of the word (*veg*)*etarian* is retained, these are all blends whose first component ends with a final *t* (*diet, fruit, meat, nut*), which overlaps with the second part of (*vege*)*tarian*. However, from a semantic viewpoint, in *meatarian* the word *vegetarian* is not included in the meaning of the blend. The OED also attests the existence of *breatharian* [1979] 'a person who consumes no nutrients other than those absorbed from the air' (OED3), whose meaning does not include the word *vegetarian* either. On the other hand, in *flexitarian* [1998] ← *flexible* + *vegetarian*, 'a person who follows a primarily but not strictly vegetarian diet' (OED3), the meaning of *vegetarian* is included. Hence, it is debatable whether these are blends or derived words from the *-arian* suffix (or secreted combining form).

Miller (2014: 89) additionally notes the frequency in use of items of jewellery with a final element *-let*: e.g., *anklet* [a1822] 'an ornament for the ankle' (OED2) was modelled on *bracelet*[17] [1438] and *frontlet* [1478] 'something worn on the forehead' (OED2), both of French origin. This series also comprises *armlet* [1535] 'an ornament or band worn round the arm' (OED2), †*earlet* [1610] 'an ear-ring' (OED2), *necklet* [1641] 'an ornamental item worn round the neck' (OED3), *leglet*

---

16 According to the OED, *vegetarian* [1842] is irregularly obtained from *veget*(*able*) + *-arian*.
17 According to Dalton-Puffer (1996: 16–17), *brac-el-et* offers a case of "double-suffixes". According to her, since Old French *bracel* was no longer felt to be diminutive, another diminutive suffix *-et* was added, ultimately resulting in one suffix *-let*.

[1836] 'an ornament for the leg' (OED2), and *wristlet* [1851] 'a bracelet' (OED2). The OED specifies that, in addition to its diminutive force, the suffix *-let* is in these words appended to nouns denoting parts of the body to form names for articles of ornament or attire.

Among frequent initial splinters, Lehrer (2007: 122) mentions *docu-*, as in *docudrama* [1961] 'a documentary drama' (OED2) and *docusoap* [1979] or *docu-opera* [n.d.] ← *documentary* and *soap opera*, 'a television documentary series following people in a particular location or occupation over a period of time' (only the former attested in OED3). Green (1991: 77) also mentions other uses of this splinter: *documusical* [1974], *docuhistory* [1981], and *docurecreation* [1983] (more examples in Algeo 1991: 38).

Interestingly, the same word *documentary* provides two splinters – an initial one (*docu-*) and a final one (*-umentary*) – neither of which is recorded in the OED as an attested combining form (see 3.2.5; cf. Table 4 in 3.1.2).

A "very popular initial splinter" (Lehrer 2007: 123) *e-*, from *electronic*, is currently a productive combining form, which is attested earlier in *email* [1979] and *e-fit* [1988] 'a computer program for creating an electronic picture based on composite photographs of facial features' (OED3). Later, it has been reused in other "dozens of items" (Lehrer 2007: 123): e.g., *e-text* [1990], *e-journal* [1991], *e-commerce* [1993], *e-publication* [1997], etc.

In computer slang, some recent blends exhibit *net* [1970] ← *Internet* (OED3) as their first component. Examples include *netiquette* [1982] ← *net + etiquette*, 'an informal code of practice regulating the behaviour of Internet users' (OED3), *netizen* [1984] ← *net + citizen*, 'a person who uses the Internet' (OED3), and *Netscape* [1988] ← *net + -scape*, 'a browser used to access and display documents on the World Wide Web' (OED3). Similarly, numerous specialised blends or compounds exhibit *Web* [1991] as their first element: e.g., *Webliography* [1995] ← *Web + bibliography*, 'a list of electronic works or documents' (OED3), *Webinar* [1997] ← *Web + seminar*, 'a seminar conducted over the Internet' (OED3), *Webzine* [1994] ← *web + magazine*, 'a magazine published on the Internet' (OED3), *Webmaster* [1993] 'the administrator of a web site' (OED3), and its analogue *Webmistress* [1994].

As the above-mentioned examples show, the present model of analogy is gradable and not a true continuum, in that it includes elements that may fluctuate between one category and another, or combine more motivations – namely, surface analogy and rule productivity. Thus, rather than a continuum, we can envisage different phases where analogical formation has occurred, with some turning points in the lexical expansion (cf. 'lexical explosion' in acquisition models). The phases of analogy include:

1. Surface analogy with one target formed on one concrete model;
2. Another similar case of surface analogy, or other single analogies whose targets are similar to 1;
3. The development of a schema in line with 2, with a series or word family as model. At least two targets, but preferably more than two constitute a series/word family;
4. The shift from a schema, with a series/word family, to a rule, with an abstract pattern.

I find these advancement phases well illustrated, for instance, by -(a)holic words in the following progression:

1. A unique case of a blend was formed by analogy with an existing one – i.e. according to a concrete model – as in *tobaccoholic* [1954] (e.g. "I am a confirmed '*tobaccoholic*'. That's like an alcoholic, only it ain't alcohol", *Daily Mail*, OED3), after *workaholic* [1947] 'a person to whom work is extremely or excessively important' (OED3);
2. Two or more blends were coined after the same pattern: e.g., *milkaholic* [1955] and *sugarholic* [1955];
3. They developed a series of blends with a recurrent splinter -(a)holic. When the lexical expansion occurred, many neologisms were formed analogously: e.g., *cake-aholic* [1957], *chocoholic* [1961] ← *chocolate + alcoholic*, 'a habitual and prolific eater of chocolate' (OED3), *foodaholic* [1965], *golfaholic* [1971], *carboholic* [1973] (from *carbohydrates*), *computerholic* [1977], *newsaholic* [1979], *spendaholic* [1982], *shopaholic* [1984] 'a compulsive shopper' (OED2), *cruise-oholic* [1989], *sexaholic* [1994], and *rage-aholic* [2008] are all attested in the OED. The fact that, in *chocoholic* and *carboholic*, -(a)holic combines with an initial splinter confirms the first attestation as blend component;
4. The productivity and regularity in use made the shift from frequent splinter to combining form. -*Aholic* is currently defined a 'suffix' in the OED and in Green (1991: 6) and 'secreted affix' in Fradin (2000). This demonstrates its diachronic change from extra-grammatical to marginal and even grammatical morphology.

Table 5 reports the results of: 1) a quantitative analysis on the token/normalised (per million words, for each decade) frequency of -(a)holic words in three corpora (COCA, BNC, TIME), and 2) a diachronic analysis of the evolution of -(a)holic from splinter status to morphemehood (either combining form or suffix) in the formation of new words.

Tab. 5: -(A)holic words and their attestation and frequency in COCA, BNC, and TIME

-(a)holic words	1960s	1970s	1980s	1990s	2000s	2010s
nymphoholic	1/0.06 TIME					
vodkaholic	1/0.06 TIME					
workaholic		25/2 TIME	22/1.99 TIME 1/0.02 BNC	58/1.38 BNC 177/0.89 COCA 33/3.5 TIME	200/1 COCA 17/2.52 TIME	28/0.7 COCA
petroholic		1/0.08 TIME				
shockaholic		1/0.08 TIME				
Coke(-)aholic			1/0.09 TIME	1/0.02 BNC		
talkaholic			1/0.09 TIME	1/0.11 TIME		
clothesaholic			1/0.02 BNC			
danceaholic			1/0.09 TIME			
drudge-aholic			1/0.09 TIME			
potaholic			1/0.02 BNC			
saltaholic			1/0.09 TIME			
shop(-)aholic				5/0.12 BNC 16/0.08 COCA 1/0.11 TIME	26/0.13 COCA 2/0.3 TIME	9/0.23 COCA
choc(k)aholic/ oholic				15/0.07 COCA 2/0.21 TIME	12/0.06 COCA	1/0.03 COCA

-(a)holic words	1960s	1970s	1980s	1990s	2000s	2010s
spendaholic				1/0.02 BNC 2/0.05 BNC 1/0.01 COCA	2/0.01 COCA	1/0.03 COCA
food(-)aholic				1/0.01 COCA	5/0.03 COCA	1/0.03 COCA
sexaholic				1/0.01 COCA	2/0.01 COCA	2/0.05 COCA
rage(-)aholic				1/0.11 TIME 3/0.01 COCA	1/0.15 TIME 2/0.01 COCA	
gambl(e)aholic				1/0.01 COCA	1/0.01 COCA	
assholic				2/0.01 COCA		
buyaholic				2/0.01 COCA		
sportsaholic				2/0.01 COCA		
auctionholic				1/0.11 TIME		
bedaholic				1/0.02 BNC		
cheesaholic				1/0.02 BNC		
creditaholic				1/0.01 COCA		
cursaholic				1/0.11 TIME		
eventaholic				1/0.01 COCA		
fatheraholic				1/0.01 COCA		
fishaholic				1/0.01 COCA		
golfaholic				1/0.01 COCA		

-(a)holic words	1960s	1970s	1980s	1990s	2000s	2010s
growthaholic				1/0.01 COCA		
hoopaholic				1/0.01 COCA		
Morseaholic				1/0.02 BNC		
owloholic				1/0.02 BNC		
pizzaholic				1/0.11 TIME		
popaholic				1/0.11 TIME		
family-oholic					1/0.15 TIME 1/0.01 COCA	
juice-aholic					2/0.01 COCA	
dealaholic					1/0.01 COCA	
Doreen-aholic					1/0.01 COCA	
elkoholic					1/0.01 COCA	
fabric-holic					1/0.01 COCA	
fruitoholic					1/0.01 COCA	
fundraise-aholic					1/0.01 COCA	
herbaholic					1/0.01 COCA	
hoardaholic					1/0.01 COCA	
snarkaholic					1/0.15 TIME	

Corpus analysis confirms that, with the exception of a few sporadic cases of -(a)holic formations already appearing in the 1960s (*nymphoholic, vodkaholic*), the first word which acted as model was *workaholic*, attested since the 1970s–80s in corpora, but especially used since the 1990s–2000s (see Figures 1 and 2).

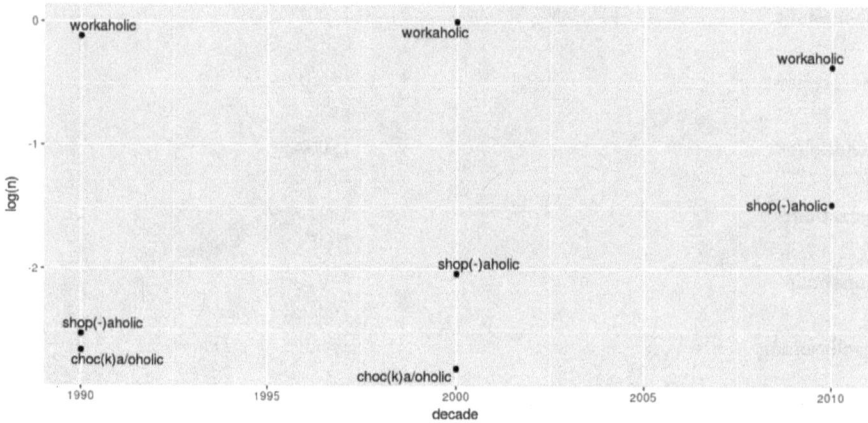

Fig. 1: Frequency of *workaholic*, *shop(a)holic*, and *choc(k)a/oholic* in COCA from 1990 to 2010

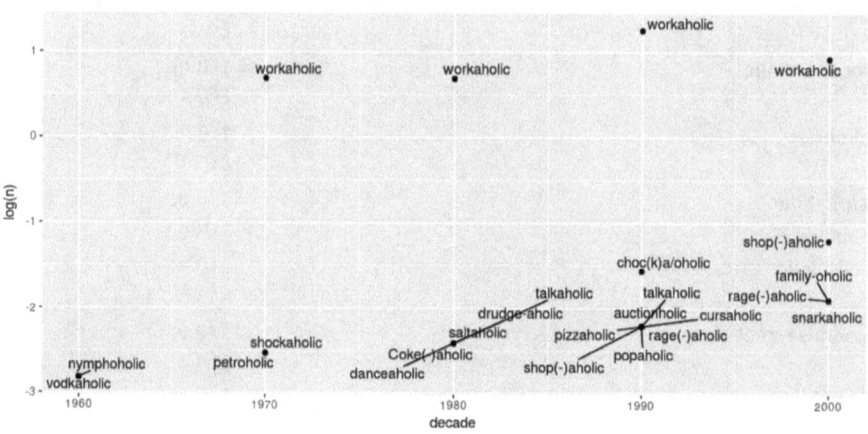

Fig. 2: Frequency of *-(a)holic* words in TIME from 1960 to 2000

3.3.2 Types of model words

The model words or sources of analogy do not constitute a homogeneous set, but can be distinguished into various types. The first distinction to be drawn is between a simplex-word model and a complex-word model:

Simplex-word model: The model may be a simplex (or monomorphemic) word, i.e. a word that has no affixes and is not part of a compound. In this case, the operation of analogy involves reanalysis, that is, the reinterpretation of the simplex word as complex (see 3.2.6). For instance, the model *safari* [1859], according to Miller (2014: 90), has generated *snowfari* [n.d.], probably used for 'a safari on the snow'. Here the noun *safari* (from the Swahili word meaning 'journey, expedition') has been reanalysed as complex (**sa +fari*), hence the substitution of the Variable Part *sa* with *snow* has been possible.

Another pertinent example is mentioned in *Wordspy*, where the verb *prespond* [2003] 'to respond to something in advance' (e.g. "Let me attempt to '*prespond*' – a new word for anticipatory response – to potential defenses of voter ignorance", 2014) is said to be coined after reanalysis of the verb *respond* as prefixed. Then, the prefix *pre-* has been added, by analogy with *pre-assign*, *pre-cook*, etc. However, in religious domains, the verb *respond* [c1555] 'to say or sing a response to a versicle' (OED3) can be analysed as from Latin *re-* + *spondēre* 'to spond; to promise or pledge'. Thus, the Latin etymology would justify the above analysis.

Similarly, in an article of *The Guardian*, the adjective *delicious* is reanalysed as having a prefix *de-*, hence, this has made it possible for the analogical nonce word *de-lovely* [n.d.] – found in the micro-context – to be formed. Indeed, although the combining form *-licious* exists, it could not be combined with a prefix, such as *de-* (cf. *babelicious*).[18]

Interestingly, in back-formation, simplex words, such as *author* [a1382], have been reanalysed as complex (i.e. **auth + -or*). This reanalysis has permitted the verb *auth* [n.d.] (Marchand [1960] 1969: 395) to be coined, by analogy with word pairs such as *act–actor*. In the latter case, the pair simplex word–derived word

---

18 Adams (1973: 163) states that elements like *del-* in *delight, delicious, delicate,* and *delovely* could be regarded "not as prefixes but as 'prefixoids'". I believe that in the Guardian text under examination ("They're *De-licious*, they're *De-Lovely*, they're sometimes plain *De-Sastrous*", Musicals, Film Section), the author wants to stress the phonological link among the three adjectives, sharing a pseudo-prefix *de-*, rather than *del-*. Graphically, this belief is confirmed by the hyphens and capital letters.

represents the model. A comparable case is the model *sordid* [1597], which has back-formed the noun *sordor* [1823] 'physical or moral sordidness' (OED2) after reanalysis, on the model of the pair *squalid–squalor* (Miller 2014: 88).

Complex-word model: The model is more commonly a complex (or polymorphemic) word, i.e. a word that typically includes a root and one or more affixes (e.g. *lord-ly*, *ac-cultur(e)-ation*), or more than one root in a compound (e.g. *black market*, *white-collar*).

Within the series of complex words that may function as models for analogy, we can further discriminate between grammatical and extra-grammatical models.

Grammatical model: Analogical formations may be created after fully grammatical models, either derived or compound words, generally, according to productive patterns. Derived words may exhibit a prefix, as in *ad-verb* [a1425], providing the pattern for the analogical formation *adnoun* [1657] 'a word added to or joined to a noun' (OED3), or a suffix, as in the above-mentioned *lord-ly* [a1000] obtaining *ladily* [c1400] 'befitting or characteristic of a lady' (OED3). In these cases, the affix (*ad-*, *-ly*) is normally kept in the analogical formation, whereas the root is semantically related to the model root (e.g. by a co-hyponymy relationship between *verb–noun*, or an antonymy relationship between *lord–lady*) (see semantic similarity in 3.2.5).

A cumulation of suffixes is also possible in grammatical models: e.g., *real-ist-ic* [1829], *natural-ist-ic* [1838], etc. provide the pattern for *actualistic* [1857] 'representative of reality' (OED3). Here *real* and *actual* stand in a paronymy relationship. Instead, the complex noun *acculturation* [1880], with a prefix *ac-* and a suffix *-ation*, has back-formed the verb *acculturate* [1917] 'to acquire through acculturation' (OED3), after word pairs such as *cultivate–cultivation*.

Grammatical models for analogical formations also include compound words. The above-mentioned compound noun *black market* [1727] and compound adjective *white-collar* [1911], for instance, have respectively established the patterns for *grey market* [1934] 'legal but arguably unethical traffic or trade in any officially controlled goods' (OED3; see also *white market* in 3.2.5) and *blue-collar* [1929] 'of or relating to manual work or workers' (OED3). Similar cases include the synthetic compound *handwriting* [1421], which is the model for the graphological term *brainwriting* [1913] 'handwriting, regarded as the product of mental characteristics' (OED3), and the astronomical compound *red dwarf* [1916], originating *brown dwarf* [1975] 'a celestial object intermediate in mass between a giant planet and a star' (OED3). Moreover, the deverbal compound noun *blackout* [1934] has originated *brown-out* [1942] 'a partial black-out' (OED2),[19] and the compound verb †*whitewash* [1576] 'to bleach' is the model of *blackwash* [1762] 'to blacken the character of' (OED3). A compound adjective is *athletically correct* [1991] 'proper or appropriate (in athletics)' (Glowka et al. 2000: 70), a pun on *politically correct* [1793].

In addition, some instances with shared non-head component are *battleship* [1794], which is the model for *battleplane* [1915] 'an aeroplane designed for use in warfare' (OED2), and *airman* [1873], providing the pattern for *airwoman* [1910] 'a woman who is engaged in the flying or operation of aircraft' (OED3). Similarly, the model words *batman* [1755], *bookman* [1618], and *busboy* [1904] have their female counterparts in, respectively, the targets *batwoman* [1941] 'a member of one of the women's auxiliary services performing the duties of a batman' (OED2), *bookwoman* [1834] 'a woman who loves literature or reading' (OED3), and *busgirl* [1914] 'a girl employed to clear tables in a restaurant' (OED3). Furthermore, the compound noun *all-nighter* [1870] has established the model for *all-dayer* [1896] 'something that lasts an entire day' (OED3). Finally, the rhyming compound *walkie-talkie* [1939] provides the pattern for *walkie-lookie* [1946] 'a portable television camera which transmits pictures and sound wirelessly' (OED3), with a shared first constituent (*walk-ie*) and co-hyponymous second constituents (*talk(-ie)–look(-ie)*). The same model also triggers *handie-talkie* [1943] 'a small, light walkie-talkie radio' (Algeo 1991: 49), with a shared second element.

Marginal model: A less common model may exhibit a (neoclassical) combining form, which is part of marginal morphology, that is, at the boundaries between derivation and composition. For instance, the model *cinematograph* [1896] shares a combining form -*graph* (and an interfix -*o*-) with the target *animatograph(e)* [1896] 'a motion picture' (OED3).[20] Similarly, the model *Eurocentric* [1927] exhibits the same combining form -*centric* as its target *Afrocentric* [1966] 'centred or focusing on Africa or on cultures of African origin' (OED3; see also *hispanocentric* [1985] and *Russocentric* [1985] in BNC).

Sometimes a complex model is resegmented and its morphological boundaries shifted to obtain reanalysis. Lehrer (2007: 120) discusses the case of *Frankfurter* [1877], whose etymon has been resegmented to obtain the series in -*furter*,

---

19 The compound *black-out* [1929] can also refer to 'temporary loss of vision experienced when a person is subjected to strong accelerative forces' (OED3). With this sense, it is the model for *red-out* [1942] 'temporary red vision' and *greyout* [1942] 'momentary diminution of vision or consciousness' (OED3).

20 See the 1896 quote in the OED, from *The Daily News* (26 March 3/6): "At a neighbouring house we have the '*cinematographe*', and by way of varying the title Mr. Paul calls his pictures the '*Animatographe*'".

including *krautfurter* [1949] 'a frankfurter topped or stuffed with sauerkraut' (OED3), and *chickenfurter* [n.d.], *turkeyfurter* [n.d.], and *shrimpfurter* [n.d.] from Lehrer (2007: 120).[21]

Extra-grammatical model: Analogical formations may also be obtained by analogy with extra-grammatical models. For instance, the model may be a blend, such as the overlapping *sexploitation* [1924], which is the model for *blax-/blacksploitation* [1972] 'the exploitation of black people' (OED2). Also, specialised *stagflation* [1965] 'a state of the economy in which stagnant demand is accompanied by severe inflation' (OED2) has established an analogical pattern with the splinter *-flation*. This pattern is used, for instance, for the production of *slumpflation* [1974] 'a state of economic depression in which decreasing output and employment in industry are accompanied by increasing inflation' (OED2) and *taxflation* [1976] 'the increase in income tax payable brought about when an inflation-linked rise in income causes a person to move into a higher tax bracket' (OED3). *Gradeflation* [n.d.] and *oilflation* [n.d.] are recorded in Algeo (1991: 6).

Acronyms can play the role of model as well. For instance, *yuppie* [1984] and *yumpie* [1984] 'young urban professional/young upwardly mobile person' (OED2) are the models for slang *woopie* [1986] ← *well-off old(er) person*, 'a member of a socio-economic group comprising affluent retired people who pursue an active lifestyle' (OED2), and for the recent *yettie* [2000] 'young, entrepreneurial, and technology-based [person]' (*The Guardian*; see also 3.1.1).

Other abbreviations can act as models, such as the initialism *HIV* [1986], which triggers *FIV* [1994] ← *feline immunodeficiency virus*, 'the cat equivalent of human HIV' (OED3, s.v. *positive*). The pair *DJ–deejay* [1946] provides the model for *VJ–veejay* [1982]: both *DJ* and *VJ* are initialisms from *disk-/video-jockey*, whereas *deejay* and *veejay* are obtained through the process of "letter pronunciation" (Mattiello 2008a: 152).

Clipped words ending with the vowel *o*, such as *intro*(*duction*) [1923], *disco*(*theque*) [1957], and medical *mono*(*nucleosis*) [1964], have been reinterpreted as having a suffix *-o*. Hence, they provide the model for analogous truncated words to which an *-o* suffix has been added: e.g., *aggro* [1969] ← *aggravation/aggression*, *lesbo* [1940] ← *lesbian*, *preggo* [1951] ← *pregnant*, etc. (Mattiello 2008a: 113–115, 2013: 52–53).[22] The same happens in the rhyming compound *evo-devo* [1997] 'evolutionary developmental biology' (OED3), where the replicatum

---

21 Lehrer (2007: 120) includes these words in blends with frequently used "splinters", but *-furter*, like *-burger*, can be considered a combining form (cf. Marchand [1960] 1969: 213).
22 However, in the latter group of suffixed clippings, the *-o* suffix seems to convey a pejorative connotative meaning (e.g. *lesb-o*), which is not in familiar *intro*, *disco*, etc.

evo(lutionary) represents the model for the replicans *dev(elopmental)* + *-o*, the suffix being crucial for the rime between model and target.[23]

3.3.3 Types of target words

While models in analogy can be either grammatical or extra-grammatical, the new analogical formation (or target) can additionally be an ungrammatical term. The latter case is especially frequent with occasionalisms, which generally require the (micro-)context to be disambiguated. Hence, the types of new target words that can be obtained through analogy include:

Grammatical target: The target may conform to English word-formation rules. For instance, within derivation, the verb *aerobicise* [1982] 'to perform aerobic exercise' (OED3) is regularly formed by adding the suffix *-ise*, as in the regular verbs *modern-ise* [1716] or *central-ise* [1801], although the OED suggests that the model is the verb *exercise* [1526]. In this case, the verb formation regularly follows the abstract pattern of *-ise* derivation, but the target is also constructed *ad hoc*, because of a phonological similarity (in the final syllable with a secondary stress) with the exact verb *exercise*, reanalysed as having a suffix *-ise* (cf. †*exerce* [c1550] OED2). Instead, the geological noun *aggradation* [1893] 'the process by which the level of a land surface is raised as a result of the deposition of detrital material by a river, current, or other agency' (OED3) is regularly obtained by adding the suffix *-ation* to the verb *aggrade*, after the model word *degradation* [1799] ← *degrade* + *-ation*. Moreover, *idealty* [1635] 'a standard of excellence' (OED3) is formed by adding a suffix *-ty* to the adjective *ideal*, after *royal-ty* [c1405].[24]

Within compounding, *aircraft* [1845] 'any of various vehicles capable of flight' (OED3) is a case of grammatical target that conforms to compounding rules, probably created after the constituent *air-* (see the compound family *air balloon* [1783], *airship* [1817], *air vessel* [1824]). Also the compounds *B-list* [1928], *C-list* [1909] 'the second/third in a series of lists' (OED3), and *Z-list* [1979] 'any list comprising only the very least celebrated or important members of a particular group' (OED3) are regularly coined after the model *A-list* [1890].

---

23 Cf. the role of interfixes in left-branching compounds in Fuhrhop (1998).
24 The similarity between the model *royal-ty* and the target *ideal-ty* seems to be more orthographic than phonological. Indeed, the final part of the two adjectives is not identical, but differs both phonologically and prosodically (cf. /ˈrɔɪəl/ vs. /aɪˈdiː.əl/).

Moreover, like the model *drive-in* [1930], the target *walk-in* [1943] 'of a cinema, shop, bank, etc.: entered on foot' (OED3) regularly comes from a phrasal verb. Finally, Joyce has regularly formed the compound *forgivemequick* [1939] (*Finnegans Wake*, p. 294) from a phrase, by analogy with the lexicalised phrase *forgetmenot* [?1533] used in the micro-context (p. 295).

Marginal target: The target, for instance, may exhibit a combining form, which is marginally set between derivation and compounding. A case in point is the neoclassical combining form *-graphy*, which is regularly added to the base *film* in *filmography* [1962] 'a list of the films of a particular director, producer, etc.' (OED2), with the interfix *-o-*, as in the model *bibliography* [1814] (see also *discography* [1930] 'a catalogue of musical recordings' OED3).

In addition, the target of analogy may be marginal between morphology and the lexicon. An illustrative example is the verb *prepone* [1913] 'to bring forward to an earlier time or date' (OED3). It has been coined from the prefix *pre-*, antonymous with *post-* in *postpone* [1496]. However, this verb is acephalous (i.e. headless), in that the head **pone* does not exist in English (yet cf. Latin *pōnere* 'to place, put'). A parallel case is *implode* [1881] 'to burst inwards' (OED2), which has been formed from the prefix *im-* after *explode* [1624], but **plode* is not a regular verbal base in English (cf. Latin *plōdĕre* 'to clap'). Still another case is *introjection* [1866] 'the action of throwing in' (OED2), formed after *interjection* [c1430] and *projection* [a1550], although **jection* is not an existing word in English (cf. Latin *jacĕre* 'to throw'). These target words belong to marginal morphology, in that they are borderline between morphologically complex words and simplex (lexicalised) items.

Extra-grammatical target: The target may be an extra-grammatical formation, namely, a blend, an abbreviation, a reduplicative, or a word which exhibits a phonaestheme. An example of a target blend which is modelled on an existing one is *Cal-Mex* [1973] ← *Californian + Mexican*, 'a type of Mexican-style cuisine originating in California' (OED3), on the pattern of *Tex-Mex* [1949] ← *Texan + Mexican*.

Other target words only involve an abbreviatory mechanism. For instance, like its model *D-day* [1918] 'the military code-name for a particular day fixed for the beginning of an operation' (OED3), the target *E-day* [1996] 'the day of official adoption of the euro as currency' (OED3) is a clipped word, *D* and *E* respectively abbreviating *day* and *Euro*. Similarly, the target *WAN* [1983] ← *Wide Area Network* (OED2) is an acronym formed after the model *LAN* [1981] ← *Local Area Network* and *CUV* [2000] ← *Crossover Utility Vehicle* (*Wordspy*) is an initialism from *SUV* [1987] ← *Sport Utility Vehicle* (OED2, s.v. *S*).

The target word can also be coined after a group of words that exhibit a phonaestheme, i.e. a group of phonemes having recognisable semantic associations, as a result of appearing in a number of words of similar meaning (Firth 1930; Marchand [1960] 1969; Anderson 1998). For instance, the noun *wumph* [1913] 'a sudden deep sound, as of the impact of a soft, heavy object' (OED2) has been attested since the beginning of the twentieth century in the OED, and the interjection *whoompf* [1958] '(expressing) a sudden, violent rushing sound' (OED2) has been recorded since the mid-twentieth century. Similar words are *whump* [1915] 'a dull thudding sound, as of a body landing heavily' (OED2) and *whomp* [1926] 'a heavy, low sound' (OED2). The origin of these words is analogical. That is, they have been coined by analogy with words such as *thump* [1552], *bump* [1611], etc., which show a final phonaestheme *ump* /ʌmp/, generally associated with 'heaviness and clumsiness' or 'heavy, awkward movements' (Mattiello 2013: 204).

Ungrammatical target: In addition, the target may not comply with the rules of English word-formation or universal grammar principles. For example, the target *Accidency* [1830] is an ungrammatical word that has been punningly coined after the model *Excellency* [?1533], and is generally used to mock somebody, as in "President Ford, mocked as '*His Accidency*', was an affable but ineffectual replacement for Nixon" (G. Troy, 2008, *Leading from Center*, OED3). Indeed, while the suffix *-ency* is regularly added to a verb in the model (*excel(l)-ency*; see Latin *excellĕre* 'to rise above others'), the string *accid* does not correspond to any English verb.

Among nonce formations, the term *complexability* [2014], found in *The Guardian* in the immediate context of the model *employability* [1889], provides another example of irregular (ungrammatical) formation.[25] Indeed, whereas in *employability* the suffix *-able* is added to a verb to form an adjective (*employ-able*) and then *-ity* is added in its turn to form the noun, in *complexability -able* is irregularly added to an adjective (**complex-able*), against the universal rule that an adjectival base cannot accept an adjectival suffix. In other words, adjectives in *-able* can be either deverbal or denominal, but cannot be deadjectival.

---

25 "'*Complexability*', not *employability*, is needed. This is having the necessary social, cultural and economic capital, along with a sophisticated creative agency, which helps graduates learn to work in different ways, with different people, places and cultures, often collaborating across disciplines and boundaries." (*The Guardian*, 2014).

By contrast, in *audile* [1886] 'a person whose mental imagery or learning process is thought chiefly to involve the sense of hearing' (OED3), the second constituent *-ile* (as in *tactile* [1615], *motile* [1857], etc.) is treated as a suffix, although it does not correspond to any regular affix in English. Here the model word *motile* – a back-formation from *motility* [1822] according to the *Online Etymology Dictionary* – is reinterpreted as having an *-ile* suffix, which is then added to a first part *aud-* (as in *auditory* [1578]).

A different case is provided by James Joyce in "the *semblance* of the *substance* for the *membrance* of the *umbrance* with the *remnance* of the *emblence*" (*Finnegans Wake*, pp. 300–301). In this extract, the words *semblance* [a1325] and *substance* [c1330] have been reanalysed as having a suffix *-ance/-ence* (cf. *perform-ance*), and, after their reanalysed model, the ungrammatical words *membrance*, *umbrance*, *remnance*, and *emblence* [1939] have been created. In the same novel, Joyce also mentions an *overlusting fear* (p. 303), but the adjective *overlusting* [1939], probably created after the model word *everlasting* [1340], is not grammatical. Indeed, while *last* is a verb and can accept the suffix *-ing* to obtain the adjective, *lust* is a noun and cannot act as base to form an adjective by adding *-ing*.[26] Another ungrammatical formation is Joyce's noun *diseasinesses* [1939] (*Finnegans Wake*, p. 303), which is formed, against the unitary output constraint, as the negative form of *easiness* [1567], in competition with grammatical *uneasiness*.

3.3.4 Types of similarity relationships

The relationships that link the new target words to their models range, as stated in 3.2.5, from phonological (segmental and suprasegmental) similarity, to morphotactic and semantic similarity. However, in most cases, the target words are motivated by a resemblance with their models at various language levels. Therefore, the sample targets discussed in the following similarity types are not exclusively motivated by one or the other likeness, but generally share various and varied similarity traits with their models.

Phonological similarity: The target may share with its model some phonological features. For instance, the target *squillionaire* [1979] /ˌskwɪljəˈneə/ 'one who is extraordinarily wealthy' (OED2, s.v. *squillion*) and its synonymous model *zillionaire* [1946] /ˌzɪljəˈneə/ share both prosodic features (both are trisyllabic words

---

[26] Admittedly, as Merlini Barbaresi (2011) remarks, in the case of Joyce's manipulations, it is difficult to identify a dividing line between ungrammaticality and anomaly.

and have the same stressed syllable at the end) and segmental features (the last two syllables are identical, the first open syllables share the nucleus /ɪ/ and have no coda).

As far as segmental phonological similarity is concerned, the relationship between target and model is frequently expressed by the formula AB ← CB, where A and C represent the Variable Part in, respectively, the target and the model, and B the Invariable Part. In other words, target and model normally share the final part, as in *simplexity* [1849] /sɪmˈplek.sɪ.tɪ/ 'simplicity' (OED2), which shares the last three syllables (and the coda in the first syllable) with the model *complexity* [1734] /kəmˈplek.sɪ.tɪ/. Target and model may even differ only for the initial phoneme (the onset) of the first stressed syllable, as in *neatnik* [1959] /ˈniːt.nɪk/ 'a person who is (excessively) neat in personal habits' (OED3) ← *beatnik* [1958] /ˈbiːt.nɪk/ 'one of the beat generation' (OED2). In *otherhood* [2014] /ˈʌð.ə.hʊd/ 'the state of being a woman who is not a mother' (*Wordspy*), the target deletes the initial phoneme from the model *motherhood* [a1500] /ˈmʌð.ə.hʊd/. The pertinent formula, therefore, is B ← AB, with a subtracted Variable Part. This is the subtype of surface analogy that we have called 'with reduction' (3.3.1).

The pattern with shared word beginning (AB ← AC) is common with blends which share an initial splinter, such as *docu-* in the series modelled on *docudrama* [1961] ← *documentary + drama*, and including *docu-fantasy* [n.d.] (cited by Szymanek 2005: 432–433), *docusoap* [1979] (OED3), and others (see 3.3.1). In these blends, the Invariable Part is represented by the first two open syllables (/ˈdɒ.kjʊ/). Instead, in the blends *batcycle*, *batplane*, and *batcopter* [n.d.] (*enTenTen12*), all Batman's vehicles coined after the model *batmobile* [n.d.] ← *Batman + automobile*, only the initial syllable – i.e. /bæt/ – is shared.

Another series with an initial Invariable Part is that marked by the phonaestheme *gl-*, which is infrequent in English, except among words with meanings related to 'vision' and 'light' (e.g. *gleam* [OE], *glint* [a1542], *glitter* [1602], *glimmer* [a1616], *glow* [1827], *glisten* [1840], etc.) (Baldi and Dawar 2000). Hence, the slang adjective *glitzy* [1966] /ˈglɪt.sɪ/ 'characterized by glitter or extravagant show; ostentatious, glamorous' (OED3) has recently been coined on the model of this schema, with which it shares the initial phonaestheme, i.e. the cluster /gl/.

Less commonly, target and model share both word beginning and word end (ABC ← ADC), as in *VBL* [2010] /ˌviːˈbiː.el/ 'visible bra line' (*The Guardian*) ← *VPL* [1977] /ˌviːˈpiː.el/ 'visible panty line' (OED2, s.v. *V*).[27] The same similarity pattern is in *infostructure* [1974] /ˈɪn.fəʊˌstrʌk.tʃə/ 'the information technology infrastructure' (OED3, s.v. *info-*), punningly coined after *infrastructure* [1927] /ˈɪn.frəˌstrʌk.tʃə/. In

---

27 Cf. *VBS* [2010] 'visible bra strap' (*The Guardian*), coined after *VBL* in the same text.

these targets, the Invariable Part is discontinuous, in that it is interrupted by an intercalated Variable Part. By contrast, in *achrist* [1584] /ˈeɪ.kraɪst/ 'a person who does not believe in the divinity of Jesus Christ' (OED3), modelled on *atheist* [?1555] /ˈeɪ.θiː.ɪst/, there is a mere orthographic overlap of the suffix *-ist* /ɪst/ of the model and the rime /aɪst/ (of *Christ*) of the target. A comparable case is the poetic adjective *adead* [1581] 'dead' (OED3), used, e.g., by Ray D. Bradbury in the line "And the last of the tarts lies *adead* on its plate" (*Dublin Sunday*, 2002). According to the OED, it reflects reanalysis of the adjective *alive* [OE]. However, their similarity is more orthographic than phonological, in that the target /əˈded/ exhibits a monophthong /e/ in the stressed syllable, whereas the model /əˈlaɪv/ has a diphthong /aɪ/ in its place.

As for suprasegmental phonology and, in particular, word length, the minimal word for analogy is a monosyllabic word, made up of an onset (one or two consonants), a nucleus (one vowel, also a short one), and a coda (one or two consonants). Although minimal words, such as *eye* /aɪ/ or *a* /ə/, exist in English, in my database there are no monosyllabic analogical words which exhibit only the nucleus (with null onset and null coda). This is clearly explainable through the fact that either nucleus or onset/coda should represent the Variable Part.

Monosyllabic targets (and models) are also uncommon. For instance, the model *bit* [1948] ← *binary* + *digit* (OED2) has originated the target *trit* [2008] (cf. the prefix *tri-* from Latin *trēs*, occurring in *trimonthly*), which is recorded in the *Rice University Neologisms Database* after its use in a computer science lecture, with the addition of a consonant in the onset (/tr/ vs. /b/) and a shared rime (/ɪt/).

By contrast, disyllabic analogical formations with disyllabic models are more frequent in my database. For instance, in the above-mentioned *audile* [1886] /ˈɔː.daɪl/ (OED3) ← *motile* [1857] /ˈməʊ.taɪl/ (3.3.3), the rime /aɪl/ of the second syllable is invariable, but the onset is voiced /d/ rather than voiceless /t/, and the first syllable has only the nucleus /ɔː/, whereas in the model the stressed syllable is made up of the body /məʊ/. In *build-down* [1983] /ˈbɪld.daʊn/ 'a systematic reduction of nuclear armaments' (OED2) ← *build-up* [1943] /ˈbɪld.ʌp/, the first stressed syllable /bɪld/ is invariable, and the second syllable /daʊn/ has both onset and coda, but a null onset /ʌp/ in the model.

Trisyllabic analogical formations with trisyllabic models are also numerous. The noun *girl Friday* [1928] /ˌɡɜːlˈfraɪ.deɪ/ 'a female assistant' (OED3) ← *man Friday* [a1809] /ˌmænˈfraɪ.deɪ/ 'someone regarded as having the characteristics of Defoe's man Friday; a servant, an attendant' (OED3) is a case in point. Polysyllabic cases also exist, such as *cacography* [1656] /kæˈkɒɡ.rə.fɪ/ 'bad writing' (OED2) ← *calligraphy* [1604] /kæˈlɪɡ.rə.fɪ/.

The general tendency of analogical formations is to maintain the same prosodic structure as their models, although the number of syllables may sometimes change, as in *acoustician* [1826] /æˌkuːˈstɪʃ.ən/ 'an expert in acoustics' (OED3), with an extra syllable with respect to its model *musician* [a1398] /mjuːˈzɪʃ.ən/.

Morphotactic similarity: The motivation for analogy can be resemblance between two morphotactic structures, i.e. when target and model are formed via the same grammatical or extra-grammatical word-formation process.

As far as morphotactic similarity is concerned, the relationship between target and model is most commonly AB ← CB.[28] In compounding, this implies that the rightmost (generally, the head) component represents the Invariable Part. This pattern is illustrated, for example, by *softcore* [1966], attributive of pornography meaning 'less obscene than hard-core pornography' (OED2, s.v. *soft*), modelled on *hardcore* [1936], and *earthshine* [1834] 'sunlight reflected by the earth' (OED3), created after *sunshine* [a1325] and *moonshine* [c1425]. However, cases with a non-head invariable constituent are not rare. The targets *handlist* [1848] 'a catalogue' (OED3) ← *handbook* [OE] and *flashforward* [1980] (Miller 2014: 90), punningly coined after *flashback* [1916] obey the formula AB ← AC, with a leftmost Invariable Part. From COCA, *straw pool* [1995] 'an apparent but not real pool' ← *straw-man* [1594] obeys the same formula.

In derivation, the formula AB ← CB entails that a (supposed) suffix or a combining form is maintained in the analogical formation, as in *ageism* [1969] 'prejudice or discrimination on the grounds of a person's age' (OED3) ← *racism* [1903] (3.3.1), or *idiolect* [1948] 'the linguistic system of one person' (OED3) ← *dialect* [1566]. The recent formation *usie* [2014] /ʌsi/ 'a group photograph taken by one of the members of the group' (e.g. "'What do you call a group selfie?' 'An *usie*, of course!'", Wordspy) keeps the *-ie* suffix of the slang model *selfie* [2002] 'a photographic self-portrait' (OED3). By contrast, when the first part is maintained (AB ← AC), this Invariable Part is a (supposed) prefix, as in *adiabolist* [1646] 'a person who does not believe in the existence of the Devil' (OED3) ← *atheist* [?1555], *adusk* [1856] 'gloomy, dark' (OED3) ← *alight* [1817], and *obround* [1668] 'roundish' (OED3) ← *oblong* [?a1425]. In all these cases, the Variable Part (either the first or the second part) is generally semantically related to the corresponding part in the model (cf. *us* vs. *self*, *dusk* vs. *light*, *round* vs. *long*).

In extra-grammatical operations, the pattern AB ← CB is illustrated, e.g., by *frappuccino* [n.d.] ← *frappé* + *cappuccino* (Lehrer 2007: 121), coined on the model of

---

28 Whereas in phonological similarity the letters A–D represent sequences of phonemes, which may happen to, but do not necessarily, coincide with morphemes, in morphotactic similarity the letters A–C may represent free morphemes (words), bound morphemes (affixes or combining forms), or word parts/series of letters in extra-grammatical formations.

mochaccino [1963] ← *mocha* + *cappuccino*, 'cappuccino coffee containing chocolate syrup' (OED3). Instead, the pattern AB ← AC is in *negatrip* [2001] ← *negative* + *trip* (Szymanek 2005: 432, also in OED3, s.v. *nega-*), created on the model of *negademand* [1995].

A grammatical process and an extra-grammatical operation can also co-occur in analogical formation, as when the noun *talkie* [1913] 'a talking film' (OED2) is created via back-clipping, like its model *movie* [1909] (originally a shortening of *moving picture*), but also exhibits a regular familiarising suffix *-ie*. Here the pattern is again AB ← CB.

Semantic similarity: The target generally shares with its model some semantic features. In particular, while one part remains constant, the Variable Part in the target is often semantically linked to a comparable part in the model. As Klégr and Čermák (2010: 236) observe, the analogical operation is signalled by "a distinct semantic link between the trigger or pattern-providing word and the neologism (typically opposition, co-hyponymy, synonymy)". In metalinguistic experimental studies on first language acquisition (e.g. Clark 1972), it has been demonstrated that antonyms and restricted sets, such as colours, are preferred responses in word association tests and effective stimuli for analogy. For instance, in their experiments, Murphy and Jones (2008) observe a wide range of opposition types in pre-school children's speech: directional or locative antonyms, such as *up–down*, gestalt size antonyms in contrary relations, such as *big–little*, the complementary gender opposition *boy–girl*, and other descriptive contraries, such as *black–white*.[29] These opposition types are also common in adults' analogical formation. For instance, one of the most common oppositions is *black–white*: e.g., *white coffee* [1873] 'coffee served with milk or cream' (OED3, s.v. *white*) ← *black coffee* [1818], and *whitemail* [1861] 'to apply moral pressure to (a person) for a good cause' (OED3, s.v. *white*) ← *blackmail* [1852]. Colours are also the source of other contrasts: e.g., *brown rice* [1916] 'unpolished rice' (OED2, s.v. *brown*) ← *white rice* [1614] (cf. *brown sugar* [1704]).

What follows is a more detailed scale of semantic relationships that link the Variable Part of the target with its corresponding part in the model:
1. Near identity with small motivation: The Variable Part of the target may be a synonym of the corresponding part in the model. For instance, in *suicide* [1732] 'one who commits self-murder' (OED2), the first Latin component *sui* 'of oneself' is synonymous with the combining form *auto-* (from Greek αὐτο-

---

29 See chapter 4 in Jones et al. (2012) for a complete account on antonyms in acquisition.

'self, one's own, by oneself') in the model *autocide* [1635] 'a person who kills himself or herself' (OED3).

2. Massive semantic overlap: The Variable Part may also be a paronym of the corresponding part in the model. A relevant case is the compound *kid-friendly* [2013] (*The Guardian*), where the Variable Part of the target – i.e. the slang word *kid* meaning 'a young child' (OED2) – is very close to its standard equivalent *child* in the model compound adjective *child-friendly* [1977] 'welcoming towards or suitable for children' (OED3, s.v. *child*).[30] A comparable case is *mouse race* [2003] 'lower-stress life-style' (*Wordspy*), from *rat race* [1937] 'urban working life regarded as an unremitting struggle for wealth, status, etc.' (OED3). In *kidflick* [1977] 'a cinematographic or video film for children' (OED2, s.v. *kid*), the right element is close to the noun *vid(eo)* in the model *kidvid* [1955] (cf. *chick flick* [1988]). In *big gun* [2001] 'an important or powerful person' (OED3, s.v. *big*), the left element is an adjective comparable to *great* in *great gun* [1657].

3. Contradictory opposition: One of the most frequent relationships is antonymy, i.e. when the target and model exhibit Variable Parts which stand in a relationship of opposition or exclusion. For instance, in the target *absentation* [1800] 'the action of absenting oneself' (OED3), the Variable Part *absent* is a simple (complementary or non-gradable) antonym of *present* in the model *presentation* [a1325] (originally used in religious and legal settings).

    In most cases, the Variable Parts are polarity antonyms, i.e. gradable terms that stand in a relationship of opposition in which the positive term does not necessarily imply the negative of the other. For instance, in *ultimogeniture* [1882] 'the mode of succession by which the right of inheritance pertains to the youngest of a family' (OED2), the Variable Part *ultimo* (from Latin *ultimus* 'last') is the opposite pole of *primo* in the model *primogeniture* [a1500] (as in post-classical Latin *primogenitura* 'right of the first-born child').

    The Variable Parts in the target and model may additionally be reverse antonyms, i.e. terms which describe movements in opposite directions. A case in point is *warm-down* [1951] 'a period of moderate physical activity undertaken to aid recovery from strenuous exercise' (OED3), where *down* is a reverse antonym of *up* in the model word *warm-up* [1915]. Two further cases are from the *Urban Dictionary* and *Wordspy*: in *hangunder* [2004] 'the funny feeling you get when you wake up after a night of not drinking and you're not hungover like usual', *under* is the opposite of *over* in the model *hangover*

---

30 See the positionally bound morpheme *-friendly* 'helpful, accommodating' found in the compounds *user-friendly, reader-friendly, listener-friendly, environment-friendly*, etc. (Olsen 2014: 31).

[1904] (see chapter 8), whereas in *beforemath* [1997] 'the events and situations that lead to a particular end', the antonymy is with *aftermath* [1656].

Lastly, the Variable Parts may be converse antonyms, i.e. terms that describe a relationship between two entities from alternate viewpoints. For instance, in the specialised target *daughterboard* [1971] 'a printed circuit board on which some of the optional components of a microcomputer are mounted' (OED2), the term *daughter* establishes a reciprocal semantic relationship with the term *mother* in *motherboard* [1965], used for 'the principal components of a microcomputer' (OED3).

It is worth noting that the semantic relationship of opposition can also involve affixes. For instance, the prefixes *under-* in the target *underloaded* [1898] 'not loaded or burdened to capacity' (OED2) and *over-* in the model *overloaded* [1671] are polarity antonyms, and the suffixes *-ful* in the nonce word *defenceful* [1864] 'full of defences; well protected' (OED2) and *-less* in the model *defenceless* [c1530] similarly stand in an opposite relationship.

4. Other contrasts: Other contrasts especially involve relationships of inclusion, as with hyponymy, hyperonymy, and (more rarely) meronymy.

Generally, the Variable Parts in the target and model are co-hyponyms, i.e. terms that are included in a common superordinate class. For instance, in the target *mandocello* [1914] 'a large mandolin' (OED3), the term *mandolin*, from which *mando-* is extracted, is a co-hyponym of *violone* (Italian for 'violon') found in the diminutive model *violoncello* [1724], in that they both belong to a superordinate 'musical instruments' set. Parallel examples illustrating co-hyponymy are *blondie* [1943] 'a small square of dense cake similar to a brownie but having a cream or golden colour' (OED3) after *brownie* [1897], *headwork* [1642] 'work done with the brain or mind' (OED3) after *handwork* [OE], and *water-quake* [1577] or *seaquake* [1680] 'a submarine eruption or seismic disturbance in the sea' (OED2) after *earthquake* [c1325]. Wordspy also offers *dog whisperer* [1998] 'a person who has, or claims to have, a natural ability to relate to or connect with dogs', in which *dog* is co-hyponymous with *horse* in *horse whisperer* [1843].

A hyponym–hyperonym relationship holds between the subordinate term *model*, which is found in the target *modelizer* [1996] 'a man who habitually goes out with fashion models' (OED3), and the superordinate term *woman* in the model word *womanizer* [1822], in that a *model* is 'a type of *woman*'.

The opposite hyperonym–hyponym relationship holds between the superordinate term *person*, which is part of the new word *chairperson* [1971] 'a chairman or chairwoman' (OED2), and the subordinate term *man* in the model *chairman* [1654]. Instead, *chairwoman* [1699] 'a woman who occupies the chair of presidency at a meeting' (OED2) holds again an antonymic relationship with its model *chairman*.

Finally, the target *nationwide* [1891] 'extending throughout a nation' (OED3) exhibits a term *nation* which stands in a meronymic (part–whole) relationship with the term *world* in the model *worldwide* [1602].

5. Small semantic overlap: A less strong semantic relationship is, for instance, between the Variable Part *garden* in the target *gardenesque* [1838] 'partaking of the character of a garden' (OED2) and the term *picture* in the model *picturesque* [1705].

As these examples show, similarity features allow an association of the target words with their models at different language levels. Most of the targets share similarity features at all levels: e.g., the above-mentioned *defenceful* and its model *defenceless* share not only semantic resemblance (opposition of the final elements), but also affinity from the phonological and morphotactic viewpoints. The fact that target and model share an Invariable Part *defence* /dɪˈfens/ implies, from the viewpoint of segmental phonology, that they share (at least) two syllables and six phonemes, and, from the morphotactic viewpoint, that they share a base *defence*, to which two opposite suffixes (*-ful* vs. *-less*) are added. Therefore, analogical formation is often the result of a combination of association processes based on resemblances from diverse viewpoints. Indeed, there is often no ambiguity (either one or the other similarity type), but intended polyvalence (both one and the other type(s)), especially in sophisticated coinages.

On some occasions, however, some types of similarity feature prevail over others, whereas other features may be absent. For instance, the adjective *blottesque* [1856] /blɒˈtesk/ 'of painting: characterized by blotted touches heavily laid on' (OED2) resembles its model *grotesque* [1561] /grəʊˈtesk/ because of morphotactic similarity features – i.e. a shared suffix *-esque* – and phonological similarity features – i.e. a shared stressed syllable. A parallel case is the noun *femocrat* [1981] /ˈfem.ə.kræt/ 'an influential female civil servant or politician' (OED3), whose morphotactic and phonological similarity with the model *democrat* [1788] /ˈdem.ə.kræt/ – with a shared combining form *-ocrat* – immediately helps the association. In both examples, however, semantic similarity features appear to be absent, at least in the Variable Parts of target and model. These marginal cases seem to invalidate the claim that a distinct semantic link between target and model is very important in analogical formation (see 1.3, also in Klégr and Čermák 2010: 236). However, in these examples we should consider the semantic meaning conveyed by the Invariable Part – i.e. respectively, the affixes *-esque* and *-ocrat* – as the semantic link activating the association between target and model. By contrast, in the compound *babymoon* [2004] attested in COCA for 'romantic vacation during a pregnancy', the semantic head 'vacation' of the model *honeymoon* [1791] is evoked. Lastly, *womanity* [1836] 'womankind', based on *humanity* [a1425], is an apparent counterexample to the generalisation that English *-ity* attaches to Latinate bases. However, here phonological and semantic similarity between *woman* and *human* plays a large role in motivating the analogy.

3.3.5 Distance between target and model

In this subsection, analogical neoformations are classified according to their distance from the model words which trigger them. To facilitate decodification (see 2.3), analogical neoformations are generally either suggested, hinted at or echoed by their model words. The former endophoric (intratextual) reference provides an anaphoric neoformation introduced by its model, whereas the latter endophoric reference is rather cataphoric, i.e. anticipates its model.

Anaphoric neoformation: The distance between model and anaphoric neoformation can be more systematically differentiated in (all exemplifications are from COCA):
a) Immediately before:

(1) Actually, my film is **Reaganomics** versus **Obamanomics**. (*PARKER SPITZER 8:00 PM EST*, 2010)

b) Same sentence:

(2) If you're wearing **high-rise** pants, don't wear **low-rise** panties. (*Good Housekeeping*, 2007)

c) Same paragraph, preceding sentence:

(3) Physicists at the CERN Laboratory in Switzerland have been trying to recreate a bit of the **big bang** for about 15 years. The project has affectionately been dubbed **little bang**. (*NPR_ATC*, 2000)

d) Preceding paragraph or longer distance:

(4) TANTAROS: Well, we have Bachmann, Newt Gingrich, Rick Santorum and now, Herman Cain. Mitt Romney is saying, oh, I'm not going to **boycott**.
PERINO: Right. That's the most interesting thing. He's like I'm not going to – you know, he's going to need Nevada if he's going to win the presidency. He would need it.
GUTFELD: It's sexist.
BECKEL: You talk about – no, it's not.
GUTFELD: It's sexist. Why isn't it called a **girl-cott**? (*Fox_Five*, 2011)

Cataphoric neoformation: The distance between cataphoric neoformation and model can be distinguished into (examples are again from COCA):
a) Immediately following:

(5) GIFFORD: No. But how's it – what's it like to feel like you're at NBC News?
NICE: NBC News, which is great. It's – what do they call it, **newsytainment? Info-tainment?**
GIFFORD: Yeah, yeah. (*NBC_Today*, 2010)

b) Same sentence:

(6) Aging is not just an accumulation of doctor visits and disability and death. It is, in fact, a very productive period for many older persons but in America we have had an **ageism** which is like **sexism** and **racism** – it's an innate, negative view of the elderly. (*CNN_News*, 1996)

c) Immediately following sentence:

(7) John Updike, in a genially confident discourse on maleness ("The Disposable Rocket"), takes the view – though he admits to admixture – that the "male sense of space must differ from that of the female, who has such interesting, active, and significant **inner space**. The space that interests men is **outer** [**space**]." (*Atlantic Monthly*, 1998)

d) Following paragraph:

(8) We were going to be operating in international waters in an area six times the size of the Mediterranean Sea, and we didn't have any indication that the Soviets would be able to detect us. On the other hand, there is always

the possibility that a "**hot war**" might break out, so we always went out prepared for war, including a full load of "war shots."
Is that why Queenfish made the trip without identity markings? It was the **Cold War,** and Queenfish was a fast-attack submarine, so we didn't want anyone to be able to positively identify us. (*Military History*, 2009)

As a universal preference, anaphoric analogies are more common than cataphoric analogies. Quantitative data on this point is given in sections 4.4, 5.4, 6.4, and 7.3.

3.3.6 Morphological categorisation of analogy

In this subsection, analogical formations are classified according to their morphological category. This morphological categorisation is meant to show the power of analogy across morphological submodules of word-formation. The types of analogy that have been identified in my database include:

The derivational type:
- Prefixation: The noun *underkill* [1964] 'insufficient capacity, esp. of nuclear weapons, to kill and effect destruction to the level of strategic requirements' (OED2) is created via prefixation, after the model word *overkill* [1957] 'the capacity, esp. of nuclear weapons, to kill and destroy many times over' (OED3).
- Suffixation: *Jewdom* [1869] 'the Jewish world or community' (OED2) is coined via *-dom* suffixation, after the model *Christendom* [c893], and *Clintonite* [1992] 'a supporter or adherent of President Clinton or his policies' (OED2) is modelled on suffixed *Nixonite* [1950]. In *oceanarium* [1938] 'a seawater aquarium in which large sea creatures can be kept and observed' (OED3), the model *aquarium* [1853] is echoed by the suffix *-arium*, yet, an English base in the target replaces a Latinate base in the model. By contrast, in *pointful* [1925] 'full of point or substance' (OED3) ← *pointless* [c1330], the base is kept, whereas the suffix is opposite. Other comparable forms are in Bauer, Lieber, and Plag (2013: 524): *fallee* [2007] ← *falling* [a1400], *haircuttee* [2001] ← *haircutter* [1694], and *snubbee* [2000] ← *snubber* [1861].
- Prefixation + Suffixation: The adjective *illatinate* [1922] 'having no knowledge of Latin' (OED2) exhibits the prefix *il-* and the suffix *-ate*, like its model *illiterate* [1556].
- Interfixation: The slang (now historical) noun *rampsman* [1859] 'a person who commits robbery with violence' (OED3) shows an interfix *-s-*, after its slang model *cracksman* [1819] 'a housebreaker' (OED3). Moreover, the noun

decelerometer [1924] 'an instrument for ascertaining the deceleration of a moving body' (OED2), formed by the addition of a combining form, exhibits the interfix *-o-*, after the pattern of the model word *accelerometer* [1875].

The combining form type:
- Neoclassical combining form: The adjective *geomorphic* [1835] 'resembling the earth in form or fashion' (OED3) ends in the final combining form *-morphic* like its model *anthropomorphic* [1827].
- Abbreviated combining form: The adjective *info-rich* [1990] 'containing, providing, or possessing a great deal of information' (OED3, also noun, s.v. *information*) exhibits a combining form *info-*, abbreviating *information*, which occurs in the schema of *infocentre* [1942], *infoline* [1982], etc. (cf. the antonym *info-poor* [1990]).
- Secreted combining form: The noun *nastygram* [1991] 'a threatening, intimidating, or insulting message, esp. one sent by electronic mail' (OED3) exhibits the final combining form *-gram* (← *telegram*), which has given birth to the series denoting 'messages delivered by a representative of a commercial greetings company, especially one outrageously dressed to amuse or embarrass the recipient' (OED2). The combining form *-gram* is earliest attested in the nonce words *Gorillagram* [1979], *bellygram* [1981], *strippergram* [1983], and *Rambogram* [1985], etc. (OED2, s.v. *-gram*). Another such formation is *kissogram* [1982] 'a novelty telegram or greetings message sent through a commercial agency, which is delivered (usu. by a provocatively-dressed young woman) with a kiss' (OED2).

The conversion type: The verb *email* [1983] 'to send (a message or file) by email' (OED3) is coined after the noun *email* [1979] 'a system for sending textual messages via a computer network' (OED3), after the model of *mail* [1827] 'to send by post' (OED3) from the respective noun [1654]. A more recent N → V zero-derivation is in *Skype* [2003] 'to have a spoken conversation over the Internet using Skype software' (OED3), from the respective proprietary name, which is comparable to the earlier verb *Google* [1998] 'to use the Google search engine to find information on the Internet' (OED3).

The compound type: The target *blamestorming* [1997] 'the process of investigating the reasons for a failure and of apportioning blame' (OED3) shares the head with the model *brainstorming* [1907]. Similarly, in *slow food* [1974] 'food prepared in a conventional or traditional manner' (OED3), the right element of the model *fast food* [1954] is maintained. By contrast, the target *weeknight* [1782] 'a night of the week other than Saturday or Sunday night' (OED3) shares the non-head component with the model word *weekday* [OE]. Similarly, the targets *acid jazz* [1988] 'a genre of dance music incorporating elements of jazz, funk, soul, and hip-hop' (OED3) and *acid house* [1988] 'a type of house music characterized by a fast beat, a spare, hypnotic, synthesized sound, and the taking of hallucinogenic drugs' (OED3) are coined after *acid rock* [1966], with a shared left element (see also *acid head* [1966]).

– The rhyming compound: The rhyming compound *pooper-scooper* [1956] 'an implement for picking up and removing litter or mess' (OED3) is humorously coined after *super-duper* [1938] (cf. *Sooper dooper pooper scooper* 'a proprietary name in the United States').
– The particle compound: The noun *fax-back* [1988] 'a service that can fax a document automatically on request' (OED3) is obtained from a phrasal verb, like its model *callback* [1960]. Similarly, in *sleep-in* [1965] 'a form of protest in which the participants sleep overnight in premises which they have occupied' (OED2), the model *sit-in* [1937] is a noun compound from a phrasal verb (see also the humorous quote from OED2 "There have been *sit-ins, lie-ins, stand-ins, eat-ins, shop-ins, sleep-ins, swim-ins,* and *sing-ins.*" New York Times, 1965, 28 March).

The blending type:
– Total blend: The total blend *liger* [1938] 'the offspring of a lion and a tigress' (OED2), in which both source words are reduced to splinters (i.e. *li*(on) and (*ti*)*ger*), follows the pattern of its model *tigon* [1927] ← *tig*(er) + (*li*)*on*, 'the offspring of a tiger and a lioness' (OED2).
– Partial blend: The partial blend *adultescent* [1996] ← *adult* + *adolescent* (1.5), in which only one source word is reduced, is coined after the model of *kidult* [1960] ← *kid* + *adult* (see Mattiello 2013: 118–120 for "total" vs. "partial blends" and other differentiations in blends along diverse parameters and language levels).

The clipping type:
– Back-clipping: The colloquial abbreviation *hetero* [1933] 'heterosexual' (OED2) is coined on the model of *homo* [1929] 'homosexual'. In *lesbo* [1940] 'lesbian', instead, the analogy is with the ending *-o* of *homo*, re-interpreted as a suffix.
– Clipped compound: The noun *Cantopop* [1988] 'a form of popular music originating in Hong Kong' (OED3) is from a compound, i.e. *Canto*(nese) *pop*(ular

music) (OED3), like its abbreviated model *Britpop* [1986] ← *British popular music*. Moreover, the abbreviated compound *Britcom* [1977] ← *British comedy* (OED3) is coined after *sitcom* [1964] ← *situation comedy* and *romcom* [1971] ← *romantic comedy*. Also the creation of abbreviated *fanfic* [1976] ← *fanatic fiction* (OED2, s.v. *fan*) may plausibly have been influenced by *fanzine* [1949] ← *fanatic magazine* (cf. the *-zine* slang suffix in Green 2010).

The acronym type: *Rafi* [1965] 'an independent political party in the state of Israel formed in 1965' (OED3), from the modern Hebrew acronym *RPY* ← *Rěšīmaṯ Pō'ălē Yiśrā'ēl* 'Israel Workers' List', is modelled on *Mapai* [1941] 'a left-wing political party in the state of Israel' (OED3), from the acronym *MP'Y* ← *Mipleget Pō'ălē 'Ereṣ Yiśrā'ēl* 'Workers' Party of Israel'. In both cases, the nouns are read as acronyms – namely, /ræˈfɪ/ and /mæˈpaɪ/ – yet the pronunciation of the target word is probably also influenced by the common male forename *Rafi*, pet form of *Raphael*. Another acronym which belongs here is *MARV* [1973] /mɑːv/ ← *manoeuvrable re-entry vehicle*, 'a missile warhead capable of altering its course during the descent phase of its flight' (OED3), coined after *MIRV* [1966] /mɜːv/ ← *multiple independent re-entry vehicle*.

The initialism type: The initialisms *SBM* [1979] and *SBF* [1978] 'single black male/female' (OED2, s.v. *S*), used in personal advertisements, are modelled on previous *SWM* [1974]/*SWF* [1976] 'single white male/female' and *SJM/SJF* [1975] 'single Jewish male/female'. Similarly, the medical term *STI* [1991] 'sexually transmitted infection' (OED2, s.v. *S*) has the initialism *STD* [1974] 'sexually transmitted disease' as its model.

The conjunct phrase type: The adjective *mix'n'match* [1960] 'of articles of clothing: capable of being coordinated in a number of different ways according to taste' (OED3) is based on similar forms, such as *pick'n'mix* [1958] 'a wide range of items or elements from which a personal selection can be made' (OED3). See also earlier *rock'n'roll* [1938], after *rhythm'n'blues* [1933].

The calque type: The adverb *ad feminam* [1839] 'on the basis of qualities, interests, or circumstances specific to a particular woman' (OED3) is coined after classical Latin *ad* 'to' + *fēminam*, accusative singular of *fēmina* 'woman', after *ad hominem* [1588] (see also *ad personam* [a1628] 'personally' OED3, after *ad rem* 'to the point or purpose' [1588]).

The morphological categorisation of analogical formations offered above confirms Klégr and Čermák's (2010) claim that:

> [R]egardless of whether a WFP [Word-Formation Process] is considered morphological, highly systematic and rule-governed (derivation, compounding) or highly idiosyncratic and arbitrary (clipping, acronymy) each is accompanied by analogical coinages.
>
> Klégr and Čermák (2010: 232)

Hence, analogy is a relevant concept to all morphological categories, disregarding the grammaticality vs. marginality vs. extra-grammaticality of the morphological process or operation through which a word is formed. In particular, surface analogies recur throughout the spectrum from rule-based to extra-grammatical formations (Mattiello 2016). However, Klégr and Čermák's (2010: 235) statement that "all word-formation ... has some kind of analogy as its underlying principle" is to some extent inaccurate. To be analogical, a formation must be based on a precise model identifiable as either one word or a series/word family, and target and model should be analysable according to a proportional equation (1.3). What can be stated, instead, is that words (or word series) belonging to all word-formation categories can function as models for the analogical process.

3.4 Psycholinguistic aspects of analogical word-formation

Hitherto, the perspective from which analogy has been dealt with is that of a linguistic classification in word-formation. However, analogy also plays a role in psycholinguistic studies. In particular, the three realms of psycholinguistics which appear to be related to analogy are first language acquisition (Clark 1981, 1982, [2003] 2009; cf. Dressler and Laaha 2012 for inflectional morphology), psycholinguistic experiments on analogical change (Thumb and Marbe 1901) and word perception and recognition (Libben 2008), and speech errors (Fromkin 1973, 1980). These different application domains depart from the primary interests of the present research, but certainly deserve mention before we turn the attention to some of the different areas where analogical new words are coined in English. Below mention is made to some of the main psycholinguistic works which may additionally be relevant to analogical word-formation.

3.4.1 Analogy in first language acquisition

Whereas research on the impact of analogy in second language learning still remains a gap in linguistic research, the impact of analogy on first language acquisition has recently been studied by Dressler and Laaha (2012), but specifically for the acquisition of German morphological inflection. In English morphology, the earliest experiments on analogy in first language acquisition were carried out by Jean Berko (1958), who focused both on inflection and on word-formation.

In the latter domain, Berko (1958) observed some tendencies of pre-school children (aged between 4–5), first-grade children (aged between 5;6–7), and college graduate adults in the coinage of new words from nonsense words, such as the verb *zib or the noun *wug. Her results show that, whereas adults may derive new words such as *zibber or *wuglet, i.e. using the common agentive pattern -er or the diminutive suffix -let, children at this stage use almost exclusively a compounding pattern. For instance, small children have coined *zibman for 'a man who *zibs for a living', after the compounds postman [1529] or milkman [1589] (although with a verb as first component), and compounds like baby *wug and little *wug for 'a very tiny *wug', after the regular pattern of baby elephant [1815] or baby bird [1841]. First graders have also created *wughouse for 'the house a *wug lives in', comparable to the model doghouse [1555].³¹

Children in their protomorphological phase of acquisition detect bound morphology and start to make successively more and more abstract generalisations.³² In line with Dressler and Laaha (2012), this phase is the most important one, since it is characterised by the simultaneous emergence of plural formation, (third person) verb inflection, diminutive formation, and compound formation. Actually, Berko's small informants seem to be aware of compounding formation, but not of diminutive suffixes. Indeed, for the diminutive of *wug, 50% of the adults have formed *wuglet, and others have offered *wuggie, *wugette, and *wugling, but no child has used a diminutive suffix. However, 52% of the children have formed

---

31 These results are comparable to what happens in inflection, where children exhibit a tendency to regularise irregular forms, such as plural nouns (e.g. foot–*foots), or strong verbs (e.g. go–*goed) (Blevins and Blevins 2009: 4). As Berko (1958: 175) suggests, since children do not have the real form rang in their lexical repertoire, they produce *ringed according to the productive rule. By contrast, surface analogies to isolated patterns have not been observed in inflection (Dressler and Laaha 2012: 115).
32 Dressler and Laaha (2012: 110) distinguish among three acquisition phases: 1) premorphology (before the child detects morphology); 2) protomorphology (when the child detects bound morphology); and 3) morphology proper, which qualitatively resembles adult morphology and starts with the subphase of core morphology.

compounds like *baby *wug*. In fact, it is commonly agreed among acquisitionists that the degree of language awareness increases slowly in acquisition, and some playful neoformations created by children in the premorphological phase may also include awareness.

Clark (1981: 303) has similarly observed that children make up new words (or new meanings) when they lack other words to express their meaning, and the new words are often compound words. For instance, a two-year-old child has coined *plate-egg* and *cup-egg* for 'fried' and 'boiled egg', and *fire-dog* for 'a dog found at the site of a local fire' (Clark 1981: 305). Agent nouns are similarly rendered through compounds, especially those combining a noun or a verb base as the first element with the noun -*man* in the second place, as in *fix-man* (for 'a car mechanic') and *garden-man* (for 'a gardener'). The latter example clearly shows that compounds with -*man* (or -*woman*, -*person*, or -*people*) in second position are more transparent for children than the -*er* suffix to express agency. Parallel compounds with -*thing* or -*machine* as their second element are coined for instruments: e.g., *eating-thing* (for 'a thing for eating with') and *hugging-machine* (for 'a thing for hugging people') have been produced by three- to five-year-olds (Clark 1981: 306). What is the role of analogy in these formations? Does Clark's data provide evidence for rule use or for analogy? As Clark (1982: 397) admits, "[t]here may be no single answer".

Although Clark (1982) mainly discusses cases of plural formation, the acquisition of word-formation appears to be comparable. Children might well begin by comparing new instances to specific model words already in their repertoires. For instance, for the coinage of *hugging-machine*, the child may have used the compound *washing-machine* [c1754], which was already in his/her lexical stock. But later, after being exposed to a large number of compounds following the same pattern, they should have a plethora of models to work from, and their use of composition may take the form of a general rule. Or they might simultaneously use rules in some domains and analogy in others. The overregularisation of the English plural suffix -*s*, as in *childs*, *fishes*, *oxes*, and *sheeps* (McMahon 1994), would seem to favour a rule interpretation. But the construction of compounds like *coffee-churn* (for 'a coffee grinder') by a child who knew *milk-churn* [1478] (Pelsma 1910) would seem to favour interpretation as analogy. As Clark (1982: 397) suggests, "analogy and rule use appear to lie on a continuum, with analogy based on single exemplars at one end, and rules abstracted over multiple exemplars at the other".

In support of the latter claim, many characteristic activity verbs[33] in English are coined by children from nouns, via conversion or zero-derivation. For instance, Clark (1982: 410) quotes in her article children's utterances of the type *It *winded* (age 3;2, noticing a picture of trees leaning in the wind) and *It's *snowflaking* (age 3;11, making dots with a crayon). The conversion of the nouns *wind* and *snowflake* to characteristic activity verbs clearly suggests interpretation as analogy, respectively with *It rained* and *It's snowing*. In other words, the existence of the model words *rain* and *snow* has encouraged children to use similar weather nouns as verbs. A parallel case is in the utterances *I'm *souping* (age 2;4, 'eating soup') and *They're *teaing* (age 5;0, 'having tea'). Again, interpretation as analogy seems to be favoured by the existence of *lunch, breakfast*, and *snack*, both as nouns and as converted verbs. A proportional analogy with these verbs – e.g., *a lunch : to lunch = a soup : X, X = to soup* – is indeed possible.

However, a set of examples from Clark's (1982) collection of characteristic activity verbs is not proportional with a concrete model. They include: *Make it *bell* (age 3;0, wanting a bell to be rung), *It *flagged* (age 3;2, looking at a drooping flag that suddenly spread out), *Don't *hair me* (age 2;4, 'don't brush my hair'), and *I'm *lawning* (age 2;9, playing with a toy lawn mower). In these cases, the children probably had an abstract model, rather than a precise lexical item, in their minds. The examples of *to bell* and *to hair* are even counted as "illegitimate" innovations (Clark 1982: 394), i.e. the innovative word is pre-empted by suppletion, because its meaning coincides with the meaning of another verb – namely, the verb *ring* or *brush* – already in the language. All of them, however, may have been created via overgeneralisation of the rule forming Noun–Verb pairings, such as *bicycle–bicycle* or *dress–dress*, rather than by surface analogy with one of these pairings.

Clearer examples of surface analogy have been provided by Anttila (1977: 19–20). He cites the case of a child who has coined the verb *nosigate* referring to 'the treatment of the nose' by analogy with medical *irrigate* [1876] referring to 'the treatment of the ear', because of the quasi-homophony between *irr* and *ear*. Another similar case of analogy is the coinage of *twomation* referring to 'two airplanes', on the model of *formation* [1914], misinterpreted as connected to the number *four* (i.e. 'four airplanes'). In both cases, reanalysis has preceded analogy.

By contrast, Liam, a bilingual child who speaks English and Italian, has provided cases of surface analogy where no reanalysis occurs. For instance, at the

---

33 Clark (1982: 410) defines "characteristic activity verbs" as verbs that "denote the characteristic activity done *by* or *to* the particular entity denoted by the parent noun of the verb" (emphasis in the original).

age of 2;6, he produced English *yogurting room* by analogy with the model *dining room* [1601], because he used to eat yogurt there. At the same age, he also coined Italian *tagliapavimento* (literally 'that mows the floor') for 'vacuum cleaner', on the model of *tagliaerba* 'lawn-mower' and similar Italian V–N compounds.[34] At the age of 3;7, the same bilingual child produced *head-mower* for 'a machine used to shave one's hair' and *dog-mower* 'a machine used to shave the dog's coat', both coined on the pattern of *lawn-mower*. On the pattern of *snowman*, he (3;7) coined *riceman* for 'a sort of snowman made of rice' (cf. *snowmouse*, from the same model, in Leo Leonni's 2004 story for children *A Busy Year*).

Children's spontaneous speech seems to be an enormous source of innovations that could be classified as surface analogies with actual words. Let me conclude this subsection with a pleasant example offered by Clark [2003] (2009):

> D (2;10, offering a pretend present to father): I bought you a tooth-brush and a *finger-brush*. Father: What's a *finger-brush*? D: It's for cleaning your nails.
> Clark ([2003] 2009: 257, emphasis added)[35]

The neosemanticism *finger-brush* seems to support both Clark's (1982) claim that compounds are more transparent than derived words, and therefore preferred by children in their early acquisition phases, and the claim that children often coin new words (or assign new meanings) after the pattern of precise words that are part of their lexical repertoire (e.g. *tooth-brush*). However, more research in this direction should be done to test these claims.

3.4.2 Psycholinguistic experiments on association in analogical change

Among psycholinguistic studies, Thumb and Marbe's (1901) monograph is now a classic. In this monograph, the psychologist Karl Marbe has designed and run the experiments and Albert Thumb has evaluated them from a linguistic perspective. In particular, the masterpiece addresses the question of whether psychological mechanisms of association leading to analogical linguistic change can be measured experimentally.

In the opening chapter, Thumb states the problem of whether analogical change must be based on association between two elements in the language

---

34 For the acquisition of Italian V–N compounds of the type *taglia-capelli* (literally 'that cuts the hair') for 'hair-dresser', see Lo Duca (1990).
35 Cf. existent *finger-brush* in OED2 (s.v. *finger*) with a different meaning, i.e. 'a brush which is dipped in the colour and drawn across the fingers'.

user's mind. For instance, since *hide* and *ride* are rime associates, as well as *hidden* and *ridden*, these associations may exert pressure to change *hid* to **hode*, like *ride–rode*.[36] Adaptations in meaning-related words could likewise occur because of psychological associations. This is the case with *October*, which could become **Octember* under the influence of the near months *September*, *November*, and *December* (Thumb and Marbe 1901: 57).

In the experimental chapters, Marbe addresses the question of whether analogical change involves the association between within-word class items. In his first experiment, for instance, Marbe used ten words from six different word classes: relational nouns (e.g. *Vater* 'father', *Mutter* 'mother'), adjectives (e.g. *gross* 'big', *klein* 'small'), personal pronouns (e.g. *ich* 'I', *du* 'you'), local adverbs (e.g. *wo* 'where', *woher* 'where from'), temporal adverbs (e.g. *wann* 'when', *jetzt* 'now'), and numerals from *eins* 'one' to *zehn* 'ten'. Marbe then called these stimuli in quasi-random order and observed the responses produced by four subjects as well as their response time.

Marbe's data shows some interesting facts. First, for all word classes, 77% of the responses belonged to the same class. Second, the subjects tended to respond in fixed pairs, such as *father–mother*, opposites for adjectives, such as *big–small*, and the next number for a numeral (*three–four*).

From the linguist's viewpoint, these findings also have linguistic relevance. Indeed, Thumb has argued that, in the history of language change, strongly associated pairs tend to become more similar in form, or may even turn up in slips of the tongue. For instance, kinship terms tend to assimilate their word endings (*father–mother–brother–sister*), as suggested by Levelt (2013: 183), or to occur in utterances such as "Where is your *father* ... er ... *mother*?" (Levelt 2013: 153).

These findings could also be interpreted from a different angle. Associated pairs, indeed, appear to be frequent Variable Parts, i.e. parts which differentiate analogical target words from existing model words. For instance, the new word *father-substitute* [1938] 'a person to whom the attachment of a child is directed in place of the father' (OED2, s.v. *father*) has been created after *mother-substitute* [1933] and *Father's Day* [1943] 'a day on which fathers are honoured' (OED2, s.v. *father*) after *Mother's Day* [1890]. A parallel case with a right Variable Part is *house-husband* [1858] 'male partner who carries out the household role and duties traditionally associated with a housewife' (OED3), coined after *housewife* [c1225]. Therefore, kinship terms can substitute their immediately associated terms in analogical

---

36 According to Paul (1880), an important countervailing power in these cases is the strength of the memory trace: since *hid* is a frequent, well-established word form in the speaker's mind, it will resist analogical change.

new words. The case of *daughterboard*, after *motherboard*, has already been mentioned (3.3.4). Similarly, opposite adjectives, such as *big–small*, may often occur as Variable Parts. For instance, *big end* [1877] '(in a piston engine) the end of the connecting rod that encircles the crankpin' (OED3, s.v. *big*) is modelled on *small end* [1846], and *big hand* [1849] 'the long hand on a clock or watch that indicates the minutes' (OED3, s.v. *big*) is coined after *small hand* [1818] (used for the short hand). Successive numerals can also help the association between model and target word and vice versa: e.g., *quartessence* [1936] 'an essence one degree less pure than a quintessence' (OED3), from Latin *quartus* 'fourth', has been created after *quintessence* [c1460] (from *quīntus* 'fifth'). A parallel example is *two-phase* [1909] (for a circuit or system, OED2, s.v. *two*), coined after *three-phase* [1892].

These remarks seem to suggest that the associations behind analogical formation have psycholinguistic (besides phonological, morphotactic, and semantic) bases, yet experiments in this area should be carried out in order to test these hypotheses.

3.4.3 Psycholinguistic experiments on compound families and the processing of compound words

Psycholinguistic experiments have also been conducted to investigate the way similar complex words are processed. Works on compound processing have brought to light clear evidence for word family effects, and this supports the idea that people make recourse to models when they form or interpret new compounds. This idea is related to the concept of analogy via schema (3.3.1).

A block of psycholinguistic studies has especially devoted attention to the interpretation and representation of English compound words (Gagné and Shoben 1997; Libben 1998, 2006, 2008; Gagné 2001; De Jong et al. 2002; Gagné and Spalding 2006; Libben and Jarema 2006). A pertinent recent study is Smith, Barratt, and Zlatev (2014), who have conducted experiments concerning the spontaneous interpretation of novel N–N food compounds (e.g. *Hawaii pizza*) in isolation and in context. Smith, Barratt, and Zlatev (2014: 105) have adopted what they call an "analogy approach". In other words, they have observed that, if the default interpretation for conventional Place–Food compounds, such as *Parma ham* [1865], is that the product originates in the place in question, this implies that other novel food compounds can be interpreted accordingly. For instance, *Parma cheese* [n.d.] will be the name for 'cheese from Parma', after the above model. However, not all novel food compounds formed after this pattern trigger the same interpretation: e.g., in *Hawaii pizza* [n.d.] 'pizza inspired by Hawaii, made with pineapple and ham' (Smith, Barratt, and Zlatev 2014:

139) the first component does not indicate physical origin, since the actual origin of this pizza is Canadian.

The study by Smith, Barratt, and Zlatev (2014) is related to the traditional psycholinguistic literature of Christine Gagné and her colleagues (see, e.g., Gagné and Shoben 1997; Gagné 2001), who have pointed out that the frequency with which the compound constituents are used with similar interpretations in already existing compounds affects the recipient's interpretation of the novel compound. However, in line with Gagné's Competition-Among-Relations-In-Nominals psycholinguistic theory (Gagné, Spalding, and Gorrie 2005), novel and conventional compounds encode a number of relations which steadily compete with each other. Therefore, this competition increases the difficulty in identifying which of all competing relations is at work for the interpretation of the novel compound under examination.

Another important line of research – represented by Gary Libben and his co-workers (e.g. Jarema et al. 1999) – explores the role of semantic transparency and morphological headedness in the processing of compounds. Jarema et al. (1999), for instance, claim that semantic transparency, morphological headedness, and position in the string interact with the processing of compounds. In their view, compounds whose morphemes are both fully transparent and whose head is the second constituent (right-headed) are easier to process than partially opaque ones, such as *strawberry* (with a transparent second component) or *jailbird* (with a transparent first component). Full transparency in compounds, however, does not seem to be related to higher probability to become a candidate model for analogy: e.g., slang *cheesecake* is fully opaque and semantically headless, and yet it is the model for analogous *beefcake* (see 1.2).

Libben (1998: 31) also claims that semantic transparency facilitates word recognition and morphological parsing, i.e. the process of determining the morphemes from which a given word is constructed. Accordingly, a semantically transparent compound, such as *birthday*, undergoes morphological decomposition (*birth* + *day*) during word recognition, whereas partially opaque compounds such as *Sunday* (with opacity in the modifier) and pseudo-compounds, such as *boycott*, do not (Sandra 1990, cited by Libben 1998: 34; cf. decomposition with only one transparent component, as in the above-mentioned *strawberry* and *jailbird*). Apropos of opacity and the interpretation of compounds, Bourque (2014: 127) has observed that the meaning of semantically opaque new compounds, such as *whitemail*, is not retrievable without knowing the (idiomatic) meaning of the model compounds, in this case *blackmail* (3.3.4).

Taft and Forster (1976) instead point to a view in which all compound words are automatically decomposed into their constituent morphemes during recognition, and, only later, the meanings of opaque constituents are rejected. Actually, a word such as *Sunday* [eOE] is nowadays lexicalised and no morphological decomposition is made in its interpretation. In other words, it is no longer treated as a composite word with the meaning 'day of the sun'. However, originally, it was probably the model for *Monday* [OE] (lit. 'day of the moon') and the other weekdays. By contrast, in the pseudo-compound *boycott*, *-cott* has first become a cranberry morph, and then a meaningful part in the analogical word *girlcott* (see 3.2.6).

Finally, Libben (2008: 5) has introduced a concept that concerns "maximization of opportunity" for activation. That is, he supports the view that compound processing not only involves both whole-word and constituent activation, but also the activation of positionally bound morphemes. For instance, for the compound *snowboard*, the whole word is activated, its constituent free morphemes are activated (*snow* and *board*), and an additional set of positionally bound morphemes (*snow-* and *-board*) are also activated. This maximisation of opportunity for activation is connected to research on morphological families in compound processing. De Jong et al. (2002), for instance, claim that compound representation involves bound morphological elements. Thus, in their view, the recognition of a compound such as *snowboard* [1983] is influenced by the type frequency of words that begin with *snow-* (e.g. *snow-storm* [1771], *snow slide* [1841]) and end in *-board* (e.g. *surfboard* [1798], *skateboard* [1964]) (see "Family Size effect" in De Jong, Schreuder, and Baayen 2000: 329).

The role played by compound constituent families is prominent for the present research on analogy. Indeed, new compounds are often formed on the basis of existing compound families organised around what Libben (2008: 7) calls "pivot constituents", i.e. positionally bound morphemes which can sometimes be the morphological head and sometimes the non-head. In analogical word-formation, the target can share either the head or the non-head with its model. For instance, *kiteboard* [1998] 'a type of surfboard designed for riding across water while harnessed to a large kite controlled by hand-held strings' (OED3) and *sandboard* [1992] 'a long narrow board on which a rider may coast down sand dunes' (OED3) share the head with *snowboard*, *surfboard*, etc. By contrast, *kiteboarding* [1996] 'a sport or pastime in which participants ride a specially adapted surfboard' (OED3) shares the modifier with earlier *kitesurfing* [1995].

Bauer, Lieber, and Plag (2013: 453) also call attention to the twentieth-century neologisms *drip-dry* [1916] 'to dry when hung up to drip' (OED2), *spin-dry* [1927] 'to remove excess water from (washing) by spinning it rapidly' (OED2), and *blow-dry* [1966] 'to style and dry (hair) with a brush or comb and hand-held hairdryer' (OED2, s.v. *blow-*). According to them, their formation has been influenced by a large constituent family of verbal compounds in *-dry* that served as an analogical model (*kiln-dry* [c1540], *sun-dry* [1695], *smoke-dry* [1704]). Algeo (1991: 7) makes an interesting distinction between "suffix-like compounds" (e.g. *home-based* [1920], *shore-based* [1927], *carrier-based* [1935], *reality-based* [1946]) and "prefix-like compounds" (e.g. *bamboo English* [1924], *bamboo government* [n.d.], *bamboo telegraph* [n.d.]). The first (*bamboo-*) or second (*-based*) elements of these compounds act as new affixes creating word families.

In addition, some general effects of morphological families with compounds concern stress. For instance, Plag, Kunter, and Arndt-Lappe (2007), Plag (2010), and Arndt-Lappe (2011) have demonstrated that stress-assignment to N–N compounds is largely predictable from the stress-behaviour of related compounds that have the same left or right constituent (e.g. *Óxford Street–Máin Street* vs. *Madison Ávenue–Fifth Ávenue*).[37] Thus, since in *snówboard* and *súrfboard* the right constituent *board* is unstressed, in analogical *skáteboard* and *kíteboard*, it will be unstressed too. However, stress on the first element is also the most common pattern in compounds.

3.4.4 Analogy in speech errors

Rudolph Meringer (1908) may be considered the father of linguistic interest in speech errors, and his published collection of over eight thousand speech, reading, and writing errors can validate this assertion. Meringer's interest in the relationship between speech errors and linguistic change has attracted many researchers, both linguists and psycholinguists. For instance, many of the contributions collected by Fromkin (1973) were inspired by Meringer's corpus. It would also be interesting to explore in more depth the role played by analogy in the production of speech errors.

In Fromkin's (1973) Introduction, a kind of error which appears to be related to analogical formation is that which produces blends or contaminations.[38] Indeed, blending is not always a conscious word-formation process, but may occur

---

[37] For English compounds, see also Arndt-Lappe and Bell (2014); for English blends, see Arndt-Lappe and Plag (2013).
[38] Here contamination is viewed as a synonym of blending (Mattiello 2013). A different view is in McMahon (1994: 74), who cites, as an illustrative example of contamination, the numeral *four* (from PIE *kwetwer-*; cf. Latin *quattuor*). This numeral, according to Grimm's Law, should have initial /h/, but it has become *four* after contamination by the immediate neighbour numeral *five*.

when two words are erroneously pronounced simultaneously (see "blend(ing) errors" in Kubozono 1990; Bertinetto 2001; Gries 2012). Spontaneous blend errors are frequently formed, for instance, with near-synonymous or semantically-related components, as in *minal* ← *minor* and *trivial*, or *beforst* ← *before* and *first*, cited by Fromkin (1973: 37). While many cases of blends are primarily due to a sharing of semantic features, others also involve words which are phonologically similar, as in *frowl* ← *frown* and *scowl*, or *herrible* ← *terrible* and *horrible* (Fromkin 1973: 261), which is analogous to its consciously-formed counterpart *torrible* [n.d.] (Gries 2004b: 425; Cacchiani 2007: 110). Blend errors with semantically related terms are comparable to conscious blends which occur, for instance, in slang *posilutely* [1914] ← *positively* + *absolutely* (OED3), generally paired with its equivalent *absotively* [1914] (1.5), and *prezactly* [1835] ← *precisely* + *exactly*, with phonetic respelling (OED3).

In her Appendix, Fromkin (1973: 243–269) mentions other types of error which are related to analogy. For instance, a frequent pattern for errors involves "Consonant Reversals" (Fromkin 1973: 245). Fromkin (1973: 245) mentions various pairs of scholars whose names have been altered as a result of initial consonant reversal. Examples include *locket or ham* 'Hockett or Lamb', *zakoffs and limmers* 'Lakoffs and Zimmers', and *fats and kodor* 'Katz and Fodor'. Analogous speech errors have occurred between the first and family names of 'Roman Jakobson' (*Yoman Rakobson*), the two parts of the city name 'New York' (*Yew Nork*), and even common compound constituents, such as 'wind mill', which is erroneously pronounced as *mind will*.

Another type includes "Haplologies and other Telescopic Errors" (Fromkin 1973: 256–257), i.e. when a word is shortened or two words are merged by deleting one or more syllables or syllable parts to ease pronunciation. Haplology generally occurs when two words are blended where they overlap, as in *muddle* ← *mud puddle*, or *nitness* ← *Nixon witness*. Overlapping blends, such as *adaptitude* [1806] ← *adapt* + *aptitude* (OED3), or *affluenza* [1973] ← *affluence* + *influenza*, 'a psychological condition including a lack of motivation, feelings of guilt, and a sense of isolation' (OED3) could have their origin or model in spontaneous phenomena like the above-mentioned haplologies.

A similar case of error that is related to analogical word-formation is provided by the word *beautify* /ˈbjuː.tɪ.fʌɪ/ (OED3), which occasionally occurs as an error for *beatify* – see, e.g., "Ignatius was afterwards *Beautified* by Pope Paul" (L. Owen, 1629, *Speculum Jesuiticum*, OED3). However, the same type of error has occurred earlier in *beautitude* [1578] /ˈbjuː.tɪ.tʃuːd/ 'supreme happiness' (OED3) for *beatitude* [a1492]. Hence, in both cases, a contamination (or haplology) seems to have occurred between *beauty* and either *beatify* or *beatitude*, although the two phenomena have occurred independently.

Other telescopic errors from Fromkin (1973) consist of the shortening of words such as *lecalization* ← *lexicalization* or *aspectal* ← *aspectual*. This pattern seems to be the model for related errors, such as *autobiographal* [1845], which is given in OED3 as an error for *autobiographical* [1807]. Also the form *accompaniment* [1669] is attested, according to the OED, as a typographical error for *accomplishment* [1425]. In this case, rather than a shortening, we have a substitution of part of the third syllable (onset–nucleus–rime /lɪʃ/), with nucleus–rime /ən/ + nucleus /ɪ/.

These errors are clearly different from the conscious folk-etymological remodelling of words like *cole/coalmouse* [?1533] (from Germanic *coal* + *mose*, 'any of several titmice with black markings' OED3, see 3.2.6), whose second element has become *mouse* by analogy with *titmouse* [1530] (with plural *titmice*, OED2). Spontaneous errors should also be distinguished from conscious word play, although the mechanisms which naturally create errors are on some occasions comparable to those originating word play. For instance, the "spoonerisms" *fight a liar* (for 'light a fire') and *queer old dean* (for 'dear old queen') cited by Fromkin (1973: 16) involve consonant reversals which are similar to the ones observed in errors. Yet, word play is purposefully used with an amusing intention, whereas speech errors are normally the result of slips of the tongue (or of the brain), and are generally performed involuntarily by persons with psychological or mental disorders (Dressler 1976).

Chapter 8 of the present work describes the results obtained from offline tests on the degree of acceptability (in terms of accessibility in or without context) of new English analogical words. These results should be corroborated by findings from offline psycholinguistic experiments.

The chapters that follow investigate analogical formations in four different domains: the specialised domain, the journalistic domain, the juvenile sphere, and the literary realm. These different domains have been selected as case studies in order to investigate whether they are comparable in terms of types of analogy, the grammatical vs. extra-grammatical formations involved, the presence vs. absence of the model in the co-text, and functions. We forecast a higher degree of regularity and predictability in the former (specialised) domain, while we expect irregularity and ungrammaticality in the latter (literary) realm, with formations that are more audacious and a higher number of occasionalisms. We also predict that the functions of analogies in these fields are dissimilar, with creativity and inventiveness used for diverse purposes, either to exclude or amuse others.

4 Analogy in specialised language

In the coinage of specialised terms, analogy has played a central role for centuries, especially in the domain of the Law, where some new words have been created on the model of existing legal items since the Middle English period. For instance, according to the etymological description provided by the OED, the origin of historical *inlaw* [1607] 'one who is within the domain and protection of the law' (OED2) is from Middle English *inlaȝe* ← *in-* + *laȝe* 'law', after *utlaȝe* 'outlaw' [OE]. Another domain for analogical coinages is that of science (Green 1991), where experts share a linguistic and cultural heritage which allows new targets to be easily understood on the basis of comparable model words. The scientific noun *omnivore* [1871] 'an omnivorous animal' (OED3) – created after the model of *carnivore* [1854], *herbivore* [1854], and *insectivore* [1863] – offers an example from the nineteenth century.

More recent analogical words pertain to the area of computer science (Green 1991). For instance, since the end of the last century, the word *little-endian* [1980] has acquired the specialised meaning of 'a person who favours a design for computer hardware in which units of data are stored or transmitted with the least significant units' (OED3).[1] Originally, the model for this word was *big-endian* [1980], which is currently used in computing for 'the most significant units'.

Another fertile area of novel analogical formation is tourism discourse (Cappelli 2013), especially tourism on the web, where, along with *last-minute* [1908] or *last-second* [1920] booking, tourists can find *first-minute* [n.d.] offers, i.e. 'occurring at the earliest possible time' (*WWW*). Another formation connected with tourism and travel is *travelogue* [1903] 'a travel documentary' (OED2), which has been coined after *dialogue* [OE], *monologue* [c1550], and a series of similar formations. According to the OED, *-logue* (from classical Latin *-logus*) is a combining form 'forming nouns denoting types of discourse', as in *prologue* [c1350], *Decalogue* [1382], *catalogue* [a1464], etc., which function as schema model for *travelogue*.

Fashion lexis is also replete with new analogical words and the *Urban Dictionary* is a veritable cornucopia of fashion's new lexicon, as demonstrated by Lopriore (2014: 250–251) for four different fashion-related fields. Among them, lexemes such as *fashionaholic* [2010] (see -(*a*)*holic* in 3.1.2 and *passim*), *SOD* [2011]

---

[1] Cf. the earlier use of *little-endian* [1749], after *big-endian* [1726], in Jonathan Swift's novel *Gulliver's Travels*, with the sense of 'a person who believes that eggs should be broken at the narrower end before they are eaten' (OED3).

'shoe obsessive disorder' (after *OCD* [1977] 'obsessive-compulsive disorder'), and *shopgasm* [2008] (after *wargasm* [2004]) represent analogies.

The language of Architecture is similarly rich in lexical neologisms (Soneira 2015: 17), which are part of the professional jargon used by design experts and other members of the architectural community, hence the labels "talkitecture" or "archispeak" (Soneira 2015: 16–17). In her study of recently-coined architectural terms in the OED, Soneira (2015: 245) has observed that 1.4% are coined via analogy. A corpus-based study shows that analogical formations include both productive series, such as those coined from *-scape* (3.3.1), and surface analogies of the type *escalator* [1900] (after *elevator* [1787]), *polychrome* [1801] (after *monochrome* [1662]), and *planar* [1850] (after *linear* [1656]) (Soneira 2015: 159–161).

The present chapter investigates specialised terminology and technical or professional jargon with the aim of showing that several new words which enrich specialists' vocabulary are motivated by the analogical process. The primary goal of this investigation is to prove that, in specialised sectors, new analogical words are generally regular, predictable, and easy to recognise (or disambiguate), especially for experts. Indeed, because of their prior knowledge of the subject, experts do not require an explicit model word in the micro-context to make the association, nor do they need to make the model word overt once they coin a new target. As a secondary goal, this investigation intends to demonstrate that analogy may have different – but all equally important – functions in the language of experts, from denomination to professional bonding, from efficiency in élite communication to group cohesion. The last subsection of the chapter shows quantitative data on the representativeness and frequency of novel specialised terms in COCA.

4.1 Types of analogical formation in specialised language

Analogical formations in specialised language conform to various types and morphological patterns. Cases of pure surface analogy, for instance, occur in different domains, including science, economics, law, information technology, and so on. Many such surface analogies belong to extra-grammatical morphology, in that they are mostly formed according to abbreviatory patterns. In psychiatry, for instance, the initialism *ADHD* [1987] ← *attention deficit hyperactivity disorder* (OED3, s.v. *A*) has been coined after the model *ADD* [1979] ← *attention deficit disorder*. Example (9), from COCA, provides an illustration of co-occurring target and model, both in bold:

(9) Students with **ADD** or **ADHD** have a severe Concentration Disorder, and, therefore, have difficulty in learning. (*Journal of Instructional Psychology*, 1997, COCA)

Other interesting neoformations are in the socio-economic sector: e.g., *G2B* [2000] ← *government to business*, 'the use of the Internet by government to provide services and information to the business sector' (OED2, s.v. *G*) is modelled on *B2B* [1994] ← *business to business*, with *to* phonetically and graphically replaced by *2* 'two'. In its turn, *G2C* [2000] ← *government to citizen*, 'the use of the Internet by government to provide services and information to private citizens' (OED2, s.v. *G*) is analogical with *G2B*.

In addition, in British law, the criminal offence *actual bodily harm* is called *ABH* [1975] (OED3), after the exact model of *G.B.H.* [1958] ← *grievous bodily harm*:

(10) ... If you don't, you are committing **ABH** or **GBH**, depending on the severity of the condition. (*The Guardian*, 2011, GloWbE)

Another surface analogy occurs in computing, where *gigaflop* [1976] 'a unit of computing speed equal to 1000 megaflops' (OED2) has been back-formed from *gigaflops*, with the initial combining form *giga-* 'giant' and re-interpretation of the final *s* (from *second*) as a plural ending:

(11) The Beowulf Project was a NASA project started in 1993 to find an option for lower-cost computing, at a time when a **gigaflop** could cost close to a million dollars. (http://www.hpcwire.com/, 2012, GloWbE)

A comparable pattern is in the back-formed model *megaflop* [1976] 'a unit of computing speed equal to one million floating-point operations per second' (OED3), with the combining form *mega-* 'very large' and the same reanalysis. In addition, the acronym *LIFO* [1968] ← *last in, first out*, 'designating a procedure in which the first item removed from a buffer, queue, etc., is the last one to have been added' (OED2) has been created in computing (but also used in accounting) as the analogical opposite of *FIFO* [1966] ← *first in, first out*, according to the same abbreviatory pattern. Example (12) is from COCA:

(12) This prevented the use of the **LIFO** or **FIFO** method of inventory calculation, both of which require that each unit of inventory be costed against the previous purchases. (*Journal of Information Systems*, 1992, COCA)

However, in specialised language, surface analogy is also often combined with rules. In politics, for instance, many grammatical terms related to the right wing have been created by analogy with their corresponding items connected to the opposition, i.e. the Left. For instance, the derived words *Rightism* [1934] 'the political views, principles, or ideas characteristic of right-wing groups or parties' (OED3) and *rightist* [1937] 'a conservative, a right-winger' (OED3) have respectively been modelled on *Leftism* [1920] and *leftist* [1924]. An example from COCA is provided in (13):

(13) This policy of political **"leftism"** and economic **"rightism"** is riddled with inconsistencies. (*Asian Affairs: An American Review*, 1999, COCA)

Similarly, the noun *New Right* [1966] 'a political movement that arose originally in response to the challenge of the New Left' (OED3) has regularly been coined after *New Left* [1955]. Other political surface analogies which also conform to rules include *minoritarian* [1930] 'a member or supporter of a minority group, esp. in politics' (OED3), after *majoritarian* [1918], *stateswoman* [1611] 'a woman who takes part in politics or public affairs' (OED3), with an interfix -s- after *statesman* [1592], and *top-down* [1969] 'that proceeds from the top downwards' (OED2, s.v. *top*), on the model of *bottom-up* [1954].[2]

In politics and business, the compound *out-tray* [1943] has also regularly been coined to denote 'a tray for outgoing and completed correspondence and other papers' (OED3), after *in-tray* [1941] used in offices for 'incoming correspondence', and *outgoing* [1622] 'money which goes out' (OED3) after *incoming* [1596] 'revenue' (OED2). In American law, a legal form of *blackmail* [1927] without demand for money is called *graymail/greymail* [1978] 'the threat of revealing government secrets, made by an accused party (esp. in cases of espionage) as a strategy to avoid prosecution' (OED3). Example (14) contextualises target and model:

(14) Lawyers on both sides used the words **"graymail"** or **"blackmail"** during conversations. (*ABA Journal*, 1995, COCA)

Other regular derived words have been created in linguistics, where 'an expert or specialist in linguistics' may be called a *linguistician* [1895], whereas 'an expert in, or student of, dialect' may be called a *dialectician* [1848] (OED3; cf. *linguist*

---

[2] According to the OED, both the model *bottom-up* and the target *top-down* have various meanings, uses, and attestations in different domains, from politics to business, computing, and linguistics.

and *dialectologist*). These formations are analogical with de-adjectival nouns ending in *-ician*, such as *logician* [1382] or *mathematician* [?a1475]. In the same realm, the noun *hypercorrection* [1934] (OED3, s.v. *hypercorrect*) has been created, by prefixation, as a synonym of *overcorrection* [1911] (see *hyper-* and *over-*), to mean 'using spelling, pronunciation, or constructions that are falsely modelled on apparently analogous prestigeful forms': e.g.,

(15)   That is probably **hypercorrection** due to the fact that British accents often drop or slur those sounds and so he over-emphasises them to sound more American, even if they're not actually emphasised that much in American. (http://tvtropes.org/pmwiki/, GloWbE)

In information technology, regular words such as *offline* [1969] 'not having access to the Internet' (OED3) and *stateful* [1989] 'of a protocol, server, etc.: that is dependent on the previous state of an application, process, etc.' (OED3) have been obtained from the models *online* [1950] and *stateless* [1987]. For the *online–offline* pair, COCA offers several examples, of which (16) is a recent one:

(16)   Twitter's president, Jack Dorsey, said this week that it would open an office in Germany, which prohibits Nazi material **online** and **offline**. (*New York Times*, 2012, COCA)

In chemistry, *buckytube* [1991] 'a cylindrical molecule of carbon consisting of two or more concentric tubes each formed of sheets of carbon atoms arranged helically' (OED2) follows the pattern of *buckyball* [1989] 'a molecule of buckminsterfullerene' (OED2). Hence, in both the target and the model, an abbreviatory mechanism (*buck* ← *buckminsterfullerene*, OED2) is combined with grammatical *-y* suffixation and compounding (*tube* vs. *ball*).

Analogy via schema is another frequent type of analogy occurring in specialised word-formation. In the jargon of politico-economy, for example, several formations are attested which indicate 'a group of five, seven, eight, ten, twenty, etc.' (i.e. *G5* [1977], *G7* [1986], *G8* [1988], *G10* [1980], *G20* [1972], etc.). These words represent a schema, with *G20* (or the variant *G-20*) attested before the others in OED2 (s.v. *G*). Example (17) is drawn from COCA:

(17)   As host nation of the **G20**, Canada says it is prioritizing the implementation of previous **G20** and **G8** donor commitments. (*Christian Science Monitor*, 2010, COCA)

Another schema is represented by words ending in *-bot* (← *robot*), which Bauer, Lieber, and Plag (2013: 526) classify as a 'splinter', but is labelled 'combining form' in OED3. The OED also specifies that *-bot* has been used with two different meanings. First, it has been used to form nouns denoting 'a type of robot or automated device', as in *mobot* [1959], originally attested as a blend ← *mobile* + *robot*. More recently, it has been used, principally in computer terminology, to form nouns denoting 'a type of program or (Internet) software, esp. one which searches out information'. With the latter meaning, we find *infobot* [1986] and its synonym *knowbot* [1988] 'any of various automated systems for providing or obtaining information' (OED3), and *cancelbot* [1993] 'a program that searches for and deletes specified postings from Internet newsgroups' (OED3). Two examples from COCA attest formations with both of the above-mentioned meanings:

(18)   The silver **gardenbot** I'd often watched tending the flowers was outside raking up the few leaves that had dared to fall on the perfectly square lawn in front of the house and depositing them in a red plastic bucket. (*Analog Science Fiction & Fact*, 2010, COCA)

(19)   Artificial-intelligence software agents, or "**knowbots**," will search through networks of databases for the desired information and deliver it either on an ongoing basis or for a specific task. (*Futurist*, 1994, COCA)

Another recent formation in computer slang is *treeware* [1993] 'material printed on paper, as opposed to material stored, published, or read in an electronic format' (OED3), humorously coined (in that 'paper' comes from *trees*) after the schema of *hardware, software*, etc. (see 3.2.3).

Moreover, in philosophy, model words such as *nulliverse* [1847] 'a world devoid of any unifying principle or plan' (OED3) and *multiverse* [1895] 'the universe considered as lacking order or a single ruling and guiding power' (OED3) have given birth to the splinter *-verse*, reused, for instance, in the cosmological term *metaverse* [1994] 'an alternative world or universe' (OED3). This target is also used in science fiction and computing with the sense 'cyberspace'.

4.2 Types of target and their relationships with the models

In the recent literature, Klégr and Čermák (2010: 233) have observed that authors such as Bauer (1983) seem to agree that genuine analogical formations are "isolated, not accounted for by any kind of rule, unpredictable to some degree". By contrast, in computational analogical theories (Skousen 1989, 1992; Skousen,

Lonsdale, and Parkinson 2002; Daelemans and van den Bosch 2005; Daelemans et al. 2007), analogy is conceptualised as a predictive mechanism. In their Introduction, Blevins and Blevins (2009: 1) similarly contradict the common misconception that all analogical formation is unpredictable: "while the recognition of analogical relations may seem like a passive process, it is in fact an aggressive process, driven by a search for predictability".

In particular, new specialised targets are often recognised and accepted – hence, reused – by specialists because of: 1) their regular form obeying morphological word-formation rules, and/or 2) their conformity to previous patterns and similarity with other related terms (i.e. the models) of the same sphere (see the criterion of regularity in 2.3).

This is demonstrated in the samples in (20)–(22), which illustrate analogical formation contextualised in three different scientific spheres (palaeontology, anatomy, and gynaecology), and belonging to diverse morphological categories (derivation, combination, and abbreviation):

(20) Early australopithecines are linked with living humans on the basis of shared characters related to bipedalism, but it has yet to be shown that their jaws and teeth differ from putative **hominine** ancestors. (*Nature*, 1993, BNC)

(21) They include mandibular **osteotomy** with genioglossus advancement and hyoid **myotomy** and suspension. (*ENT: Ear, Nose & Throat Journal*, 1999, COCA)

(22) In July 1986, two more specialists and numerous samples later, it was recommended that the Forts consider a mixture of Artificial Insemination by Husband (**AIH**) and Donor (**AID**). (*Good Housekeeping*, 1992, BNC)

What these three cases of scientific/medical targets share is the absence of the model word in either the context or the micro-context, i.e. the sentence length. Indeed, here interpretation does not depend on intratextual information, but on prior knowledge of the subject involved.

For instance, in (20) the interpretation of the word *hominine* [1957] 'characteristic of hominines' (OED3) is not merely connected to the previous text, where we find the noun *humans* (from the same etymology, i.e. classical Latin *hūmānus*). It is rather connected to the model series of *canine* [1623], *asinine* [1624], *feline* [1681], and similar adjectives, as well as to the abstract model of *-ine* adjectival suffixation (reproducing Latin *-īnus, -īna, -īnum*).

Similarly, in (21), the words *osteotomy* [1740] 'anatomical dissection of the bones' (OED3) and *myotomy* [1676] 'the surgical division of a muscle' (OED3) come from the combination of two initial combining forms – namely, *osteo-* (from ancient Greek ὀστέον 'bone') and *myo-* (from ancient Greek μῦς 'muscle') with a final combining form *-tomy* (τομή 'cutting'). The latter is a splinter obtained from *anatomy* [?1541], which acts as unmentioned model for the above-mentioned targets.

A comparable case is offered in (22) by the targets *AIH* [1945] and *AID* [1945]. They are initialisms obtained through the abbreviation of two phrases – i.e. *Artificial Insemination by Husband* and *Artificial Insemination by Donor* (OED3, s.v. A) –, but the model initialism *AI* [1945] ← *Artificial Insemination* is absent from the microcontext (see analogy with enlargement in 3.3.1).

These three examples show that, in specialised contexts, the model word does not need to be made explicit (in the previous or following text) for disambiguation, since, in general, experts are aware of the model whose pattern was used to obtain the target (cf. decodification in 2.3).

By contrast, in (23)–(25), from the domains of mathematics, botany, and finance, the model words are included either in the same sentence or in the same paragraph, preferentially in two consecutive sentences. The co-presence of model and target in the same text guarantees accessibility and the model's recoverability also to non-experts:

(23) In its simplest form, DIVISION is defined as an operation between a **binary** relation (the dividend) and a **unary** relation (the divisor) which produces a **unary** relation (the quotient) as its result. (*Information Systems Development*, 1992, BNC)

(24) Chromophils are subdivided into **acidophils** (40% of all cells) and **basophils** (10% of all cells). (*Histology*, courseweb.edteched.uottawa.ca, enTenTen 2012)

(25) A '**Eurocurrency**' is any currency being traded outside its country of origin. Thus there are **Eurofrancs, Euromarks, Euroyen**. Similarly, '**Eurosterling**' is sterling which is traded in other financial centres, outside the UK. By far the most plentiful form of **Eurocurrency** is the **Eurodollar**. (*Financial Markets and Institutions*, 1990, BNC)

In (23), for instance, the target adjective *unary* [1931] ← Latin *ūnus* 'one', 'involving or operating on a single element' (OED2) is anaphoric in respect to its model *binary* [1796] ← *bīnī* 'two together', 'of, pertaining to, characterized by, or compounded of, two' (OED2; see also *ternary* [1860] and *n-ary* [1964]). The similarity between target and model is primarily morphotactic (the suffix *-ary* is shared), but also phonological (the last two unstressed syllables are shared), and semantic ('one' and 'two' are successive numbers in a list). Anaphoric reference to the model is the clearest mode of analogical word-formation, in that the origin of the target is clarified by the resemblance with a previously specified model.

In (24), however, the target noun *acidophil* [1900] 'a cell or cell component that can be readily stained with an acid dye' (OED3) is cataphoric in respect to its interfixed model word *basophil* [1898] 'a cell or other structure having an affinity for basic substances' (OED2). Target and model words exhibit the same neoclassical combining form *-phil(e)* (from ancient Greek φίλος 'loving'), the same interfix *-o-*, and two antonymous (complementary) components (*acid* vs. *base*). However, the target here cataphorically anticipates its model, which is clarified immediately afterwards.

Lastly, in (25), the target *Eurosterling* [1974] (OED3, s.v. *Euro-*) is coined after the series which includes the combining form *Euro-* (← *European*), and the names of individual currencies, earliest in *Eurodollar* [1960] and in more general *Eurocurrency* [1961], but also in *Eurofranc* [1980], *Euromark* [1974], and *Euroyen* [1974]. In (25), *Eurosterling* can be compared both with an antecedent model (*Eurocurrency*) and with a following one, i.e. *Eurodollar*. In other words, the new target is both anaphoric and cataphoric in respect to the model words which act as schema.

4.3 The functions of analogical specialised words

Specialised language is highly specific, precise, and normally monoreferential (Gotti [2005] 2008: 33). In other words, every specialised term signals a concept and effectively condenses a semantic value which is unique, not conveyed or expressible by other words in the same specialised domain. The ideal of "biuniqueness" (one-to-one correspondence between *signans* 'word' and *signatum* 'meaning', Dressler et al. 1987: 111) concerns the same specialised area. That is, there is a tendency towards avoidance of homonymy and polysemy in the same domain, but not necessarily in two different specialised fields (cf. *erosion* as 'a natural or human-induced process affecting the Earth' vs. 'a medical condition affecting the human body' vs. 'a stock price reduction', Faber 2009: 71–72). As a consequence, experts who share the same terminology can invent new analogical formations for three main reasons: 1) to denominate new concepts, discoveries, alliances, etc.; 2) to communicate efficiently and effectively with other specialists in their sector; and 3) to establish or reinforce in-group cohesion.

The denomination function, for instance, is illustrated in (26) by the initialism *GST* [1985] ← *goods and services tax*, 'a value-added tax levied on consumer goods and services' (OED2, s.v. *G*).

(26) Although it was unable to veto legislation, the Liberal majority in the Senate – led by former Deputy Prime Minister Allan MacEachan – blocked a key piece of government legislation: a bill to implement the highly unpopular goods and services tax (**GST**), a new 7 per cent value added tax due to take effect on Jan. 1, 1991. (*Keesing's Contemporary Archives*, 1990, BNC)

In this text, the new target *GST* is used for the first time in brackets, with its full form immediately preceding it, with the aim of labelling a new tax. The model initialism *VAT* [1966],[3] short for the *value added tax* cited in the micro-context, is not mentioned explicitly, but experts and non-experts can certainly recover it from its morphotactic and phonological similarity with the target. Moreover, the semantic link between the two names related to the economic sector can confirm the analogical origin of *GST*.

Communicating specialised information efficiently and effectively at the same time is another purpose of analogical words, such as the word *before-tax* [1944] (generally referred to profit) in (27):

(27) Under a typical health saving account, the employer can save money by offering a health-insurance plan with a high annual deductible – say, $2,000 – and the employee and employer can pay into the HSA, in **before-tax** dollars, an amount equal to the high deductible. (*Change*, 2006, COCA)

The target *before-tax* 'prior to the deduction of tax' (OED3, s.v. *before*) has an exophoric model word, i.e. the adjective *after-tax* [1944] 'remaining after tax has been deducted' (OED3, s.v. *after-*). Although in the OED both adjectives are attested earliest in 1944, the distribution of the two terms in COCA – *before-tax* (17 occurrences) vs. *after-tax* (373 occurrences) – suggests that the former is coined after the latter. Thus, although the model is absent from the context, specialists can immediately associate the new compound adjective with the pattern of the

---

[3] Sometimes *VAT* is pronounced as one word, as an acronym, but letter-by-letter pronunciation increases, in this case, its resemblance with the target *GST*.

model word, with which it shares the right element *tax* and an antonymic left element (cf. *post-tax* [1934] after *pre-tax* [1917] OED3).

Another function of analogical specialised words is establishing or reinforcing social or professional bonds. Thus, for instance, linguists use the combining form *-lect* (← *dialect*) to designate a regional or social variety within a language, as in *idiolect* [1948] 'the linguistic system of one person' (OED3), *sociolect* [1963] 'a variety of a language used by a particular social group or class' (OED3), and a number of more recent technical terms, such as *acrolect*, *basilect*, and *mesolect*:

(28)   Thus speakers do not randomly mix **acrolect** features with those from the **basilect** to create a **'mesolect'**; each 'lect' is discrete and ordered with respect to the other lects in the continuum. (Mark Sebba, *London Jamaican*, 1993, BNC)

The target *mesolect* [1971] (OED3) has been created, therefore, as an intermediate form between *acrolect* [1965] 'the most prestigious dialect or variety of a particular language' (OED3) and *basilect* [1965] 'the least prestigious or 'lowest' variety of any language' (OED3). Experts use these terms – and also the free form *lect* – to create professional closeness, that is, to maintain group cohesion and to strengthen their relationship with the other group members.

4.4 Distribution of analogical specialised words

This section shows the distribution and frequency of the analogical specialised words mentioned in this chapter in COCA – distinguished into various genres (Spoken, Fiction, Magazine, Newspaper, Academic) – and GloWbE. In Table 6, quantitative data is provided concerning: a) the distributional token/normalised frequency of the items in each section of COCA (abbreviated, for reasons of space, as Spok, Fic, Mag, News, Acad), b) the total token/normalised frequency in GloWbE, and c) the possible presence of the model word in both corpora. In the latter two columns regarding the model, the overall (also normalised) number of examples (in COCA and GloWbE) are indicated in which the target is either Ana(phoric) (preceding the model) or Cata(phoric) (following it) (see 3.3.5 for the distance between target and model).

As for the methodology, a few words of explanation are in order. The first remark concerns acronyms and initialisms. The detection of these types of words in corpora may give misleading results, in that some of these words are ambiguous and may stand for different source phrases. In an effort to address this issue, I adopted a two-pronged approach: 1) automated corpus analysis based on the acronym/initialism search string to retrieve all items, and 2) close reading of all occurrences in context to detect their exact meaning. This procedure enabled the exclusion of 47.43% of the occurrences of *ABH* in GloWbE, excluding labels which stood for *Association of Business Historians*, or source phrases other than *Actual Bodily Harm*.

The second remark concerns the sections of COCA. The query system available at http://corpus.byu.edu/ allows for either a random search or a more specific search of the items in the various sections. I selected the latter option, which gave me both the overall and partial frequency in the sections. Each section of COCA accounts for 88 million words, GloWbE accounts for 1.9 billion words, and the two corpora total 2.34 billion words. Therefore, normalised frequencies per million words (pmw) were also provided. The grey box in Table 6 indicates the section of COCA with a higher token frequency/normalised frequency of the corresponding item. The detailed timeframe of the occurrences was ignored.

The last remark concerns the identification of the model words. The query system also allows for the retrieval of collocates occurring up to a maximum nine-word distance, either before or after the item under query. This query option allowed for 1) the retrieval of the model words in the micro-context, 2) the differentiation between anaphoric and cataphoric analogical words. The light grey box in the last two columns of Table 6 signals the type of endophoric (ana- vs. cataphoric) reference to the model which was found more commonly in the two corpora under examination according to normalised frequencies. For the items which are triggered by a whole series, rather than a precise item, a string query such as **bot* (for *cancelbot* and *knowbot*) or **verse* (for *metaverse*) was entered in the collocation slot.

The results of the query are given in Table 6.

Tab. 6: New analogical specialised words (Anaphoric vs. Cataphoric) and their frequency in COCA and GloWbE

New words	COCA					GloWbE	Model	
	Spok	Fic	Mag	News	Acad		Ana	Cata
ABH			11/0.12			82/0.04	5/0.002	6/0.002
acidophil						1/0.0005		
AID					3/0.03	3/0.001		
AIH		4/0.04			27/0.30	48/0.02		
before-tax			10/0.11	3/0.02	4/0.04	85/0.04	7/0.002	12/0.005

New words	COCA					GloWbE	Model	
	Spok	Fic	Mag	News	Acad		Ana	Cata
buckytube		6/0.06	11/0.12					
cancelbot						14/0.007		
dialectician		2/0.02			3/0.03	45/0.02	2/0.0008	
escalator	76/0.86	354/4.02	89/1.01	130/1.47	39/0.44	1,982/1.043	56/0.02	32/0.01
Eurosterling						6/0.003		
fash-ionaholic								
first-minute						15/0.007		
gardenbot		6/0.06						
G2B						16/0.008		
G2C						35/0.01	1/0.0004	6/0.002
G5		5/0.05	61/0.69	25/0.28	198/2.25	469/0.24		
G7	38/0.43	3/0.03	11/0.12	16/0.18	22/0.25	1,542/0.81	13/0.005	39/0.01
G8	104/1.18	3/0.03	66/0.75	51/0.57	65/0.73	2,567/1.35	45/0.01	162/0.06
G10		1/0.01	25/0.28	3/0.03	1/0.01	151/0.07	1/0.0004	3/0.001
gigaflop						3/0.001		
graymail/greymail	1/0.01				6/0.06	28/0.01		2/0.0008
GST	2/0.02	1/0.01	33/0.37	10/0.11	12/0.13	9,035/4.75	31/0.01	38/0.01
hominine						4/0.002		
hypercorrection						17/0.008		
infobot								
inlaw			2/0.02			157/0.08	2/0.0008	
knowbot			1/0.01					

New words	COCA					GloWbE	Model	
	Spok	Fic	Mag	News	Acad		Ana	Cata
LIFO	1/0.01	2/0.02	2/0.02	8/0.09	6/0.06	148/0.07	10/0.004	16/0.006
linguistician						2/0.001		
little-endian						28/0.01	6/0.002	2/0.0008
mesolect						12/0.006	9/0.003	
metaverse		13/0.14	4/0.04	3/0.03	4/0.04	130/0.06	7/0.002	6/0.002
minoritarian	1/0.01		2/0.02		5/0.05	22/0.01	3/0.001	2/0.0008
myotomy					17/0.19	8/0.004	1/0.0004	
n-ary						13/0.006	1/0.0004	4/0.001
New Right	34/0.38	5/0.05	51/0.57	19/0.21	52/0.59	564/0.29		
offline	86/0.97	58/0.65	197/2.23	90/1.02	80/0.90	14,247/7.49	3,452/1.47	1,342/0.57
omnivore	9/0.10	24/0.27	39/0.44	23/0.26	5/0.05	388/0.20	21/0.008	17/0.007
osteotomy					63/0.71	54/0.02	1/0.0004	4/0.001
out-tray						8/0.004	2/0.0008	
outgoing	495/5.62	174/1.97	521/5.92	521/5.92	264/3	9,704/5.10	899/0.38	317/0.13
planar		9/0.10	58/0.65	2/0.02	161/1.82	505/0.26	8/0.003	9/0.003
polychrome	2/0.02	10/0.11	52/0.59	6/0.06	49/0.55	79/0.041	4/0.001	1/0.0004
post-tax			1/0.01	3/0.03	3/0.03	209/0.11	12/0.005	3/0.001
Rightism		1/0.01			1/0.01	24/0.01	4/0.001	1/0.0004
rightist	25/0.28	5/0.05	23/0.26	95/1.07	108/1.22	618/0.32	74/0.03	32/0.01
shop-gasm								
SOD								
stateful						159/	4/0.001	9/0.003

New words	COCA					GloWbE	Model	
	Spok	Fic	Mag	News	Acad		Ana	Cata
states-woman	3/0.03	1/0.01	1/0.01	5/0.05	1/0.01	0.08 54/0.02	6/0.002	
ternary		2/0.02			30/0.34	136/0.07	21/0.008	13/0.005
top-down	49/0.55	10/0.11	136/1.54	87/0.98	495/5.62	3,394/1.78	182/0.07	306/0.13
treeware			3/0.03					
unary					8/0.09	163/0.08	22/0.009	21/0.008

The data reported in Table 6 shows the distribution of the specialised terms selected for qualitative analysis. In particular, it shows that the words occur in various genres and modes, rather than being confined to academic written text. As far as COCA is concerned, in order of frequency, 53.70% occur in academic texts, 46.29% in magazines, 42.59% in fiction texts, 35.18% in newspapers, and 27.77% in spoken discourse. Interestingly, 85.18% of the specialised terms selected occur in GloWbE, while only one term (*infobot*) is unattested in either corpora, despite its being recorded in the OED, whereas *fashionaholic*, *SOD*, and *shopgasm* are only attested in the *Urban Dictionary*.

The data of Table 6 is visualised in Figures 3 and 4. The former includes all new analogical words in Table 6, whereas the latter shows only the most frequent ones.

The massive occurrence of some of these terms in corpora – *outgoing* records 1,975 occurrences (4.48 pmw) in COCA and 9,704 (5.10 pmw) in GloWbE, *top-down* occurs 777 times (1.76 pmw) in COCA, and *offline* occurs even 14,247 (7.49 pmw) in GloWbE – confirms their actual level of representativeness as intended neologisms. There are very few exceptions of unattested words in COCA, such as *Eurosterling* or *cancelbot*, and yet whose establishment is documented in the OED (cf. *Euro-* and *-bot*).

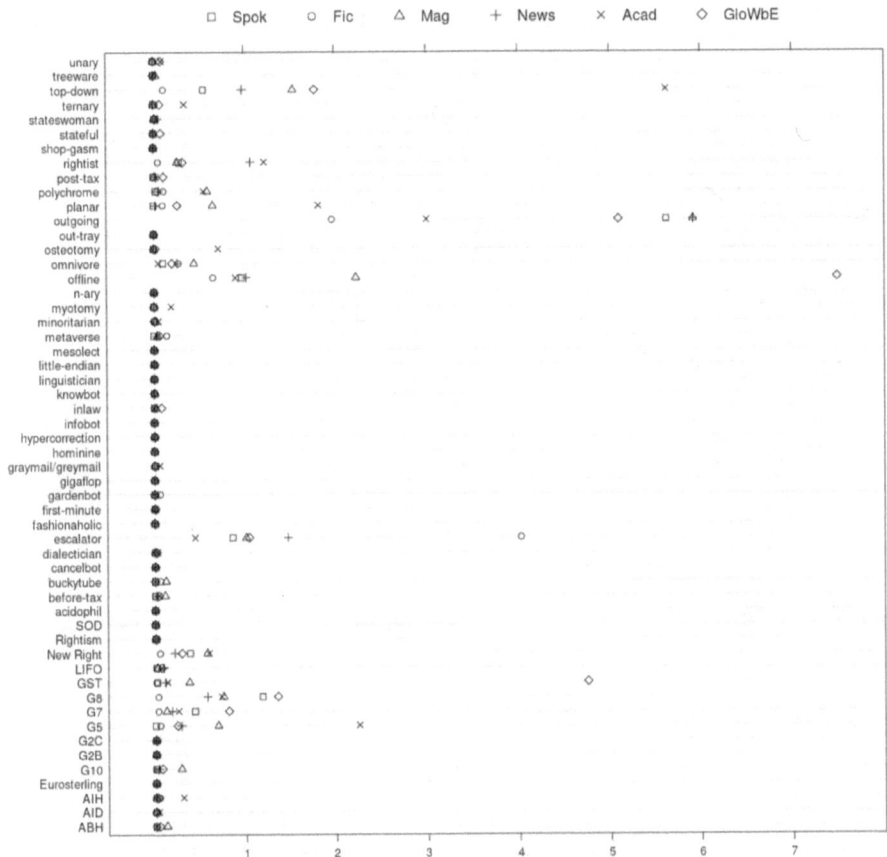

Fig. 3: Visualisation of all data from Table 6

As far as the model words are concerned, 59.25% of the new words occur together with their models, either/both as anaphoric analogies (100%) or/and as cataphoric anticipations of the model words (84.37%). The percentage of words which occur both as anaphoric and as cataphoric analogies is 75%, although some specialised terms (27.77% in my list) exophorically allude to an external model with no need for its explicit mention.

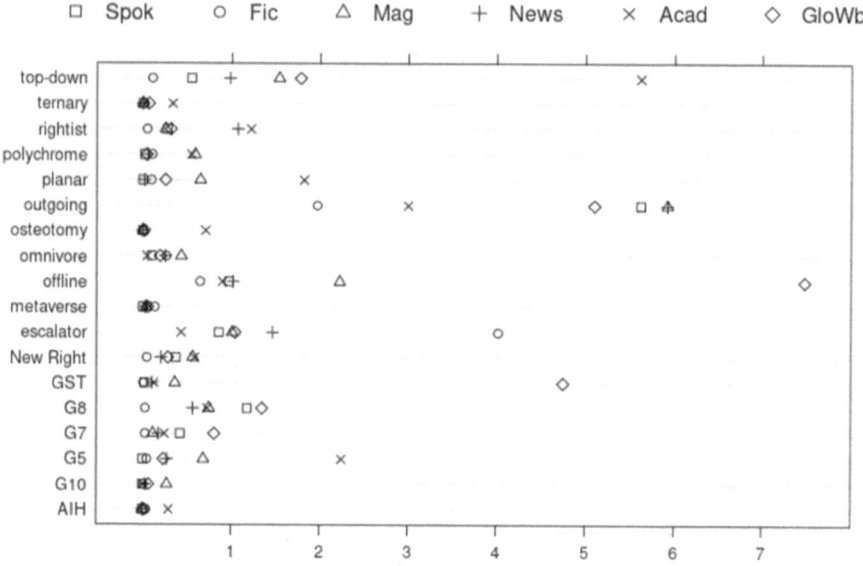

Fig. 4: Visualisation of the most frequent words in Table 6

4.5 Final remarks on analogy in specialised words

This examination of the specialised lexicon of science, economics, information technology, politics, and the Law from the viewpoint of analogical word-formation has been profitable for various reasons. First, the identification of the types of analogy which occur in specialised sectors (4.1) has demonstrated that surface analogy can take place both in isolation (e.g. *ABH*, *LIFO*) and combined with rule patterns (e.g. *minoritarian*, *offline*, *Rightism*, *stateful*). In addition, analogy via schema seems to play an important role in experts' language (e.g. *-bot* in computer science, *-ary* in mathematics, *Euro-* in finance), as confirmation of the regularisation process that many recurrent splinters or combining forms are undergoing in English word-formation.

Second, the identification of the specialised targets and their relationships with the words that act as model (4.2) have shown that specialised vocabulary may require explicit models only when it is addressed to non-experts, since expert readers or hearers do not necessitate endo-/ana-phoric reference to a previously mentioned model word to recognise the new target word. Exophoric reference is more often made to the experts' presumed knowledge, which is a prerequisite to access all new terminology occurring in specialised domains.

Third, the identification of the primary functions of analogical word-formation in specialised jargons (4.3) has proved that analogy may help experts both to name new abstract concepts or concrete objects which are created in their field, and to keep in-group cohesion and communicate efficiently and competently with their colleagues or other specialists. All the new specialised words mentioned in the present chapter are attested in the OED as (mostly recent) neologisms and several attestations of their actual use are given in COCA and GloWbE. This shows that in technical, scientific, or economic language, new terminology is mainly made up of intended neologisms which are meant to enrich the lexicon of English for Special Purposes.

It is also interesting to notice that some of these neologisms are not necessarily meant to cover a lexical or conceptual gap. For instance, *linguistician* and *dialectician* have their equivalent terms in *linguist* and *dialectologist*, *hypercorrection* has mostly the same meaning as *overcorrection*, and *post-tax* is synonymous with *after-tax* in the same way as *before-tax* has its synonym in *pre-tax*. Yet, the reason for these new coinages may be an interest in increasing precision: e.g., the suffix *-ician* conveys higher expertise in an art or science than agentive *-ist*, and *hyper-*, from Greek, seems to show a shade of excess which is less strong/evident in Germanic *over-*. However, similarity with an actual specialised model word, as in *post-tax* created after *pre-tax*, motivates analogical formation more than the existence of a synonym *after-tax* may prevent its coinage.

A final remark concerns the actual distribution of new specialised words in corpora of English (4.4). In particular, the frequency of specialised neologisms in the different genres identified in COCA – from spoken language to academic written text passing through magazines and newspapers – corresponds to the modes of text production (distinguishing between written and oral, with the former subdivided into composed and spontaneous) within a specialised language. In particular, in the field of specialised discourse, there are four different situations in which a specialist may address a topic (Gotti [2005] 2008: 25).[4] These four different situations, with varied requirements of explicitness, correspond to four levels of specificity in language use (the first three are taken from Widdowson 1979), namely:

---

[4] Altieri Biagi (1974) adds to these four situations a fifth (higher) level of 'formalisation/condensation into formulae' referring to a situation in which specialists address other specialists in theoretical works, using formulae, symbols, diagrams, and other non-verbal conventions to condense information.

- *Scientific exposition*: When specialists address other specialists to expose theories, debate issues within their disciplinary field, describe a research project, or report results, they can make frequent use of specialised terminology whose semantics is opaque, although this level of specificity follows precise ideals, such as monoreferentiality/biuniqueness within the same field. Specialists can also decide to coin novel formations which may require a definition, unless their morphotactics is clear from the analogy with other specialised terms. For this level, we can envisage new analogical formations which either exophorically refer to extra-textual models already shared among experts or follow well-established schemas.
- *Scientific instruction*: When specialists address semi- or non-specialists to explain notions pertaining to their discipline, as in academic textbooks and instruction manuals, they can make use of specialised terms. Whether they are old or new, for educational purposes specialised terms are explained whenever they occur for the first time. For this level, we can predict a high concentration of new analogical formations which anaphorically refer to a previously specified model, or cataphorically anticipate an immediately following one.
- *Scientific journalism*: When specialists provide information of a technical nature drawing on the layman's everyday knowledge and experience, as in newspaper or magazine articles presenting scientific/technical information, they mainly introduce specialised concepts through everyday lexicon (see popularisation discourse). Since the purpose here is to reach out to a wider audience, but also to attract the audience's attention, new terms may be allusive to previously mentioned terms, after which they have been created, by analogy. We can also predict, on the journalist's part, a lower attention to the well-formedness and grammaticality of the new analogical words, in that what matters is their effectiveness.
- *Scientific jargon*: When specialists address other specialists using the oral mode and spontaneous style, as in doctors' conversation, specialised terminology does not need to be defined or explained. New specialised terms may have the purpose, in this case, of establishing or increasing cohesion among experts. Knowledge of the models for new analogical words is often taken for granted, and the model's recoverability is therefore presumed as an automatic operation.

The specialised words analysed in the present chapter seem partly to reflect this heterogeneous classification. Example (21), for instance, is taken from *ENT Journal* and provides a case of scientific exposition where two targets – i.e. *osteotomy* and *myotomy* – occur with an absent model (*anatomy*). The latter has produced the combining form *-tomy*, which is well-recognised among experts. Example (24), from a textbook on histology, is instead a situation of scientific instruction, where the target *acidophil* and the model *basophil* are specified for semi-/non-experts within the same explanatory text. Finally, in example (10), an extract from *The Guardian* illustrates scientific journalism, with the analogy *ABH* immediately preceding the model *GBH*, which is made clear to all readers.

5 Analogy in juvenile language

Adolescents are an immense resource for new vocabulary items (Eble 1996; Coleman 2014), and many innovative terms that they create are inexorably based on the vocabulary that they already use. Recent instances of analogical neologisms and nonce words used by teenagers are collected in the *Urban Dictionary*. One of these is the word *neargasm* [2014] 'the frustrated feeling of being on the brink of something fantastic but never actually tasting that satisfaction', posted in December 2014 after the known pattern of *wargasm*, and similar neoformations having -*gasm* (← *orgasm*) as their second constituent. This seems to constitute a series in *Urban Dictionary*'s juvenile speech, with words such as *joygasm* [2005] 'moment of intense, unfiltered joy or passion', *cutegasm* [2007] 'the reaction one feels when being exposed to something overly cute', and *cakegasm* [2008] 'a mind blowing double orgasm induced by cakes' having consolidated the blending pattern (see 5.1).

Two frequent functions for the coinage of new juvenile words are following fashion and creating a distance from adults and their world. The effect that teenagers wish to produce by coining new analogical items is often humour. Indeed, when they form a new target word which resembles its model word for some shared trait, they make allusion to the model, or even want to satirise, parodise its meaning. For instance, the *Rice University Neologisms Database* contains the word *bitchdar* [2008], which has been defined by the young compiler as 'a method of determining how big a bitch somebody (usually a girl) is'. This formation is unattested in recognised dictionaries such as the OED, but it can be associated with an attested blend – i.e., slang *gaydar* [1988] 'an ability, attributed esp. to homosexual people and likened humorously to radar, to identify a (fellow) homosexual person by intuition' (OED3) – which combines *gay* with the acronym *radar* (← *radio detection and ranging*). Blending and acronyms, as we will see, are particularly useful extra-grammatical operations that help adolescents not only to coin innovative and unusual words, but also to create a vocabulary that is cryptic, ambiguous, and enigmatic for those who are not familiar with it.

The present chapter explores analogy in juvenile language or adolescents' slang (Mattiello 2008a). The primary aim of this study is to show that teenagers are inventive, original, and can use analogy to create new extra-grammatical formations, such as the above-mentioned blends. Yet, at the same time, their analogical formations can be perfectly regular, with model words which comply with well-established word-formation rules. Whereas analogical new words in the *Urban Dictionary* defy quantitative analyses, the *Rice University Neologisms Database* gives us significant data to support these claims (Mattiello 2016).

Among the 6,755 entries in the database collected by Rice students,[1] 398 (5.89%) are analogy-based terms, with 12.56% recent neologisms. These percentages become even more significant if we consider that many of the words included in this collection are essentially neosemanticisms (i.e. existing words with a new meaning) rather than actual new words. The types of analogy in the Rice collection are varied:

- 34.42% (137 items) are pure surface analogies obtained via extra-grammatical operations (e.g. *BFFL* [2010] 'best friend for life' ← *BFF* [1987] 'best friend forever', OED2, s.v. *B*; see 3.3.1), or reanalysis (e.g. *eighthead* [2013] 'a forehead that is larger than normal' ← *forehead* [c1000] reanalysed as *four-head*). 4.41% are attested neologisms, the remaining are occasionalisms.
- 16.58% (66 items) are surface analogies which also comply with rules (e.g. *Failbook* [2013] 'derogatory expression for Facebook' or *Pink Friday* [2008], coined after *Black Friday* [1961] for 'the Friday after Thanksgiving, on which participating major retailers cut prices and make a donation from sales to help fight breast cancer'). The percentage of regular recent neologisms attested in the OED is 27.69%.
- 48.99% (195 items) are analogies via schema, with 13.33% attested headwords (recent neologisms) in the OED (e.g. *Webinar* [1997], see *web-* in 3.3.1), and 73.84% exhibiting well-established combining forms (e.g. *flexitarian* [2011, earlier in the OED] 'a person who eats meat less often than an average American', see *-arian* in 3.3.1).

Another aim of this study is to show the range of functions that analogical formations can serve, both from the insiders' (i.e. the adolescent's) viewpoint and from the outsiders' (i.e. the adult's) viewpoint. On the one hand, new analogical formations can be used by teenagers to show off, to boast that their slang (in-group) language is up to date, original, even artistic, and this language helps them create a verbal connection with their peers. On the other hand, their language is a means to establish social closeness and to exclude those who are not part of the group, because they belong to a different generation or social class.

---

1 The actual number of entries in the Rice collection is 9,016, yet, since some of the entries coincide, 6,755 is the number of words contained in the lemma list, with overlapping items deleted.

5.1 Types of analogical formation in juvenile language

Analogical formations in adolescents' talk are varied, with types of analogy which belong to different morphological categories. As already said, many pure surface analogies are collected in the *Rice University Neologisms Database*. They include, for instance, the complex word *e-pal* [2008] 'a friend which communicates with one by e-mails'. Indeed, since the first element *e-* from *electronic* is now an attested combining form, *e-pal* is both coined on the exact model of *pen-pal* [1925], by substitution of the left element, and on the schema of words such as *e-mail*, *e-shopping*, etc., by substitution of the right element.

In addition, at the Rice University Department, a commonly used reduplicative is *ling-ling* [2008] ← *linguistics*, as in:

(29)   How is **ling-ling** going? (*Rice University Neologisms Database*)

A compiler has suggested the analogical origin of this nonce word, probably modelled on hip-hop slang *bling-bling* [1999] 'ostentatious jewellery' (OED3). Although the meaning associated with the model word *bling-bling* is completely unrelated to that of the copy reduplicative *ling-ling* (cf. 1.3 and 3.3.4 for semantic similarity), the same word-formation pattern and phonological resemblance may have triggered the neoformation. However, the sound symbolism conveyed by *bling-bling* – apparently representing the visual effect of light being reflected off precious stones or metals (cf. *ting* [1495] and *ping* [1855] containing the same final phonaestheme) – seems not to be expressed by the new form *ling-ling*, nor is the disparaging connotation which in the model is connected with wealth.

Many blends are also attested in the Rice database. Some examples include *Blindian* [2010] ← *Black* + *Indian*, created after *Windian* [2008] ← *White* + *Indian*, and *Chrasian* [2013] ← *Christian* + *Asian*, after *Wasian* [2008] ← *White* + *Asian*. Another set of semantically related words is made up of *brinner* [2008] 'dinner that consists of breakfast food', *linner* [2010] 'a meal between lunch and dinner', and the recent *lupper* [2013]:

(30)   Yesterday afternoon we were pretty hungry so we went ahead and had **lupper** instead of waiting for dinner. (*Rice University Neologisms Database*)

The form of *brinner*, *linner*, and *lupper* is in perfect accordance with the way the majority of blends are formed in English (cf. Gries 2004a; Trommer and Zimmermann 2010; Arndt-Lappe and Plag 2013). However, their semantic link with the lexicalised model *brunch* [1896] is evident from the co-hyponymy relationship among *breakfast*, *lunch*, *dinner*, and *supper* (see 1.2 and 3.3.1).² As for the Invariable Part, *brinner* maintains the first initial cluster *br-* of *brunch*, *linner* in its turn keeps the second part of *brinner*, and *lupper* the first letter of *linner*.

With semantically related components, we have *gimongous* [2008] ← *gigantic/giant* + *humongous*, after the model *ginormous* [1948] (with a shared left splinter), and *niftabulous* [2008] ← *nifty* + *fabulous* or *superbulous* [2008] ← *super(b)* + *fabulous*, both after *fantabulous* [1959] (with a shared right splinter, see 1.1). The blend *slungry* [2011] ← *sleepy* + *hungry* acts as model for both *sangry* [2013] ← *sad* + *angry* and *tangry* [2013] ← *tired* + *angry*. The right component *angry*, however, is semantically, morphotactically, and (partially) phonologically different from the model's splinter *-ungry*. Consider the *tangry* example in a conversational context offered by a Rice database compiler:

(31) Girl 1: Stop typing so loud!
      Girl 2: Dang, someone's **tangry**.
      Girl 1: I only had one hour of sleep last night! (*Rice University Neologisms Database*)

The model word *vodkatini* [1955] 'a martini cocktail in which vodka is substituted for gin' (OED2) has triggered two further blends: namely, *midnitini* [2008] 'a midnight martini' and *tiratini* [2008] 'a tiramisu-flavored martini', with different types and degrees of similarity and two shared final syllables in the splinter *-tini*. Recent coinages in the Rice collection are connected with the new technologies and social networks: e.g., *Twittizen* [2010] ← *Twitter* + *citizen* and *Twetiquette* [2011] ← *Twitter* + *etiquette* are respectively created after *netizen* [1984] and *netiquette* [1982] (see 3.3.1), and *Twitterverse* [2013] 'the collection of all social media activity on the website Twitter' exhibits a final element *-verse* (cf. 4.1). The recent *vlogger* [2013] combines *video* with *blogger*, like its model *vlog* [2005] (← *video* + *blog*) recorded both in the *Urban Dictionary* and in the Rice database. This is a contextualised example from Rice:

---

2 The use of such analogies as *linner* and *brinner* is not confined to young people's language, as the following extract from the newspaper *USA Today* (2011) seems to confirm: "Desserts are now eaten any time, sometimes even before breakfast. Lunch and dinner are increasingly combined into "*linner*". Many consumers insist on breakfast for dinner, forcing restaurants to keep the breakfast grills fired all day to serve "*brinner*," says Nancy Kruse, president of The Kruse Company, who consults for food companies on our topsy-turvy eating habits." (COCA).

(32) I work as a composer, but I hate my job, so I am also a **vlogger**. (*Rice University Neologisms Database*)

Still in the Rice collection, an analogical word which involves reinterpretation is *writeo* [2008], used by a professor to indicate 'a misspelling in handwriting'. Indeed, the slang back-clipping *typo* [1892], which is often used for 'a typographical error' (OED2), has been reanalysed as a complex model (*type* + *-o*), and this reanalysis has conducted to the target *write-o*. In *Wordspy*, analogical *speako* [2001] 'an error in speaking' involves the same reanalysis. Bauer, Lieber, and Plag (2013: 527) include *-o*, with the meaning 'language production error', among splinters with a moderate productivity.

Furthermore, in the *Urban Dictionary*, many acronyms and intialisms are created by analogy with existing ones. For instance, the model word *LOL* [1989], from the initial letters of *Laughing Out Loud*, used on the Internet 'to draw attention to a joke or humorous statement' (OED3), has triggered the initialism *LQTM* [2006] ← *Laughing Quietly To Myself*, and the acronym *ROFL* [2002] ← *Rolling On the Floor Laughing*.[3] Similar coinages are recorded in the Rice collection: i.e. *IDL* [2011] ← *I Die Laughing* and *FOFL* [2011] ← *Fall On the Floor Laughing*.

Most of the above-mentioned analogical formations belong to extra-grammatical morphology, in that they involve reduplicative, abbreviatory, or blending patterns, yet the *Rice University Neologisms Database* as well as the *Urban Dictionary* also include grammatical surface analogies. For instance, a regular analogy is the compound *wake-and-bake* [2008], created by a Rice student to refer to 'the process or act of smoking marijuana right upon waking up in the morning':

(33) I'm pre-packing this bowl tonight. Tomorrow's gonna be **wake-and-bake** for me. (*Rice University Neologisms Database*)

This formation is coined from two verbs, after the precise model of *shake-and-bake* [1981], generated after a phrase to indicate 'something compared in some way to the product Shake'n Bake, esp. as being quick or simple to use or perform' (OED3; see the proprietary name *Shake'n Bake*).

Analogical compounds also occur in the *Urban Dictionary*, where in 2003 the vulgar compound word *dick flick* was included to refer to 'the testosterone-driven opposite of a 'chick flick'':

---

3 According to an article in *The Guardian* (May 28, 2014), French people use *MDR* ← *mort de rire* 'died of laughter' as an analogical coinage after English *LOL*.

(34) There was no way that John's date was going to watch a **dick flick** with him. (*Urban Dictionary*)

The model here is a compound noun – namely, slang *chick flick* [1988] – commonly used, especially by teenagers, to refer to 'a film perceived, or marketed, as appealing particularly to women' (OED2, s.v. *chick*). In both the model and the target, the left component is a shortened word, namely, *chick* is abbreviated from *chicken*, and *dick* is a playful alteration of *Ric-* (← *Richard*) (cf. *buddy movie* [1978], OED2, s.v. *buddy*).

From the same model, but with an abbreviated second constituent, the *Urban Dictionary* records *chick lit* [1988] 'literature by, for, or about women' (OED2, s.v. *chick*), as in:

(35) Guy 1: Dude, you can't read *The Notebook* in public!
Guy 2: Why not?
Guy 1: It's **chick-lit**! (*Urban Dictionary*, 2015)

Here the similarity between the right elements *lit* and *flick* is both phonological and semantic.

A comparable analogical pair is *babe magnet* [1989] 'a man who is attractive to women' (OED3, s.v. *babe*), also recorded in the *Urban Dictionary* and probably modelled on earlier *chick magnet* [1970] 'a man who attracts women the way a magnet attracts iron shavings' (OED2).

The type of analogy that follows a schema model is amply represented by the examples collected in the Rice database. For instance, a student has suggested *Potteresque* [2008] as a grammatical analogical formation on the pattern of adjectives ending in *-esque* and having a surname as base, such as *Dantesque* [1813], *Browningesque* [1880], *Audenesque* [1940], etc. Indeed, the latter series functions as schema for *Potteresque*, which has been coined to describe something 'that captures the essence of Harry Potter's personality', as in:

(36) I didn't think the fourth Harry Potter movie was very **Potteresque**! (*Urban Dictionary*)

Frequent splinters can also contribute to analogy via schema. The following are quite productive splinters in the Rice database:
– *-orexia* (← *anorexia*), as in *bridorexia* [2008] 'the bride's regimen of restricted diet for the purpose of weight loss', *manorexia* [2008] 'an eating disorder affecting men', *orthorexia* [2008] (earlier, 1997, in OED3) 'excessive concern

with consuming a diet considered to be correct in some respect', *tanarexia* [2008] 'disorder in which a person obsessively tans', *bulimarexia* [2011] 'a disorder that is the combination of bulimia and anorexia', and *Halloweenorexia* [2011] 'the self-induced eating disorder common in mostly teenage women caused by the desire to look good in a Halloween costume'.
- *-ccino* (← *cappuccino*), as in *fiberccino* [2008] 'a cappuccino that has a fiber supplement in it' and *crappuccino* [2013] 'an overpriced caffeinated beverage that basically tastes awful' (cf. folk-etymological *cuppaccino* [2008] from Italian *cappuccino*).
- *-gasm* (← *orgasm*), as in *laughgasm* [2008] 'an orgasm from laughing', *sargasm* [2008] 'an orgasm that derives its pleasure from (quasi-homophone) sarcasm', *Swirllgasm* [2008] 'a state of ecstasy achieved during the consumption of Swirll frozen yogurt', *peegasm* [2011] 'a feeling of euphoric relief experienced when you finally use the bathroom', and the above-mentioned *joygasm* [2005].

Combining forms are also frequently used to coin new analogical words. Examples of secreted/abbreviated combining forms used in Rice university vocabulary include:
- *-licious*, as in *awesomelicious* [2008] 'used to describe a person or thing that is marvelous, stunning, great', *beerlicious* [2008] 'having the quality of being both delicious and alcoholic', *coolicious* [2008] 'describing cool with a more modern connotation', *freshalicious* [2008] 'having an enhanced flavor when warm or freshly made' (e.g. "Those cookies you made last night were *freshalicious*"), *Hooterlicious* [2008] ← *Hooters*, 'sexually suggestive, provocative, or stimulating', and *fruitlicious* [2011] 'having a fresh and fruity taste' (see 1.2).
- *-rific* (← *terrific*), as in *fantabulific* [2008] (with dropped *r*) 'fantastic, fabulous, and terrific', *magrific* [2008] 'magnificent and terrific', *scandilific* [2008] 'describing someone who is terrific at spreading scandal', *scarific* [2008] (from *scary*) 'causing both fright and a pleasant feeling', *splendorific* [2008] (from *splendor*) 'amazing, awesome', and *wonderific* [2011] (from *wonderful*) 'describing extremely good feelings' (more examples in Bauer, Lieber, and Plag 2013: 527, also in OED3).
- *-(a)holic*, as in *assaholic* [2008] 'chronically inconsiderate, cruel, or obnoxious to others', *barkaholic* [2008] (e.g. "My dog JJ is such a *barkaholic*. I've got so many complaints from our neighbors because JJ barks all night long."), *cameraholic* [2008] 'one who is addicted to taking pictures', *drunkoholic* [2008] 'one who is known to habitually become intoxicated with alcoholic

substances', *caffeineaholic* [2010] 'a person who is addicted to caffeine', and *gameaholic* [2011] 'one who is addicted to playing video games' (see also 3.3.1 and 5.2).
- *-(a)thon*, as in *drinkathon* [2008] 'an extended party involving the consumption of alcohol', *hackathon* [2013] (from *hacking*) 'an event in which computer programmers and others involved in software development collaborate intensively on software projects', and *PDA-athon* [2008] 'a large amount of public display of affection', with an initialism as its base. In *Dananathon* (*sic*) [2011] 'the birthday celebration held by Charles Dana for himself' and *LeBron-a-thon* [2008] 'the saturating sports media coverage of all things having to do with James LeBron's first season in the NBA', the bases are family names (see also 3.3.1).
- *-zilla*, as in *Bridezilla*, *groomzilla* already discussed in 3.2.6.

The combining element *-sphere* – earlier an independent noun – is used at Rice in *blogosphere* [1999] 'the cultural or intellectual environment in which blogs are written and read' (also in OED3), coined after *atmosphere* [1638], *biosphere* [1899], *ecosphere* [1953], etc. Another combining form which has originated a schema is *-phobia* (from post-classical Latin), which is commonly used to form nouns with the sense 'fear of –', such as *hydrophobia* [1547], *Anglophobia* [1793], and psychological *school phobia* [1930] 'excessive and apparently irrational fear of attending school' (OED3, s.v. *school*). New formations in the Rice collection are *Diet-sodaphobia* [2008] 'the fear of drinking diet sodas' and *lovephobia* [2008] 'fear of love'.

The combining form *-rrhea*, first attested in *diarrhœa* [1398] and forming medical terms 'denoting (usually excessive) flow or secretion, as logorrhœa, mucorrhœa, etc.' (OED3) has given birth to *cyberrhea* [2008] 'a connection problem in the computer network', with nearly the same pronunciation of *er* and *ar*. However, in the Rice database, the meaning of the combining form has been extended from 'excessive flow' to 'a more general problem'.

Analogy via schema is actually represented in other web resources, as well as in dictionaries on teenagers' slang. In a study on slang compounds in online and paper slang dictionaries (Mattiello 2003), it was noted that adolescents tend to use word families to express concepts that frequently occur in their lives. For instance, they coin new words by analogy with compounding patterns which exhibit a constant right element, such as a body part. Some examples are *motormouth* [1955] 'a person who talks fast and incessantly' (OED3), which has probably been coined after *big mouth* [1834] 'a talkative, indiscreet, or boastful person' (OED3, s.v. *big*), and *potty mouth* [1969] 'a tendency to be foul-mouthed' (OED3, s.v. *potty*), after *foulmouth* [1692] 'a person who uses obscene, profane, or scurrilous language' (OED2). Other comparable cases include slang *airhead* [1971] 'a foolish, unintelligent, or frivolous person' (OED3, cf. 3.3.1 with a different meaning), which is modelled on *fat-head* [1835] 'a stupid dolt' (OED2), and *bird brain* [1943] '(a person with) a small brain' (OED2, s.v. *bird*), created on the pattern of *beetle-brain* (attested since 1593 in the OED). With a different meaning connected to drug addiction, slang *crackhead* [1986] 'a person who is addicted to crack cocaine' (OED2, s.v. *crack*) has probably been formed on the model of *acid head* [1966] 'a person who takes acid' (OED3, s.v. *acid*; see also the colloquial meaning of *head* 'an addict' in OED3) (more examples in Mattiello 2008a; Green 2010). Two examples of such formations recorded in the *Urban Dictionary* are:

(37)   Most blondes have a reputation for being **air heads**. (*Urban Dictionary*, 2003)

(38)   That **crack head** asked me for a smoke. (*Urban Dictionary*, 2006)

In another study on slanguage (or teenage talk, Mattiello 2005), experimental tests were conducted on native English speaker students in order to investigate the way they typically intensify common action verbs, such as *to dance* or *to drink*. Results from these tests show that adolescents tend to use the analogical mechanism to coin new intensifying expressions too. For instance, some students suggested using *your socks off* or *your tits off* (modelled on *your ass off*) as possible collocates with the verb *to dance*. Others declared that they used many novel expressions metaphorically alluding to the destructive effects of alcohol: among them, *to get hammered* and *to get trashed* 'to get drunk or intoxicated' are analogical with slang *to get smashed* [1962] and *to get wasted* [1968–1970], both attested in the OED. Although expressions and phrases are beyond the scope of this book, their connection with the analogical mechanism corroborates the findings concerning new analogical juvenile words.

Interestingly, the innovative nature of adolescents and students' slang has also produced ungrammatical targets. An illustrative example of ungrammaticality in the Rice collection is the adjective *prettiful* [2008] 'having beauty' used in Internet correspondence to emphasise the idea of attractiveness by drawing attention to the adjective *pretty*. The model of this target may be the adjective *beautiful* [c1443], regularly formed from a noun (*beauty*) and the suffix *-ful*. By contrast, *prettiful* is irregularly formed from an adjective, which is an impossible base for the *-ful* suffix. However, another possible analysis for this neoformation – i.e.

a blend from *pretty* and *beautiful* (cf. *Urban Dictionary*) – would exclude analogy as the operating word-formation mechanism.

5.2 Types of target and their relationships with the models

The types of target words that are part of adolescents' vocabulary are less predictable – and often more idiosyncratic – than the analogical targets that make up specialised jargon. Many of these new targets are peculiar to a small minority, and the model words from which they are created remain obscure and inaccessible, especially when they are not specified in the immediate context.

The three conversational excerpts in (39)–(41), drawn from the *Urban Dictionary*, show different degrees of difficulty in identifying an absent model word:

(39)   I told my dad he needs to start watching something other than the O'Reilly Factor. All that **insultainment**'s no good for his blood pressure! (*Urban Dictionary*, 2007)

(40)   Ben: Excuse me, what time is it, please?
Girl with iPad, using zoom feature, staring at photo on screen of Lake Atitlan in Guatemala and not really paying attention: (Hrmmmphhh!)
Rachel: I don't think that girl's really paying attention. She's a **tablet potato**! Ask someone else ... (*Urban Dictionary*, 2010)

(41)   A: Let's go to a movie.
B: Alright, I'll come pick you up.
A: Alright, **ttys**. (*Urban Dictionary*, 2004)

In (39), for instance, the existence of the series which exhibits a combining form *-tainment* (← *entertainment*) can help the association of *insultainment* [2007] with model words such as *docutainment*, *infotainment*, and so on (see 2.2). Like its model nouns denoting genres of broadcasting, journalism, etc., in which entertainment is combined with aspects of the genre, *insultainment* has been coined for 'print, broadcast or online content which is so devoid of actual news or information that it can only be considered an insult to the intelligence of the viewer'. Although the first element *insult* is not as abbreviated as *docu*, *info*, etc., the similarity between this target and the schema formed by *-tainment* words is evident from both the morphotactic viewpoint and the phonological viewpoint (e.g. word length and overlap of the last two syllables with the models).

Similarly, in (40) the existence of the attested analogical formation *mouse potato*, created on the model of *couch potato* (1.2), can help identify the association of *tablet potato* [2010] with this same model. Indeed, from the morphological viewpoint, *tablet potato* shares the second constituent with *couch/mouse potato*, and, semantically, they all refer to 'an idle person who spends most of his/her leisure time performing a repetitive activity'. In particular, a *tablet potato* refers to 'a person who uses a tablet, especially on a train, airplane, boat, or bus, and is oblivious to everything around him or her'. In this case, the analogical target substitutes the first component (*couch* or *mouse* vs. *tablet*) in order to specify the type of (technological) device the person is addicted to.

Finally, the model in (41) is nearly unrecognisable and its analogical target is hard to disambiguate due to its extra-grammaticality. Indeed, the full phrase which underlies the target initialism *ttys* [2004] – i.e. *Talk To You Soon* – is not expanded in the text and this obstructs its disambiguation. Furthermore, the model's recognition presupposes prior knowledge of both the vocabulary item *ttyl* [2002] and its expanded form *Talk To You Later*. Extra-grammatical formations, unlike the grammatical *tablet potato*, display an increased difficulty in recognition and understanding.

Like specialised jargons, therefore, adolescents' slang presumes specific vocabulary knowledge. This means that very often only teenagers can have direct access to the new analogical formations used by their peers, because the vocabulary that they share can help the association of new targets with well-known models. Adults, by contrast, have difficult access to the new generation's analogical language, unless they find some hints to the model words in the micro-context. Examples (42)–(43) show target words that are endophoric in respect to their model words:

(42)   Your momma's so ugly she's not a **MILF** she's a **MIRF**! (*Urban Dictionary*, 2006)

(43)   Page: Girl that hat on him was so sexy, I need to hook up with that **Dilf**.
Candace: How many kids does he have?
Page: One ... Maybe two, IDK, I just heard he was a dad. There more prepared in life. Hey, men call us **Milfs**! (*Urban Dictionary*, 2009)

In both cases, the model word is the acronym *MILF* [1992] ← *Mother I'd Like to Fuck*, 'a sexually attractive woman who is a mother' (OED3). However, in (42) the target *MIRF* [2006] – i.e. an acronym for *Mom I'd Run From* – is anaphoric to its model, whereas in (43) the target *Dilf* [2003] ← *Dad I'd Like to Fuck* cataphorically anticipates its female counterpart (*Milf(s)*). In the latter case, the Variable Part in the target (*dad*) is also made explicit. In both cases, the similarity between target and model word is clearly morphotactic (both are acronyms), but also phonological (*MILF* and *MIRF* only differ for a consonant sound in the coda, *Milf* and *Dilf* for a consonant sound in the onset). In *Dilf–Milf*, the semantic opposition between *D(ad)* and *M(other)* also helps the association of the target with its model.

Adolescents have actually created a variety of acronyms which follow this same model and act as a schema. Other neoformations attested in the *Urban Dictionary* include *bilf* [2003] ← *Babysitter I'd Like to Fuck*, *gilf* [2003] ← *Grandmother/Granny I'd Like to Fuck* (also in Green 2010), *tilf* [2003] ← *Teacher I'd Like to Fuck*, and *wilf* [2003] ← *Wife I'd Like to Fuck*. The existence of a word set, as in this case, can evidently reinforce the association of the target with the model schema.

In (44)–(45), however, the targets only show an endophoric hint to their Variable Parts:

(44)   Gracie, you have to leave that **camera** at home! You are becoming a **cameraholic**! (*Rice University Neologisms Database*, 2008)

(45)   Joe has **VOCD**; he must adjust the **volume** on any television in which it is not set to a perfect number. (*Urban Dictionary*, 2009)

In (44), indeed, the model schema – i.e. words ending in -(*a*)*holic*, such as *workaholic* and *shopaholic* – is not mentioned in the text. Yet, the target *cameraholic* is partially anaphoric, in that it refers to its Variable Part *camera*, which occurs earlier, at a six-word distance, in the previous sentence.

Similarly, in (45), the model word *OCD* [1977] ← *Obsessive-Compulsive Disorder* (OED3, s.v. *O*) is not mentioned. Nonetheless, the target *VOCD* [2009] is cataphoric in respect to its Variable Part *volume*, which is made explicit later, at a four-word distance, in the following sentence (see 3.3.5 for target–model distance, 3.3.1 for surface analogy with enlargement).

5.3 The functions of analogical slanguage words

Adolescents' slang has been attributed various functions (and effects) in the literature. They range from the need to create or express intimacy with their peers (Eble 1996; see "group-restriction" and "privacy" in Mattiello 2008a: 214–217) to the jocular/mocking function, which involves plays on (especially vulgar) words or use of offensive expressions to scorn the group's outsiders (Stenström, Andersen, and

Hasund 2002; see "vulgarity" and "playfulness" in Mattiello 2008a: 218–224). Another reason why teenagers are in constant search of novel forms of expression is their desire for creativity, innovation, and originality (see "freshness" and "novelty" in Mattiello 2008a: 224–225). In other words, they want to show off, both to their friends and to their parents or other adults, such as educators, who are part of their daily lives (Coleman 2014).

The function of creating intimacy with their friends is illustrated, for example, by the use of a neoformation in (46):

(46)   This day started out **SNAFU**, but then my machine went all **TARFUN**. (*Urban Dictionary*, 2004)

In this text, the target acronym *TARFUN* [2004] ← *Things Are Really Fucked Up Now* is anaphoric to its model word *SNAFU* [1942] ← *Situation Normal: All Fouled* (or *Fucked*) *Up*, which originally belonged to military slang, but later extended its meaning, and has been used, since the 1940s, to refer to something which is 'confused, chaotic' (OED2). Here the similarity between target and model is more orthographic than phonological, in that, in the second syllable, the body *FU* is pronounced differently in the two words (/fʌ/ vs. /fuː/). However, target and model mainly resemble each other morphotactically, in their both being acronyms.

Acronymic formation is indeed a privileged choice among young coiners, because abbreviations are often vague, cryptic, and hard to disambiguate for outsiders. Hence, the use of acronymic terms aids teenagers to establish an intimate and private connection, often without being too explicit or understood by adult people.

The second function that is served by new analogical formations involves jocularity, playfulness, and humour. Consider, for instance, the nonce word in (47):

(47)   Of course she looks perfect in that photo, she was **PHOBAR**. (*Urban Dictionary*, 2010)

The word *PHOBAR* [2010] appearing in the *Urban Dictionary* is coined after the pattern of the acronym *fubar* [1944] ← *Fouled* (or *Fucked*) *Up Beyond All Recognition*, 'ruined, messed up' (OED3).[4] In particular, it is a mixed formation that retains the initial (and also some non-initial) letters of *PHOtoshopped Beyond All Recognition*. Therefore, its reference to the exophoric model *fubar* is humorous,

---

4 According to the OED, *fubar* [1944] is in its turn analogical with the model *snafu* [1942] ← *Situation Normal: All Fouled* (or *Fucked*) *Up*.

in that *PHOBAR* refers to an image, usually a photo of a person, 'which has been airbrushed with digital image manipulation software so significantly that the person in the photo is barely recognisable'. Morphotactic resemblance and phonological similarity – especially, overlap of the second unaccented syllable /bɑː/ – between target and model can facilitate the disambiguation of the word play. Language puns, as in this case, often correspond to acts of mockery and ridicule towards somebody, such as an absent addressee (*she*).

In (48), the pun is similarly towards an absent addressee (*my cousin/he*):

(48) My cousin's jaws were slightly agar, almost drooling, eyes glazed on the computer monitor. He had a total **computer face**. (*Urban Dictionary*, 2010)

The nonce word *computer face* [2010] 'a person's face becoming too relaxed as a result of looking at a computer screen for too long' has probably been coined on the pattern of *TV face* [2009] 'a person's face becoming too relaxed as a result of watching TV for too long'. Indeed, the latter has been introduced in the *Urban Dictionary* before the former, and could have acted as model word (in spite of its ephemerality). However, the jocularity of the target *computer face* works especially well if it is associated with *TV face*, and this association greatly depends on the interpreter's group membership and prior knowledge of adolescents' language.

Innovation and originality are other functions that novel analogical words can serve. For instance, when a young man or young woman refers to his/her father in these terms:

(49) Dad, that story in your email message left me **typeless**! (*Urban Dictionary*, 2004)

(s)he clearly intends to appear original, creative, and innovative. The originality of the neologism *typeless* [2004] is linked to its being a target word created on the pattern of one exact model word – i.e. *speechless* [a1000] – to indicate 'the state of being so astounded that one cannot type'.[5] Target and model here show both morphotactic and phonological likeness, which may facilitate the father's understanding of the new word. The micro-context citing an *email message* can also help the addressee's comprehension. Yet the language remains unique and inventive, and analogical formations such as *typeless* or *computer face* run the risk

---

[5] The adjective *typeless* [1845] is also attested in the OED, yet with a different meaning, i.e. as a nonce formation for 'untyped, unprinted'.

of not becoming established new words if they are not reused by adolescents, or extended to a larger part of the speech community, although both forms are grammatical and completely transparent.

5.4 Distribution of analogical juvenile words

This section shows the distribution and frequency of the analogical juvenile words mentioned in this chapter in COCA and GloWbE. The methodology that was adopted for the compilation of Table 7 is the same as that which was used for Table 6. For instance, as for acronyms and initialisms, a two-pronged approach enabled the exclusion of many occurrences of *IDL* and *Tilf*, which never (or rarely) in the corpora corresponded to the source phrases *I Die Laughing* and *Teacher I'd Like to Fuck*. Therefore, only the acronyms/initialisms with the pertinent juvenile sense have been selected: e.g., *ttys* occurred three times with the meaning *Talk To You Soon* in GloWbE, but 69 with a different (irrelevant) sense. However, for Table 7 some further remarks are in order.

Firstly, a close reading approach was also necessary for other types of formations. These include the reduplicative *ling-ling*, the compound *Pink Friday*, and the derived word *typeless*, which are all attested in both corpora, but not with the meaning with which they are used by teenagers/students. Hence, despite the fact that the query system gave some occurrences for these items, they were considered unattested.

Another remark concerns the detection of combining forms. For neoclassical ones, such as *-phobia*, *-rrhea*, or *-sphere*, the overall attestation in the two corpora was beyond our scope. Therefore, I only checked specific novel words which exhibited these forms, such as *lovephobia*, *Twitterrhea*, and *blogosphere*. By contrast, for abbreviated and secreted combining forms, such as *-licious*, *-rific*, *-tainment*, and *-zilla*, an automated corpus analysis based on the query strings **licious*, **rific*, etc. was followed by a close check of all the pertinent words. This procedure excluded *delicious* and *malicious* from the count, but included *bootylicious*, *girlicious*, and others.

Distribution of analogical juvenile words — 147

Tab. 7: New analogical juvenile words (Anaphoric vs. Cataphoric) and their frequency in COCA and GloWbE

New words	COCA					GloWbE	Model	
	Spok	Fic	Mag	News	Acad		Ana	Cata
-(a)holic	120/1.36	45/0.51	170/1.93	171/1.94	27/0.30	1,927/1.01	77/0.03	76/0.03
airhead	8/0.09	29/0.32	17/0.19	8/0.09	1/0.01	368/0.19		
-(a)thon	123/1.39	21/0.23	109/1.23	17/0.19	19/0.21	904/0.47	43/0.01	38/0.01
babe magnet	3/0.03	5/0.05	8/0.09	2/0.02		15/0.007		
BFFL						10/0.005		1/0.0004
bilf						1/0.0005		
bird brain	2/0.02		3/0.03			39/0.02		
bitchdar								
Blindian								
blogosphere	89/1.01	5/0.05	60/0.68	60/0.68	23/0.26	4,786/2.51	3/0.001	1/0.0004
brinner				1/0.01		7/0.003		
-ccino	5/0.05	20/0.22	25/0.28	16/0.18		16/0.008	1/0.0004	6/0.002
chick lit	7/0.07	5/0.05	6/0.06	9/0.10	94/1.06	434/0.22		1/0.0004
Chrasian								
computer face								
crackhead	6/0.06	1/0.01	1/0.01	2/0.02		91/0.04	1/0.0004	1/0.0004
dick flick								
Diet-sodaphobia								
Dilf			1/0.01			12/0.006	1/0.0004	
eighthead						1/0.0005		

New words	COCA					GloWbE	Model	
	Spok	Fic	Mag	News	Acad		Ana	Cata
e-pal						11/0.005		
Failbook						8/0.004		1/0.0004
flexitarian			7/0.07				1/0.0004	2/0.0008
FOFL								
-gasm		3/0.03	4/0.04	3/0.03	3/0.03	116/0.06	5/0.002	1/0.0004
gimongous						2/0.001		
IDL								
-licious	10/0.11	30/0.34	49/0.55	41/0.46		513/0.27	27/0.01	25/0.01
ling-ling								
linner			3/0.03			3/0.001		2/0.0008
lovephobia								
LQTM	1/0.01					3/0.001		
lupper		1/0.01				1/0.0005		
midnitini								
MIRF								
motormouth	5/0.05	5/0.05	10/0.11	7/0.07	1/0.01	131/0.06		
niftabulous								
-orexia			3/0.03		1/0.01	119/0.06	15/0.006	10/0.004
PHOBAR								
Pink Friday								
Potteresque			1/0.01			5/0.002		
potty mouth	3/0.03	6/0.06	10/0.11	6/0.06		126/0.06		
prettiful						2/0.001		
-rific	4/0.04	8/0.09	16/0.18	2/0.02		135/0.07	18/0.007	19/0.008
ROFL						842/0.44	37/0.01	12/0.005
Twitterrhea			1/0.01					

New words	COCA					GloWbE	Model	
	Spok	Fic	Mag	News	Acad		Ana	Cata
sangry						1/0.0005		
speako								
superbulous								
tablet potato								
-tainment	27/0.30	4/0.04	75/0.85	42/0.47	18/0.20	1,034/0.54	17/0.007	10/0.004
tangry						1/0.0005	1/0.0004	
TARFUN								
tilf						1/0.0005	1/0.0004	
tiratini								
ttys						3/0.001		
Twetiquette						2/0.001		
Twitterrhea			1/0.01					
Twitterverse			6/0.06	5/0.05	1/0.01	440/0.23		2/0.0008
Twittizen								
typeless								
vlogger				1/0.01		50/0.02	11/0.004	
VOCD								
wake-and-bake								
Webinar		3/0.03		1/0.01	8/0.09	3,151/1.65	8/0.003	15/0.006
wilf								
writeo								
-zilla	32/0.36	33/0.37	32/0.36	25/0.28		787/0.41	4/0.001	

The data reported in Table 7 shows the distribution of the juvenile terms selected for qualitative analysis in COCA and GloWbE. The results confirm the expectations that, in adolescents' language, many novel words are mere occasionalisms. Indeed, 36.61% of the terms are neither attested in COCA nor in GloWbE, and

15.49% occur infrequently – 1 or 2 occurrences (or 0.0004/0.0008 pmw) – and only in the latter corpus. However, the oral mode also plays a role in this case. Given that spoken data is underrepresented in COCA (i.e. one fifth of the texts belongs to spoken language), and that the spoken part of COCA mostly contains scripted words rather than spontaneous conversation, these aspects could have influenced the results.

The data of Table 7 is visualised in Figure 5, which includes all the new analogical words in the table, and Figure 6, with only the most frequent ones.

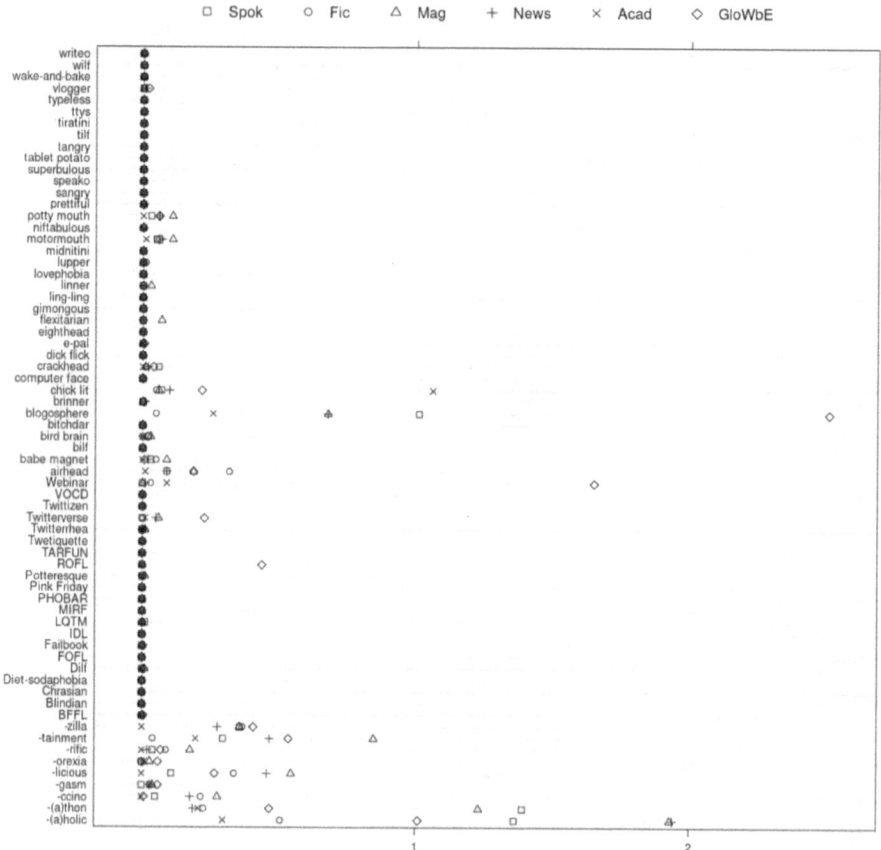

Fig. 5: Visualisation of all data from Table 7

On the other hand, the occurrence of the combining forms and splinters that make up one fifth of the above lemma list is relatively high. The overall high token/normalised frequency of -(a)holic words (2,460 occurrences/7.05 pmw, 63.97% in the news and magazines) and -(a)thon words (1,193 occurrences/3.72 pmw, 42.56% in spoken discourse) does not strike. However, the normalised frequency of such splinters as -gasm (129 occurrences/0.19 pmw), -orexia (123/0.1 pmw), and -ccino (82/0.73 pmw) in novel words of both corpora is lower. Secreted or abbreviated combining forms, such as -licious, -rific, -tainment, and -zilla, also play a considerable role in novel word-formation. COCA and GloWbE collectively include 909 occurrences of -zilla words (1.78 pmw), 643 of -licious words (1.73 pmw), 165 of -rific words (0.4 pmw), and 1,200 of -tainment words (2.4 pmw), all of which (excluding the latter) are completely absent from academic discourse.

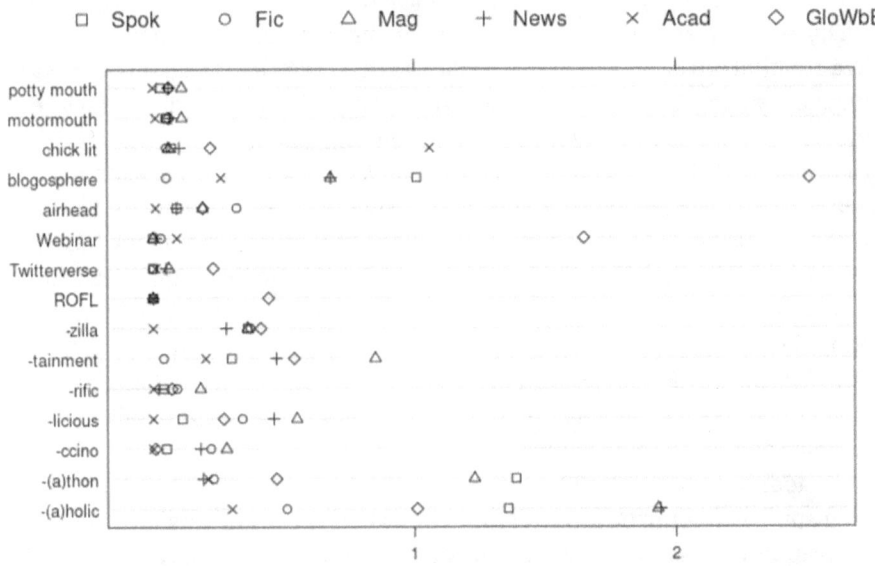

Fig. 6: Visualisation of the most frequent words in Table 7

Another remarkable fact is related to the considerable presence of compound words in the lemma list. Nearly a quarter of the list is made up of compound nouns and 3% of this list also includes derived words which perfectly comply with word-formation rules. These findings suggest that, in spite of their search for innovation and creativity, teenagers often coin new words by applying the rules of composition and derivation that they already know, besides using analogy. These findings also mesh quite well with Clark's (1981: 303) observations in first-language acquisition (3.4.1), especially with children's tendency to coin new compound words, which are more transparent than derived words.

As far as the model words are concerned, of the 63.38% attested words in the corpora, a half occurs together with their models, with a balance of 50% between anaphoric and cataphoric analogies.

5.5 Final remarks on analogy in juvenile words

This analysis of juvenile language, or slang(uage), from the viewpoint of analogical formation has helped understand the role played by analogy in the coinage of adolescents' neologisms and nonce words. Firstly, the types of analogical formations that teenagers coin (5.1) range from surface analogies that are also based on productive patterns (e.g. *Potteresque, babe magnet*) to extra-grammatical formations (e.g. *lupper, vlogger, LQTM*), and even to ungrammatical ones, e.g. *prettiful*, which has a doubtful origin. Analogy via schema is another principal mechanism of word-formation among teenagers, with subtypes that include combining forms (e.g. *-licious, -rific*), frequent splinters (e.g. *-gasm, -orexia*), and word families with pivot head components (e.g. *motormouth, potty mouth*). These results show, on the one hand, that students and adolescents tend to coin regular new words in line with their morphological competence and awareness, but, on the other hand, they also create neologisms and (especially) occasionalisms that are extra-grammatical, as an attempt to appear original, creative, and inventive. Acronyms (e.g. *LOL, MILF*) and initialisms (e.g. *ttyl*) are specifically selected as models for new targets (e.g. *ROFL; Dilf, tilf, MIRF; ttys*) for their brevity, easy memorisation, and difficult recoverability at the same time (Mattiello 2013: 109), in this case, recoverability both of the model and of the source phrase.

In addition, the analysis of juvenile analogical targets, of the model words that inspire their formation, and of their contextual or extra-textual interrelations (5.2) has shown that, in slanguage, the model's recoverability may be facilitated by prior knowledge and group membership. Thus, exophoric reference to the model word is only possible in conversations among adolescents or insiders, whereas an explicit endophoric reference can encourage the adults' disambiguation and understanding. Other verbal hints in the text can anaphorically or cataphorically allude to the Variable Part of the target, stressing its relevance in the identification of the model. Indeed, both Variable and Invariable Part in the target can aid outsiders' comprehension.

Finally, the investigation of the crucial functions of analogical word-formation in juvenile talk (5.3) has proved that adolescents use analogy both as a mechanism of ingroupiness, and as a means of exclusion. Indeed, although analogical formations in juvenile language may seem ambiguous, unclear, and inaccessible to most adult people, they are viewed by teenagers as cohesive devices, in that they refer to model words (series or word families) that the adolescents already share. Analogical language, therefore, serves to consolidate the use of already existing patterns and, at the same time, to create a funny and innovative vocabulary that may distinguish new generations from old ones.

Lastly, a corpus analysis of the novel words discussed in this chapter (5.4.) has shown the relevance of occasionalisms and nonce formations in adolescents' vocabulary, as well as a regularisation of abbreviated and secreted combining forms, such as *-licious*, *-rific*, *-tainment*, and *-zilla*, most of which are typical of the juvenile sphere. Other neoclassical combining forms, such as *-phobia*, *-rrhea*, or *-sphere*, confirm their productivity by adding to new bases.

6 Analogy in journalistic language

Journalistic language, especially in its recent popularising genres on the web, is prolific in analogical formations. Journalists create neologisms and occasionalisms everyday (for some lexical innovations in the *Times*, see Baayen and Renouf 1996), with the purpose of attracting and amusing their readership. In newspaper texts, the role of analogy is especially intra-textual, in that the hilarious effect that new target words attain is primarily obtained as an echo to their model words.

In an article published in *The Guardian*, for instance, the headline states "*Brexit, Grexit*, with the possibility of *Spexit*. Whose bright idea was this?" (2015, emphasis added). This clearly suggests that the former words (both attested in *Wordspy* [2012] for 'the exit of Great Britain/Greece from the European Union'), are model blends for the latter occasionalism, referring in its turn to 'the exit of Spain'. In the same article, the journalist suggests six more portmanteaus inspired by the same model words: namely, *Portugexit* (from *Portugal*), *Irelexit* (from *Ireland*), *Luxembexit* (from *Luxembourg*), *Cyprexit* (from *Cyprus*), *Frexit* (from *France*), and *Germexit* (from *Germany*). In spite of the temporary character of these six occasionalisms, the columnist seems to be sure that they will catch the attention of his/her readers, encouraging them to read more or even the whole piece.

New journalistic terms with the same function have also been collected in *Neologisms – New Words in Journalistic Text*. For instance, words such as *shockvertising* [2008] ← *shock + advertising*, 'the advertising industry's attempt to get the public to sit up and take notice', probably modelled on *shockumentary* (3.1.2), or *e-portfolio* [2004], which follows a schema with an initial combining form *e-*, can both attract the readers' attention and help writers to establish a closer relationship with their public.

The present chapter is an examination of some journalistic analogies which occur in online newspapers, such as *The Guardian* and *The Observer,* or have been selected from newspapers' archives, such as the above-mentioned *Neologisms – New Words in Journalistic Text*. The key purpose of this examination is to show the importance of the (micro-)context for the disambiguation of the analogies that appear in the press. Indeed, the context – either sentence or paragraph – generally includes the model word of the new target. This is normally the author's deliberate choice, because (s)he intends to facilitate his/her readers' comprehension process. Thus, an explicit (endophoric) reference to the model word can function as an ironic mention, although the target may act as a parody, a distortion, or bad imitation of the model. As a result, analogical formations in the press can be word plays, puns, and occasionalisms coined on the spot to allude, amuse, or deride. Journalistic analogies can also be ungrammatical, or be consequences of reanalysis, because what is more irregular, or unusual, attracts more.

This chapter therefore shows that the pragmatic functions of newspaper analogies range from the (humorous) attraction of readers' attention to the construction of social closeness.

6.1 Types of analogical formation in journalistic language

Analogical formations abound in the press, with nonce words which mainly prosper in online newspapers, where journalists' language includes, in terms of types, both pure surface analogies and analogies via schemas, and, in terms of morphological categories, grammatical, extra-grammatical, and ungrammatical formations.

A close investigation of the collection *Neologisms – New Words in Journalistic Text* can provide evidence of the relevance of analogical word-formation to journalistic language. This collection includes 819 novel words selected from *The Independent* and *The Guardian* in a timeframe spanning from 1997 to 2012 and identified as being 'new' by the software developed by the Research and Development Unit for English Studies (Birmingham City University) during the APRIL project.

The investigation has produced the following results:
- The database totals 95 analogies out of 819 items. In other words, 11.59% of the neoformations are analogy-based, and 21.05% are headwords in the OED. Among analogy-based neoformations:
    a. 13.68% (13 items) are pure surface analogies, such as the acronymic formation *nimf-ism* [2006] ← *not in my front seat* + *-ism*, after *Nimbyism* [1986] ← *not in my back yard*. The recent neologisms of this type include *beefalo* [1974] ← *beef* + *buffalo* (OED2), based on *catalo* [1894] ← *cattle* + *buffalo*, and *prepone* [1913] discussed in 3.3.3.
    b. 22.10% (21 items) are surface analogies which also conform to rule patterns. Examples of attested neologisms of this type include *alphabetism* [1978] 'prejudice or discrimination resulting from a person's position on an alphabetical list' (OED3) ← *sexism* [1866] (also *racism*), and *refoliate* [1932] (OED3, s.v. *re-*) ← *defoliate* [1793].
    c. 64.21% (61 items) are analogies via schema, with more than 90% that exhibit attested combining forms (e.g. *-athon*, *-scape*, *e-*, *eco-*, etc.).

As far as morphological categories are concerned, both the investigation of *Neologisms* and a random search in *The Guardian* have demonstrated the variety of word-formation processes illustrated by journalistic analogical formations.

Grammatical formations in the *Neologisms* database are illustrated by both compound words, such as the compound *café-bar* [1938] (OED2, s.v. *café*), coined after *café-restaurant* [1926], and derived words, such as *Blairese* [1998], created after *Johnsonese* [1843] or *Carlylese* [1858], to designate 'the diction of Tony Blair' (see *-ese*, OED2). In the latter case, the original pattern, with authors' names as bases, has been extended to a derivative from a politician's name. From a regular combining form *cyber-*, *cyberbar* [1997] 'a bar in which customers may use computer terminals to access the Internet' has been coined as a synonym of its model *cybercafé* [1994]:

(50) Spain has Europe's lowest take-up of the Internet, but many cities have flourishing **'cyberbars'** where would-be netties can log on while enjoying the more familiar pleasures of sinking a beer or a generous Spanish measure of whisky. (*Neologisms*, 1997)

Another regular process which combines with pure surface analogy is conversion. For instance, *eBay* [1995], the name of an American multinational corporation and e-commerce company providing sales services via the Internet, has been converted into a verb, as the following extract from *Neologisms* illustrates:

(51) Accordingly, eBay has made the ultimate transformation from trademarked proper noun to verb: I may **eBay** that vase later tonight; my decorator spends all his evenings **eBaying** for a 1982 BMW. (*Neologisms*, 2004)

Parallel examples of N → V zero-derivation are attested in the OED: e.g., *to Google* and *to Skype* discussed in 3.3.6.

Similarly, the compound verb *wait-list* [1960] 'to put (a person) on a waiting list' (OED2) comes from the noun *wait-list* [1897], and like the simplex verb *list* derives from the corresponding noun.

The Guardian likewise offers regular analogical formations, such as *dairy-free* [1983] 'that does not contain milk or products derived from milk' (OED2, s.v. *dairy*), formed on *gluten-free, sugar-free*, etc. (Olsen 2014: 31), and *black-collar* [2010], modelled on *white-collar* [1911] and *blue-collar* [1929] (3.3.2):

(52) This is scarcely the first crisis involving what an Australian victims' group, Broken Rites, has termed **black-collar** crime. (*The Guardian*, 2010)

Extra-grammatical analogical formations are also common, both in the *Neologisms* collection and in newspapers. For instance, the blend *politisoap* [2005], probably from *politi(cal)*, or *politi(cs)*, and *soap (opera)*, is modelled on *docusoap* [1979] (3.3.4):

(53)   A variety of readers have been in touch about minor inaccuracies in *The Deal*, the **politisoap** shown on Channel 4 on Sunday night. (*Neologisms*, 2005)

and the acronym *Mads* [2006] ← *mums and dads* is humorously created in a Guardian article entitled "Come on you Wags!":

(54)   Naturally, they [the Wags] could not have done it without their **Mads** (mums and dads, of whom more later). (*The Guardian*, 2006)

The model word *Wags* [2002] 'the wives and girlfriends of a group of professional football players' (OED3), occurs sixteen times in the text, the first occurrence is six paragraphs before the target *Mads*.

In addition, a newspaper headline states, "First bank accounts for teens and tweens" (*The Guardian*, 2014). Hence, it shows the target *tween* [1946], short for *tweenager* 'a person who is nearly, or has only just become, a teenager' (OED3), immediately after its model clipping *teen* [1818], short for *teenager* 'a young person in the teens' (OED2).

Ungrammatical analogies are also illustrated by a Guardian article where the author comments on the use of the suffix *-th*, used in the past to coin words such as *stealth* [a1325] or †*blowth* [1602] (cited in the article), and which is now unproductive. The author wanting to 'revive' this suffix concludes his/her piece in this way:

(55)   Who now will join me in reviving this useful feature of the English language? Will it be young men, barely out of their **boyth**? Or older people, in the wise days of their **greyth**? Come now, there's no need for **coyth**. (*The Guardian*, 2006)

In this quote, the words in bold are all analogical nonce formations, but one of them – *boyth* – is ungrammatical. Indeed, while adjectival bases, such as *grey* or *coy*, can accept the nominal *-th* suffix, the noun *boy* cannot, hence, its humorous effect in the article.

The type of analogy via schema occurs in journalistic language both through combining forms and through splinters. For instance, the schema with the *-tainment* combining form (see 2.2) has originated new words attested in *The Guardian*: i.e., *histo-tainment* [2009], *sport-o-tainment* [2012], and *opinio-tainment* [2013]. A comparable schema is that with the *-licious* combining form, obtaining creative *Excelicious* [2014] ← *Microsoft Excel*, 'the name of a blogger', and *Sweetie-licious* [2012] 'the name of a bakery'. In addition, the combining form *-(o)rama* (3.3.1) has triggered the hilarious word *chaterama* [2015] (from *chat* 'familiar and easy talk', with a different interfix *-e-*). This nonce formation is mentioned in an article on David Cameron, who has used it to define 'a kind of informal meeting which does not involve the reading of the documents that an adviser had brought with him or her' (*The Guardian*, 2015).

The splinter *-ercise* has also triggered new targets, as the following extract from *The Guardian* shows:

(56) **Dancercise, boxercise** and even **hulercise** [from *hula* 'an Hawaiian dance'] are all now well established, and who is to say that **textercise, shopercise** and **callcentrercise** will not shortly follow? Surely there is a place among them for **party gamercise**? (*The Guardian*, 2008)

The productivity of this splinter makes it a potential candidate for the role of combining form (3.3.1).

A series having an acronymic name as its model word – i.e. the British *Esa* [2009] 'European Space Agency' centre – includes *Estec* 'European Space Research and Technology Centre', *Esoc* 'European Space Operations Centre', *Esrin* 'European Space Research Institute', and *Esac* 'European Space Astronomy Centre'. Hence, in a newspaper article, the author Ian Sample has suggested a new target *Escort* 'European Space Curators of Rare Tat', which is analogical (sharing the first two letters) with the above set:

(57) But back to Britain's new Esa centre. The space agency has facilities in all of the major member states. There is Estec in Noordwijk, in the Netherlands; there's Esoc in Darmstadt, Germany; Esrin in Frascati, Italy and Esac in Villanueva de la Cañada near Madrid in Spain. And there are more besides.
At the press conference to mark the opening of the British facility, the BBC's Jonathon Amos asked Dordain if Esa had an acronym for the centre yet. They don't. He asked us if we had any ideas. We didn't.

But I'm sure we can come up with something to help Esa out. It looks like the first two characters have to be ES for European Space. The rest is all to play for though.
I propose **Escort** (European Space Curators of Rare Tat). It recognises the new centre's future role in curating moon rock and meteorites, with a nod to the favoured mode of transport in the region. I can say that, I grew up there. (*The Guardian*, 2009)

It is worth noting that the neoformation occurs at a three-paragraph distance from its model words (see 3.3.5).

A similar word set mentioned in *The Guardian*'s sister Sunday newspaper – *The Observer* – includes acronyms built on the pattern of *Yuppies* [1984] 'young upwardly mobile professionals', namely, *Buppies* [1984] 'black upwardly mobile professionals' and *Yuffers* [2006] 'young urban females'. In the same newspaper article, *Dinkies* [1986] 'dual income, no kids' is the model for the nonce formation *Orchids* [2006] 'one recent child, hideously in debt':

(58) It started with the Yuppies, those endlessly aspiring young upwardly mobile professionals who drove fast cars, wore expensive suits, got their hair streaked, bought flats in London's Docklands and tried to make as much money as fast as possible. After that we faced an avalanche of social acronyms to match the times. These included the **Buppies**, who turned out to be black upwardly mobile professionals. Then the Yuppies married, gave up their Armani suits and Porsches and took to life together. Then they became Dinkies (dual income, no kids) or had children, thus turning themselves into **Orchids** (one recent child, hideously in debt).
But now a new breed of urban professionals has appeared on the block. Meet the **Yuffers**: young urban females who typically spend more than they earn, enjoy weekends at country houses or health spas, and who normally have at least two maxed-out credit cards. (*The Guardian*, 2006)

6.2 Types of target and their relationships with the models

The types of target word in journalistic terminology are innovative, inventive, and odd, especially for the comical (or even hilarious) effect that they are meant to produce on readers. What characterises journalistic analogies is their connection with the (micro-)context, where a model is expected for disambiguation. In other words, when the reader meets a new potentially analogical word in the article which (s)he is reading, (s)he is expected to remember, or search for the model word within the same article. This may be both the author's strategy to get all his/her article read, and the author's intention to facilitate his/her readers' comprehension. Whatever the reason, model and target words generally tend to co-exist in the same (micro-)context. Examples (54)–(58) have illustrated (with various distances) this co-existence between model and analogical formation.

Similarly, examples (59)–(61) show anaphoric targets, with models which immediately precede them:

(59)   Mods, Hippies, Yuppies, Sloanes, Dinkies, Lombards, New Men, Soft Lads, New Laddettes, **Generation X-ers**, **Generation Y-ers**, Wide-boys, Young Fogeys, New Agers, Permakids ... the list of the labels we hang on ourselves grows almost daily. (*The Observer*, 1999)

(60)   Thomas Cook promises to become more '**hi-tech** and **high-touch**' as it rolls out turnaround strategy and another £50m of cost cuts (*The Guardian*, subheading, 2013)

(61)   It is a simple matter of making sure you know your **dot-coms** from your **dot-co-dot-uks.** (*Neologisms*, 1999)

In (59), for instance, *Generation Y-ers* [1996] 'members of Generation Y' (OED3, see also *Generation Y* [1992]) has been used for people born in the 1980s and 1990s, regarded as having attitudes or values which are in direct contrast to those of the members of the preceding generation (*Generation X-ers* [1989]). The two compound words resemble each other from all viewpoints, yet the journalist has chosen to make their analogical relationship more explicit by presenting them as two subsequent words in a list.

Similarly, in (60), target and model are joined by a coordinator (*and*) and offered between inverted commas in the same expression. From the morphotactic viewpoint, the two compounds are different. Indeed, the model (*hi-tech* [1972]) is a clipped compound from *high technology*, whereas the target (*high-touch* [1980]) is a regular compound formed by substituting the second part (*tech* with *touch*) to designate 'direct personal contact with customers' (OED3, s.v. *high*).[1] Model and target also differ orthographically – cf. the spelling *hi* vs. *high* – but not phonologically, in that in both cases the first syllable is identically pronounced /haɪ/.

Finally, in (61) the new target *dot-co-dot-uks* [1999] is coined after the model of the preceding *dot-coms* [1994]. They denote Internet addresses for commercial

---

[1] *High-tech* is also the model for *low-tech* [1979] 'simple or basic technology' (OED3).

sites expressed in terms of the final part *.com* (*com* is shortened from *commercial*) or the British *.co.uk*. The morphological process forming the model and target words is 'symbol pronunciation', in that in both cases the symbol '.' is read expanded, as *dot*.

By contrast, examples (62)–(63) show cataphoric targets, with models which follow them in the micro-context:

(62) **Googleware**, the seamless union of **hardware** and **software**, gives the search company the largest computer system in the world and keeps it ahead of the competition. (*Neologisms*, 2006)

(63) Name: The **yummy**. Age: Young. Appearance: Urban and male. **Yummy** is a sort of acronym, like **yuppie**, or **buppie**, or ... Guppy? That's a kind of fish. (*The Guardian*, 2014)

Googleware [2006] in (62) belongs to the series of *hardware* and *software* (3.2.3 and *passim*), with an evident substitution of the first element *hard/soft* with *Google*, a proprietary name for an Internet search engine launched in 1998. The presence of an explicit model schema in this case seems more useful for providing a definition of what *Googleware* is, than for showing the exact model words on which the new target is constructed.

Similarly, in (63), the acronyms *yuppie* and *buppie* (see (58) in 6.1) are explicitly given in the text as models for the preceding *yummy* [2014], coined to refer to 'a young, urban male obsessed with personal grooming and health'. The similarity between the target and its models is primarily morphotactic: *young/black urban professional* + *-y/-ie* : *yuppie/buppie* = *young urban male* + *-y/-ie* : *yummy*. Yet, *yuppie* and *yummy* are also very close phonologically: cf. /ˈjʌ.pɪ/ with /ˈjʌ.mɪ/.

Absent model words are rarer in journalistic text. Example (64) offers a new target whose model word is not made explicit in the text:

(64) The Future Laboratory, for example, is churning them out faster than high street stores can close down. 'Chiconomic' is one of their better efforts, while 'homedulging' is just flagrant **lexploitation** (noun. Taking advantage of dire circumstances to create new words). (*The Observer*, 2009)

The blend *lexplotation* [2009], presumably from *lexicon* + *exploitation*, is modelled on similar blends, such as *sexploitation* [1924] or *blaxploitation* [1972] (3.3.2), with similarities that are not only morphotactic, but also phonological. Indeed, *lexploitation* differs from *sexploitation* only for the initial consonant sound, and this resemblance can aid the model's recoverability without a necessary intratextual reference.

6.3 The functions and effects of analogical journalistic words

The language of newspaper writers is intended to be attractive, entertaining, and effective at the same time, but also suggestive and evocative, as seen in sections 6.1–6.2. Analogy, therefore, is one of the main mechanisms that journalists use to create 1) eye-catching occasionalisms vs. 2) new terms, i.e. intended neologisms with a labelling function.

In online newspapers, in particular, reporters and journalists tend to create occasionalisms to establish a closer social connection with the reading public. In other words, the freshness of the journalist's neoformations contributes to lowering the level of discourse to informal language, and thus reinforces the writer–reader relationship.

The novel nonce words offered in (65)–(66), for instance, can help social closeness:

(65) Are you a BOurgeois BOhemian?
We've had Hippies, **Yuppies**, **Buppies** and **Dinkies**. Now it's time for the **Bobos**. Melinda Wittstock in New York reports on the rise of the new urban upper class. (*The Observer*, 2000)

(66) So now we have OTK (over the knee, generally applied to boots but can also be used for hemlines); **VPL** is well known but there is now also **VBL** (visible bra line) and **VBS** (visible bra strap) and then the particularly marvellous TFFF (too fat for fashion). (*The Guardian*, 2010)

The use of extra-grammatical model words, such as the acronyms *Yuppies* [1984], *Buppies* [1984], and *Dinkies* [1986], or the initialism *VPL* [1977] 'visible panty line' (OED2, s.v. *V*), makes the new occasionalisms modelled on them more eccentric and unconventional than regular neologisms. Like their model words, the new targets are abbreviations – specifically, a (rhyming/copy) clipped compound (*Bobo* [2010]) and an initialism (*VBL* [2010]), whereas the third initialism highlighted in (66) (*VBS* [2010]) is coined, in its turn, after *VBL*. Since the use of abbreviations, such as *Bobo* or *VBL*, is generally connected with lack of formality, the register in these extracts is more familiar than in more traditional newspapers, and the relaxed tone may make readers feel at their ease. Clippings, from a general observation of the data in chapters 4–6, are less common models than acronyms for analogical formations.

Analogical journalistic words with a denominative/labelling function are instead suitable for specialised – more formal – contexts, as observed in chapter 4. Journals are carriers of popularising innovation in science, technology, and specialised fields. Therefore, the new terminology that they offer includes intended neologisms. In (67), for instance, the acronyms *Pigs* [2010] and *Stupid* [2010] represent new labels respectively used in economics for 'an association of major emerging national economies' and 'the union of countries with deficits', as specified in this extract:

(67) First there were the '**Brics**' – Brazil, Russia, India, China – and the 'Next 11' emerging economies. Now enter the **Pigs**, or should that be **Piigs**?
The struggling European economics of Portugal, Ireland, Greece and Spain have quickly become known collectively as the **Pigs**. But there is some debate as to whether to include Italy, in which case the acronym becomes a more shrill-sounding **Piigs** ...
But as one acronym dies, another is born. Financial markets are already coining the term **Stupid** for countries with the most unwieldy deficits, and that is where the UK comes in. The new acronym stands for Spain, Turkey, United Kingdom, Portugal, Italy and Dubai. (*The Guardian*, 2010)

However, it is worth noting that, like the model *Brics* (homophonous with *bricks*),[2] these new targets are so-called "punning acronyms" or "acrostics" (Mattiello 2013: 90–91), i.e. combinations that intentionally give rise to homophones with existing words. Hence, the labels *Pigs* and *Stupid*, with different degrees and types of similarity with their model *Brics*, may help establish a more familiar tone, in spite of the specialised environment.

In addition, when newspaper articles are published on the web, the text becomes more popularised, and analogical formations with a denominative function may turn out to be unserious occasionalisms. In (68), for example, the new targets *intrapreneur* and *me-lancer* have a humorous purpose, besides having a labelling function:

(68) My thesis was that we mistakenly equate 'working for yourself' with 'being self-employed'. So what I needed was a new word to help capture this different sense.

---

[2] The homophony evokes the connotation of the building of a new anti-American force.

Had I come up with a catchy one, it is possible that the idea itself would have had longer legs. But I couldn't. I tried **'intrapreneur'**, but as is often the case, someone had already used it, to mean something else. In the end, I settled on the ugly **'me-lancer'**. No wonder the concept has sunk without trace. (*The Observer*, 2009)

The word *intrapreneur* [1978] attested in OED2 with the sense 'an employee given the freedom to work independently within a company' is created with a prefix *intra-*, after reanalysis of *entrepreneur* [1852], which is not mentioned in the text. Similarly, *me-lancer* [2009], coined on the pattern of the absent compound *freelancer* [1924], exhibits both phonological and morphological likeness with its model. Analogy is used to find a new label which can express a new concept, but the journalist's primary aim is less connected with denomination than with the readers' amusement. Hence, the function of establishing a closer social connection with the reading public appears to dominate here.

The effect that analogical journalistic words more commonly produce is indeed playfulness or fun, especially when the new targets function as echoes to model words that are either explicitly mentioned in the text or implied, or when their formation involves reanalysis.

An example of punning is provided in (69), where the author plays on the model word *ebooks*, and offers a series of analogical formations which exhibit the same combining form *e-* (from *electronic*, see 3.3.1):

(69) If **ebooks** have **ejackets** then I can perhaps add an **ewarning** about **ebloody estrong elanguage**. All we can hope for in the lead up to publication is that Colin goes **e-asy** on us. (*The Guardian*, 2003)

Here the journalist shows that the *e-* combining form can be used to form not only new analogical nouns (*ejackets, ewarning, elanguage*), but also ungrammatical adjectives (*estrong*), and even intensifiers (*ebloody*). Moreover, the nonce word *e-asy* involves reinterpretation of the initial letter of the adjective *easy* as a combining form. Thus, unlike other cases that involve reinterpretation of the model word before analogy applies, this case involves reanalysis of the target. Indeed, *e-asy* is not a new complex word coined on the model *e-* series, but an existing word resegmented as complex and meant to echo the preceding series. In other words, it is a purely orthographic analogy.

The overall effect produced by ungrammatical nonce words, such as *estrong*, and morphological resegmentation, as in *e-asy*, is punning. Therefore, the (pseudo-)morphological similarity among the novel words in (69) can capture readers' curiosity, and amuse them because of grammatical anomaly.

6.4 Distribution of analogical journalistic words

This section shows the distribution and frequency of the analogical journalistic words mentioned in this chapter in COCA and the *TIME Magazine Corpus* (abbreviated in Table 8 as TMC). Despite its smaller size (100 million words), the latter corpus is more pertinent in this case than GloWbE (1.9 billion words) used for corpus analysis in Tables 6–7.

The approach adopted for Table 8 is again a combination of automated corpus analysis to retrieve all items and close reading of all occurrences in context to detect their exact meaning and pertinence. For instance, the acrostic *Escort* could be confused with the homophonous noun meaning 'bodyguard, etc.', or with Ford's Eurocar.

In general, the lemmata rather than the inflected forms have been the object of quantitative analysis, with the exception of some acronyms in which the final *s* either stands for the name of a country (*Pigs* ← *Portugal, Ireland, Greece, and Spain*) or is a plural concept (*Mads* ← *mums and dads*).

Moreover, for converted verbs such as *eBay* and *waitlist*, an automated query selecting the PoS (Part-of-Speech) was possible.

Tab. 8: New analogical journalistic words (Anaphoric vs. Cataphoric) and their frequency in COCA and TIME Magazine Corpus

New words	COCA					TMC	Model	
	Spok	Fic	Mag	News	Acad		Ana	Cata
alphabetism								
beefalo		4/0.04		1/0.01		2/0.02		
black-collar								
Blairese								
bobo			2/0.02		2/0.02			
boyth								
buppie	1/0.01	4/0.04	7/0.07	1/0.01		2/0.02		
café-bar								
coyth								
cyberbar	3/0.03			1/0.01			1/0.001	

New words	COCA					TMC	Model	
	Spok	Fic	Mag	News	Acad		Ana	Cata
dairy-free	3/0.03		248/2.81	15/0.17		2/0.02	5/0.009	4/0.007
dot-co-dot-uk								
e-asy								
eBay (v)								
ebloody								
ejacket								
elanguage								
e-portfolio					27/0.30		1/0.001	
-ercise	3/0.03	4/0.04	15/0.17	19/0.21	4/0.04	8/0.08		
Escort								
estrong								
ewarning								
Generation Y	5/0.05		26/0.29	43/0.48	12/0.13	6/0.06	12/0.02	2/0.003
Googleware								
greyth								
high-touch	1/0.01		6/0.06	5/0.05	4/0.04		4/0.007	
intrapreneur			2/0.02			1/0.01		
lexploitation								
-licious	10/0.11	30/0.34	49/0.55	41/0.46		10/0.1		
Mads								
me-lancer								
nimf-ism								
-(o)rama	5/0.05	6/0.06	22/0.25	42/0.47	8/0.09	29/0.29		
Orchid								
Pigs								
politisoap								
refoliate			2/0.02					
shockvertising								
Stupid								
-tainment	27/0.30	4/0.04	75/0.85	42/0.47	18/0.20	46/0.46		1/0.001

New words	COCA					TMC	Model	
	Spok	Fic	Mag	News	Acad		Ana	Cata
tween	21/0.24	5/0.05	67/0.76	51/0.57	2/0.02	1/0.01	3/0.005	3/0.005
VBL								
VBS								
wait-list (v)								
yuffer								
yummy								

The data reported in Table 8 shows the distribution of the journalistic terms selected for qualitative analysis in COCA and *TIME Magazine*.

The findings confirm that media language is overflowing with occasionalisms, which are coined on the spot and used only once by the journalists to attract their readers and be innovative or amusing. More specifically, 67.39% of the terms under examination are neither attested in COCA nor in the *TIME Magazine*, including regular formations, such as *Blairese*, *Googleware*, *alphabetism*, and *café-bar*, the latter two being nonetheless in the OED. Occasionalisms abound, especially blends (e.g. *lexploitation*, *politisoap*, *shockvertising*), acronyms (e.g. *yuffer*, *yummy*), and initialisms (e.g. *VBL*, *VBS*). Nor are there occurrences of acrostics with a denominative function, such as *Pigs* or *Stupid*, in corpus analysis, at least with the sense used by the reporter in example (67). Of course, words such as *Mads* or *Orchid* occur frequently in both corpora, but not as acronyms. *Tween* also occurs frequently, but often, especially in the *TIME Magazine Corpus*, as a fore-clipping for *between* rather than as a back-clipping for *tweenager*. The acronym *yummy* is attested 592 times in COCA, but only once (0.002 pmw) as an acronym for *Young Urban Marxist Manager* (cf. (63)).

Derived words with unproductive suffixes, such as *coyth*, *greyth*, and *boyth* (the latter ungrammatical), are clearly used as nonce terms in media language, whereas words such as *ejacket* or *ebloody*, in spite of their regular formation from a combining form *e-*, are mere puns. The orthographic analogy *e-asy* is not attested with hyphenation.

Of the remaining 32.60% words, especially attested in magazines and newspapers, nearly 9% are either combining forms (e.g. *-licious*, *-(o)rama*, *-tainment*) or recurrent splinters (i.e. *-ercise*). It is worth noting that *-licious* and *-tainment* are two combining forms that journalistic language shares with the language of adolescents. However, these forms are less frequent in the *TIME Magazine Corpus* (*-licious* 10 occurrences/0.1 pmw, *-tainment* 46 occurrences/0.46 pmw) than in GloWbE (respectively, 513/0.27 pmw and 1,034/0.54 pmw occurrences), partly due to the smaller size of the former corpus compared to the latter, as shown by normalised frequencies.

As for the model words, they rarely co-occur with their targets in corpora, with anaphoric analogies which clearly dominate over cataphoric ones.

The data of Table 8 is visualised in Figure 7, which includes all the new analogical words in the table.

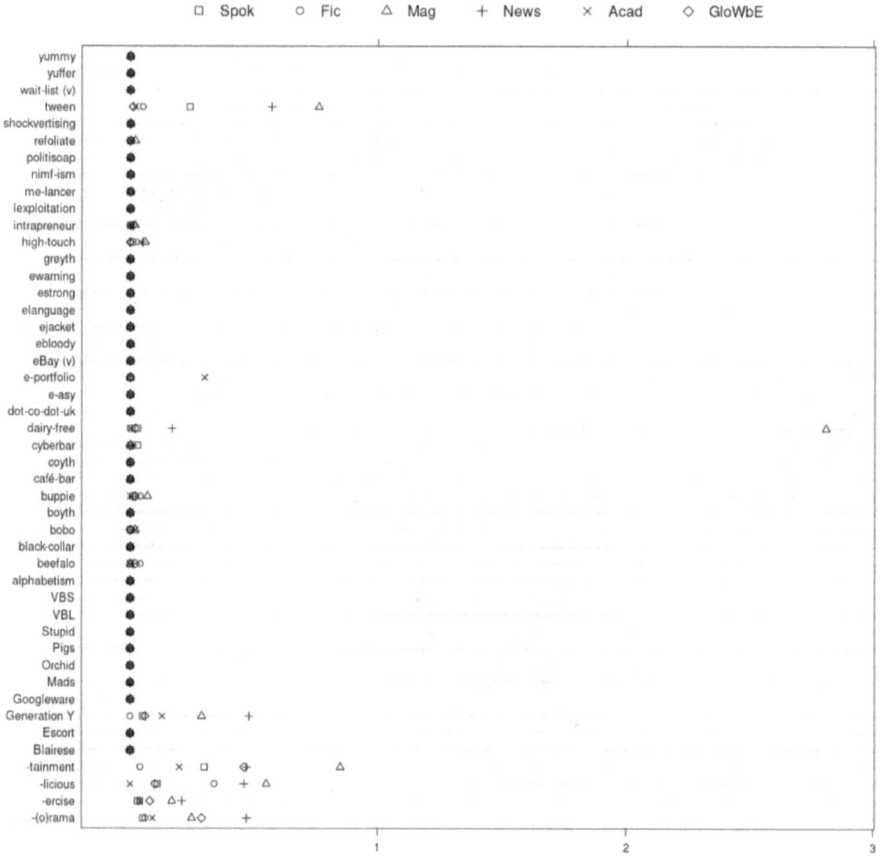

Fig. 7: Visualisation of all data from Table 8

Figure 8 is a selection of the most frequent words in Table 8.

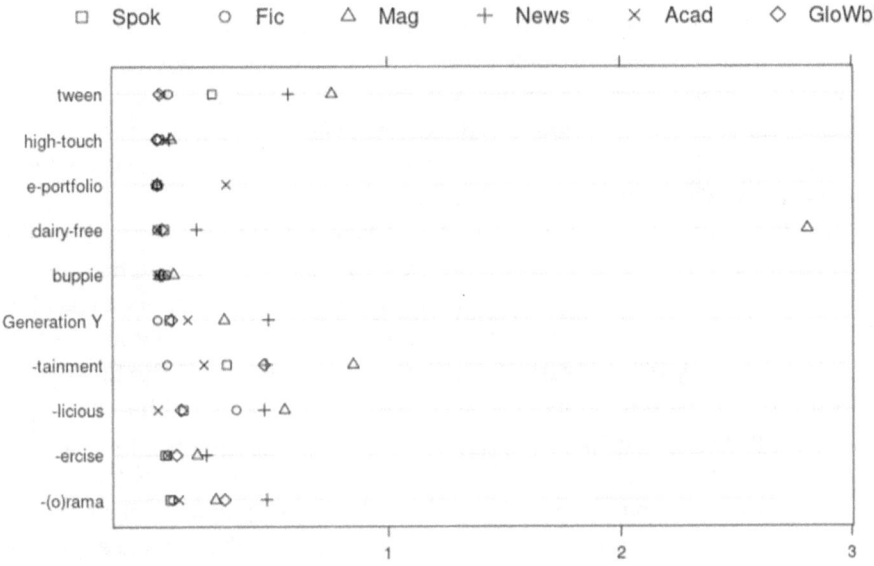

Fig. 8: Visualisation of the most frequent words in Table 8

6.5 Final remarks on analogy in journalistic words

This examination of journalistic language in the press, especially in online newspaper archives and collections of journalistic texts, has confirmed that analogy is a central mechanism of word-formation for the new terminology coined by journalists. Indeed, journalists tend to use analogy to create novel words, above all occasionalisms that belong to grammatical, extra- and un-grammatical morphology. As for types of analogy (6.1), surface analogy frequently occurs in newspaper articles, and analogy via schema is primarily obtained by means of combining forms or frequent blend splinters. The innovative character of newspaper vocabulary is clearly shown by 1) productive processes that apply to irregular bases (*ebloody*), 2) unproductive processes that apply to unusual bases (*boyth*), making the whole formation ungrammatical, or 3) a combination of extra-grammatical base and regular derivation (*nimf-ism*).

For occasionalisms, journalists prefer to show their new analogical formations in combination with the model words which trigger them (6.2), generally in the same context or micro-context. The model's recoverability is essential for extra- or un-grammatical targets, because the presence of the model word helps readers' comprehension and facilitates interpretation. Endophoric reference to the model word can be either anaphoric or cataphoric, but the distance between target and model commonly remains within the paragraph range. The exophoric (situational) context may, on some occasions, favour the association between the new target and its model. For instance, in (68), specialised terminology, such as the term *self-employed* mentioned in the extract, may build a situation where the context is related to economics, thus facilitating the interpretation of *intrapreneur* and *me-lancer* after absent *entrepreneur* and *freelancer*.

The presence of the model word in journalistic texts is also essential from the pragmatic viewpoint, in that most new targets are plays or puns on their model words, series, or word families. Indeed, one of the focal effects of analogical formations in the press is playfulness, which is often obtained by humorous allusion to the model word, which is distorted, resegmented, or reanalysed to function as word-formation pattern for the new target (see *nimf-ism*, *e-asy*). Other pragmatic functions include the creation of social closeness with the reading public and the attraction of readers' interest (6.3). To lay more emphasis on the new targets and focus readers' attention on them, journalists often use typographical strategies, such as single quotation marks (e.g. *'hi-tech and high-touch'*, *'me-lancer'*) or hyphens (*e-asy*). The latter is an especially useful marker of reanalysis.

All functions converge in making media language more innovative than many other genres, such as scientific articles or academic handbooks. However, compared to juvenile language, where novelty and originality are more central as functions (5.3), in journalistic language innovation is more prone to create new labels (*yuffer*, *Pigs*, *Orchid*), and possibly new terms which may become stable in the future. In this respect, journalistic language is comparable to scientific and specialised language (4.3).

7 Analogy in literary works

In literary works, writers often exploit the power of analogy to colour their language with neoformations, and poets or dramatists may create novel words, principally for rhetorical purposes. As observed by Salmon (1987), analogy was also widely used by William Shakespeare. For instance, in *Troilus & Cressida*, Shakespeare coined *exposure* [1609] 'the state or fact of being subjected to any external influence' (OED2) – "To weaken our discredit, our *exposure*" (i. iii. 195) – after the model of *enclosure* [1574]. By contrast, in *Coriolanus*, he experimented with another version of the word *exposure* – i.e. †*exposture* [a1616] – in "A wilde *exposture*, to each chance" (iv. i. 37), formed by analogy with *posture* [a1586], *composture* [1614], etc. (OED2).

Shakespeare's novel words have been a cornerstone for the English lexicon and its enrichment, via analogy, although most of these words have remained mere occasionalisms. For instance, in some of his dramas, Shakespeare used the word *fathered* [1608] 'having a father' (OED2), which is labelled as a "rare" adjective in the OED. Its origin is analogical, from its antonym *fatherless* [?c1225] ("*Father'd* he is, and yet he's *fatherless*", *Macbeth*, in Salmon 1987: 199). But it also acted as model word for its analogical co-hyponym *husbanded* [a1616] ("Thinke you, I am no stronger than my Sex Being so *Father'd*, and so *Husbanded*?", *Julius Caesar*, ii. i. 296). In addition, the new compound *sun-beamed eyes* served in Shakespeare's comedy *Love's Labour's Lost* as model for a comparable compound: "Once to beholde with your *sun-beamed eyes* ... You were best call it '*daughter-beamed eyes*'" (Salmon 1987: 199). Nonetheless, the model compound †*sun-beamed* [1598] has been labelled an "obsolete" novel word in OED2 (only in Shakespeare), whereas its target *daughter-beamed* [1598] has remained an occasionalism.[1]

Shakespeare also used existing model words to create Latinate novel words (see Garner 1987: 220). A relevant case modelled on *speechless* [a1000] and *tongueless* [1447] is *languageless* [1609] 'without language' (OED2), firstly used in *Troilus & Cressida* ("Hees growne a very land-fish *languagelesse*, a monster", iii. iii. 256). More recently, other authors have reused this analogical word: e.g., Nathaniel Hawthorne ("Toolless, houseless, *languageless*, except for a few guttural sounds", *Our Old Home*, 1863, I. 28) and Steven Pinker ("here is no record

---

1 See Boase-Beier (1987) for more on poetic compounds, especially in modern English poets. See Neuhaus (1989) for more on Shakespeare's neologisms.

DOI 10.1515/978-3-11-055141-9

that a region has served as a 'cradle' of language from which it spread to previously *languageless* groups", *Language instinct*, 1994, ii. 26).

It is worth noting that the types of analogy – e.g., grammatical vs. un-/extragrammatical – that intervene in novel word-formation may vary from literary genre to literary genre and from author to author. In this regard, Salmon (1987) has observed that Shakespeare's lexical creativity was mainly directed towards poetic or dramatic – rather than grammatical – ends. In other terms, rather than using word-formation with a grammatical or lexical function, he used it for metrical reasons, such as adjusting the words' length to the requirements of the verse (e.g. *vasty* [1598] substituted *vast* in *vasty deepe*, Salmon 1987: 196). For this reason, Shakespeare's analogical novel words are different from prose authors' ones.

In general, many literary analogical formations seem to be governed by what has been called "Poetische Lizenz" (Dressler and Panagl 2007). In poetry and prose, indeed, novel words are often motivated by some literary purpose and/or accepted because of the author's authority. Thus, Boase-Beier (1987: 2–3) has introduced the concept of "deviation" (vs. linguistic norms), according to which poetic and literary language is "the result of an interaction of certain poetic principles with the grammar of standard language". For instance, Shakespeare's *vasty* can be seen as a deviation from rules of word-formation, specifically of derivation, because an adjectival suffix -*y* is added to an adjective, whereas James Thurber's *kissgranny* deviates from compounding norms, in that the Verb + Noun pattern is productive in Romance languages, but unproductive in English (Dressler 1993: 5028).

For the analysis of literary analogies, in the present chapter two different authors have been selected: namely, an English poet – Gerard Manley Hopkins (1844–1889) – and an Irish novelist – James Augustine Aloysius Joyce (1882–1941). As we will see, deviation occurs in both authors, but especially in Joyce's novel *Finnegans Wake* (1939), where nonce words are often the result of anomaly. Unlike previous chapters where specialised, juvenile, or journalistic analogies are presented in general, here Hopkins' analogies (7.1) are kept distinct and analysed separately from Joyce's ones (7.2).

7.1 Analogy in Gerald Manley Hopkins

Gerald Manley Hopkins was principally a poet, so his poems have been the primary source of neologisms and occasionalisms. However, he was also the author of journals, papers, notebooks, and letters, where he provided additional examples of analogical new words. Hence, I have explored most of his works in search of analogy, although his poems remain the focus of this section. Unless otherwise specified, the examples discussed in 7.1.1–7.1.3 refer to the 1967 edition of the *Poems* (the lines are given in round brackets) and are all attested in the OED.

7.1.1 Types of analogy

As far as types of analogy are concerned, Hopkins' works predominantly offer cases of surface analogy which do not deviate from norms of word-formation. Grammatical analogies proliferate in his *Poems*, especially in the form of compounds. For instance, the compound *fire-folk* [1877] "O look at all the *fire-folk* sitting in the air!" (66) (OED2, s.v. *fire*) shares its head with model words such as *countryfolk* [c1325] or *townfolk* [c1325], while *martyr-master* [1876] is modelled on regular *martyr-maid* [1854], with a shared non-head component:

(70)　Thy unchancelling poising palms were weighing the worth, Thou **martyr-master**. (58)

Another relevant example is the adjective *ill-balanced* [1864] used in "The clouds come, like *ill-balanced* crags" (118) and modelled on its opposite *well-balanced* [a1616] (cf. the pair *ill-intentioned–well-intentioned*).

Grammatical surface analogies also occur in derivation. For example, the derived adjective *museless* [1644] 'uninspired' (OED3, "My mind is dull and *museless*", *Further Letters*, 159) is regularly created as the antonym of the model word *museful* [1597]. By contrast, the adverb *leafmeal* [c1880] 'with leaves fallen one by one' (OED2, s.v. *leaf*, "Though worlds of wanwood *leafmeal* lie", 89) is obtained by adding the unproductive suffix *-meal* to a noun base (OED3), after †*flock-meal* [c893] and †*drop-meal* [c1000].

A deviation in morphological inflection is in Hopkins' *Further Letters*, where he creates an irregular past form of the verb *comprehend* ("She *comprehood* who I was by my photographeme", 1864, 211), probably on the model of the strong paradigm of *understand–understood–understood*, not with a pure rime, but identical syllable coda and same prosodic structure.[2]

Remarkably, Hopkins' poetic new words are often his model for other analogical nonce words. For instance, *May-mess* [1867] used in "Look, look: a *May-mess*, like on orchard boughs!" (67) is the model word after which he forms *May-hope* [a1889] found in "*May-hope* of our darkened ways!" (38).

---

[2] Since the verbs *comprehend* and *understand* are often used synonymously, Hopkins' *comprehood* could also be interpreted as a blend of *comprehended* and *understood*.

A comparable case is the obsolete adjective †*passion-pastured* [c1865] only found in Hopkins' verse "How turn my *passion-pastured* thought" (125). This functions as model word for his †*passion-plunged* [1876] found in "Our *passion-plungèd* giant risen" (62). In both cases, similarity is between the non-head components. Moreover, in his *Journals and Papers*, he has coined both the model *inscape* [1868] 'the individual or essential quality of a thing' (OED2) and its target *outscape* [1868] 'the outward appearance of a region' (OED3).

Analogy via schema is another type of analogy that we can observe in Hopkins' works. For instance, *lovescape* [1876] 'view, depiction, or evocation of love' (OED3)[3] and *waterscape* [1826] 'a view or piece of scenery consisting largely of water' (OED3) are neologisms respectively used in his *Poems* and *Letters to Robert Bridges*, after the series *city-scape, riverscape, sea-scape*, etc. (see the combining form *-scape* already discussed in 3.3.1).[4] Another series with the cranberry morph *yester-* is *yesterday, yesternight, yestermorning*, etc. (3.3.1), to which Hopkins adds *yester-tempest* [1888]:

(71)   Delightfully the bright wind boisterous ropes, wrestles, beats earth bare
       Of **yestertempest**'s creases. (105)

Another case of analogy via schema is provided by the Pronoun *she* + Noun pattern, which is often used in compounds to modify animals' names (*she-wolf* [c1450], *she-lion* [1568], *she-dog* [1624]), or common gender nouns, such as *she dancer* [1624], *she-doctor* [1775], or *she-cousin* [1808], to indicate the female counterpart. In Hopkins' *Sermons and Devotional Writings*, *she-being* [1881] is opposed to *she-man* [1640]:

(72)   The woman, that is **she-being**, not she-man, of the Apocalypse. (170)

In Hopkins' *Further Letters*, the pattern *ready* + infinitive Verb, as in the adjective *ready-to-perish* [1855], is the model for his *ready-to-read* [1887]:

---

[3] According to the OED, both *outscape* and *lovescape* are apparently modelled on the unique model of *inscape* [1868]. However, whereas the semantic connection between *in* and *out* is closer, the etymology of *lovescape* is clearly from the series ending in *-scape*.

[4] The word *scape* is also used independently in Hopkins, in the sense of 'a reflection or impression of the individual quality of a thing or action' (OED2). Hence, his *scapeless* [1874] in "Scapeless aimless background of tapestry, a cannon, and so on" (*Journals and Papers*, 245) is coined to refer to something 'without distinctive and individual quality'.

(73) Publishers 'tapped a stratum' ... of almost untouched reading or **ready-to-read** public. (379)

Cf., later *ready-to-use* [1893], *ready-to-serve* [1935], *ready-to-cook* [1959], etc. constituting a word family (OED3, s.v. *ready*).

Therefore, many of Hopkins' analogical formations are regular compounds or derived words obtained on the model of other well-formed words. He often provides both the model and the target of analogical formation, but both are regularly created according to productive word-formation rules. However, analogy may also be connected with ungrammatical formations in his poetry. For instance, an illegal formation is in the following extract from *The Note-books and Papers of Gerard Manley Hopkins*:

(74) He would raise man ... infinitely above **manself** to the divine justice. (271)

The target *manself* [1880] 'the natural state or condition of a human being' (OED3), modelled on *himself* [eOE], is ungrammatical and well illustrates his deviation from rules of word-formation.

7.1.2 Types of target–model relationship

In Gerald Manley Hopkins' works, the relationship between the target and the model is generally explicit. In Ladányi's (2000: 18) terminology, his surface analogies are often "in context", in that the (micro-)context frequently provides the model word along with the analogical formation.

The model is usually specified earlier in the text – with an anaphoric relationship with the target – and this helps both the model's recoverability and the target's understanding. Anaphoric analogy occurs, for instance, in his *Sermons and Devotional Writings*:

(75) Sloth, in some sense sin of frailty, inaction, only appearing not so much in **non-resistance** to evil as in **non-execution** of good. (133)

where the prefixed noun *non-execution* [1883] 'the omission or failure to execute a law or perform a task' (OED3) is formed after previous *non-resistance* [1748].

It also occurs in the Preface to Hopkins' *Poems*:

(76) The poems in this book are written some in **Running Rhythm**, the common rhythm in English use, some in **Sprung Rhythm**, and some in a mixture of the two. (1)

where the expression *Running Rhythm* [a1887] used to label the conventional English poetic metre is probably the model for the analogical new term *Sprung Rhythm* [1877] 'a poetic metre which approximates to the rhythm of speech' (OED2, s.v. *sprung*), although the OED gives an earlier attestation for the latter.

By contrast, in one of Hopkins' *Poems*, the new verb *disremember* [1815] 'to forget' (OED2) cataphorically anticipates the model *dismember* [1297]:

(77) Qúite **Disremembering, dismémbering** áll now. (97)

with an evident phonological and morphotactic similarity between the two.

Another example of cataphoric analogy is provided in this extract from *The Letters of Gerard Manley Hopkins to Robert Bridges*:

(78) Two strains of thought ... the **overthought** that which everybody, editors, see ... which might for instance be abridged or paraphrased ... the other, the **underthought**, conveyed chiefly in the choice of metaphors etc. used and often only half realised by the poet himself. (105)

Here the prefixed noun †*overthought* [1883] 'conscious thought' (OED3) has been created as the opposite of *underthought* [1602], attested earlier in the OED. Besides morphotactic and phonological similarity, in this case target and model also exhibit a semantic connection of antonymy (*over-* vs. *under-*).

On some occasions, Hopkins is the coiner of two nonce words which resemble each other and appear together, in the same micro-text (the second extract is from *The Journals and Papers of Gerard Manley Hopkins*):

(79) Tongue true, **vaunt-** and **tauntless**. (82)

(80) The others [pigeons] are dull **thundercolour** or **black-grape-colour**. (232)

For instance, from the morphotactic viewpoint, the adjectives *vauntless* [c1879] and *tauntless* [c1879] in (79), modelled on *dauntless* [a1616] mentioned in the previous verse, share the same privative suffix *-less*, and, from the phonological viewpoint, they share the rime of the stressed syllable /ɔːnt/ and the entire unstressed syllable /lɪs/. However, the nouns *thundercolour* [1873] and *black-grape-*

colour [1873] in (80) share above all the second compound head constituent *colour*, but the latter has a multiword lexical unit (*black grape*) as first constituent. In these cases, however, it is difficult to determine which is the model and which is the target, since the creation of these words is probably simultaneous and only attested in Hopkins.

Examples of "surface analogy without context" (Ladányi 2000: 18), that is, analogy which makes reference to an external – exophoric – model word, are frequent, although disambiguation of the target is in this case obstructed by the absence of an explicit model. Some examples of exophoric analogy are in (81)–(85):[5]

(81) The grey lawns cold where gold, where **quickgold** lies! (66)

(82) Mary's photographs are of Snowdon, Cadair Idris, and Valley Crucis Abbey: in the foreground of the last is the **show-woman** Miss Lloyd in her green shade, a quaint old character. (147)

(83) The youngest boy Leo is a remarkably winning **sweetmannered** young fellow. (183)

(84) And this whether I speak of human nature or of my individuality, my **self-being**. (122)

(85) In returning the sky in the west was in a great wide winged or shelved rack of **rice-white** fine pelleted fretting. (216)

Hopkins' novel compounds generally share one of the two components with their model. In (81), for instance, *quickgold* [1877] 'liquid gold' (OED3, s.v. *quick*) shares its non-head with *quicksilver* [eOE] 'the liquid metal mercury' (OED3), but is also anaphoric with previous *gold*. A comparable case is exophoric *show-woman* [1820] 'a woman who conducts a show' (OED2, s.v. *show*), created after *showman* [1742]. By contrast, in (83)–(85), the new words share their head with their models, namely *good-mannered* [1715] → *sweetmannered* [1887], *well-being* [1561] → *self-being* [1587] 'independent existence' (OED2), and *snow-white* [c1000] (as adjective) → *rice-white* [1856].

---

5 Examples (82)–(83) are from *Further Letters of Gerald Manley Hopkins*, (84) is from *Sermons and Devotional Writings*, (85) from *The Journals and Papers of Gerard Manley Hopkins*. (81) is from the *Poems*.

7.1.3 Functions and effects

Hopkins' analogical words are essentially created for poetic purposes. His novel words have two primary functions. One of them is condensing meaning in the length of the verse. In particular, his novel compound words allow the expression of condensed meaning, thus complying with the number of syllables and stresses of the poetic metre. Some examples of new compounds are reported in (86)–(89):

(86) Stigma, signal, cinquefoil token For lettering of the lamb's fleece, rud-dying of the **rose-flake**. (58)

(87) Which, lightening o'er the body **rosy-pale**, Like shiver'd rubies dance. (10)

(88) Not that the **sweet-fowl, song-fowl,** needs no rest. (71)

(89) **Star-eyed strawberry-breasted** Throstle. (77)

The novel word *rose-flake* [1876] in (86),[6] probably modelled on *snowflake* [1734], with an identical stressed syllable nucleus /əʊ/, is a disyllabic creative formation which suits Hopkins' poetry, as well as the neologism *rosy-pale* [1862] in (87),[7] coined after the family of compound adjectives expressing colour and tone (e.g. *rosy bright* [1725], *rosy-purple* [1770], *rosy-white* [1832], *rosy-crimson* [1845], etc.). The non-head component *rosy* is a key word in the poem "A Vision of the Mermaids". It is repeated eight times in the poem, as well as in *rosy-pale*, either in compound adjectives (*rosy turn'd, rosy-lipp'd, rosy-budded*) or in noun phrases (*rosy weed, rosy foam, rosy floating cloud, rosy isles*). Hence, it functions as a central concept referring back (anaphorically) and forward (cataphorically) to related concepts.

According to the OED, the poetic occasionalism *song-fowl* [1877] in (88) is created after *song-bird* [1774], with identity of the non-head component, but it may also be the target of the antecedent model *sweet-fowl* [1877], with a shared head component. Whether or not *song-fowl* belongs to the word set *song-X* or *X-fowl*,

---

[6] The noun *rose-flake* has been reused by D. M. Wright (*Irish Heart*, 1918, 41, "But no wind the near air stirred. Lightly as a spoken word Breathed within a lover's ear Dropt *rose-flakes* my casement near.", OED3, s.v. *rose*).

[7] Later also in *New York Magazine* (1978, 3 April, "The terrine de poisson, a *rosy-pale* slice of fish pâté.", OED3, s.v. *rosy*).

meaning in this verse is condensed as a result of the two nonce words *sweet-fowl* and *song-fowl*.

Two further novel words are in (89), where a thrush is described as *star-eyed* [1646], a neologism attested in other authors, and *strawberry-breasted* [1878], only in Hopkins. Both parasynthetic compounds acquire a simulative sense, but the former is coined, according to the OED, after *star-wise* [1608] (cf. later *star-leaved* [1711] and *star-shaped* [1861]), whereas the latter is probably after *strawberry-coloured* [1688] and *strawberry-like* [1862]. A model word family *X-breasted* also exists which may have functioned as model for *strawberry-breasted*, but the non-head component is again a key word in the line, producing alliteration of the syllable onset /st/.

Another function of Hopkins' analogies is, indeed, producing alliteration or rhyme, especially in his *Poems*. An emblematic example is the neologism *sloggering* [1876] in (90):

(90) The inboard seas run swirling and hawling; The rash smart **sloggering** brine Blinds her. (57)

It belongs to the phonaesthetic series of *slide* [a950], *slither* [c1200], and so on, with an initial cluster *sl-* suggesting the idea of "sliding movement" (Mattiello 2013: 203). This is the interpretation given to the word by J. Milroy in *The language of Gerard Manley Hopkins* (1977): "Certainly imitative, belonging to phonaesthetic series (*slither*, etc.), a derivative (*slog*, etc.), and a blend ... Complex associations suggest the meaning: 'dashing (against the ship) repeatedly and drawing back with a sucking gurgling noise'." (OED2). Furthermore, the word contributes to the alliteration of initial /s/ in *seas ... swirling ... smart sloggering*. Rhyme among *swirling*, *hawling*, and *sloggering* reinforces the musicality of the verse.

In another of his *Poems*, "The Loss of the Eurydice", Hopkins has also generated the compound *Walsingham Way* [c1878] (from the name of a town in Norfolk), modelled on its synonym *Milky Way* [c1450] (suggested by the antecedent *Milk*):

(91) That a starlight-wender of ours would say The marvellous Milk was **Walsingham Way**. (75)

The alliteration of initial /w/ in this neologism contributes to the rhythm of these verses, and echoes other words showing the same sound (*wender*, *would*, *was*). Other authors have used this compound noun, among whom James Joyce, in

Ulysses ("The waggoner's star: *Walsingham way*: the chariot of David: the annular cinctures of Saturn", 1922, 653, in OED2).

It is probably for the same reason – i.e. alliteration of initial /s/ in *spirit* and *sours* – that Hopkins coins the occasionalism *selfyeast* [a1889], on the model of *self-want* [1669] and *self-taste* [1880] (the latter again in Hopkins) in the verse provided in (92):

(92)　**Selfyeast** of spirit a dull dough sours. (101)

7.2 Analogy in James Joyce

James Joyce was considered to be one of the most influential writers in the modernist avant-garde of the early twentieth century. Of his numerous works, the novel *Finnegans Wake* (1939) has been selected for the analysis of analogy because of its innovative character and experimental language. In this novel, Joyce creates many nonce words that are borderline between morphologically motivated formations and grammatical anomalies. Many neologisms and occasionalisms are mere word distortions, with vowel or consonant changes/insertions in respect to their original words, such as the Hibernicism *illigant* [1819] 'elegant' (OED2), attested in several authors before Joyce, or the anomaly *refreskment* [1939], with a cluster /sk/ that substitutes /ʃ/, probably influenced by Italian *rinfresco* 'refreshment'. Others, by contrast, are (regular) formations modelled on existing compounds or derived words. The focus in the next sub-section is both on neologisms and on occasionalisms.

7.2.1 Types of analogy

Joyce's novel *Finnegans Wake* offers various types of analogy. The type that we have defined surface analogy is illustrated, for instance, by grammatical compounds. Examples include the compound noun *bookstaff* [OE] 'a letter of the alphabet' (OED3), which is modelled on (and literally translated from) German *Buchstabe* (with the same meaning), probably also influenced by *roun-staff* [OE] 'a runic letter or symbol' (OED3, s.v. †*roun*), and the adverb *nowanights* [1672] 'at night at the present time' (OED3), created after *nowadays* [?1387]. The well-established analogical compound *ear-witness* [1539] is likewise used in his novel (see 1.2):

(93)　Our cubehouse still rocks as **earwitness** to the thunder of his arafatas ... (p. 4)

As far as derived words are concerned, in *Finnegans Wake* the noun *sonny* [1850] 'a small boy' (OED2) appears immediately before its model *sissy* [1846] 'a sister' (OED2), and both exhibit a suffix *-y/-ie* used to form pet names and familiar hypocoristics (see also the antecedent *mabby* and *sammy*):

(94)   ... Holispolis went to Parkland with mabby and sammy and **sonny** and **sissy** and mop's varlet de shambles and all to find the right place for it by peep o'skirt or pipe a skirl ... (p. 446)

Another grammatical surface analogy involves the process of conversion or zero-derivation. In "He would *pen* for her, he would *pine* for her" (p. 400), Joyce uses the noun *pen* [1904] 'to use a pen, to write' (OED3) with a verbal syntactic function, by analogy with *pine* (noun and, in the above-mentioned sentence, converted verb).

Surface analogies in *Finnegans Wake* may also entail the process of reanalysis. For instance, in the creation of *spattee* [1926] ← *spat*, 'an outer stocking or legging worn by women for protection against wet and cold' (OED2), the model *puttee* [1882] (from Hindi *paṭṭī* 'bandage') has been reinterpreted, by folk-etymology, as having a patient suffix *-ee*, as if from *to put*.

In *Finnegans Wake*, surface analogies may also entail extra-grammatical operations. The extract in (95), for instance, offers relevant cases of reduplication:

(95)   Here, and it goes on to appear now, she comes, a peacefugle, a parody's bird, a peri potmother, a pringlpik in the ilandiskippy, with peewee and **powwows** in **beggybaggy** on her bickybacky and a flick flask **fleckflinging** its pixylighting pacts' huemeramybows, picking here, pecking there, pussypussy plunderpussy. (p. 12)

This passage is entirely constructed on sound symbolism, especially on reduplicatives and words consisting of meaningful phonaesthemes, as well as on alliterating labials: namely, /p/, /b/, and /f/. An analogical rhyming reduplicative is *powwow* [1939],[8] which exhibits the same consonant alternation as its antecedent model *peewee* [1793]. The ablaut reduplicative *beggybaggy* [1939], however, seems to reproduce the following *bickybacky* [1939], although the prototypical alternation /ɪ/ ~ /æ/ is slightly modified into /e/ ~ /æ/. In this case, it is difficult to

---

[8] The word *powwow* has been attested in the OED since 1624, but the meaning 'a priest, shaman, or healer' is completely unrelated to Joyce's context. Here the word is clearly modelled on its coordinated noun, with vowel substitution.

establish if the model word is *beggybaggy* or, as stated, *bickybacky* (neither attested in the OED), yet the prototypicality of the latter occasionalism makes it a more potential candidate for the model role.

In (95), analogy is also in the creation of the nonce term *fleckflinging* [1939], probably after the model words *flick* [1447] and †*flask* [a1300]. These words indeed exhibit an initial phonaestheme *fl-* /fl/, which is generally associated with 'phenomena of movement, flying, flowing', as in the series consisting of *flag*, *flee*, *flow*, *fly*, etc. (Mattiello 2013: 203). The echo word *fleckflinging* also constitutes an irregular exception, in that the second vowel is generally more back and lower than the first one.

The type of analogy via schema is illustrated in Joyce's novel by a parasynthetic derivative – in "To anyone who knew and loved the christlikeness of the big *cleanminded* giant H. C. Earwicker" (p. 44) –, which follows the pattern of the word family with the *clean-* adjective as first member: e.g., *clean-legged* [1568], *clean-armed* [1592], and so on (OED2).

Furthermore, in the passage reported in (96), Joyce creates a new word family with the *-little* adjective as second member:

(96) It's a **candlelittle** houthse of a month and one windies. Downadown, High Downadown. And nummered quaintlymine. And such reasonable weather too! The wagrant wind's awalt'zaround the piltdowns and on every blasted knollyrock (if you can spot fifty I spy four more) there's that gnarlybird ygathering, a **runalittle, doalittle, preealittle, pouralittle, wipealittle, kicksalittle, severalittle, eatalittle, whinealittle, kenalittle, helfalittle, pelfalittle** gnarlybird. (p. 12)

The word family also includes sentence compounds (*run-a-little* [1939], *do-a-little* [1939], etc.) and nonce words such as *candlelittle* [1939], in which the adjective irregularly follows the referring noun.

In addition, Joyce creates ungrammatical analogies. An example is the adverb *faithly* [a1375] 'indeed, certainly, surely' (OED3) in "I *faithly* sincerely believe so indeed" (p. 676). This poetic neologism recorded in other authors, both before and after Joyce, represents a deviation from derivation rules. In particular, instead of adding the adverbial suffix *-ly* to an adjective, as in *faithful-ly* [a1382] and *sincere-ly* [1597] (used in the micro-context), Joyce adds the suffix to a nominal base, departing from regularity and predictability, but motivated by his poetic licence.

The author's licence also motivates his deviation from the norms of inflection. As for nominal inflection, he coins the noun *strongers* [1939] – an occasionalism only found in Joyce – to indicate 'strong drinks' (OED2):

(97) Swiping rums and beaunes and sherries and ciders and negus and citronnades too. The **strongers**. (p. 79)

Therefore, he adds the plural suffix *-s* to the comparative form of an adjective (*strong-er*) rather than to a noun (cf. *rum-s, strong drink-s*, etc.) (cf. the slang suffix *-ers*, as in *preggers*, in Mattiello 2008a: 100–101). As for verbal inflection, in "I *thunk* I told you" (p. 677) Joyce replaces the irregular form of the verb *think* in the past – i.e. *thought* – with a subregular unproductive pattern which is based on the paradigm of verbs such as *stink–stunk–stunk*. These deviations confirm his authority as artist and his audacity as coiner.

In this section, it is also worth mentioning the linguistic anomalies that Joyce creates to make adjacent words closer to each other from the phonological (and graphic) viewpoint. For instance, in "the *alltitude* and *malltitude*" (p. 4), the two nouns *altitude* /ˈæl.tɪ.tjuːd/ and *multitude* /ˈmʌl.tɪ.tjuːd/, which already share the *-tude* suffix, are made more similar because of the shared rime /ɔːl/ in the first syllable and the parallel orthography.

Another anomaly which deserves attention is in the coordinated noun phrase "*muertification* and *uxpiration* and *dumnation* and *annuhulation*" (p. 79), where some vowels in *aspiration, damnation*, and *annihilation* are modified after the vowel alteration in the supposed model *muertification* [1939] 'mortification' (cf. Spanish *muerte* 'death'). In this case, the nouns sharing the suffix *-ation* are only graphically made more alike, although their pronunciation remains different.

An anomaly that concerns composition is in the complex nonce words *romekeepers* [1939], *homesweepers* [1939], and *domecreepers* [1939]. They are probably all modelled on, and rhyme with, the existing compound *home keeper(s)* [1574], none of them being attested in the OED. In the first nonce word, the inexistent noun *rome* substitutes *home* in the analogy. By contrast, in the second nonce word, the agent noun *sweeper* substitutes *keeper*, whereas in the last one, *dome* and *creeper* respectively replace *home* and *keeper*. It is evident that the similarity between model and targets is here primarily phonological.

By contrast, some occasionalisms that Joyce coins in *Finnegans Wake* are not proper cases of analogy. For instance, in "That he was only too *cognitively conatively cogitabundantly* sure of it" (p. 120), the latter formation is not created on the model of the previous adverbs, but rather by blending the two overlapping adverbs *cogitabundly* and *abundantly* and repeating in alliteration the initial stressed syllable /kɒ/. Something similar happens in the noun *bisexycle* [1939], where the word *sex* is intercalated within *bicycle*, and in the adverb *contrawatchwise* [1939], where *watch* is inserted into *contrariwise* by replacing the syllable /rɪ/. These are not types of analogy, but types of blend.

7.2.2 Types of target–model relationship

In James Joyce's novel *Finnegans Wake*, the relationship between the target and the model is often explicit. Thus, it is possible to identify analogical formations because they are either preceded or, more rarely, followed by their models.

An anaphoric surface analogy is clearly recognisable in extract (98):

(98) … twolips have pressed togatherthem by sweet Rush, townland of twinedlights, the **whitethorn** and the **redthorn** have fairygeyed the mayvalleys of Knockmaroon … (p. 18)

where the compound *redthorn* [1939] is obtained on the model of existing *whitethorn* [a1300], with which it shares morphotactic similarity (i.e. the second compound constituent *thorn*) and semantic similarity (i.e. *red* and *white* are co-hyponyms of 'colours'). In the same extract, the blend *togatherthem* [1939] ← *together + to gather them* is preceded by *twolips* [1939] ← *two + tulips*, the latter functioning as model for the former.

By contrast, a cataphoric analogy is offered by *moon night* [1939] in (99):

(99) … loses weight in the **moon night** but gird girder by the **sundawn** … (p. 188)

which is created after the poetic noun compound *sundawn* [1835] 'dawn, daybreak' (OED2, s.v. *sun*) mentioned immediately afterwards, but also from a literal translation of German *Mondnacht*.

The model words are also recoverable in (100):

(100) The mixer, accordingly, was bluntly broached, and in the best basel to boot, as to whether he was one of those lucky cocks for whom the **audible-visible-gnosible-edible** world existed. (p. 120)

where the nonce formation *gnosible* [1939] – from *gnosis* 'a special knowledge of spiritual mysteries' (OED2) – refers both back, to the models *audible* [1483] and *visible* [a1340], and forward, to *edible* [1611]. Here *gnosible* may recall the broader meaning of Ancient Greek *gnosis* 'recognition' and therefore mean 'recognisable'. However, *gnos-* is also homophonous with *nose*, which has a clear semantic link to the other formations in the sentence.

In many cases, both the model and the target are occasionalisms specifically created for artistic purposes from various juxtapositions. In (101)–(103), for instance, it is hard to discriminate the model from the target word:

(101) … there is in fact no use in putting a tooth in a snipery of that sort and the amount of all those sort of things which has been going on **onceaday in** and **twiceaday out** every other nachtistag among all kinds of promiscious individuals at all ages in private homes … (p. 89)

(102) Well, this freely is what must have occurred to our missive (there's a sod of a turb for you! please wisp off the grass!) unfilthed from the boucher by the sagacity of a **lookmelittle likemelong** hen. (p. 152)

(103) (**youthsy, beautsy**, hee's her chap and shey'll tell memmas when she gays whom) (p. 126)

The adverbial phrase *twiceaday out* [1939] in (101) is presumably modelled on the antecedent *onceaday in* [1939], which is semantically related to its target because of the opposition between *once* and *twice* as well as between *in* and *out*.

The complex adjectives *lookmelittle* [1939] and *likemelong* [1939] in (102) are both from clauses, but the latter is probably coined after the former, with the sharing of morphotactic similarity (Verb–*me*–Adverb), phonological similarity, especially in the lateral approximant /l/ (/lʊk.miː.lɪt.l/ vs. /laɪk.miː.lɒŋ/), and semantic similarity (*little* vs. *long* and co-hyponymy of the verbs *look–like*).

Finally, *beautsy* [1939] in (103) is the result of the addition of the diminutive suffix *-sy* to *beaut(y)*, by analogy with the model *youthsy* [1939].

Some of the occasionalisms created by Joyce have a relationship with their model that is primarily based on sound symbolism. As illustrative examples, consider the extracts in (104)–(105):

(104) But all they are all there scraping along to sneeze out a likelihood that will solve and salve life's robulous rebus, hopping round his middle like kippers on a griddle, O, as he lays dormont from the **macroborg** of Holdhard to the **microbirg** of Pied de Poudre. (p. 15)

(105) **Drink a sip, drankasup,** for he's as sooner buy a guinness than he'd stale store stout. (p. 10)

In (104), the nonce word *microbirg* [1939] is in anaphoric relationship with its model *macroborg* [1939]. Here target and model differ for their vowel sounds, i.e., in *microbirg*, the combining form *micro-* and the long vowel /ɜː/ replace *macro-* and /ɔː/ in *macroborg*.

By contrast, in (105), the anaphoric target *drankasup* [1939] exhibits soundsymbolic *-a-* /æ/ and *-u-* /ʌ/, which seem to suggest a longer focus upon the action (vs. *-i-* /ɪ/ in the model *drink a sip*). The latter is not attested as a compound word, but it may be an imperative clause, since it is not spelt as one word.

Exophoric analogies may also occur in *Finnegans Wake*. As a result, the model's recoverability is decreased in (106)–(109):

(106) ... shows Early English tracemarks and a marigold window with manigilt lights, a **myrioscope,** two remarkable piscines and three wellworthseeing ambries. (p. 174)

(107) The Diggins, **Woodenhenge,** as to hang out at. (p. 803)

(108) Lean neath stone pine the pastor lies with his crook; young pricket by pricket's sister nibbleth on returned viridities; amaid her rocking grasses the herb trinity shams lowliness; skyup is of **evergrey.** (p. 17)

(109) And, be dermot, who come to the keep of his inn only the **nieceof-his-inlaw,** the prankquean. (p. 26)

In (106), the word *myrioscope* [a1877] 'a kind of kaleidoscope in which patterns are produced by continuous movement of a flat object of fixed design in front of an arrangement of mirrors' (OED3) is coined after *kaleidoscope* [1817] showing the same neoclassical combining form *-scope* (see Latin *-scopium* ← Greek σκοπεῖν 'to look at, examine').

In (107), the target *Woodenhenge* (cf. *woodhenge* [1927] 'a henge believed to have contained a circular timber structure', OED2) is modelled on a proper name, *Stonehenge* [1297], with which it mainly shares morphotactic and semantic similarity (i.e. same right component *henge* and related left component *wood(en)* vs. *stone*).

Finally, the compound *evergrey* [1939] in (108) resembles its absent model *evergreen* [1555], and *nieceof-his-in-law* [1939] in (109) is humorously modelled on the word set consisting of *brother-in-law* [c1300], *mother-in-law* [a1382], *father-in-law* [c1385], etc. In the latter case, the existence of the combining form *-in-law* (OED2) helps the disambiguation.

7.2.3 Functions and effects

Joyce's analogical words are effective and provide his novels with a touch of originality. Word plays, in particular, pervade the whole text of *Finnegans Wake* conferring innovation to it, although they mainly consist of ephemeral occasionalisms.

The most important function served by Joyce's analogical occasionalisms is the readers' involvement and the attraction of their interest. While some analogies seem more regular and do not arouse a lot of interest, others are especially attractive and do arouse the readers' curiosity. Consider, for instance, the words in bold in (110)–(113):

(110) Mr Wallenstein Washington Semperkelly's **immergreen** tourers in a command performance by special request with the courteous permission for pious purposes the homedromed and enliventh performance of problem passion play of the **millentury**, running strong since creation ... (p. 43)

(111) ... in the case of the littleknown periplic **bestteller** popularly associated with the names of the wretched mariner ... (p. 168)

(112) Because it is a horrible thing to have to say to say to day but one dilalah, Lupita Lorette, shortly after in a fit of the unexpectednesses drank carbolic with all her dear placid life before her and paled off while the other soiled dove that's her **sister-in-love**, Luperca Latouche ... (p. 92)

(113) ... Parr aparrently, to whom the **headandheelless** chickenestegg bore some Michelangiolesque resemblance ... (p. 111)

In these examples, the model word of the analogy is left unexpressed, and this is deliberately done to attract the readership. Joyce's readers are invited to reanalyse words such as *century* [1533] (from Latin *centuria* 'a company of 100 men') as complex, and to interpret *millentury* [1939] in (110) as a surface analogy modelled on it. His readers are also invited to disambiguate *bestteller* [1939] in (111) as a compound obtained on the quasi-homophone model *bestseller* [1864], or to appreciate the jocularity offered by *sister-in-love* [1939], which is phonologically adjacent to its model *sister-in-law* [c1440] (cf. /lʌv/ vs. /lɔː/) (cf. (109)). Lastly, they are invited to grasp the meaning of the synthetic compound *headandheelless* [1939] as originated from the model word *headless* [OE], but with a phrase as base.

Moreover, the occasionalism *immergreen* in (110) is an eye-catching adaptation of the German name of a plant (*Immergrün*, literally 'always green'), and may be viewed as an analogy on English *evergreen* [1555] (cf. (108)). Another occasionalism which deserves attention is the blend *enliventh* [1939] ← *enliven* + *eleventh*, whose formation is modelled on various overlapping blends.

Word distortions also occur in Joyce's *Finnegans Wake*, again with the author's intention to attract readers. For instance, in:

(114) Breakfates, **Lunger, Diener** and **Souper** (p. 178)

the names of the meals are altered, their letters are mixed up, and additions are made, analogically, on the model of others. The mid-day meal *lunch*, in particular, appears to take an extra suffix *-er*, on the model of *dien-er* and *soup-er* (cf. French *din-er*, *soup-er*, and the orthography of German *Diener* 'servant'). This is semantically and orthographically comparable to the suffix introduced into slang to make jocular formations, such as *brekker* 'breakfast' (OED2; Mattiello 2008a: 100). The morning meal, *breakfast*, has also been altered as *breakfates*, by using graphically identical vowels in the right component.

Another function that is served by Joyce's novel words is the display of creativeness, innovation, and originality. His originality offers its best in complex formations, ranging from the regular neologism *blackthorn* [a1325] in (115):

(115) Oblige with your **blackthorns**; gamps, degrace! (p. 78)

which is modelled on its opposite *whitethorn* [a1300] (cf. (98)), to the more innovative phrase-based derivations in (116):

(116) the **toomuchness**, the **fartoomanyness** of all those fourlegged ems ... who thus at all this marvelling but will press on hotly to see the vaulting feminine libido of those interbranching ogham sex upandinsweeps sternly controlled and easily repersuaded by the uniform **matteroffactness** of a meandering male fist? (p. 167)

the former of which – i.e. *toomuchness* [1875] (OED2, s.v. *too*) – playing the model role for the other two. These derived words are grammatical, but part of an elegant and cultivated language.

Lastly, rhythm is the main effect produced by Joyce's analogical nonce words. Rhythm is most evidently generated by reduplication, which intervenes, for instance, in extract (117):

(117)   ... threatens thunder upon malefactors and sends whispers up **fraufrau**'s **froufrous** ... (p. 173)

Here the cataphoric analogy *fraufrau* [1939] (from German *Frau* 'woman') anticipates its model – i.e. the copy reduplicative *froufrou* [1870] 'a rustling' (OED2) – activating sound symbolism through the consonant cluster *fr-* /fr/.

In extract (118), analogy occurs as a regular substitution of consonant sounds:

(118)   If Dann's **dane**, Ann's dirty, if he's **plane** she's purty, if he's **fane**, she's flirty, with her auburnt streams, and her coy cajoleries, and her dabblin drolleries, for to rouse his rudderup, or to drench his dreams. (p. 189)

Indeed, in this extract, *dane* [1939] /deɪn/ and *fane* [1939] /feɪn/ are modelled on *plane* [1666] /pleɪn/,[9] whereas *purty* /ˈpɜː.tɪ/ [1682] – a regional variant of 'pretty' according to OED3 – rhymes with *dirty* /ˈdɜː.tɪ/ and *flirty* /ˈflɜː.tɪ/, and alliterates with <u>r</u>ouse his <u>r</u>udderup. Rhythm is also reinforced by the alliteration in <u>c</u>oy <u>c</u>ajoleries, <u>d</u>abblin <u>d</u>rolleries, <u>r</u>ouse his <u>r</u>udderup, and <u>d</u>rench his <u>d</u>reams.

The examples provided in this section validate the hypothesis that the author's audacity is generally combined with creativity, ungrammaticality, and unpredictability on the one hand, but also with sound, rhythm, and effectiveness on the other.

7.3 Quantitative data on literary analogies

The data discussed in sections 7.1 and 7.2 provides two case studies of analogy in literary tradition. All Hopkins' analogies mentioned in 7.1 are recorded in the OED, but only 37.14% are actual neologisms, whereas 62.85% are occasionalisms.

---

[9] Actually, *dane* and *fane* are attested in the OED, but as nouns rather than as adjectives.

The OED itself specifies that terms such as *leafmeal*, *vauntless*, and *tauntless* are nonce words, whereas others are considered as obsolete (e.g. †*passion-plunged*).

Neologisms include both surface analogy and analogy via schema types. Surface analogies amount to 61.53% and also conform to rule patterns, both derivation (e.g. *disremember, museless, non-execution*), and compounding (e.g. *quick-gold, self-being, show-woman, Sprung Rhythm*). Analogies obtained via a schema model amount to 38.46%. Some of them are well-established and have been re-used by several authors (e.g. *lovescape, outscape, water-scape* after the final combining form *-scape*, see 3.3.1). Others are less common among authors, but belong to attested word families, such as *rosy-X* (*rosy-pale*) and *star-X* (*star-eyed*). The latter cases show the importance of left (non-head) components in analogical formation.

Occasionalisms are for the most part (63.63%) regular surface analogies, with an evident incidence of compounds (e.g. *fire-folk, martyr-master, thundercolour*), but also derived words (e.g. †*overthought, vauntless*). Un-/Extra-grammatical analogical words (e.g. *manself, sloggering*) and derived words with unproductive suffixes (e.g. *leafmeal*) play a marginal role in Hopkins' poetry – i.e. 13.63% in my database. Analogy via schema is slightly more common (22.72%), with examples confirming the importance of non-head components in analogical formation: e.g., *yester-tempest* is from a cranberry morph, *ready-to-read* obeys the pattern *ready* + infinitive, *she-being* belongs to the family *she-X*, and parasynthetic *sweet-mannered* and *strawberry-breasted* are respectively from the *strawberry-X* and *sweet-X* word sets. Although, for *strawberry-breasted*, an *X-breasted* word set may also have functioned as model, the Variable Part does not belong to the typical part of speech of the set – i.e. adjective in *big-breasted, flat-breasted, narrow-breasted, open-breasted, wide-breasted*. This suggests that, as in the other examples of analogy via schema, the leftmost element plays the role of Invariable Part in the substitution.

A final remark regarding occasionalisms in poetic and literary works concerns the availability and profitability of such new words. While some of them are attested only in Hopkins, others have been reused by other authors of whom mention is made in the OED. For instance, in 1999, Sondra Horton Fraleigh wrote "Her *rice-white* face" (106) in *Dancing into Darkness*, and, in 1956, Kenneth Clark reused *ill-balanced* in *The Nude* ("Could fill an *ill-balanced* nature with destructive envy", 284). Similarly, *Walsingham way* is gaining its way towards establishment and recognition among other authors (see James Joyce, Michael John Petry Herne).

Joyce's analogies mentioned in 7.2 are for the most part occasionalisms (81.96%), whereas the number of actual neologisms recorded in the OED amounts to 18.03%. Neologisms include both grammatical (e.g. *black-thorn, ear-witness*) – more than 80% – and ungrammatical formations, such as *faithly* and *strongers*. The latter is labelled 'slang' in the OED.

Occasionalisms in Joyce illustrate heterogeneous types of analogy and various degrees of audacity. Types range from pure surface analogy (*millentury* on *century*) to analogy combined with rule patterns (*redthorn, gnosible, sister-in-love*), and even to analogy via schema. For instance, the set of words with a *-little* right element constitutes a word family (e.g. *runalittle, doalittle, preealittle, pouralittle*, etc.) and *nieceof-his-in-law* belongs to the *-in-law* series.

As for models, 71.87% of Hopkins' analogies are exophoric, i.e. without a model word in the (micro-)context. Of the remaining 28.12% endophoric analogies, one third is cataphoric and two thirds are anaphoric.

By contrast, only 25.92% of Joyce's analogies are exophoric. There is indeed a prevalence of endophoric analogies (74.07%), four fifths of which are anaphoric, that is, refer to a previously mentioned model word, and one fifth is cataphoric. The necessity of an explicit model word in Joyce is proportional with the difficulty in disambiguating his audacious formations.

7.4 Final remarks on analogy in literary works

This analysis of literary analogies in Hopkins' poetry and in Joyce's novel has shown two central points concerning analogy in word-formation. On the one hand, the generalisation that literary analogies are often irregular and unpredictable because of the author's deviation from linguistic rules and norms is too broad. The literature offers both cases of linguistic anomalies, such as some of the nonce words created by James Joyce in *Finnegans Wake* (e.g. *annuhulation, lunger*), but also perfectly regular analogical neologisms, such as the compounds or derived words coined by Hopkins in his *Poems* (e.g. *show-woman, overthought*).

Hopkins and Joyce mainly create occasionalisms that have no chance to be reused (although some of them are recorded in the OED), or which may be adopted by other authors for artistic/poetic purposes. Analogical occasionalisms in Hopkins are mainly grammatical surface analogies (e.g. *rose-flake, rosy-pale*), as well as analogies via schemas (e.g. *she-being, yester-tempest*), whereas Joyce's analogies are more inventive, and may also involve loans (e.g. *fraufrau*) and loan adaptations (e.g. *bookstaff, moon night*, both from German), anomaly (e.g. *annuhulation*), and sound symbolism (e.g. *microbirg, dane, fane*). Therefore, the present chapter has demonstrated that – although ungrammatical novel words occur in both authors (e.g. *manself, strongers*) – the novelist deviates from linguistic norms and rules more than the poet does.

In Hopkins, analogy may be in context, in that it may refer back (anaphora) or forward (cataphora) to its model. Yet exophoric analogy (i.e. without context) prevails in the poet's works. Thus, while endophoric analogy contributes to the rhythm of the poems, with repetition of the model's sounds in the target, exophoric analogy allows the poet to condense information in the length of the verse.

In Joyce's *Finnegans Wake*, both endo- and exo-phoric analogy are exemplified, with a remarkable prevalence of the former over the latter. Endophoric analogy allows for the model's recoverability, and contributes to the playfulness and rhythm of the novel. Exophoric analogy increases the readers' interest, and makes the language more enigmatic, cryptic, and difficult to disambiguate. Analogy is a mechanism that Joyce especially adopts to show his audacity.

Different degrees of audacity can be identified in Joyce's novel, exemplified by the following formations:

- Clause-based compounds (*likemelong, drankasup*) and phrase-based derived words (*fartoomanyness, matteroffactness*);
- Extra-grammatical formations, such as reduplicatives (*powwow, beggybaggy*) and blends (*togatherthem, enliventh*);
- Loans or loan adaptations, such as *immergreen*, from German, or *diener* and *souper*, from French;
- Orthographic and/or phonological distortions, as in *malltitude, uxpiration*, and *romekeepers*;
- Combinations of some of the above, as in *fraufrau*, a reduplicative from German *Frau*.

8 Acceptability of new analogical words

This chapter is based on an experiment that has been conducted on native English speakers to test the (degree of) acceptability of new analogical words. To the best of my knowledge, there are no previous studies which investigate new analogical words using quantitative data on their acceptability, either in isolation or in context. Admittedly, this is a small-scale study, whose goal is neither providing statistical results nor measuring reaction times for psycholinguistic aims. The chapter rather uses quantitative data to understand how native speakers regard analogical words, if they are able to recognise and interpret them, and if they would admit the use of such new words in an adequate context. The focus in this chapter is on the role played by the type of analogy (e.g. surface vs. via schema), the type of target (e.g. grammatical vs. extra-/un-grammatical), and the context (i.e. the presence vs. absence of the model) in the assessment of new analogical words. In particular, the acceptability of analogical words is assessed by the participants in the experiment in terms of the words' accessibility or easy interpretation, and of the recognisability of a word, word form, series, or family that could have acted as model.

The first section of the chapter describes the methodology of the experiment, including the participants, materials, and procedure. The second section presents some problems evidenced by pilot tests and puts forward some hypotheses concerning the impact of the variables of both the first and the second part of the experiment on the new words' acceptability assessment. The last section discusses quantitative results in terms of: 1) tendencies in the rating of analogical words on a scale ranging from fully acceptable to unacceptable, and 2) criteria that can lead speakers to accept (or reject) a new word formed by analogy. More generally, the acceptability assessment of analogical words can help us discriminate between cases of analogy that are easier to recognise, process, and understand and cases that are inaccessible, difficult to recognise, and hard to comprehend even for native speakers. I expect that the former are more stable cases of analogy, such as those formed via a schema model or conforming to rule patterns, whereas the latter are more creative formations, which may involve either reanalysis or extra-grammatical operations.

8.1 Method

8.1.1 Participants

Twenty-six native English speakers (fifteen females and eleven males, age range 31–68 years) participated in the experiment.

The participants in the pilot test were two females and a male. One of the females, aged fifty-nine, came from the United States and had been living in Italy for thirty years. Her education level was high, in that she held a Ph.D. in linguistics and worked as an Associate Professor of English linguistics. The other female participant, aged fifty, came from Canada and had spent thirty-seven years in Italy. Her education level was lower – middle school level – and she worked as a shopkeeper. The male participant in the pilot test was younger (31 years), came from the UK, had a Bachelor of Arts (B.A.) Degree, and worked as a librarian in London.

The twenty-three participants tested in the actual experiment (thirteen females and ten males) had university-level education. In particular, they had at least a B.A. Degree; two of them had a Bachelor of Science (B.Sc.) Degree; four had a Master's Degree; three held a Ph.D. Most of them had spent several years in Italy (range 22–40 years) working in different Universities as English teachers. However, they came from different English-speaking countries (i.e. UK, USA, and Canada).

8.1.2 Materials

On the basis of previous theoretical accounts and the working model presented in 3.3, ten new analogical words in English were selected and used as targets in the experiment. The words were heterogeneous in terms of:
- *Grammaticality*: three targets were grammatical nouns (a derived word, a compound from a phrasal verb, a loose compound); three targets were extragrammatical formations (two blends, an alphabetism); one was ungrammatical; one involved reanalysis; two were formed from two recognised combining forms (*-licious*, *-adelic*). The blends exhibited recurrent splinters (i.e. *-arian* from *vegetarian*, *-flation* from *inflation*).
- *Type of analogy*: six targets belonged to the surface analogy type, three of which also conformed to rules, the others being cases of pure surface analogy. The remaining four targets belonged to the type obtained through analogy via schema.

- *Source*: two targets belonged to the specialised language of economics; two were taken from teenagers' speech (one was typical of text and e-mail messages); two were from journalistic language; two from the literature (minor authors were preferred over famous ones so as not to influence the informants); two were general. All the words were attested either in COCA or in other corpora, dictionaries, or collections.

The heterogeneity of the targets guaranteed that the participants could not be influenced by antecedent examples in their assessment of acceptability. The number of words was limited to ten to avoid any saturation effect, i.e. a top-down and habituation effect in the acceptability rating (see problems in 8.2).

The target words were presented first in isolation, i.e. within a word list, and then in contexts, which were either actual or adapted from corpora. The texts were heterogeneous in terms of register (formal vs. informal vs. slang), genre (e.g. newspaper article, specialised research book, book for music fans, conversation, etc.), and mode (spoken vs. written language). The context length also varied from one-clause sentence to two paragraphs, as shown in (119)–(128):

(119) As Bushism segued into **Obamaism**, political caricature continued its rebirth. (adapted from COCA, 1996)

(120) The graduates in this research thought that government-led employability strategies had little relevance to them. They said creative work is different; they won't have one job so one size never fits all, and their work is about creative interaction and finding solutions within a global environment.
"**Complexability**" is actually needed. This is having the necessary social, cultural and economic capital, along with a sophisticated creative agency, which helps graduates learn to work in different ways, with different people, places and cultures, often collaborating across disciplines and boundaries. The graduates said they want to be supported to develop this **complexability** because without it the privileged circles of paid work remained impenetrable. (*The Guardian*, 2014)

(121) A: Lol ... man that was hilarious!!
B: Yeah I know ... **rofl** ... (*Urban Dictionary*, 2007)

(122) O-M-G! She is so bootylicious, she is so sexilicious, she is so gorgeoulicious, she is so completely licious with her **weavealicious**

hair! (adapted from *Urban Dictionary*, 2008; *weavealicious* is attested in COCA, 2007)

(123) So-called stagflation and **slumpflation** are the inevitable reflection of the progressive divergence between a rising nominal and a falling real supply of money. (OED2, 1974)

(124) "The idea was to ask women not to spend money on themselves over a weekend. No shopping, no eating out, no beauty parlour visits – all weekend activities that shop owners benefit from. Instead of a boycott, it was a **girlcott**," she explains. (*Deccan Herald*, http://www.countercurrents.org/rahman151112.htm, 2015)

(125) Clearly, as the article itself mentions, this is declared money. In other words, this is **white money**. The amount of black money is still unaccounted for. (http://www.thehindu.com/, GloWbE)

(126) There are categories for everything educated or not, foreign car or not ... English-speaking or not, meatarian or not, if vegetarian then whether an **eggitarian** or strict, if strict then too strict to eat Western desserts with egg or not. (adapted from COCA, 2005)

(127) A: My roommate came back from the party with a hangover last night!
B: I didn't go to the party last night, I woke up this morning with a wicked **hangunder**. (adapted from *Urban Dictionary*, 2004)

(128) I remember the Droogs putting out rock-solid **punkadelic** indie records. (OED3, 1997)

Additionally, a native speaker who did not participate in the actual experiment rated the contexts for their efficiency, since a more efficient context might have a higher impact on the acceptability assessment than a less efficient one.

8.1.3 Procedure

The experiment was divided into two parts, which were compiled by the twenty-six participants in a ten/fifteen-minute timespan (average 30–45 seconds per word). The first and second parts were compiled separately, one after the conclusion of the other, and with no opportunity to revise the first part after having inspected the second part. Overall, the latter part was completed more rapidly than the first part. Reaction times were not measured.

In the first part, the participants were asked to rate the ten new English analogical words described in 8.1.2 on the following scale: 1 (= fully acceptable), 2 (= probable), 3 (= possible), 4 (= improbable), 5 (= unacceptable). The participants were told that the words under examination were 'new' and 'analogical', and that they were not being tested on their knowledge of English, but on the words' acceptability. Acceptability was assessed in terms of accessibility, easy interpretation, and recognisability of a potential model word, series, or family. Thus, criteria for considering a form 'acceptable' could be that the form was clearly understandable, or that it was similar, opposite, or close in meaning/form to one that they already knew, or to a set of comparable words. Only for the words that the participants rated as fully acceptable (i.e. 1), were they asked to justify their choice.

Acceptability was variously defined by the participants in terms of easy understanding (14), clear etymology (10), and similarity with (9), reminiscence of (3), opposition to (6), or punning on (4) existing words. Evaluations based on prior – either active or passive – knowledge of the new words (13) were excluded from quantitative results. The participants were also asked to illustrate fully acceptable words with a possible invented example. The examples provided gave me a more precise idea of the informants' actual recognition and interpretation of the new analogical words. Interestingly, some of the informants' examples (15) included both the target words and their models.

The independent variables for the first part were:
1. Conformity vs. nonconformity to rule patterns; or the grammaticality vs. ungrammaticality vs. extra-grammaticality vs. marginality of the targets;
2. Belonging to either surface analogy or analogy via schema type;
3. Semantic neighbourhood between the targets and their models;
4. Phonological neighbourhood of the targets to possible model words.

In the second part of the experiment, the participants were asked to reassess the acceptability of the same new words, providing an actual or adapted context where they were used.

The additional variables for the second part were:
5. Reference of either endophoric (8 anaphoric/1 cataphoric) or exophoric (1) targets to their model words;

6. Target–model distance, from immediately before (a in 3.3.5) to preceding paragraph (d in 3.3.5) for anaphoric targets, to same sentence (b in 3.3.5) for cataphoric targets;
7. Context length (long and complex vs. short and condensed) and efficiency.

8.2 Problems and hypotheses after pilot tests

The pilot tests evidenced some problems and constraints in the experiment and imposed some restrictions on the participants' characteristics. The pilot tests also served to put some hypotheses forward in order to develop more precise criteria of acceptability for novel analogical words.

8.2.1 Problems and constraints

As for target words, the most evident problem was related to their actual novelty for the participants. Previous active/passive knowledge of one of the words could determine its acceptability rating. In other terms, if an interviewee knew one of the targets, (s)he would probably evaluate it as fully acceptable. Therefore, as said in 8.1.3, when the words were rated 1 (fully acceptable) because they were either used by the participants themselves or had been heard from other users, these results were excluded from the distribution figures.

Another problem was determined by the opaqueness of some, especially extra-grammatical formations. For instance, the participants had some difficulties in identifying blend bases from splinters, or in rating the acceptability of the alphabetism without knowing the full form from which it had been shortened. While for blends the identification of a recurrent splinter could be one of the factors determining acceptability, for acronyms the full phrase could help the association with an existing model word. Hence, for the acronym *ROFL* offered in the target list, a footnote was added indicating the full phrase from which it might potentially come.

A related constraint was determined by the number of targets used in the experiment. A larger number of words would have given more reliable results, but at the same time could compromise the results due to attention deficits or fatigue in top-down processing results, especially in the second part involving contexts. The overall number of words used (10) both allowed for heterogeneity in the targets (see 8.1.2) and avoided saturation effects. For the same reasons, the words were submitted in different random orders.

As for participants, pilot tests evidenced the necessity to restrict the participants to a homogeneous group in terms of education, but heterogeneous in terms of age and English variety. In particular, a university degree (or higher) was considered as a basic prerequisite for participation in the experiment. A lower level of education could influence or compromise the results.

On the other hand, the participants' age range varied from 31 to 68, thus excluding teenagers from the experiment. This constraint could have some effects on the rating of analogical words from teenagers' speech, such as *hangunder*, but not on the evaluation of specialised, journalistic, literary, or general items. Moreover, some of the older participants declared that they knew the young generation's acronym *ROFL*, so age was not considered as a fundamental limitation influencing the results.

An additional constraint concerning the participants was their origin and the variety of English that they spoke. This constraint had some effects on the participants' previous knowledge of some terms, which may be unfamiliar in the UK, but already in use in the USA. Hence, data based on the informants' prior knowledge of the words was deleted from the results.

To summarise, the reference interviewees in the present study 1) were all English mother tongue speakers, 2) came from different English-speaking countries, 3) had at least a B.A. Degree, and 4) were all adults.

8.2.2 Hypotheses

On the basis of the independent variables and of the partial results obtained in the pilot tests, some hypotheses may be put forth about the acceptability rating in the first part (isolated targets) and in the second part (contextualised targets), as well as about the effect that context may have on the improvement of acceptability rating.

As for the first part, acceptability of isolated targets may be connected with the independent variables (1)–(4) identified in 8.1.3:

1'. If a target is obtained by surface analogy, but also conforms to rules, then it will be more acceptable than an analogical target that is either irregular or involves reanalysis. In other terms, grammatical analogical words will be considered by native speakers as more acceptable than both extra-grammatical words and ungrammatical words formed by analogy.

2'. If a target is obtained by analogy via schema or rule, with a set of prototype words as model, then native speakers will find it less difficult to recognise the analogical pattern and will be more prone to accepting the new word. In other terms, analogical words from a schema model will be considered by native speakers as more acceptable than surface analogies with just one precise item as model.

3'. If a target is closer from the semantic viewpoint to its model, then native speakers will find it less difficult to recover the model and will be more inclined to accept the new word. Semantic neighbourhood affects the Variable Part of the complex test item, which is more likely to be in opposition to, or a co-hyponym with the corresponding part in the model. Clearer semantic oppositions will encourage acceptability on the native speakers' part. There were no synonymous relationships included between the targets provided and their models, in order to avoid lexical blocking effects.

4'. If a target is closer from the phonological viewpoint to its model, then native speakers will find it less difficult to recover the model and will be more inclined to accept the new word. Phonological neighbourhood affects the Invariable Part, which may be identified with one or more syllables corresponding to an affix, a combining form, a splinter, a word, or word part. The larger the number of phonemes that are shared between target and model, the easier the model's recoverability from the native speakers' perspective, the higher the likelihood of accepting the target.

As for the second part, acceptability of contextualised targets may also be connected with the additional variables (5)–(7) identified in 8.1.3:

5'. The association between target and model word and the consequent acceptability of the former will be easier if there is an endophoric reference, i.e. if the target refers to an antecedent or following model, than if there is no cotextual reference to the model (exophoric reference).

6'. The target–model association will be more rapid if the distance between the two is shorter than if it is longer. Immediately before or immediately following is thought to be the ideal distance for easier association and acceptability of the new target.

7'. A short and condensed context will favour association and acceptability more than a long and complex context will. Moreover, a more efficient context will have a more robust impact on the improvement of acceptability rating between first and second part.

However, it should be noted that the participants in the experiment had no time limits. Therefore, the target–model distance or the context length were not considered essential variables for the impact of the context on the acceptability of the new words.

As for the improvement of acceptability rating, we can additionally hypothesise that:

8'. From a comparison between the results obtained in the first part and those obtained in the second part, there will be either a confirmation or an upgrading (never a downgrading) of the acceptability rating by native speakers.

8.3 Results and discussion

Results from the first and second parts of the experiment were analysed using Microsoft Excel spreadsheets in order to test the hypotheses (1')–(8') put forward in 8.2.2. Results obtained from a male participant who rated most of the targets as unacceptable (5) in both parts because of misspelling or supposed incorrectness were removed from the data prior to analysis. The remaining results emerged from twenty-two participants' responses.

An Excel function that calculates the sum of acceptability data and the Average Degree of Acceptability per target in Isolation [ADAI] and in Context [ADAC] was used to answer quantitative needs. Since full acceptability was rated 1 and unacceptability 5, the lower the average score obtained, the higher the target acceptability.

A further clarification concerns both ADAI and ADAC scores. In the quantitative analyses, only mean ratings are shown and discussed. This decision results from the fact that there were no substantial variations between the participants' assessments when judging the targets in isolation and in context. Given the low number of participants in the experiment, homogeneity in responses provided additional evidence for the legitimacy of hypotheses (1')–(8').

8.3.1 First part of the experiment

The results of the first part of the experiment [ADAI] are presented in Graph 1.

The data reported in Graph 1 appears to validate (most of) the hypotheses (1')–(4') set forth in 8.2.2.

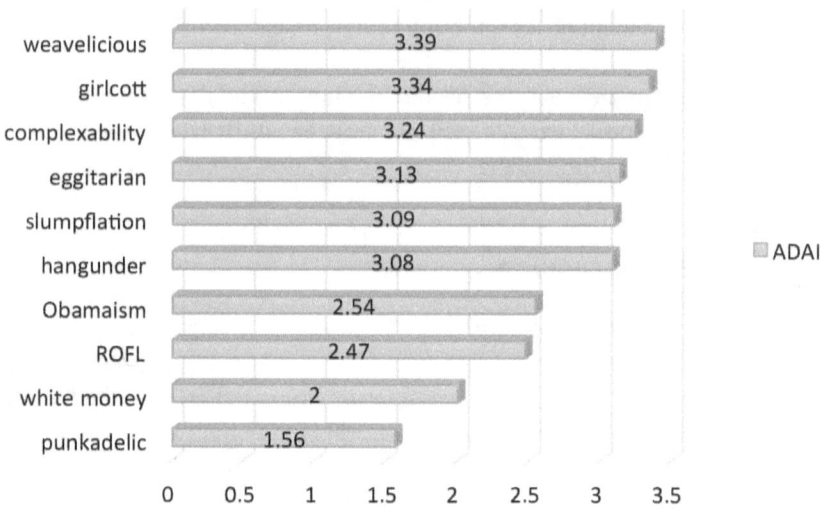

Graph 1: Average Degree of Acceptability per target in Isolation [ADAI]

The first hypothesis (1') concerning the grammaticality (vs. un- or extra-grammaticality) of the targets is corroborated by the data in Graph 1. The loose compound *white money* [ADAI 2], regularly formed on *black money*, as well as the derived word *Obamaism* [ADAI 2.54], which is modelled on the schema of *Reaganism, Bushism, Clintonism,* etc., are more acceptable than both ungrammatical and extra-grammatical words.

More specifically, grammatical targets (*white money, Obamaism*) are more acceptable than ungrammatical targets (i.e. *eggitarian* [ADAI 3.13] ← *egg* + Latin *-i-* + *-(t)arian* from *vegetarian, complexability* [ADAI 3.24], see 3.3.3, *weavelicious* [ADAI 3.39], irregularly formed from a verb), and also more than extra-grammatical targets (*slumpflation* [ADAI 3.09] ← *slump* + *-flation* from *inflation*).

Furthermore, grammatical targets such as *white money* and *Obamaism* are also more acceptable than the target *girlcott* [ADAI 3.34], which involves reanalysis, but not more acceptable than *punkadelic* [ADAI 1.56], which is obtained from a combining form.

A counterexample that contradicts hypothesis (1') is extra-grammatical *ROFL* [ADAI 2.47] ← *Rolling On the Floor Laughing*, whose acceptability degree is higher than that of grammatical *Obamaism*. However, this result is not surprising: i.e. *ROFL* is commonly used nowadays by teenagers in their text messages, so the informants might have met this acronym before without declaring it.

The second hypothesis (2') concerning the type of analogy involved (surface vs. via schema) is also partly substantiated by the data in Graph 1. In particular, the target *punkadelic*, with a combining form *-adelic* from *psychedelic*,[1] is modelled on the series comprising *funkadelic* [1970] 'the name of a pop group formed in 1968 by George Clinton', *grunge-edelic* [1991], etc. (OED3, see also later *swingadelic* [2006]). A schema model identified with a series is easier to recover than a precise item, as in surface analogy. In the case of *Obamaism* – unattested in the OED but attested in COCA (4 occurrences) – the pattern is *-ism* suffixation added to a president's surname, as in *Nixonism* [1952], *Reaganism* [1966], *Clintonism* [1992], *Bushism* [1980], the latter case being phonologically less similar than the others to *Obamaism* because of a smaller number of syllables (three vs. five).

A counterexample that disconfirms hypothesis (2') is *weavelicious*. In this case, the schema model of *-licious* formations (see 1.2), normally coined from nouns (as in *bootylicious, babelicious*), conflates with an irregular (ungrammatical) verbal base *weave* (the noun is a conversion from the verb). Hence, hypothesis (2') is here refuted by hypothesis (1').

Another counterexample that deserves attention is *eggitarian*, whose schema model – based on *-arian*, as in *fruitarian, meatarian*, etc. (see 3.3.1) – is obscured by the presence of a Latinate element *-i-*, which is absent from the models. While this element may have been added to make the target more euphonious, its presence makes the formation ungrammatical. Hypothesis (1') is again in conflict with hypothesis (2').

The third hypothesis (3') on semantic neighbourhood between target and model is for the most part validated by at least the most acceptable words. Indeed, the Variable Part *punk* in the target *punkadelic* is semantically related to the model bases *funk* in *funkadelic* and *grunge* in *grunge-edelic*, in that they are co-hyponyms of 'types of music'. An equivalent co-hyponymous relationship is between *Obama* and *Nixon, Reagan, Clinton*, etc. respectively in the target *Obamaism* and the models *Nixonism, Reaganism, Clintonism*. By contrast, *white money* is related to its model *black money* by a relationship of semantic opposition.

However, *hangunder* [ADAI 3.08], *girlcott*, and *eggitarian* were considered as less acceptable by the informants, in spite of their semantic relationship of opposition (*under* vs. *over*, *girl* vs. *boy*) or co-hyponymy (*egg* vs. *fruit, nut, meat*) with

---

[1] According to OED3, the combining form *-adelic* 'forms adjectives designating or relating to a style of music which combines psychedelic characteristics with the style or genre indicated by the first element' (cf. *shagadelic* 'sexy, esp. in a psychedelic way' OED3 with a different meaning). The spelling for the reduced vowel /ə/ varies between *-a-* and *-e-*, although *-adelic* is the most common form.

their model words (*hangover*, *boycott*), and series ending in -*arian* (*fruitarian*, *nutarian*, *meatarian*).

In *weavelicious*, however, there is no semantic connection with *bootylicious* or *babelicious*, which are therefore difficult to identify and accept as prototypical model words. Similarly, there is no connection, from either semantic or syntactic viewpoint, between *complex* (in the target *complexability*) and *employ* (in the model *employability*). Finally, in *slumpflation*, the semantic connection between *slump* 'a sudden decline in the price of commodities' and *stag*- (← *stagnation* 'an absence of growth') in *stagflation* is obscured by the abbreviation in the model, although the two words share the same economic field.

The fourth hypothesis (4') on phonological neighbourhood between target and model is again corroborated. The targets exhibit a phonological connection (Invariable Part) with their models. The Invariable Part may be a word (*money*, *hang*), a combining form (-*licious*, -*adelic*), a splinter (-*arian*, -*flation*), a cumulation of suffixes (-*ability* from -*able* + -*ity*), or a suffix (-*ism*). When it is a series of sounds that do not correspond to any English morpheme, such as *cott* in *girlcott* (cf. ME *cott* as an alternative spelling of *cot*), it is more difficult to identify the model word.

In *punkadelic* /ˌpʌŋk.əˈde.lɪk/, (especially) modelled on *funkadelic* /ˌfʌŋk.əˈde.lɪk/, the Invariable Part consists of three entire syllables and rime in the first syllable. The fact that the two words differ only for one sound helps association and encourages acceptability of the target. In the case of *ROFL*, by contrast, phonological continuity with the model *LOL* is difficult if not impossible to identify. The distinction between Variable Part and Invariable Part is in this case indiscernible, so that the two words can resemble each other only graphically because of some shared (capital) letters (*O*, *L*). Furthermore, to increase ambiguity, while in the *Urban Dictionary ROFL* is read by native speakers as one word (/rɒfl/), the model *LOL* can be read either letter-by-letter (/ˌel.əʊˈel/) or as one word (/lɒl/).

Hitherto, the various causes of acceptability rating of the neoformations and their results in ranking order have been discussed individually according to the variables (1)–(4). However, it also emerges from the results that some of the causes may converge while others are in conflict with one another. For instance, *punkadelic* and *white money* show the highest ADAI because they are grammatical, obtained after a schema/regular model, and exhibit high similarity with their model words from both semantic and phonological viewpoints. In particular, the phonological overlap between *punkadelic* and *funkadelic* makes the latter easily recoverable and the former highly acceptable by most informants. Similarly, the semantic opposition between *white* and *black* helps the recoverability of *black money*. This convergence of positive factors may have encouraged acceptability on the informants' part.

Interestingly, the cases of the surface analogy *ROFL* and the analogy via schema *Obamaism* show very close ADAI, although the former is extra-grammatical and the latter is grammatical, and the similarity between *Obamaism* and *Reaganism*, *Bushism*, etc. is more evident than the similarity between *ROFL* and *LOL*, both semantically and phonologically. In other words, many positive factors encourage the acceptability of *Obamaism*, whereas many negative factors discourage the acceptability of *ROFL*. However, the motivation behind the relatively high ADAI of *ROFL* may be connected with the fact that a possible full form for this acronym was provided in a footnote to help its disambiguation and association with the model, or, as stated above, it may be connected with the informants' undeclared prior knowledge of the acronym.

Moreover, both *white money* and *ROFL* show a higher ADAI than the extra-grammatical surface analogy *slumpflation*, whose phonological connection with the model *stagflation* is rather evident, whereas semantically the abbreviation of *stagnation* in the model may obscure the semantic link and obstruct the association.

Unlike *slumpflation*, the more acceptable surface analogy *hangunder* is grammatical and the semantic relationship of opposition between *under* and *over* in its model *hangover* is clear, although not as clear as the opposition between *white* (*money*) and *black* (*money*). Also phonologically, target and model share a syllable recognisable as one word (*hang*) and the final schwa in the second syllable. A convergence of positive factors normally encourages acceptability, but this prediction is disconfirmed by the mid-low ranking of this neoformation in Graph 1.

The case of *girlcott*, a surface analogy after *boycott*, shows both positive and negative factors. As for positive factors, *girlcott* is semantically similar to *boycott* in the first syllable (*girl* is opposite to *boy*), whereas it is phonologically similar to its model in the second syllable (*cott*), which is not an existing morpheme. As for negative factors, the reanalysis of *boycott* as a complex word and the ungrammaticality of the target *girlcott* discourage the acceptability of the latter neoformation.

Similarly, the other three neoformations – i.e. *eggitarian*, *complexability*, and *weavelicious* – are ungrammatical. This negative factor prevails over other positive factors in rating acceptability: e.g., the schema model with formations ending in *-arian* and *-licious*, the semantic similarity between the base *egg* and its co-hyponyms *fruit*, *meat*, *nut*, or the phonological resemblance between targets and models, especially in the final syllables. Here the conflict between the negative factor and all the other positive factors shows how the grammaticality vs. ungrammaticality of the neoformations plays a fundamental role in acceptability rating and ranking order.

8.3.2 Second part of the experiment compared with the first part's results

Graph 2 shows a comparison between the results of the first part of the experiment and those of the second part. In other words, it shows the Average Degree of Acceptability of the targets both in Isolation [ADAI] and in Context [ADAC]. The second part of the experiment was meant to test whether the targets could be more easily accepted by the participants if found in an appropriate context where the model was provided than if offered in isolation.

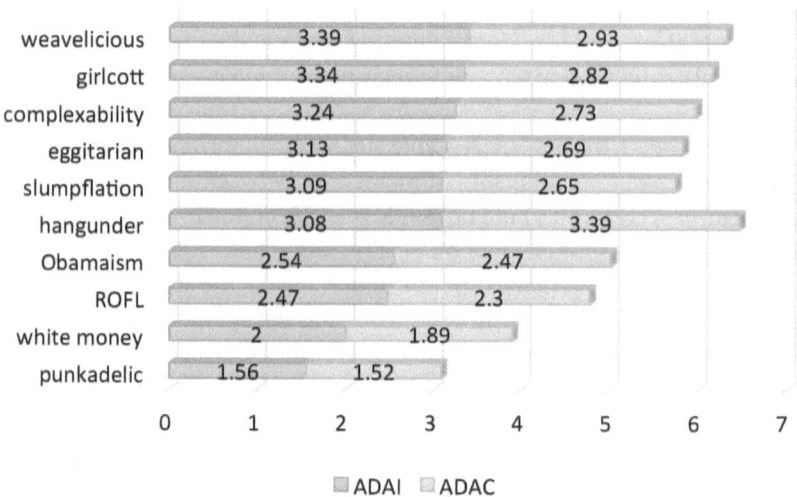

Graph 2: Average Degree of Acceptability per target in Isolation [ADAI] and in Context [ADAC]

In this second part of the experiment, both the independent variables (1)–(4) discussed in 8.1.3 and the additional variables (5)–(7) introduced in 8.1.3 are relevant to acceptability rating. Indeed, Graph 2 shows that the ranking order of the neoformations only varies in one case (for *hangunder*), whose acceptability in context does not improve, as in all the other examples, but decreases.

Hence, the data reported in Graph 2 shows that hypothesis (8') is confirmed by nearly all targets. In all cases except *hangunder*, there was an upgrading of acceptability rating by native speakers if the targets were provided in context. There was no participant who kept all acceptability ratings unchanged. By contrast, on four occasions, the acceptability of the targets *white money*, *Obamaism*, *girlcott*, and *weavelicious* was downgraded in context, but, in spite of this fact, the average acceptability rating in context [ADAC] improved. On those occasions, however, the downgrading was not connected with the difficulty in recovering the model. It was rather connected with the different meaning that the participants associated with the new targets when they first saw them, and the meaning that the targets actually had in the contexts offered.

It is not unexpected that the average upgrading concerned not so much grammatical targets – e.g., *white money* [ADAC 1.89] improved by 0.11 points and *Obamaism* [ADAC 2.47] by 0.07 – as, especially, extra-grammatical targets (*ROFL* [ADAC 2.30] improved by 0.17 and *slumpflation* [ADAC 2.65] by 0.44), and even ungrammatical targets. For instance, *girlcott* [ADAC 2.82], which in (124) was presented immediately after its model *boycott*, upgraded by 0.52 ("Instead of a *boycott*, it was a *girlcott*").[2] This result may signal that not all participants were able to recover the model obtained after reanalysis of the verb/noun *boycott*, yet most of them accepted *girlcott* once they had discovered that it might be an analogical pun from the corresponding verb/noun.

A comparable case was provided by irregular *complexability* [ADAC 2.73], whose model *employability* was offered in the previous paragraph in (120). It indeed upgraded by 0.51 when found in context. Similarly, ungrammatical *weavelicious* [ADAC 2.93] upgraded by 0.46 when it was offered at the end of a sentence which also included *bootylicious* and other irregular analogies ("She is so *bootylicious*, she is so *sexilicious*, she is so *gorgeoulicious*, she is so completely *licious* with her *weavealicious* hair!", see (122)). Indeed, the ungrammaticality of *weavelicious* appears to be more acceptable in this context, since it is motivated by the similarly with irregular formations, such as *sexilicious* and *gorgeoulicious*, both de-adjectival (i.e. from *sexy* and *gorgeous*).

In determining acceptability, the presence of the model either before or after the target (hypothesis 5') proved to be an important factor. For instance, *eggitarian* [ADAC 2.69] upgraded by 0.44 when presented in context ("There are categories for everything educated or not, foreign car or not ... English-speaking or not, *meatarian* or not, if *vegetarian* then whether an *eggitarian* or strict ...", see (126)).

---

[2] In this context, *girlcott* [1891] 'a boycott carried out by a woman or group of women' (OED3) is a converted noun from the verb. Cf. the model noun *boycott* [1880] converted from the verb.

Anaphoric reference to previous model words, such as *meatarian*, and to *vegetarian*, from which the splinter *-arian* is obtained, helped association and inspired acceptability.

Anaphoric reference especially helped association in cases of short target–model distance (hypothesis 6'). For instance, in "As *Bushism* segued into *Obamaism* ..." (119) or "So-called *stagflation* and *slumpflation* ..." (123), the model's recoverability was undemanding. However, reference to a model in the previous sentence also activated association and improved acceptability: e.g., in "A: *Lol* ... man that was hilarious!! B: Yeah I know ... *rofl* ..." (121), the participants probably had a confirmation that the model that they had in their mind in the first part of the experiment was *LOL*. By contrast, anaphoric reference to the model *hangover* did not contribute to improving acceptability in the case of *hangunder*.

Longer target–model distances, as in *complexability* referring to the model *employability* found in the antecedent paragraph (120), might require more time, but since the participants in the experiment had no temporal limits, identification of the model was in most cases straightforward.

Cataphoric reference to the model also helped association (hypothesis 5'). For instance, in "In other words, this is *white money*. The amount of *black money* is still unaccounted for." (125), the model's recoverability was a rather simple task for the participants, as substantiated by the upgrading of acceptability in context.

Finally, also in the case of exophoric reference the model's recoverability was not a demanding task for the participants. For instance, the association of *punkadelic* with the series obtained after *funkadelic* was facilitated in a context involving music, although the model word(s) did not occur ("I remember the Droogs putting out rock-solid *punkadelic* indie records.", see (128)). However, compared with the isolated target, the average acceptability did not upgrade considerably. This partly confirms hypothesis (5'), in that, in *punkadelic*, the difference between the averages in isolation and in context (ADAI – ADAC = 0.04) was not as noticeable as in previous cases.

As for hypothesis (7'), the impact of a short, condensed, or more efficient context on acceptability upgrading was not more substantial than the impact of a long and complex context. A native speaker, for instance, valued the context of *Obamaism* as efficient – "As *Bushism* segued into *Obamaism*, political caricature continued its rebirth." (119), whereas the context of *complexability* (120), involving two paragraphs, was too long and complex for him. Yet, acceptability upgrading was not more striking in the former (0.07 points) compared with the latter (0.51 points), but rather vice versa.

More precisely, for *Obamaism*, in fifteen cases the participants confirmed the same acceptability rating, in six cases they upgraded acceptability by 1 or 2 points, and in one case they downgraded it by 4 points. For *complexability*, however, we had fourteen confirmations and eight upgrading by 1–3 points. Of course, these different results may be influenced by the grammaticality of *Obamaism* [ADAI 2.54] vs. the ungrammaticality of *complexability* [ADAI 3.24], as a further confirmation that the independent variables (1)–(4) still continued to work in this second part of the experiment. Yet, there was no important effect obtained by context efficiency that might imply a correlation between this efficiency and the upgrading of acceptability rating.

The general tendency seems to be that the difference between ADAI and ADAC – that is, between the average degree of acceptability of the neoformations in isolation and in context – gradually increases as the neoformation exhibits more negative than positive factors in variables (1)–(4). In other words, new target words that are grammatical (1), have a schema model (2), and resemble their model both semantically (3) and phonologically (4) do not considerably increase their acceptability degree from the first to the second part of the experiment: e.g., in *punkadelic* [ADAI 1.56] – [ADAC 1.52] = 0.04 points. By contrast, new targets that are ungrammatical (1) surface analogies (2) with a low degree of similarity with their models (3)–(4) more noticeably improve their acceptability: e.g., in *complexability* [ADAI 3.24] – [ADAC 2.73] = 0.51 points and in *weavelicious*, despite its schema model, [ADAI 3.39] – [ADAC 2.93] = 0.46 points. This tendency shows the greater importance of context for ungrammatical than for grammatical neoformations, both for the model's recoverability and for the target's disambiguation.

The only example that in the second part of the experiment changes its position in ranking order is *hangunder*, whose acceptability degree in context [ADAC 3.39] is higher than the ADAC of ungrammatical words, such as *eggitarian* [ADAC 2.69], *complexability* [ADAC 2.73], and *weavelicious* [ADAC 2.93], despite its being grammatical.

Therefore, if only acceptability in context is taken into account, *hangunder* loses its fifth position in ranking order and acquires the last (tenth) position, after *weavelicious*. This factor could be partly explained by a lack of clarity of the context provided in (127) ("A: My roommate came back from the party with a *hangover* last night! B: I didn't go to the party last night, I woke up this morning with a wicked *hangunder*."). This context may have sounded odd to native speakers and the meaning of *hangunder* 'the funny feeling you get when you wake up after a night of not drinking and you're not hungover as usual' may have remained obscure in spite of its similarity with and anaphoric reference to its explicit model *hangover*.

8.3.3 Final remarks on the experiment

The experiment conducted in this chapter was meant to test the degree of acceptability of various new English analogical words, both in isolation and in context. In particular, this experiment was meant to investigate how native speakers view analogical words, if they are able to recognise and interpret them, and if they would accept the use of such new words in general or in a given context. Attention was focused on the role played by the type of analogy (e.g. surface vs. via schema), the type of target (e.g. grammatical vs. extra-/un-grammatical), and the context (i.e. the presence vs. absence of the model) in the assessment of new analogical words. In particular, the main criteria for the acceptability of analogical words were found to be the words' accessibility, regularity, familiar etymology, and the recognisability of a word, series, or word family that could have acted as model.

Although results are far from having statistical reliability, the quantitative analyses show that most of the hypotheses put forward on the basis of theoretical assumptions and of some pilot tests with a random sample of native speakers are for the most part substantiated by empirical data.

A selected sample of well-educated native speakers of English who live in different English-speaking countries participated in the experiment. The participants were tested on the degree of acceptability of ten analogical words both alone [Average Degree of Acceptability in Isolation] and in provided contexts [Average Degree of Acceptability in Context].

The hypotheses put forth in (1')–(4') concerned the isolated words and the way variables such as target grammaticality (vs. ungrammaticality), type of analogical formation, and semantic/phonological neighbourhood with the model could affect target acceptability [ADAI]. Results show that grammatical targets are better candidates for acceptability than extra- or un-grammatical targets. They also corroborate the hypotheses that the model's recoverability is facilitated by a) the presence of a schema with various prototypical words as model, b) semantic similarity with the model in the Variable Part, and c) phonological similarity with the model in the Invariable Part. Continuity between target and model has proved to be an essential precondition for recoverability and acceptability. In general, if the participants were able to recognise the model, they were more prone to accept the target triggered by it.

The hypotheses put forth in (5')–(8') concerned the same words in context and the way variables such as endo- (vs. exo-phoric) reference to the model, target–model distance, context shortness and efficiency could affect (especially, upgrade) the degree of acceptability [ADAC]. Results show that, although anaphoric reference to a close model is the ideal condition for association and acceptability of the target, cataphoric reference and even exophoric reference may help association as well. In all cases except one, context upgraded average acceptability levels, and this was especially the case with ungrammatical targets, whose ADAC significantly outdid ADAI. By contrast, for grammatical targets or targets obtained from schema models, the difference between ADAI and ADAC proved to be less significant.

A comparison between the two rankings of acceptability – with the words in isolation [ADAI] and in context [ADAC] – reveals that the interaction of various intermingled factors has an impact on the acceptability of a new analogical word that native speakers have never heard or used. As participants themselves declared when they were asked the reasons why they would accept such new words, the morphological and/or semantic transparency of the words, the regular word-formation pattern, and the identification of an opposite existing word that could act as model are all possible answers. Contextualised examples where the models were also provided could support the native speakers' opinions, or facilitate their understanding. From the viewpoint of analogy, all the answers and assessments connected with the relationship between target and model are noteworthy.

A final remark concerns the different sources of the selected targets. As stated before (see materials in 8.1.2), two targets belonged to the economics field and were used by specialists (*white money*, *slumpflation*), two were teenagers' analogies commonly used in oral conversation or text messages (*ROFL*, *hangunder*), two were journalistic analogies used in newspaper articles (*Obamaism*, *complexability*), two were used by minor authors in literature (*eggitarian*, *weavelicious*), and two were general (*punkadelic*, *girlcott*). Different sources for targets and different genres or modes are variables that have not been taken into consideration so far, but may deserve some attention in the discussion of results.

For instance, general analogies, such as *punkadelic* and *girlcott*, are not necessarily more acceptable than specialised or journalistic analogies. Indeed, while *punkadelic* is the most acceptable word in the ranking, *girlcott* is less acceptable than *white money*, *Obamaism*, and *slumpflation*. Juvenile analogies, such as *ROFL* and *hangunder* when considered in isolation, are also more acceptable in the ranking than general *girlcott* or literary *eggitarian* and *weavelicious*.

These results suggest that native speakers' evaluation of new targets' acceptability is not affected by the type of coiners (e.g. experts, teenagers, journalists, or authors) or genre of discourse (e.g. specialised book vs. text message vs. conversation vs. newspapers and magazines vs. fiction). Acceptability evaluation is especially driven by morphological factors related to the type of analogy involved and the regularity of the analogy-based words, as well as to co-textual factors connected with the presence or absence of the model triggering the new words. In general, the identification of a word, a series, or word family which could have acted as model encouraged the new words' acceptability.

However, as observed, the small-scale experiment carried out in this chapter had an exploratory nature and generalisations cannot be made until a larger-scale study provides statistically significant data confirming the preliminary findings discussed here.

9 Conclusions

The research questions that I posed in the Introduction to the book were:
1. What is the overall role played by analogy in English word-formation?
2. How can we associate newly coined analogical formations with their models? How is the model recoverable? Are some models preferred or dispreferred for analogical formation?
3. To what extent is the coinage of a new analogical word predictable and to what extent is it not? Are some types of target word more possible, probable, or acceptable than others?
4. What are the contexts and textual genres which favour and motivate analogical word-formation? Why do speakers choose to coin a new word which bears a resemblance to another particular item rather than using only word-formation rules?

As to the first question, this book shows that analogy is a versatile concept in English word-formation, in that it is transversely relevant to grammatical and marginal morphology, extra-grammatical morphology, and even to ungrammatical word forms, the latter often involving reanalysis. A quantitative investigation of the database shows that:

− Within grammatical morphology, 23.9% of the analogical formations are compounds, 11.8% are derived words, and 0.5% are N → V converted words;
− Within extra-grammatical morphology, blends account for 13.9% of the database, acronyms or initialisms for 7.8%, reduplicatives, clippings, and back-formations for 0.8%, and phonaesthemes for 0.6%.
− Within marginal morphology, especially in regard to the transition between derivation and compounding, 35.1% of the database is obtained via combining forms. Other less frequent transitions are between complex noun phrases and prototypical compounds (e.g. loose compounds), or between morphology and the lexicon (e.g. submorphemes) (see marginal morphology in Dressler 2000: 6–7);
− The remaining 4 percentage includes ungrammatical formations, either because they do not comply with morphological rules or because they involve reanalysis.

Moreover, analogical formations belong to a spectrum of types and subtypes (3.3.1) which are illustrated in this work both through institutionalised neologisms (54%), attested in dictionaries, collections, and corpora, and through nonce words or occasionalisms (46%) that are still waiting for acceptance and recognition by the English speech community. These neoformations belong to heterogeneous morphological categories (3.3.6), but can be assimilated because of a morphological relatedness to a concrete model (3.2.5).

As to the relationship between target and model words, the book discusses target analogical formations as part of what Bauer, Lieber, and Plag (2013) call 'paradigmatic morphology'. Indeed, most of them cannot be analysed in terms of a concatenation process – or, at least, this is not their primary motivation – but have to be considered in terms of a paradigmatic substitution of a Variable Part, either in an exact model word or in a grid of related words. Thus, for instance, the coinage of slang *beefcake* can be explained by the proportional equation *cheese* : *cheesecake* = *beef* : X (X = *beefcake*), where *beef* (vs. *cheese*) accounts for the Variable Part. In this case, however, the neoformation is also a regular N–N compound complying with word-formation rules, that is, it is the subtype of 'surface analogy combined with rule'.

A different subtype of surface analogy (called 'pure') is in *duckwich* and *turkeywich*, obtained after the reanalysis of *sandwich* as a complex word, although there is no *sand* in a *sandwich*.

A still different type is in *beefburger*, whose model is not a precise word, but a series represented by related words, i.e. *chickenburger*, *cheeseburger*, etc., and triggered by the morphological resegmentation of *Hamburg-er* as *ham* + *burger*, again with no *ham* inside. The latter type of analogy is obtained via a schema model.

As to the model's recoverability and the target's interpretation, these are facilitated by that portion of the analogy termed 'Invariable Part', since it is shared by new targets and their models. In other words, target words generally preserve a segment of their models, which may correspond either to an existing morpheme, such as the compound component *cake* in *beefcake* or the combining form *-burger* in *beefburger*, or to a meaningless sequence of letters, such as *wich* in *duckwich*.

Statistically, the neoformations collected in this book show a tendency of analogical target words to preserve the final part of their models. In particular, 31.3% of formations preserve a final combining form (vs. 3.7% preserving an initial combining form), 10.6% of derived words preserve a suffix (vs. 1.2% preserving a prefix), and 16.2% of compounds retain their right constituent (vs. 7.6% retaining the left constituent). This shows the great importance of the morphological head, another indicator of the impact of grammatical structures on analogical formation. Blends also confirm this same tendency, with 9% final splinters reproduced in analogical blends (vs. 2% initial splinters). In general, these findings may signal the salience of word ends over word beginnings in analogical word-formation.

In addition, the book shows that, in analogical word-formation, similarity is not confined to the Invariable Part, but also comprises an array of affinities at various language levels, namely, phonological, morphotactic, and semantic features [f_n], which are owned by both the target and the model. From the phonological viewpoint, similarity features include segmental affinities in onset, nucleus, coda, body, or rime, and suprasegmental aspects, such as word length and stress. From the morphotactic viewpoint, similarity features involve the grammaticality vs. extra-grammaticality of the formations, as well as their morphological and syntactic categorisation. Lastly, from the semantic viewpoint, similarity features consist of near identity (synonymy), massive semantic overlap (paronymy), contradictory opposition (antonymy), or other contrasts (especially, co-hyponymy) concerning the Variable Part in models–targets. More often than not, new analogical words exhibit an intended polyvalence, i.e. simultaneous display of similarity features from diverse viewpoints.

Therefore, preferred models in analogical formation are those that resemble their targets from various viewpoints, so that the model–target association is immediate and, consequently, the model's recoverability is favoured. Preferred models are also series, in that the existence of accepted sets of words sharing the same formation process is another factor helping and encouraging model–target association. Finally, models that are complex (or reanalysable as complex words) may be preferred in analogical formation, in that this may help the substitution that is typical of the analogical proportion.

As to the predictability of novel analogical words, analogy is not fully unpredictable, as some scholars (e.g. Bauer 1983; Dressler and Karpf 1995 *inter alia*) claim, but partially predictable on the basis of the availability of a certain word (or word pattern) and of its potential to become the model for the creation of new words. However, a distinction should be made between the type of analogy based on a unique exemplar and the type based on several prototypes.

The model of analogy described in this book is gradual, with surface analogy – i.e. analogy created on a unique exemplar, such as *software* after *hardware* – being at the one end of the scale, and analogy via schema – i.e. with several prototypes – at the other end. In other words, analogical words may be formed on the pattern of either an exact model (e.g. *hardware*), or more similar words that constitute a series or word set. The shift from surface analogy to analogy via schema is a gradual process, which entails ever more words modelled on the same item, and, later, on more prototypical items, that is, a schema. In *-ware* formations, *software, firmware, adware, spyware* become prototypes for the creation of later *malware, bloatware, vapourware*, and similar others. Therefore, unlike rules, schemas are not abstract in nature, but rather consist of concrete words, such as the above set.

Moreover, in such a complex case as the one in question, a compound analysis of the prototypical set, including *firmware, adware, spyware*, etc. does not seem to be convincing. As observed by Bauer, Lieber, and Plag (2013: 528), *-ware* is more plausibly a bound splinter with a distinct meaning 'software' than a free compound component (cf. *hard + ware*). The regularity of *-ware* formations and the predictability of new similar forms make it a potential candidate for interpretation as a final combining form. This case illustrates not only the trend to coin new words on series of existing others which are accepted, recognised, and institutionalised, but also the relevance of analogy to the diachronic development of the English lexicon.

The dividing line between recurrent splinters and combining forms is also very subtle and it is often difficult to discriminate between the two categories, if not, again, by resorting to diachronic reasons. For instance, there must have been a moment when the splinter *-(a)holic*, as in *workaholic, sugarholic, chocoholic*, etc. became a recognised combining form. Indeed, the fact that it combines with another blend component in *chocoholic* (← *choco*(*late* + *alco*)*holic*) confirms its splinter status, at least initially. However, the fact that in *workaholic* or *chocoholic* only part of the meaning of *alcoholic* is retained suggests that *-(a)holic* may have evolved – as it actually has – towards a combining form status; specifically, it is a secreted combining form (Warren 1990). Its productivity has even led to the label 'suffix' in dictionaries such as the OED or Green (1991), or 'secreted affix' in Fradin (2000).

Interestingly, *-(a)holic* is not an isolated case where researchers and lexicographers do not agree with the interpretation of a morpheme. For instance, *-ati* (in *literati*), often added to words ending in *-er* (hence the variant *-erati*), as in *niggerati, glitterati*, etc., is labelled 'combining form' in the OED, and Jonathon Green (2010) even describes it as a slang 'suffix', conferring more regularity upon this bound morpheme. However, both Klégr and Čermák (2010) and Miller (2014) offer a blending analysis for analogical words such as *glitterati* and *jazzerati*, thus interpreting *-erati* still as a blend component or 'splinter'.

Many splinters discussed in this book on analogy have originated series, and may be candidates for the status of combining forms. They include, for instance, *-ercise* ← *exercise* (as in *boxercise, dancercise, computercize*), which Baldi and Dawar (2000) define an 'unconventional suffix', and *-arian*, which, in line with Adams (1973), is a 'suffix' that occurs in a subgroup of words inspired by *vegetarian*, i.e. *breatharian, dietarian, flexitarian, fruitarian, nutarian*, etc.

Two case studies – i.e. -*sitter* as in analogical *dog-sitter* and -*napping* as in *dognapping* – have also been quantitatively investigated in English corpora (3.1.2), using corpus linguistics tools, in order to show that, in contrast with Bauer (1983), analogy can give rise to productive series. Analogical words modelled on such productive patterns are not only predictable, but also possible and acceptable.

It is on the basis of these premises that I have decided to test the degree of acceptability of new analogical words with a sample of native English speakers. Given the small number of participants, the quantitative analysis cannot provide statistically reliable results, but it shows some tendencies in native speakers' attitude towards analogical neoformations. The participants in the experiment were tested on the degree of acceptability of ten analogical words both in isolation and in provided contexts.

First, some hypotheses were put forth after pilot tests, but before the actual experiment. They concerned the isolated words and the way variables such as target grammaticality (vs. ungrammaticality), type of analogical formation (surface vs. via schema), and semantic/phonological neighbourhood with the model could affect target acceptability. Results show that grammatical targets are better candidates for acceptability than extra- or un-grammatical targets. They also corroborate the hypotheses that the model's recoverability is favoured both by the presence of a schema model, and by the semantic and phonological similarity between model and target, both in the Variable and in the Invariable Part. In general, tests show that, if the informants are able to recognise the model, they are also more inclined to accept its analogical target.

Second, additional hypotheses were put forth concerning the same words in context and the way variables such as endo- (vs. exo-phoric) reference to the model, target–model distance, and context efficiency could affect (especially, increase) the mean degree of acceptability. Results show that anaphoric reference to a close model is the ideal condition for association of the target, but also cataphoric reference may help such an association. In all cases except one, context upgraded average acceptability levels, and upgrading was especially evident and significant with ungrammatical targets.

In general, a new English analogical formation can gain acceptance in a speech community if its pattern is recognisable, either because there is a series or word family conforming to it, or because the analogical target also complies with word-formation rules. Other co-textual factors, mainly the occurrence of the model word in the same (micro-)context, can contribute to the processes of recoverability, disambiguation, and acceptance.

Finally, as to the contexts and textual genres which favour and motivate analogical word-formation, new English analogical words are currently coined in a gamut of areas and domains, including specialised discourse, juvenile speech, journalistic language, and literary works. Each of these domains, of course, has its own reasons for neologising and, more precisely, for creating novel formations that resemble existing ones.

In specialised discourse, a large number of such formations are intended neologisms, as the words selected for qualitative and quantitative analyses in chapter four demonstrate. Indeed, among them, 94.4% are attested in the OED, and 64.8% also occur in COCA, whereas only 14.8% are unattested in GloWbE. In corpora, 59.2% of the new words occur together with their models, either/both as anaphoric analogies (100%) or/and as cataphoric anticipations of the model words (84.3%), while 27.7% exophorically allude to an external model with no need of its explicit mention. The reasons behind intended specialised neologisms range from the denomination function to the necessity to communicate ever more efficiently and effectively with other experts in one's sector, or to reinforce social and professional bonds with one's group.

In juvenile language, dealt with in chapter five, the number of new words attested in corpora corresponds to 63.4%, with only a half occurring together with their models, with a balance of 50% between anaphoric and cataphoric analogies.

Remarkably, analogy via schema seems to be often opted for by young speakers as a word-formation mechanism. Indeed, alongside well-established combining forms, such as *-(a)holic* and *-(a)thon*, adolescents recurrently use such splinters as *-gasm*, *-orexia*, and *-ccino*, and such combining forms as *-licious*, *-rific*, and *-zilla* to create new words. The motives for such analogical formations range from the need to express intimacy with their peers to the desire to exclude outsiders, especially parents and educators. Other reasons involve jocularity, playfulness, and humour, as well as a search for creativity, innovation, and originality.

In journalistic language, 67.3% of the terms under examination are neither attested in COCA nor in *TIME Magazine*, and most of them are nonce words including puns, ungrammatical formations, derived words displaying unproductive suffixes, and even orthographic analogies meant to attract readers' attention. The residual neologisms (32.6%) mostly include formations obtained via combining forms, such as *-licious* and *-tainment*, or recurrent splinters (e.g. *-ercise*). The model words rarely occur together with their targets, with anaphoric analogies which clearly dominate over cataphoric ones.

As for functions, in newspapers, especially electronic ones, journalists tend to create occasionalisms to reduce formality and establish a closer social connection with the reading public. Journalistic analogical nonce words are commonly used to capture readers' curiosity, and amuse them through grammatical anomaly. Other journalistic analogies used in more formal contexts, such as science popularisation texts, are intended neologisms obeying a denominative/labelling function.

Lastly, in literary language, generalisations are not possible, since this book focuses on two authors only, nor can corpus analysis be conducted with meaningful results. Yet, a comparison between the two authors seems to be conceivable. This comparison shows that all analogical formations found in Hopkins' *Poems* are recorded in the OED, although only 37.1% of them are actual neologisms and 62.8% are occasionalisms. By contrast, only 18% of Joyce's analogies in *Finnegans Wake* are OED entries, and the percentage of ephemeral occasionalisms amounts to 81.9%.

Moreover, whereas Hopkins' analogies are for the most part novel compounds, Joyce's ones are both grammatical neologisms and ungrammatical occasionalisms, illustrating various degrees of audacity, from clause-based compounds and phrase-based derived words to extra-grammatical formations and loans, or loan adaptations, and even to orthographic and/or phonological distortions. As a consequence, whereas 71.8% of Hopkins' analogies are exophoric, i.e. without a necessary model word in the (micro-) context, 74% of Joyce's analogies are endophoric, with a predominance of anaphoric over cataphoric targets. Indeed, an explicit model is in Joyce essential for disambiguation.

In both authors, however, analogy is mainly used for effective reasons, especially, for poetic purposes, such as producing alliteration, rhyme, creating rhythm, as well as for arousing the audience's curiosity, playing on words, and spicing poems or novels with original formations.

Overall, the study conducted in this book both revives the ancient prominence of the notion of analogy and confers new dignity on it. First, it shows that analogical formations should not be neglected or dismissed from morphological accounts, because they are far from infrequent and multifarious in English word-formation, ranging from regular compounds or derived words to linguistic anomalies. Second, it shows that analogy is not fully unpredictable, since novel analogical target words can be partially predicted on the basis of existing word forms, word families, and series (or schemas) which can act as models. Thus, analogical neoformations are not chaotic, but limited by probabilistic factors. Third, it shows the contextual suitability and polyvalence of analogy, which may be adopted in numerous dissimilar spheres as an efficient and effective word-formation mechanism.

References

Adams, Valerie. 1973. *An introduction to Modern English word-formation*. London: Longman.
Adams, Valerie. 2001. *Complex words in English*. Harlow: Longman.
Aitchison, Jean. 2003 [1987]. *Words in the mind: An introduction to the mental lexicon*, 3rd edn. Oxford: Blackwell.
Algeo, John (ed.). 1991. *Fifty years among the new words: A dictionary of neologisms, 1941–1991*. Cambridge: Cambridge University Press.
Altieri Biagi, Maria L. 1974. Aspetti e tendenze dei linguaggi della scienza. In Centro per lo studio dell'insegnamento all'estero dell'italiano, *Italiano d'oggi: Lingua non letteraria e lingue speciali*, 67–110. Trieste: LINT.
Amiot, Dany. 2008. Analogy vs rules: How can diachronic and synchronic perspectives be made to work together? In Geert Booij, Angela Ralli & Sergio Scalise (eds.), *Morphology and dialectology. On-line proceedings of the sixth Mediterranean Morphology Meeting (MMM6)*, Ithaca, 27–30 September 2007, 123–133. University of Patras, Greece.
Anderson, Earl R. 1998. *A grammar of iconism*. Madison, NJ: Fairleigh Dickinson University Press.
Anttila, Raimo. 1977. *Analogy*. The Hague, Paris & New York: Mouton.
Anttila, Raimo. 2003. Analogy: The warp and woof of cognition. In Brian D. Joseph & Richard D. Janda (eds.), *The handbook of historical linguistics*, 425–440. Oxford: Blackwell.
Arndt-Lappe, Sabine. 2011. Towards an exemplar-based model of stress in English noun–noun compounds. *Journal of Linguistics* 47 (11). 549–585.
Arndt-Lappe, Sabine. 2014. Analogy in suffix rivalry: The case of English -*ity* and -*ness*. *English Language and Linguistics* 18 (3). 497–548.
Arndt-Lappe, Sabine. 2015. Word-formation and analogy. In Peter O. Müller, Ingeborg Ohnheiser, Susan Olsen & Franz Rainer (eds.), *Word-formation. An international handbook of the languages of Europe*, vol. 2, 822–841. Berlin: De Gruyter Mouton. https://manling.files.wordpress.com/2014/03/47_arndt-lappe_hsk_toappear.pdf (accessed 29 May 2015).
Arndt-Lappe, Sabine & Melanie J. Bell. 2014. Analogy and the nature of linguistic generalisation: Locality, generality, and variability in English compound stress. Manuscript, Heinrich-Heine-Universität Düsseldorf and Anglia Ruskin University. Submitted for publication. https://www.phil-fak.uni-duesseldorf.de/anglistik3/arndt-lappe/publications_arndt_lappe/ (accessed 25 September 2014).
Arndt-Lappe, Sabine & Ingo Plag. 2013. The role of prosodic structure in the formation of English blends. *English Language and Linguistics* 17 (3). 537–563.
Aronoff, Mark. 1976. *Word formation in generative grammar*. Cambridge, MA: The MIT Press.
Aronoff, Mark. 1983. Potential words, actual words, productivity and frequency. In Shirō Hattori & Kazuko Inoue (eds.), *Proceedings of the thirteenth International Congress of Linguistics*, 163–171. Tokyo: Permanent International Committee on Linguistics.
Aronoff, Mark & Kristen A. Fudeman. 2011 [2005]. *What is morphology?*, 2nd edn. Malden, MA, Oxford & Chichester: Wiley-Blackwell.
Austin, John L. 1962. *How to do things with words: The William James lectures delivered at Harvard University in 1955*. Oxford: Claredon Press.
Baayen, Harald & Antoinette Renouf. 1996. Chronicling 'the Times': Productive lexical innovations in an English newspaper. *Language* 72 (1). 69–96.

Baldi, Philip & Chantal Dawar. 2000. Creative processes. In Geert E. Booij, Christian Lehmann, Joachim Mugdan, Wolfgang Kesselheim & Stavros Skopeteas (eds.), *Morphologie–morphology: An international handbook of inflection and word-formation*, vol. 1, 963–972. Berlin & New York: Walter de Gruyter.

Bat-El, Outi. 2000. The grammaticality of extragrammatical morphology. In Ursula Doleschal & Anna M. Thornton (eds.), *Extragrammatical and marginal morphology*, 61–84. München: Lincom Europa.

Bauer, Laurie. 1983. *English word-formation*. Cambridge: Cambridge University Press.

Bauer, Laurie. 2001. *Morphological productivity*. Cambridge: Cambridge University Press.

Bauer, Laurie. 2003 [1988]. *Introducing linguistic morphology*, 2nd edn. Edinburgh: Edinburgh University Press.

Bauer, Laurie, Rochelle Lieber & Ingo Plag. 2013. *The Oxford reference guide to English morphology*. Oxford: Oxford University Press.

Becker, Thomas. 1990. *Analogie und morphologische Theorie* (Studien zur theoretischen Linguistik). München: Fink.

Becker, Thomas. 1993. Back-formation, cross-formation and 'bracketing paradoxes' in paradigmatic morphology. In Geert Booij & Jaap van Marle (eds.), *Yearbook of morphology 1993*, 1–25. Dordrecht: Kluwer.

Benczes, Réka. 2006. *Creative compounding in English*. Amsterdam & Philadelphia: John Benjamins.

Berko, Jean. 1958. The child's learning of English morphology. *Word* 14. 150–177.

Bertinetto, Pier Marco. 2001. Blends and syllabic structure: A four-fold comparison. In Mercè Lorente, Núria Alturo, Emili Boix, Maria-Rosa Lloret & Lluís Payrató (eds.), *La gramàtica i la semàntica en l'estudi de la variació*, 59–112. Barcelona: Promociones y Publicaciones Universitarias.

Blevins, James P. & Juliette Blevins. 2009. Introduction: Analogy in grammar. In James P. Blevins & Juliette Blevins (eds.), *Analogy in grammar. Form and acquisition*, 1–12. Oxford: Oxford University Press.

Bloomfield, Leonard. 1933. *Language*. New York: Henry Holt and Company.

Boase-Beier, Jean. 1987. *Poetic compounds: The principles of poetic language in Modern English poetry*, reprinted 2010. Tübingen: Max Niemeyer Verlag GmbH & Co KG.

Booij, Geert E. 2005. *The grammar of words*. Oxford: Oxford University Press.

Booij, Geert E. 2010. *Construction morphology*. Oxford: Oxford University Press.

Bosch, Antal van den & Walter Daelemans. 2013. Implicit schemata and categories in memory-based language processing. *Language and Speech* 56 (3). 309–328.

Bourque, Stephen Y. 2014. *Toward a typology of semantic transparency: The case of French compounds*. Canada: University of Toronto PhD thesis.

Brinton, Laurel J. & Elizabeth Closs Traugott. 2005. *Lexicalization and language change*. Cambridge: Cambridge University Press.

British National Corpus. 2010. BNC Webmaster. University of Oxford. http://www.natcorp.ox.ac.uk/.

Bybee, Joan L. 1988. Morphology as lexical organization. In Michael Hammond & Michael Noonan (eds.), *Theoretical morphology. Approaches in modern linguistics*, 119–141. San Diego: Academic Press.

Bybee, Joan L. 2010. *Language, usage and cognition*. Cambridge: Cambridge University Press.

Bybee, Joan L. & David Eddington. 2006. A usage-based approach to Spanish verbs of 'becoming'. *Language* 82. 323–355.

Cacchiani, Silvia. 2007. Discourse-pragmatic features of novel evaluative blends. In Laura Jottini, Gabriella Del Lungo & John Douthwaite (eds.), *City-scapes: Islands of the self. Language studies*, vol. 2, 103–114. Cagliari: CUEC.

Cappelli, Gloria. 2013. Travelling words: Languaging in English tourism discourse. In Alison Yarrington, Stefano Villani & Julia Kelly (eds.), *Travels and translations. Anglo-Italian cultural transactions*, 353–374. New York & Amsterdam: Rodopi.

Chapman, Don & Royal Skousen. 2005. Analogical modeling and morphological change: The case of the adjectival negative prefix in English. *English Language and Linguistics* 9 (2). 333–357.

Chomsky, Noam. 1957. *Syntactic structure*. The Hague: Mouton.

Christofidou, Anastasia. 1994. *Okkasionalismen in poetischen Texten*. Tübingen: Narr.

Clark, Eve V. 1972. On the child's acquisition of antonyms in two semantic fields. *Journal of Verbal Learning and Verbal Behavior* 2. 750–758.

Clark, Eve V. 1981. Lexical innovations: How children learn to create new words. In Werner Deutsch (ed.), *The child's construction of language*, 299–328. New York & London: Academic Press.

Clark, Eve V. 1982. The young word maker: A case study of innovation in the child's lexicon. In Eric Wanner & Lila R. Gleitman (eds.), *Language acquisition: The state of the art*, 390–425. Cambridge: Cambridge University Press.

Clark, Eve V. 2009 [2003]. *First language acquisition*, 2nd edn. Cambridge: Cambridge University Press.

Coleman, Julie. 2014. Slang used by students at the University of Leicester (2004–11). In Julie Coleman (ed.), *Global English slang: Methodologies and perspectives*, 49–61. London & New York: Routledge.

Concise Oxford English Dictionary. 2011. Oxford: Oxford University Press.

Corpus of Contemporary American English. 1990–2012. COCA. Brigham Young University. http://corpus.byu.edu/coca/.

Crawford Camiciottoli, Belinda B. 2015. 'All those Elvis-meets-golf-player looks': A corpus-assisted analysis of creative compounds in fashion blogging. *Discourse, Context and Media*. http://dx.doi.org/10.1016/j.dcm.2015.10.002 (accessed 23 November 2015).

Daelemans, Walter & Antal van den Bosch. 2005. *Memory-based language processing*. Cambridge: Cambridge University Press.

Daelemans, Walter, Jakub Zavrel, Ko van der Sloot & Antal van den Bosch. 2007. *TiMBL: Tilburg memory based learner, version 6.0, reference guide* (LK Technical Report 04–02). Tilburg: ILK.

Dalton-Puffer, Christiane. 1996. *The French influence on Middle English morphology. A corpus-based study of derivation*. Berlin & New York: Mouton de Gruyter.

De Jong, Nivja H., Laurie B. Feldman, Robert Schreuder, Matthew Pastizzo & R. Harald Baayen. 2002. The processing and representation of Dutch and English compounds: Peripheral morphological and central orthographic effects. *Brain and Language* 81 (1). 555–567.

De Jong, Nivja H., Robert Schreuder & R. Harald Baayen. 2000. The morphological family size effect and morphology. *Language and Cognitive Processes* 15 (4/5). 329–365.

Derwing, Bruce L. & Royal Skousen. 1989. Morphology in the mental lexicon: A new look at analogy. In Geert Booij & Jaap van Marle (eds.), *Yearbook of Morphology 2*. 55–71. Dordrecht & Providence RI: Foris.

De Smet, Hendrik. 2013. Change through recombination: Blending and analogy. *Language Sciences* 40. 80–94.

Dressler, Wolfgang U. 1976. Tendenzen in kontaminatorischen Fehlleistungen (und ihre Beziehung zur Sprachgeschichte). *Die Sprache* 22. 1–10.
Dressler, Wolfgang U. 1977. Elements of a polycentristic theory of word formation. *Wiener Linguistische Gazette* 15. 13–32.
Dressler, Wolfgang U. 1981. General principles of poetic license in word formation. In Horst Geckeler, Britigitte Schlieben-Lange, Jürgen Trabant & Harald Weydt (eds.), *Logos semantikos. Studia linguistica in honorem Eugenio Coseriu 1921–1981*, vol. 2, 423–431. Berlin: Mouton de Gruyter.
Dressler, Wolfgang U. 1993. Word-formation: Poetic licence. In Ronald E. Asher & James M. Y. Simpson (eds.), *The encyclopedia of language and linguistics*, vol. 9, 5028–5029. Oxford: Pergamon Press.
Dressler, Wolfgang U. 2000. Extragrammatical vs. marginal morphology. In Ursula Doleschal & Anna M. Thornton (eds.), *Extragrammatical and marginal morphology*, 1–10. München: Lincom Europa.
Dressler, Wolfgang U. 2003. Degrees of grammatical productivity in inflectional morphology. *Italian Journal of Linguistics / Rivista di Linguistica* 15 (1). 31–62.
Dressler, Wolfgang U. 2007. Produktivität und poetische Lizenz. In Wolfgang U. Dressler & Oswald Panagl (eds.), *Poetische Lizenzen*, 87–98. Wien: Praesens Verlag.
Dressler, Wolfgang U. & Annemarie Karpf. 1995. The theoretical relevance of pre- and protomorphology in language acquisition. In Geert E. Booij & Jaap van Marle (eds.), *Yearbook of Morphology 1994*, 99–122. Dordrecht: Kluwer.
Dressler, Wolfgang U. & Sabine Laaha. 2012. The impact of types of analogy on first language acquisition. *Lingue e Linguaggio* 11 (2). 107–121.
Dressler, Wolfgang U. & Mária Ladányi. 1998. On grammatical productivity of word formation rules (WFRs). *Wiener Linguistische Gazette* 62/63. 29–55.
Dressler, Wolfgang U. & Mária Ladányi. 2000. Productivity in word formation (WF): A morphological approach. *Acta Lingistica Hungarica* 47 (1). 103–145.
Dressler, Wolfgang U., Willi Mayerthaler, Oswald Panagl & Wolfgang U. Wurzel. 1987. *Leitmotifs in natural morphology*. Amsterdam & Philadelphia: John Benjamins.
Dressler, Wolfgang U. & Lavinia Merlini Barbaresi. 1994. *Morphopragmatics: Diminutives and intensifiers in Italian, German, and other languages*. Berlin & New York: Mouton de Gruyter.
Dressler, Wolfgang U. & Oswald Panagl (eds.). 2007. *Poetische Lizenzen*. Wien: Praesens Verlag.
Eble, Connie. 1996. *Slang and sociability: In-group language among college students*. Chapel Hill & London: The University of North Carolina Press.
English TenTen web corpus. 2012. enTenTen12. Lexical Computing Ltd. https://www.sketchengine.co.uk/ententen-corpus/.
Faber, Pamela. 2009. The pragmatics of specialized communication. *Entreculturas* 1. 61–84.
Fertig, David L. 2013. *Analogy and morphological change*. Edinburgh: Edinburgh University Press.
Firth, John R. 1930. *Speech*. London: Ernest Benn.
Fischer, Olga. 2007. *Morphosyntactic change: Functional and formal perspectives*. Oxford: Oxford University Press.
Fischer, Roswitha. 1998. *Lexical change in Present-day English. A corpus-based study of the motivation, institutionalization, and productivity of creative neologisms*. Tübingen: Gunter Narr Verlag.
Fleischer, Wolfgang. 1975. *Wortbildung der deutschen Gegenwartssprache*. Tübingen: Niemeyer.

Fradin, Bernard. 2000. Combining forms, blends and related phenomena. In Ursula Doleschal & Anna M. Thornton (eds.), *Extragrammatical and marginal morphology*, 11–59. München: Lincom Europa.
Fromkin, Victoria A. 1973. *Speech errors as linguistic evidence*. The Hague & Paris: Mouton.
Fromkin, Victoria A. 1980. Introduction. In Victoria A. Fromkin (ed.), *Errors in linguistic performance. Slips of the tongue, ear, pen, and hand*, 1–12. New York & London: Academic Press.
Fuhrhop, Nanna. 1998. *Grenzfälle morphologischer Einheiten*. Tübingen: Stauffenburg.
Gagné, Christina. 2001. Relation and lexical priming during the interpretation of noun–noun combinations. *Journal of Experimental Psychology: Learning, Memory, and Cognition* 27 (1). 236–254.
Gagné, Christina & Edward J. Shoben. 1997. Influence of thematic relations on the comprehension of modifier–noun combinations. *Journal of Experimental Psychology: Learning, Memory, and Cognition* 23 (1). 71–87.
Gagné, Christina & Thomas L. Spalding. 2006. Conceptual combination: Implications for the mental lexicon. In Gary Libben & Gonia Jarema (eds.), *The representation and processing of compound words*, 145–168. Oxford: Oxford University Press.
Gagné, Christina, Thomas L. Spalding & Melissa C. Gorrie. 2005. Sentential context and the interpretation of familiar open-compounds and novel modifier–noun phrases. *Language and Speech* 48 (2). 203–221.
Gardani, Francesco. 2013. *Dynamics of morphological productivity. The evolution of noun classes from Latin to Italian*. Leiden: Brill.
Garner, Bryan A. 1987. Shakespeare's Latinate neologisms. In Vivian Salmon & Edwina Burness (eds.), *A reader in the language of Shakespearean drama*, 207–228. Amsterdam & Philadelphia: John Benjamins.
Global Web-Based English. 2012–2013. GloWbE. Brigham Young University. http://corpus.byu.edu/glowbe/.
Glowka, Arthur Wayne, Brenda K. Lester, Rachel Duggan-Caputo, Jeff Drye & Barry A. Popik. 2000. Among the new words. *American Speech* 75 (2). 184–198.
Glowka, Arthur Wayne & Megan Melançon. 2002. Among the new words. *American Speech* 77 (3). 313–324.
Gotti, Maurizio. 2008 [2005]. *Investigating specialized discourse*, 2nd edn. Bern: Peter Lang.
Green, Jonathon. 1991. *Neologisms. New words since 1960*. London: Bloomsbury Publishing.
Green, Jonathon. 2010. *Green's dictionary of slang*, 3 vols. Edinburgh: Chambers. Digital edition 2016 at https://beta.greensdictofslang.com/.
Gries, Stefan Th. 2004a. Shouldn't it be *breakfunch*? A quantitative analysis of blend structure in English. *Linguistics* 42 (3). 639–667.
Gries, Stefan Th. 2004b. Isn't that *fantabulous*? How similarity motivates intentional morphological blends in English. In Michel Achard & Suzanne Kemmer (eds.), *Language, culture, and mind*, 415–428. Stanford: CSLI Publications.
Gries, Stefan Th. 2012. Quantitative corpus data on blend formation: Psycho- and cognitive-linguistic perspectives. In Vincent Renner, François Maniez & Pierre Arnaud (eds.), *Cross-disciplinary perspectives on lexical blending*, 145–168. Berlin & New York: Mouton de Gruyter.
The Guardian Online. 2017. Guardian News and Media Ltd. http://www.theguardian.com/uk.
Haspelmath, Martin. 2002. *Understanding morphology*. London: Arnold Publications.

Hermann, Eduard. 1931. *Lautgesetz und Analogie*. Berlin: Weidmannsche Buchhandlung.
Hill, Eugen. 2007. Proportionale Analogie, paradigmatischer Ausgleich und Formerweiterung. Ein Beitrag zur Typologie des morphologischen Wandels. *Diachronica* 24 (1). 81–118.
Hock, Hans H. 1991 [1938]. *Principles of historical linguistics*, 2nd edn. Berlin & New York: Mouton de Gruyter.
Hockett, Charles F. 1968. *The state of the art*. The Hague & Paris: Mouton.
Hohenhaus, Peter. 1996. *Ad-hoc-Wortbildung. Terminologie, Typologie und Theorie kreativer Wortbildung im Englischen*. Frankfurt am Main: Peter Lang.
Hohenhaus, Peter. 2007. How to do (even more) things with nonce words (other than naming). In Judith Munat (ed.), *Lexical creativity, texts and contexts*, 15–38. Amsterdam & Philadelphia: John Benjamins.
Hopkins, Gerard Manley. 1935. *The letters of Gerard Manley Hopkins to Robert Bridges*. London: Oxford University Press.
Hopkins, Gerard Manley. 1937. *The note-books and papers of Gerard Manley Hopkins*. Humphry House (ed.). London & New York: Oxford University Press.
Hopkins, Gerard Manley. 1956. *Further letters of Gerard Manley Hopkins: Including his correspondence with Coventry Patmore*. London & New York: Oxford University Press.
Hopkins, Gerard Manley. 1959a. *The journals and papers of Gerard Manley Hopkins*. London & New York: Oxford University Press.
Hopkins, Gerard Manley. 1959b. *Sermons and devotional writings*. London & New York: Oxford University Press.
Hopkins, Gerard Manley. 1967. *Selected poems of Gerard Manley Hopkins*. James Reeves (ed.). London: Heinemann.
Hopper, Paul J. & Elizabeth Closs Traugott. 2003 [1993]. *Grammaticalization*, 2nd edn. Cambridge: Cambridge University Press.
Iamartino, Giovanni. 1999. L'innovazione lessicale nei testi letterari e nelle loro traduzioni: Puntualizzazioni concettuali e indicazioni metodologiche. In Gabriele Azzaro & Margherita Ulrych (eds.), *Anglistica e …: Metodi e percorsi comparatistici nelle lingue, culture e letterature di origine europea*, vol. 2, 257–269. Trieste: EUT.
The Independent Online. 2017. Independent Print Ltd. http://www.independent.co.uk/.
Itkonen, Esa. 2005. *Analogy as structure and process. Approaches in linguistics, cognitive psychology and philosophy of science*. Amsterdam & Philadelphia: John Benjamins.
Jarema, Gonia, Céline Busson, Rossitza Nikolova, Kyrana Tsapkini & Gary Libben. 1999. Processing compounds: A cross-linguistic study. *Brain and Language* 68. 362–369.
Jones, Steven, M. Lynne Murphy, Carita Paradis & Caroline Willners. 2012. *Antonyms in English. Construals, constructions and canonicity*. Cambridge: Cambridge University Press.
Joyce, James. 1939. *Finnegans wake*. London: Faber and Faber.
Kastovsky, Dieter. 1986a. Diachronic word-formation in a functional perspective. In Dieter Kastovsky & Aleksander Szwedek (eds.), *Linguistics across historical and geographical boundaries. In honour of Jacek Fisiak on the occasion of his fiftieth birthday*, 409–421. Berlin: Mouton de Gruyter.
Kastovsky, Dieter. 1986b. The problem of productivity in word formation. *Linguistics* 24. 585–600.
Kemmer, Suzanne. 2003. Schemas and lexical blends. In Hubert C. Cuyckens, Thomas Berg, René Dirven & Klaus-Uwe Panther (eds.), *Motivation in language: From case grammar to cognitive linguistics. Studies in honour of Günter Radden*, 69–97. Amsterdam & Philadelphia: John Benjamins.

Kilani-Schoch, Marianne & Wolfgang U. Dressler. 2002. Affinités phonologiques dans l'organisation de la morphologie statique: l'exemple de la flexion verbale française? *Folia Linguistica* 36 (3/4). 297–312.
Kilani-Schoch, Marianne & Wolfgang U. Dressler. 2005. *Morphologie naturelle et flexion du verbe français*. Tübingen: Gunter Narr Verlag.
Kiparsky, Paul. 1968. Linguistic universals and linguistic change. In Emmon Bach & Robert T. Harms (eds.), *Universals in linguistic theory*, 171–202. London & New York: Holt, Rinehart and Winston.
Kiparsky, Paul. 1974. Remarks on analogical change. In John M. Anderson & Charles Jones (eds.), *Historical linguistics*, 257–275. Amsterdam: North Holland.
Klégr, Aleš & Jan Čermák. 2010. Neologisms of the 'on-the-pattern-of' type: Analogy as a word-formation process? In Martin Procházka, Markéta Malá & Pavlína Šaldová (eds.), *The Prague school and theories of structure*, 229–241. Göttingen: V&R unipress.
Koefoed, Geert & Jaap van Marle. 2000. Productivity. In Geert E. Booij, Christian Lehmann, Joachim Mugdan, Wolfgang Kesselheim & Stavros Skopeteas (eds.), *Morphologie–morphology: An international handbook of inflection and word-formation*, vol. 1, 303–311. Berlin & New York: Walter de Gruyter.
Köpcke, Klaus-Michael. 1993. *Schemata bei der Pluralbildung im Deutschen: Versuch einer kognitiven Morphologie*. Tübingen: Gunter Narr Verlag.
Köpcke, Klaus-Michael. 1998. The acquisition of plural marking in English and German revisited: Schemata versus rules. *Journal of Child Language* 25. 293–319.
Korecky-Kröll, Katharina, Gary Libben, Nicole Stempfer, Julia Wiesinger, Eva Reinisch, Johannes Bertl & Wolfgang U. Dressler. 2012. Helping a crocodile to learn German plurals: Children's online judgment of actual, potential and illegal plural forms. *Morphology* 22 (1). 35–65.
Krott, Andrea. 2009. The role of analogy for compound words. In James P. Blevins & Juliette Blevins (eds.), *Analogy in grammar. Form and acquisition*, 118–136. Oxford: Oxford University Press.
Krott, Andrea, R. Harald Baayen & Robert Schreuder. 2001. Analogy in morphology: Modeling the choice of linking morphemes in Dutch. *Linguistics* 39 (1). 51–93.
Krott, Andrea, Peter Hagoort & R. Harald Baayen. 2004. Sublexical units and supralexical combinatorics in the processing of interfixed Dutch compounds. *Language and Cognitive Processes* 19 (3). 453–471.
Krott, Andrea, Gary Libben, Gonia Jarema, Wolfgang U. Dressler, Robert Schreuder & Harald Baayen. 2004. Probability in the grammar of German and Dutch: Interfixation in triconstituent compounds. *Language and Speech* 47 (1). 83–106.
Krott, Andrea, Robert Schreuder, R. Harald Baayen & Wolfgang U. Dressler. 2007. Analogical effects on linking elements in German compound words. *Language and Cognitive Processes* 22 (1). 25–57.
Kubozono, Haruo. 1990. Phonological constraints on blending in English as a case for phonology–morphology interface. In Geert E. Booij & Jaap van Marle (eds.), *Yearbook of Morphology 1990*, 1–20. Dordrecht: Kluwer.
Küpper, Tim. 2007. *Neologism in Early Modern English*. Norderstedt: GRIN Verlag.
Laaha, Sabine, Dorit Ravid, Katharina Korecky-Kröll, Gregor Laaha & Wolfgang U. Dressler. 2006. Early noun plurals in German: Regularity, productivity or default? *Journal of Child Language* 33. 271–302.
Ladányi, Mária. 2000. Productivity, creativity and analogy in word formation (WF). Derivational innovations in Hungarian poetic language. In Gábor Alberti & Istvaìn Kenesei (eds.),

Approaches to Hungarian: Papers from the Pécs Conference, vol. 7, 73–90. Szeged: JATEPress. http://ladanyi.web.elte.hu/derivational_innovations.pdf (accessed 5 August 2013).

Lahiri, Aditi. 2000. Introduction. In Aditi Lahiri (ed.), *Analogy, levelling, markedness. Principles of change in phonology and morphology*, 1–14. Berlin & New York: Mouton de Gruyter.

Lamb, Sydney M. 1998. *Pathways of the brain. The neurocognitive basis of language*. Amsterdam & Philadelphia: John Benjamins.

Lehrer, Adrienne. 1996. Identifying and interpreting blends: An experimental approach. *Cognitive Linguistics* 7 (4). 359–390.

Lehrer, Adrienne. 2003. Understanding trendy neologisms. *Italian Journal of Linguistics / Rivista di Linguistica* 15 (2). 369–382.

Lehrer, Adrienne. 2006. Neologisms. In Keith Brown (ed.), *Encyclopedia of language and linguistics*, 2nd edn, 590–593. Oxford: Elsevier.

Lehrer, Adrienne. 2007. Blendalicious. In Judith Munat (ed.), *Lexical creativity, texts and contexts*, 115–133. Amsterdam & Philadelphia: John Benjamins.

Leonni, Leo. 2004. *A busy year*. New York: Knopf Books for Young Readers.

Levelt, Willem J. M. 2013. *A history of psycholinguistics: The pre-Chomskyan era*. Oxford: Oxford University Press.

Libben, Gary. 1998. Semantic transparency in the processing of compounds: Consequences for representation, processing, and impairment. *Brain and Language* 61. 30–44.

Libben, Gary. 2006. Why study compound processing? An overview of the issues. In Gary Libben & Gonia Jarema (eds.), *The representation and processing of compound words*, 1–22. Oxford: Oxford University Press.

Libben, Gary. 2008. Compounding and cognition. *ICCS Proceedings*, 27–29 July 2008, Seoul, Korea.

Libben, Gary & Gonia Jarema (eds.). 2006. *The representation and processing of compound words*. Oxford: Oxford University Press.

Lieber, Rochelle. 1992. Compounding in English. *Italian Journal of Linguistics / Rivista di Linguistica* 4 (1). 79–96.

Lieber, Rochelle. 2005. English word-formation processes. Observations, issues, and thoughts on future research. In Pavol Štekauer & Rochelle Lieber (eds.), *Handbook of English word-formation*, 375–427. Dordrecht: Springer.

Lindsay, Mark & Mark Aronoff. 2013. Natural selection in self-organizing morphological systems. In Fabio Montermini, Gilles Boyé & Jesse Tseng (eds.), *Morphology in Toulouse: Selected proceedings of the 7th Décembrettes*, 133–153. München: Lincom Europa.

Lipka, Leonhard. 2000. English (and general) word-formation – The state of the art in 1999. In Bernhard Reitz & Sigrid Rieuwerts (eds.), *Anglistentag 1999 Mainz: Proceedings*, 5–20. Trier: WVT.

Lo Duca, Maria Giuseppa. 1990. L'acquisizione dei composti V–N dell'italiano. In Monica Berretta, Piera Molinelli & Ada Valentini (eds.), *Parallela 4. Morfologia/Morphologie*, 305–315. Tübingen: Narr.

Lopriore, Lucilla. 2014. Norm and usage in online open-source dictionaries: The case of fashion lexis in Urban Dictionary. In Alessandra Molino & Serenella Zanotti (eds.), *Observing norm, observing usage. Lexis in dictionaries and in the media*, 241–258. Bern: Peter Lang.

Lyster, Roy & Masatoshi Sato. 2013. Skill acquisition theory and the role of practice in L2 development. In María del Pilar García-Mayo, María Junkal Gutiérrez Mangado & María Martínez Adrián (eds.), *Contemporary approaches to second language acquisition*, 71–91. Amsterdam & Philadelphia: John Benjamins.

Marchand, Hans. 1969 [1960]. *The categories and types of Present-day English word-formation: A synchronic-diachronic approach*, 2nd edn. München: Beck.

Marle, Jaap van. 1990. Rule-creating creativity: Analogy as a synchronic morphological process. In Wolfgang U. Dressler, Hans C. Luschützky, Oskar E. Pfeiffer & John R. Rennison (eds.), *Contemporary morphology*, 267–273. Berlin & New York: Mouton de Gruyter.

Mattiello, Elisa. 2003. Slang compounds as one case of morphological complexity. In Lavinia Merlini Barbaresi (ed.), *Complexity in language and text*, 343–377. Pisa: Edizioni Plus.

Mattiello, Elisa. 2005. *A bomb* and *un casino*: Intensifiers in English and Italian slanguage. In Marcella Bertuccelli Papi (ed.), *Studies in the semantics of lexical combinatory patterns*, 279–326. Pisa: Edizioni Plus.

Mattiello, Elisa. 2007. Combining forms and blends: The case of *scape*. In Laura Jottini, Gabriella Del Lungo & John Douthwaite (eds.), *Cityscapes: Islands of the self. Language studies*, vol. 2, 115–130. Cagliari: CUEC.

Mattiello, Elisa. 2008a. *An introduction to English slang: A description of its morphology, semantics and sociology*. Monza: Polimetrica International Scientific Publisher.

Mattiello, Elisa. 2008b. From *sexgate* to *vallettopoli*: Contrasting English and Italian combining forms. In Carla Vergaro (ed.), *Dynamics of language contact in the twenty-first century*, vol. 2, 177–190. Perugia: Guerra.

Mattiello, Elisa. 2013. *Extra-grammatical morphology in English. Abbreviations, blends, reduplicatives, and related phenomena*. Berlin & Boston: De Gruyter Mouton.

Mattiello, Elisa. 2014. Analogical nonce words and L2 learning. Paper presented at the 12th ESSE Conference, Seminar on Non-words, Nonce-words and Morphology Teaching, Košice, Slovakia, 29 August–2 September.

Mattiello, Elisa. 2015. The impact of figuration on word-formation: The role of figurative language in the production and interpretation of novel analogical compounds. Paper presented at the 2nd International Symposium on Figurative Thought and Language, University of Pavia, Italy, 28–30 October. Accepted for publication in *Textus* 2017.

Mattiello, Elisa. 2016. Analogical neologisms in English. *Italian Journal of Linguistics / Rivista di Linguistica* 28 (2), 103–142.

Mazzaferro, Gerardo. 2009. Language change and variation in English. In Virginia Pulcini (ed.), *A handbook of Present-day English*, 21–62. Roma: Carocci.

McCarthy, John J. & Alan Prince. 1993. *Prosodic morphology: Constraint interaction and satisfaction*, Technical Report 3, Rutgers University Center for Cognitive Science, Rutgers University. http://scholarworks.umass.edu/cgi/viewcontent.cgi?article=1013&context=linguist_faculty_pubs (accessed 19 February 2012).

McMahon, April M. S. 1994. *Understanding language change*. Cambridge: Cambridge University Press.

Meringer, Rudolph. 1908. *Aus dem Leben der Sprache: Versprechen, Kindersprache, Nachahmungstrieb*. Berlin: Behr's Verlag.

Merlini Barbaresi, Lavinia. 2011. Outstanding features of the Italian language: Evaluatives, alteratives, blends, and compounds in the Italian rendition of Joyce's ALP. In Raffaella Baccolini, Delia Chiaro, Chris Rundle & Sam Whitsitt (eds.), *A Joyceful of talkatalka from friendshapes for Rosa Maria Bollettieri Bosinelli*, vol. 1, 195–216. Bologna: Bononia University Press.

Miller, Gary D. 2014. *English lexicogenesis*. Oxford: Oxford University Press.
Motsch, Wolfgang. 1981. Der kreative Aspekt in der Wortbildung. In Leonhard Lipka (ed.), *Wortbildung*, 94–118. Darmstadt: Wissenschaftliche Buchgesellschaft.
Munat, Judith. 2007. Lexical creativity as a marker of style in science fiction and children's literature. In Judith Munat (ed.), *Lexical creativity, texts and contexts*, 163–185. Amsterdam & Philadelphia: John Benjamins.
Munat, Judith. 2016. Lexical creativity. In Rodney H. Jones (ed.), *The Routledge handbook of language and creativity*, 92–106. London: Routledge.
Murphy, M. Lynne & Steven Jones. 2008. Antonyms in children's and child-directed speech. *First Language* 28 (4). 403–430.
Neologisms. 2003. Rice University. http://www.ruf.rice.edu/~kemmer/Words04/neologisms/a.html.
Neologisms – New Words in Journalistic Text. 1997–2012. Birmingham City University. http://rdues.bcu.ac.uk/neologisms.shtml.
Neuhaus, Joachim H. 1989. The Shakespeare dictionary database. *ICAME Journal* 13. 3–11.
Nosofsky, Robert M. 1986. Attention, similarity, and the identification-categorization relationship. *Journal of Experimental Psychology: General* 115. 39–57.
Nosofsky, Robert M. 1990. Relations between exemplar similarity and likelihood models of classification. *Journal of Mathematical Psychology* 34. 393–418.
The Observer Online. 2017. Guardian News and Media Limited or its affiliated companies. http://www.theguardian.com/observer.
Olsen, Susan. 2014. Delineating derivation and compounding. In Rochelle Lieber & Pavol Štekauer (eds.), *The Oxford handbook of derivational morphology*, 26–49. Oxford: Oxford University Press.
Online Etymology Dictionary. 2001–2017. Douglas Harper. http://www.etymonline.com/.
Oxford English Dictionary Online, 2nd edn. 1989. OED2. Oxford: Oxford University Press. http://www.oed.com/.
Oxford English Dictionary Online, 3rd edn. OED3. Oxford: Oxford University Press. http://www.oed.com/.
Paul, Hermann. 1880. *Prinzipien der Sprachgeschichte*. Tübingen: Max Niemeyer.
Pelsma, John R. 1910. A child's vocabulary and its development. *Pedagogical Seminary* 17. 328–369.
Plag, Ingo. 1999. *Morphological productivity. Structural constraints in English derivation*. Berlin & New York: Mouton de Gruyter.
Plag, Ingo. 2003. *Word-formation in English*. Cambridge: Cambridge University Press.
Plag, Ingo. 2010. Compound stress assignment by analogy: The constituent family bias. *Zeitschrift für Sprachwissenschaft* 29 (2). 243–282.
Plag, Ingo, Gero Kunter & Sabine Arndt-Lappe. 2007. Testing hypotheses about compound stress assignment in English: A corpus-based investigation. *Corpus Linguistics and Linguistic Theory* 3 (2). 199–233.
Prasada, Sandeep & Stephen Pinker. 1993. Generalization of regular and irregular morphological patterns. *Language and Cognitive Processes* 8. 1–56.
Rainer, Franz. 1988. Towards a theory of blocking: The case of Italian and German quality nouns. In Geert E. Booij & Jaap van Marle (eds.), *Yearbook of morphology 1988*, 155–185. Dordrecht: Foris.
Rainer, Franz. 2007. Zur Typologie poetischer Lizenzen in der Wortbildung. In Wolfgang U. Dressler & Oswald Panagl (eds.), *Poetische Lizenzen*, 99–115. Wien: Praesens Verlag.

Rainer, Franz. 2012. Morphological metaphysics: Virtual, potential and actual words. *Word Structure* 5 (2). 165–182.
Rainer, Franz. 2013. Formación de palabras y analogía: Aspectos diacrónicos. *Anexos de Revista de Lexicografía* 19. 141–172.
The Rice University Neologisms Database. 2004–2014. Rice University. http://neologisms.rice.edu/.
Ronneberger-Sibold, Elke. 2000. Creative competence at work: The creation of partial motivation in German trade names. In Ursula Doleschal & Anna M. Thornton (eds.), *Extragrammatical and marginal morphology*, 85–105. München: Lincom Europa.
Ronneberger-Sibold, Elke. 2008. Word creation. Definition – function – typology. In Franz Rainer, Wolfgang U. Dressler, Dieter Kastovsky & Hans C. Luschützky (eds.), *Variation and change in morphology. Selected Papers from the 13th International Morphology Meeting*, 201–216. Amsterdam & Philadelphia: John Benjamins.
Rundblad, Gabriella & David B. Kronenfeld. 2000. Folk-etymology: Haphazard perversion or shrewd analogy? In Julie Coleman & Christian J. Kay (eds.), *Lexicology, semantics and lexicography: Selected papers from the 4th G. L. Brook symposium*, 19–34. Amsterdam & Philadelphia: John Benjamins.
Salmon, Vivian. 1987. Some functions of Shakespearian word-formation. In Vivian Salmon & Edwina Burness (eds.), *A reader in the language of Shakespearean drama*, 193–206. Amsterdam & Philadelphia: John Benjamins.
Saussure, Ferdinand de. 1995 [1916]. *Cours de linguistique générale*, 2nd edn. Paris: Payot.
Scalise, Sergio. 1984. *Generative morphology*. Dordrecht: Foris.
Scalise, Sergio. 1988. The notion of 'head' in morphology. In Geert E. Booij & Jaap van Marle (eds.), *Yearbook of morphology 1988*, 229–245. Dordrecht: Kluwer.
Scalise, Sergio. 1992. Compounding in Italian. *Italian Journal of Linguistics / Rivista di Linguistica* 4 (1). 175–199.
Schironi, Francesca. 2007. Analogía, *analogia, proportio, ratio*: Loanwords, calques, and reinterpretations of a Greek technical word. In Louis Basset, Frédérique Biville, Bernard Colombat, Pierre Swiggers & Alfons Wouters (eds.), *Bilinguisme et terminologie grammaticale gréco-latine*, 321–338. Louvain: Peeters.
Schmid, Hans-Jörg. 2008. New words in the mind: Concept-formation and entrenchment of neologisms. *Anglia* 126 (1). 1–36.
Schmid, Hans-Jörg. 2011. *English morphology and word-formation. An introduction*. Berlin: Erich Schmidt Verlag.
Skehan, Peter. 1998. *A cognitive approach to language learning*. Oxford: Oxford University Press.
Sketch Engine. 2003–2013. Lexical Computing Ltd. East Sussex, United Kingdom. https://the.sketchengine.co.uk/.
Skousen, Royal. 1975. *Substantive evidence in phonology*. The Hague & Paris: Mouton.
Skousen, Royal. 1989. *Analogical modeling of language*. Dordrecht: Kluwer Academic Publishers.
Skousen, Royal. 1992. *Analogy and structure*. Dordrecht: Kluwer Academic Publishers.
Skousen, Royal. 2009. Expanding analogical modeling into a general theory of language prediction. In James P. Blevins & Juliette Blevins (eds.), *Analogy in grammar. Form and acquisition*, 164–184. Oxford: Oxford University Press.
Skousen, Royal, Deryle Lonsdale & Dilworth B. Parkinson (eds.). 2002. *Analogical modeling*. Amsterdam & Philadelphia: John Benjamins.
Skousen, Royal & Thereon Stanford. 2007. *AM: Parallel*. Provo, UT: Brigham Young University.

Smith, Viktor, Daniel Barratt & Jordan Zlatev. 2014. Unpacking noun–noun compounds: Interpreting novel and conventional food names in isolation and on food labels. *Cognitive Linguistics* 25 (1). 99–147.
Soneira, Begoña. 2015. *A lexical description of English for architecture. A corpus-based approach*. Bern: Peter Lang.
Spencer, Andrew. 1991. *Morphological theory: An introduction to word structure in generative grammar*. Oxford: Blackwell.
Stenström, Anna-Brita, Gisle Andersen & Ingrid K. Hasund. 2002. *Trends in teenage talk: Corpus compilation, analysis and findings*. Amsterdam & Philadelphia: John Benjamins.
Szymanek, Bogdan. 2005. The latest trends in English word-formation. In Pavol Štekauer & Rochelle Lieber (eds.), *Handbook of word-formation*, 429–448. Dordrecht: Springer.
Taft, Marcus & Kenneth I. Forster. 1976. Lexical storage and retrieval of polymorphemic and polysyllabic words. *Journal of verbal learning and verbal behavior* 15. 607–620.
Thumb, Albert & Karl Marbe. 1901. *Experimentelle Untersuchungen über die psychologische Grundlagen der sprachliche Analogiebildung*. Leipzig: Engelmann.
TIME Magazine Corpus. 1923–2006. Brigham Young University. http://corpus.byu.edu/time/.
Traugott, Elizabeth Closs & Bernd Heine (eds.). 1991. *Approaches to grammaticalization*, 2 vols. Amsterdam & Philadelphia: John Benjamins.
Trommer, Jochen & Eva Zimmermann. 2010. Portmanteaus as generalized templates. Paper presented at the 14th International Morphology Meeting, Budapest, 16 May.
Urban Dictionary. 1999–2017. http://www.urbandictionary.com/.
Wanner, Dieter. 2006. *The power of analogy. An essay on historical linguistics*. Berlin & New York: Mouton de Gruyter.
Warren, Beatrice. 1990. The importance of combining forms. In Wolfgang U. Dressler, Hans C. Luschützky, Oskar E. Pfeiffer & John R. Rennison (eds.), *Contemporary morphology*, 111–132. Belin & New York: Mouton de Gruyter.
Widdowson, Henry G. 1979. *Explorations in applied linguistics*. Oxford: Oxford University Press.
Wiechmann, Daniel, Elma Kerz, Neal Snider & T. Florian Jaeger. 2013. Introduction to the special issue: Parsimony and redundancy in models of language. *Language and Speech* 56 (3). 257–264.
Wiktionary – A Wiki-based Open Content Dictionary. 2017. http://en.wiktionary.org/wiki/Wiktionary:Main_Page.
Wordspy – The Word Lover's Guide to New Words. 1995–2017. http://www.wordspy.com/.
Zemskaja, Elena A. 1992. *Slovoobrazovanije kak dejatel'nost'* [word-formation as activity]. Moskva: Nauka.
Zemskaja, Elena A., Margarita V. Kitajgorodskaja & Evgenij N. Širjaev. 1981. *Russkaja razgovornaja reč': Obščie voprosy, slovoobrazovanie, sintaksis* [colloquial spoken Russian: general issues, word-formation, syntax]. Moskva: Nauka.
Zwicky, Arnold M. & Geoffrey K. Pullum. 1987. Plain morphology and expressive morphology. In Jon Aske, Natasha Beery, Laura Michaelis & Hana Filip (eds.), *Proceedings of the 13th annual meeting of the Berkeley linguistics society, general session and parasession on grammar and cognition*, 330–340. Berkeley: Berkeley Linguistics Society.

Lexical index

The present index includes my total database of analogical words, arranged in alphabetical order. For each entry, the index provides the target, its model, and the first attestation of both in the sources consulted (see 2.4). The entries indicated as 'after' a specific word count as surface analogy, whereas those indicated as 'from' a more general element count as analogy via schema.

ABH [1975], after *G.B.H.* [1958]
absentation [1800], after *presentation* [a1325]
Accidency [1830], after *Excellency* [?1533]
acculturate [1917] ← *acculturation* [1880], after *cultivate–cultivation*
✝*achage* [1875], after *breakage* [1775]
achrist [1584], after *atheist* [?1555]
acid house [1988], after *acid rock* [1966] and *acid head* [1966]
acid jazz [1988], after *acid rock* [1966] and *acid head* [1966]
acidophil [1900], after *basophil* [1898]
ACIDS [n.d.], after *AIDS* [1982]
acoustician [1826], after *musician* [a1398]
acrolect [1965], from *-lect*
actualistic [1857], after *realistic* [1829]
Adamhood [1828], after *manhood* [c1225]
adead [1581], after *alive* [OE]
ad feminam [1839], after *ad hominem* [1588]
ADHD [1987], after *ADD* [1979]
adiabolist [1646], after *atheist* [?1555]
adnoun [1657], after *adverb* [a1425]
ad personam [a1628], after *ad rem* [1588]
adultescent [1996], after *kidult* [1960]
adulthood [1850], after *childhood* [OE]
adusk [1856], after *alight* [1817]
advertainment [1999], from *-tainment*
adware [1983], from *-ware*
aerobicise [1982], after *exercise* [1526]
Aerobie [1985], after *Frisbee* [1957]
Afrocentric [1966], after *Eurocentric* [1927]
ageism [1969], after *sexism* [1866] and *racism* [1903]
aggradation [1893], after *degradation* [1799]
aggro [1969], after *intro* [1923]
AID [1945], after *AI* [1945]
AIH [1945], after *AI* [1945]

aircraft [1845], after *air balloon* [1783] and *airship* [1817]
airhead[1] [1943], after *bridge-head* [1812] and *beachhead* [1940]
airhead[2] [1971], after *fat-head* [1835]
air-rage [1996], after *road rage* [1988]
airsick [1785], after *sea-sick* [a1566]
airwoman [1910], after *airman* [1873]
all-dayer [1896], after *all-nighter* [1870]
alphabetism [1978], after *sexism* [1866]
animaliculture [1879], from *-culture*
animatograph(e) [1896], after *cinematograph* [1896]
anklet [a1822], after *bracelet* [1438]
annuhulation [1939], after *muertification* [1939]
apartotel [1965], after *motel* [1925]
apiculture [1864], from *-culture*
armlet [1535], after *bracelet* [1438]
arterati [n.d.], from *-erati*
art-napping [1978], from *-napping*
ass(a)holic [1990s], from *-(a)holic*
athletically correct [1991], after *politically correct* [1793]
auctionholic [1990s], from *-(a)holic*
audile [1886], after *tactile* [1615] and *motile* [1857]
audiorama [1954], from *-(o)rama*
auth [n.d.] ← *author* [a1382], after *act–actor*
awesomelicious [2008], from *-licious*
babe magnet [1989], after *chick magnet* [1970]
babymoon [2004], after *honeymoon* [1791]
baby-napping [1992], from *-napping*
baby-sit [1946] ← *baby-sitter* [1937], after *mix–mixer*
bamboo English [1924], from *bamboo-*

bamboo government [n.d.], from *bamboo-*
bamboo telegraph [n.d.], from *bamboo-*
barkaholic [2008], from *-(a)holic*
basilect [1965], from *-lect*
batcopter [n.d.], after *batmobile* [n.d.]
batcycle [n.d.], after *batmobile* [n.d.]
batplane [n.d.], after *batmobile* [n.d.]
battleplane [1915], after *battleship* [1794]
battle-worthy [1889], after *seaworthy* [1807]
batwoman [1941], after *batman* [1755]
beautsy [1939], after *youthsy* [1939]
bedaholic [1990s], from *-(a)holic*
beefalo [1974], after *catalo* [1894]
beefburger [1940], from *-burger*
beefcake [1949], after *cheese-cake* [1934]
beerlicious [2008], from *-licious*
beforemath [1997], after *aftermath* [1656]
before-tax [1944], after *after-tax* [1944]
belief [c1175], after *belyfan*
bellygram [1981], from *-gram*
bestteller [1939], after *bestseller* [1864]
Beyoncégate [2013], from *-gate*
BFFL [2010], after *BFF* [1987]
bickybacky [1939], after *beggybaggy* [1939]
big end [1877], after *small end* [1846]
big gun [2001], after *great gun* [1657]
big hand [1849], after *small hand* [1818]
bikathon [n.d.], from *-(a)thon*
bike-napping [2003], from *-napping*
bilf [2003], after *Milf* [1992]
Billygate [1980], from *-gate*
bird brain [1943], after *beetle-brain* [1593]
bird cafeteria [2011], after *bird-house* [1855]
birdnapping [2011], from *-napping*
bitchdar [2008], after *gaydar* [1988]
biznapping [1993], from *-napping*
black-collar [2010], after *white-collar* [1911] and *blue-collar* [1929]
black-grape-colour [1873], after *thundercolour* [1873]
blackthorn [a1325], after *whitethorn* [a1300]
blackwash [1762], after *†whitewash* [1576]
Blairese [1998], after *Johnsonese* [1843] and *Carlylese* [1858]
blamestorming [1997], after *brainstorming* [1907]
blandspeak [n.d.], from *-speak*

blax-/blacks-ploitation [1972], after *sexploitation* [1924]
Blazerati [n.d.], from *-erati*
blendalicious [2007], from *-licious*
Blindian [2010], after *Windian* [2008]
B-list [1928], after *A-list* [1890]
bloatware [1991], from *-ware*
blogosphere [1999], from *-sphere*
blogspeak [n.d.], from *-speak*
blondie [1943], after *brownie* [1897]
blottesque [1856], after *grotesque* [1561]
blow-dry [1966], after *kiln-dry* [c1540] and *sun-dry* [1695]
blue-collar [1929], after *white-collar* [1911]
boatel [1956], after *motel* [1925]
boatnapping [1981], from *-napping*
Bobos [2010], after *Yuppies* [1984], *Buppies* [1984], and *Dinkies* [1986]
bookstaff [OE], after G. *Buchstabe* and *rounstaff* [OE]
bookwoman [1834], after *bookman* [1618]
Bosszilla [1988], from *-zilla*
boxcar-napping [1963], from *-napping*
boxercise [1985], after *sexercise* [1942]
boyth [2006], after *stealth* [a1325] and †*blowth* [1602]
brainwriting [1913], after *handwriting* [1421]
breatharian [1979], after *vegetarian* [1842]
Bremain [2016], after *Brexit* [2012]
Bridezilla [1995], from *-zilla*
bridorexia [2008], from *-orexia*
brinner [2008], after *brunch* [1896]
Britcom [1977], after *sitcom* [1964] and *romcom* [1971]
brown dwarf [1975], after *red dwarf* [1916]
brown-out [1942], after *blackout* [1934]
brown rice [1916], after *white rice* [1614]
buckytube [1991], after *buckyball* [1989]
build-down [1983], after *build-up* [1943]
bulimarexia [2011], from *-orexia*
Buppies [1984], after *Yuppies* [1984]
busgirl [1914], after *busboy* [1904]
buyaholic [1990s], from *-(a)holic*
cacography [1656], after *calligraphy* [1604]
café-bar [1938], after *café-restaurant* [1926]
caffeineaholic [2010], from *-(a)holic*
cake-aholic [1957], from *-(a)holic*

cakegasm [2008], after *wargasm* [2004]
callcentrercise [2008], after *sexercise* [1942]
Cal-Mex [1973], after *Tex-Mex* [1949]
cameraholic [2008], from *-(a)holic*
cancelbot [1993], from *-bot*
candlelittle [1939], from *-little*
Cantopop [1988], after *Britpop* [1986]
carboholic [1973], from *-(a)holic*
carrier-based [1935], from *-based*
carsick [1908], after *sea-sick* [a1566]
cartnapping [1964], from *-napping*
catnapping [1939], from *-napping*
cat sitter [1948], from *-sitter*
chaindrink [n.d.], after *chainsmoke* [1934]
chairperson [1971], after *chairman* [1654]
chairwoman [1699], after *chairman* [1654]
Charlestoner [1927], after *waltzer* [1811]
chaterama [2015], from *-(o)rama*
chatterati [1990], from *-erati*
cheesaholic [1990s], from *-(a)holic*
cheeseburger [1938], from *-burger*
chickenburger [1936], from *-burger*
chickenfurter [n.d.], after *Frankfurter* [1877]
chick lit [1988], after *chick flick* [1988]
chicknapping [1995], from *-napping*
Chinglish [1957], after *Spanglish* [1954]
chocoholic [1961], from *-(a)holic*
Chrasian [2013], after *Wasian* [2008]
Cinerama [1951], from *-(o)rama*
city-scape [1856], from *-scape*
cleanminded [1939], after *clean-legged* [1568], *clean-armed* [1592], etc.
Clintonism [1992], after *Nixonism* [1952], *Reaganism* [1966], and *Bushism* [1980]
Clintonite [1992], after *Nixonite* [1950]
Clintonomics [1992], from *-nomics*
C-list [1909], after *A-list* [1890]
clothesaholic [1980s], from *-(a)holic*
cloudscape [1868], from *-scape*
Coke-aholic [1980s], from *-(a)holic*
cole/coalmouse [?1533], after *titmouse* [1530]
collapsar [n.d.], after *quasar* [1964]
commutercize [n.d.], after *sexercise* [1942]
complexability [2014], after *employability* [1889]
computercize [n.d.], after *sexercise* [1942]
computer face [2010], after *TV face* [2009]

computerholic [1977], from *-(a)holic*
computeritis [n.d.], from *-itis*
computer-speak [1968], from *-speak*
coolicious [2008], from *-licious*
coolth[1] [1547], after *warmth* [c1175]
coolth[2] [1966], after *warmth* [1600]
copumentary [2008], from *-umentary*
copyleft [1976], after *copyright* [1735]
corpsenapping [1991], from *-napping*
couch rat [1988], after *couch potato* [1979]
couch tomato [1988], after *couch potato* [1979]
coyth [2006], after *stealth* [a1325] and †*blowth* [1602]
crackhead [1986], after *acid head* [1966]
crappuccino [2013], from *-ccino*
creditaholic [1990s], from *-(a)holic*
cruise-oholic [1989], from *-(a)holic*
cuppaccino [2008], from *-ccino*
cursaholic [1990s], from *-(a)holic*
cutegasm [2007], after *wargasm* [2004]
CUV [2000], after *SUV* [1987]
cyberbar [1997], after *cybercafé* [1994]
cyberrhea [2008], from *-rrhea*
Cyprexit [2015], after *Brexit* [2012] and *Grexit* [2012]
dairy-free [1983], after *sugar-free* [1924], *gluten-free* [1927], etc.
Dallasgate [1975], from *-gate*
Dananathon [2011], from *-(a)thon*
danceaholic [1980s], from *-(a)holic*
danceitis [n.d.], from *-itis*
dancercise [1967], after *sexercise* [1942]
dancethon [n.d.], from *-(a)thon*
dane [1939], after *plane* [1666]
daughter-beamed [1598], after *sun-beamed* [1598]
daughterboard [1971], after *motherboard* [1965]
dealaholic [2000s], from *-(a)holic*
decelerometer [1924], after *accelerometer* [1875]
defenceful [1864], after *defenceless* [c1530]
de-lovely [n.d.], after *delicious* [c1300]
designerati [n.d.], from *-erati*
deskercise [n.d.], after *sexercise* [1942]
dessert-napping [1996], from *-napping*

devo in *evo-devo* [1997], after *evo*
dialectician [1848], after *logician* [1382] and *mathematician* [?a1475]
dick flick [2003], after *chick flick* [1988]
dietarian [1880], after *vegetarian* [1842]
Diet-sodaphobia [2008], from *-phobia*
digerati [1992], from *-erati*
Dilf [2003], after *Milf* [1992]
dinkie/-y [1986], after *yuppie* [1984]
diseasinesses [1939], after *easiness* [1567]
Disorient Express [2008], after *Orient Express* [1883]
disremember [1815], after *dismember* [1297]
doalittle [1939], from *-little*
docu-fantasy [n.d.], after *docudrama* [1961]
docuhistory [1981], after *docudrama* [1961]
documusical [1974], after *docudrama* [1961]
docu-opera [n.d.], after *docudrama* [1961]
docurecreation [1983], after *docudrama* [1961]
docusoap [1979], after *docudrama* [1961]
docutainment [1978], from *-tainment*
dog whisperer [1998], after *horse whisperer* [1843]
dognapping [1921], from *-napping*
dog-sitter [1942], after *baby-sitter* [1937] (see later *-sitter*)
dogumentary [2006], from *-umentary*
dolphin-napping [2001], from *-napping*
domecreepers [1939], after *home keeper(s)* [1574]
donutorama [1992], from *-(o)rama*
Doreen-aholic [2000s], from *-(a)holic*
dot-co-dot-uks [1999], after *dot-coms* [1994]
doublespeak [1957], from *-speak*
doubleton [1906], after *singleton* [1876]
drankasup [1939], after *drink a sip*
dreamscape [1858], from *-scape*
drinkathon [2008], from *-(a)thon*
drip-dry [1916], after *kiln-dry* [c1540] and *sun-dry* [1695]
drudge-aholic [1980s], from *-(a)holic*
drunkoholic [2008], from *-(a)holic*
duckwich [1943], after *sandwich* [1762]
dumnation [1939], after *muertification* [1939]
†*earlet* [1610], after *bracelet* [1438]

earthshine [1834], after *sunshine* [a1325] and *moonshine* [c1425]
ear-witness [1539], after *eyewitness* [1539]
e-asy [2009], from *e-*
eatalittle [1939], from *-little*
ebloody [2003], from *e-*
eco-art [1970], from *eco-*
e-commerce [1993], from *e-*
E-day [1996], after *D-day* [1918]
edutainment [1983], from *-tainment*
eggburger [1960], from *-burger*
eggitarian [2005], after *vegetarian* [1842]
eighthead [2013], after *forehead* [c1000]
ejackets [2003], from *e-*
e-journal [1991], from *e-*
elanguage [2003], from *e-*
elkoholic [2000s], from *-(a)holic*
emblence [1939], after *substance* [c1330] and *semblance* [a1325]
end-of-the-semesteritis [2008], from *-itis*
e-pal [2008], after *pen-pal* [1925] and from *e-*
e-portfolio [2004], from *e-*
e-publication [1997], from *e-*
e-reader [1999], from *e-*
Esac [2009], after *Esa* [2009]
escalator [1900], after *elevator* [1787]
Escort [2009], after *Esa* [2009]
Esoc [2009], after *Esa* [2009]
Esrin [2009], after *Esa* [2009]
Estec [2009], after *Esa* [2009]
estrong [2003], from *e-*
e-text [1990], from *e-*
Eurofranc [1980], from *Euro-*
Euromark [1974], from *Euro-*
Eurosterling [1974], from *Euro-*
Euroyen [1974], from *Euro-*
eventaholic [1990s], from *-(a)holic*
evergrey [1939], after *evergreen* [1555]
ewarning [2003], from *e-*
Excelicious [2014], from *-licious*
†*exposture* [a1616], after *posture* [a1586]
exposure [1609], after *enclosure* [1574]
extrapolation [1872], after *interpolation* [1763]
fabric-holic [2000s], from *-(a)holic*
facebookitis [n.d.], from *-itis*
fad-tastic [1962], from *-tastic*

Failbook [2013], after *Facebook*
faithly [a1375], after *-ly* adverbs (cf. *sincerely* in the micro-context)
fallee [2007], after *falling* [a1400]
family-oholic [2000s], from *-(a)holic*
fane [1939], after *plane* [1666]
fanfic [1976], after *fanzine* [1949]
fantabulific [2008], from *-rific*
fartoomanyness [1939], after *toomuchness* [1875]
fashionaholic [2010], from *-(a)holic*
fatheraholic [1990s], from *-(a)holic*
fathered [1608], after *fatherless* [?c1225]
Father's Day [1943], after *Mother's Day* [1890]
father-substitute [1938], after *mother-substitute* [1933]
fax-back [1988], after *callback* [1960]
femocrat [1981], after *democrat* [1788]
fiberccino [2008], from *-ccino*
filmfest [1970], from *-fest*
filmography [1962], after *bibliography* [1814]
fire-folk [1877], after *countryfolk* [c1325] and *town folk* [c1325]
firmware [1968], from *-ware*
first-minute [n.d.], after *last-minute* [1908]
fishaholic [1990s], from *-(a)holic*
FIV [1994], after *HIV* [1986]
flashforward [1980], after *flashback* [1916]
fleckflinging [1939], after *flick* [1447] and †*flask* [a1300], also from *fl-* /fl/
flexitarian [1998], after *vegetarian* [1842]
Floodgate [1978], from *-gate*
FLOTUS [1983], after *POTUS* [1895]
fluorescence [1852], after *opalescence* [1805]
FOFL [2011], after *ROFL* [2008]
foodaholic [1965], from *-(a)holic*
forgivemequick [1939], after *forgetmenot* [?1533]
foxnapping [2001], from *-napping*
Frankenfruit [1992], from *Franken-*
Frankenplant [1998], from *Franken-*
Frankenscience [1999], from *Franken-*
frappuccino [n.d.], after *mochaccino* [1963] and from *-ccino*
fraufrau [1939], after *froufrou* [1870]
freshalicious [2008], from *-licious*

Frexit [2015], after *Brexit* [2012] and *Grexit* [2012]
fruitarian [1893], after *vegetarian* [1842]
fruitlicious [2011], from *-licious*
fruitoholic [2000s], from *-(a)holic*
fundraise-aholic [2000s], from *-(a)holic*
fun-tastic [1939], from *-tastic*
G10 [1980], after *G20* [1972]
G2B [2000], after *B2B* [1994]
G2C [2000], after *G2B* [2000]
G5 [1977], after *G20* [1972]
G7 [1986], after *G20* [1972]
G8 [1988], after *G20* [1972]
gaily [a1375], after *daily* [OE]
Galwegian [1870], after *Norwegian* [1607]
gambl(e)aholic [1990s], from *-(a)holic*
gameaholic [2011], from *-(a)holic*
gardenbot [2010], from *-bot*
gardenesque [1838], after *picturesque* [1705]
Gategate [1987], from *-gate*
Generation Y-ers [1996], after *Generation X-ers* [1989]
geomorphic [1835], after *anthropomorphic* [1827]
Germexit [2015], after *Brexit* [2012] and *Grexit* [2012]
gigaflop [1976] ← *gigaflops*, after *megaflop–megaflops*
gilf [2003], after *Milf* [1992]
gimongous [2008], after *ginormous* [1948]
girl(-)cott [1884], after *boycott* [1880]
girl Friday [1928], after *man Friday* [a1809]
glitterati [1956], from *-erati*
glitzy [1966], from *gl-* /gl/
gnosible [1939], after *visible* [a1340] and *audible* [1483]
golfaholic [1971], from *-(a)holic*
golfnapping [1998], from *-napping*
Googleware [2006], from *-ware*
Gorillagram [1979], from *-gram*
gosling-napping [2008], from *-napping*
gradeflation [n.d.], after *stagflation* [1965]
grandmother [1483], after *grandfather* [1424]
granny-sitter [1985], from *-sitter*
graymail/greymail [1978], after *blackmail* [1927]

gray market/grey market [1934], after black market [1727]
grayout/greyout [1942], after black-out [1929]
greyth [2006], after stealth [a1325] and †blowth [1602]
GRID [n.d.], after AIDS [1982]
groomzilla [2003], from -zilla
groovalicious [2002], from -licious
groundhog-napping [1993], from -napping
growthaholic [1990s], from -(a)holic
GST [1985], after VAT [1966]
guppie [1984], after yuppie [1984]
hackathon [2013], from -(a)thon
haircuttee [2001], after haircutter [1694]
half-caf [1990], after decaf [1956]
Halloweenorexia [2011], from -orexia
handie-talkie [1943], after walkie-talkie [1939]
handlist [1848], after handbook [OE]
hands-on [1905], after hands-off [1860]
hangunder [2004], after hangover [1904]
headandheelless [1939], after headless [OE]
headwork [1642], after handwork [OE]
helfalittle [1939], from -little
hen fest [1963], from -fest
herbaholic [2000s], from -(a)holic
herstory [1970], after history [OE]
hetero [1933], after homo [1929]
high-touch [1980], after hi-tech [1972]
Hinglish [1967], after Spanglish [1954]
hispanocentric [1985], after Eurocentric [1927]
histo-tainment [2009], from -tainment
hit lady [1980], after hit man [1970]
hoardaholic [2000s], from -(a)holic
Hollywoodgate [1978], from -gate
home-based [1920], from -based
homesweepers [1939], after home keeper(s) [1574]
hominine [1957], after canine [1623] and asinine [1624]
hoopaholic [1990s], from -(a)holic
Hooterlicious [2008], from -licious
hot war [1947], after cold war [1945]
househusband [1858], after housewife [c1225]
house-sitter [1949], from -sitter
hulercise [2008], after sexercise [1942]
husbanded [a1616], after fathered [1608]

hypercorrection [1934], after overcorrection [1911]
idealty [1635], after royalty [c1405]
idiolect [1948], from -lect
illatinate [1922], after illiterate [1556]
ill-balanced [1864], after well-balanced [a1616]
IMBY [1989], after NIMBY [1980]
immergreen [1939], after evergreen [1555] (see G. Immergrün)
IMO [1989], after IMHO [1984]
implode [1881], after explode [1624]
infobot [1986], from info- and -bot
info-poor [1990], from info-
info-rich [1990], from info-
infostructure [1974], after infrastructure [1927]
infotainment [1980], from info- and -tainment
inlaw [1607], after outlaw [OE]
inner space [1958], after outer space [1842]
insultainment [2007], from -tainment
intrapreneur [1978], after entrepreneur [1852]
introjection [1866], after interjection [c1430]
Irangate [1986], from -gate
Irelexit [2015], after Brexit [2012] and Grexit [2012]
irritainment [1993], from -tainment
Japlish [1960], after Spanglish [1954]
jazzerati [2000], from -erati
Jewdom [1869], after Christendom [c893]
jogathon [n.d.], from -(a)thon
joygasm [2005], after wargasm [2004]
juice-aholic [2000s], from -(a)holic
junk-fooditis [n.d.], from -itis
kenalittle [1939], from -little
kicksalittle [1939], from -little
kidflick [1977], after kidvid [1955] (cf. chick flick [1988])
kid-friendly [2013], after child-friendly [1977]
kissogram [1982], from -gram
kiteboard [1998], after snowboard [1983]
kiteboarding [1996], after kitesurfing [1995]
knee-mail [2000], after e-mail [1979]
knowbot [1988], from -bot
Koreagate [1976], from -gate
krautfurter [1949], after Frankfurter [1877]
ladily [c1400], after lordly [a1000]

languageless [1609], after *speechless* [a1000] and *tongueless* [1447]
lase [1962] ← *laser* [1960], after *mix–mixer*
laughgasm [2008], after *wargasm* [2004]
laughing post [1810], after *laughing stock* [?1518]
†*laughing stake* [1630], after *laughing stock* [?1518]
leafmeal [c1880], after †*flock-meal* [c893] and †*drop-meal* [c1000]
LeBron-a-thon [2008], from *-(a)thon*
leglet [1836], after *bracelet* [1438]
lesbo [1940], after *homo* [1929]
lexplotation [2009], after *sexploitation* [1924]
LIFO [1968], after *FIFO* [1966]
liger [1938], after *tigon* [1927]
likemelong [1939], after *lookmelittle* [1939]
ling-ling [2008], after *bling-bling* [1999]
linguistician [1895], after *logician* [1382] and *mathematician* [?a1475]
linner [2010], after *brunch* [1896]
liquor-fest [1952], from *-fest*
little bang [2000], after *big bang* [1949]
little-endian [1980], after *big-endian* [1980]
lovephobia [2008], from *-phobia*
lovescape [1876], from *-scape*
low-rise [1948], after *high-rise* [1908]
LQTM [2006], after *LOL* [1989]
lunarscape [1965], from *-scape*
lunger [1939], after *diener* and *souper* [1939]
lupper [2013], after *brunch* [1896] and *linner* [2010]
Luxembexit [2015], after *Brexit* [2012] and *Grexit* [2012]
Mads [2006], after *Wags* [2002]
magrific [2008], from *-rific*
malltitude [1939], after *alltitude* [1939]
malware [1990], from *-ware*
mandocello [1914], after *violoncello* [1724]
mankini [21st cent.], after *bikini* [1947]
manorexia [2008], from *-orexia*
manself [1880], after *himself* [eOE]
mariculture [1867], from *-culture*
martyr-master [1876], after *martyr-maid* [1854]
MARV [1973], after *MIRV* [1966]

matteroffactness [1939], after *toomuchness* [1875]
May-hope [a1889], after *May-mess* [1867]
meatarian [n.d.], after *vegetarian* [1842]
me-lancer [2009], after *freelancer* [1924]
membrance [1939], after *substance* [c1330] and *semblance* [a1325]
Merkozy [2011], after *Bennifer* [2008] and *Brangelina* [2011]
mesolect [1971], from *-lect*
metaverse [1994], after *nulliverse* [1847] and *multiverse* [1895]
microbirg [1939], after *macroborg* [1939]
middlebrow [1924], after *highbrow* [1898] and *lowbrow* [1901]
midnitini [2008], after *vodkatini* [1955]
milkaholic [1955], from *-(a)holic*
mill [1786], after *cent* [1782]
millentury [1939], after *century* [1533]
minification [1894], after *magnification* [1672]
minoritarian [1930], after *majoritarian* [1918]
MIRF [2006], after *MILF* [1992]
mix'n'match [1960], after *pick'n'mix* [1958]
mobot [1959], from *-bot*
mockumentary [1965], from *-umentary*
modelizer [1996], after *womanizer* [1822]
mom-zilla [2005], from *-zilla*
Monicagate [1998], from *-gate*
monokini [1964], after *bikini* [1947]
monologue [c1550], after *dialogue* [c1450]
moon night [1939], after *sundawn* [1835] (see G. *Mondnacht*)
moonquake [1906], after *earthquake* [c1325]
moonscape [1907], from *-scape*
morpheme [1896], after *phoneme* [1879]
Morseaholic [1990s], from *-(a)holic*
Motorama [1947], from *-orama*
motormouth [1955], after *big mouth* [1834]
mouse potato [1994], after *couch potato* [1979]
mouse race [2003], after *rat race* [1937]
moviethon [1954], from *-(a)thon*
mRNA [1961], after *RNA* [1942]
museless [1644], after *museful* [1597]
myrioscope [a1877], after *kaleidoscope*
narrowcast [1978], after *broadcast* [1921]
n-ary [1964], after *binary* [1796]

nastygram [1991], from -gram
nationwide [1891], after worldwide [1602]
naturopathy [1901], from -pathy
neargasm [2014], after wargasm [2004]
neatnik [1959], after beatnik [1958]
necklet [1641], after bracelet [1438]
negatrip [2001], after negademand [1995]
netiquette [1982], from net
netizen [1984], from net
Netscape [1988], from net
nettitis [1999], from net and -itis
New Right [1966], after New Left [1955]
newsaholic [1979], from -(a)holic
newsy-tainment [2010], from -tainment
nieceof-his-in-law [1939], from -in-law
niftabulous [2008], after fantabulous [1959]
niggerati [1932], from -(er)ati
nilky [n.d.], after yuppie [1984] and dinkie/-y [1986]
nimf-ism [2006], after Nimbyism [1986]
NOMG [2013], after OMG [1917]
non-execution [1883], after non-resistance [1748]
nounspeak [n.d.], from -speak
nowanights [1672], after nowadays [?1387]
numerati [n.d.], from -erati
nutarian [1909], after vegetarian [1842]
nymphoholic [1960s], from -(a)holic
Obamaism [1996], after Nixonism [1952], Reaganism [1966], etc.
Obamanomics [2010], from -nomics
obround [1668], after oblong [?a1425]
oceanarium [1938], after aquarium [1853]
octant [1672], after quadrant [?c1400]
offline [1969], after online [1950]
oilflation [n.d.], after stagflation [1965]
oldster [1818], after youngster [1608]
omnivore [1871], after carnivore [1854] and herbivore [1854]
opinio-tainment [2013], from -tainment
Orchids [2006], after Dinkies [1986]
orienteer [1965], after mountaineer [1599]
orthorexia [1997], from -orexia
osteotomy [1740], after anatomy [?1541] and myotomy [1676]
otherhood [2014], after motherhood [a1500]
outgoing [1622], after incoming [1596]

outro [1967], after intro [1923]
outscape [1868], after inscape [1868]
out-tray [1943], after in-tray [1941]
overlusting [1939], after everlasting [1340]
†overthought [1883], after underthought [1602]
owloholic [1990s], from -(a)holic
oxnapping [1952], from -napping
party gamercise [2008], after sexercise [1942]
†passion-plunged [1876], after †passion-pastured [c1865]
PDA-athon [2008], from -(a)thon
peegasm [2011], after wargasm [2004]
pelfalittle [1939], from -little
performancethon [n.d.], from -(a)thon
petnapping [1967], from -napping
petroholic [1970s], from -(a)holic
pet sitter [1976], from -sitter
PHOBAR [2010], after fubar [1944]
pianothon [1963], from -(a)thon
Pigs/Piigs [2010], after Brics [2010]
Pink Friday [2008], after Black Friday [1961]
pisciculture [1807], from -culture
pizzaholic [1990s], from -(a)holic
planar [1850], after linear [1656]
pointful [1925], after pointless [c1330]
politerati [n.d.], from -erati
politisoap [2005], after docusoap [1979]
polychrome [1801], after monochrome [1662]
pomiculture [1852], from -culture
poolathon [1963], from -(a)thon
pooper-scooper [1956], after super-duper [1938]
popaholic [1990s], from -(a)holic
poptastic [1992], from -tastic
Portugexit [2015], after Brexit [2012] and Grexit [2012]
post-tax [1934], after pre-tax [1917]
potaholic [1980s], from -(a)holic
Potteresque [2008], after Browningesque [1880], Audenesque [1940], etc.
potty mouth [1969], after foulmouth [1692]
pouralittle [1939], from -little
powwow [1939], after peewee [1793]
preealittle [1939], from -little
preggo [1951], after lesbo [1940]
prepone [1913], after postpone [1496]

prespond [2003], after *respond* [a1538]
prettiful [2008], uncertain origin, perhaps after *beautiful* [c1443]
prooflisten [2000], after *proofread* [1845]
pulsar [1968], after *quasar* [1964]
punkadelic [1980], from *-adelic*
pupnapping [1934], from *-napping*
quadrilogue [c1475], after *dialogue* [c1450]
quartessence [1936], after *quintessence* [c1460]
quickgold [1877], after *quicksilver* [eOE]
Rafi [1965], after *Mapai* [1941]
rage-aholic [2008], from *-(a)holic*
Rambogram [1985], from *-gram*
rampsman [1859], after *cracksman* [1819]
ready-to-read [1887], after *ready-to-perish* [1855]
reality-based [1946], from *-based*
red-out [1942], after *black-out* [1929]
redthorn [1939], after *whitethorn* [a1300]
refoliate [1932], after *defoliate* [1793]
remnance [1939], after *substance* [c1330] and *semblance* [a1325]
rice-white [1856], after *snow-white* [c1000]
Rightism [1934], after *Leftism* [1920]
rightist [1937], after *leftist* [1924]
riverrun [1927], after *riverbed* [1781]
riverscape [1854], from *-scape*
rock'n'roll [1938], after *rhythm'n'blues* [1933]
rockerati [1900], from *-erati*
rockerthon [1963], from *-(a)thon*
rockumentary [1969], from *-umentary*
ROFC [2011], after *ROFL* [2008]
ROFL [2002], after *LOL* [1989]
romekeepers [1939], after *home keeper(s)* [1574]
roofscape [1891], from *-scape*
rose-flake [1876], after *snowflake* [1734]
rosy-pale [1862], after *rosy bright* [1725], *rosy-purple* [1770], etc.
rotavate [1950] ← *Rotavator* [1936], after *act–actor*
rRNA [1962], after *RNA* [1942]
runalittle [1939], from *-little*
Russocentric [1985], after *Eurocentric* [1927]
saltaholic [1980s], from *-(a)holic*
sandboard [1992], after *snowboard* [1983]

sangry [2013], after *slungry* [2011]
sargasm [2008], after *wargasm* [2004]
SBF [1978], after *SWF* [1976] and *SJF* [1975]
SBM [1979], after *SWM* [1974] and *SJM* [1975]
scandilific [2008], from *-rific*
scarific [2008], from *-rific*
schlockumentary [2005], from *-umentary*
sea-foodetarian [n.d.], after *vegetarian* [1842]
seaquake [1680], after *earthquake* [c1325]
sea(-)scape [1799], from *-scape*
self-being [1587], after *well-being* [1561]
selfyeast [a1889], after *self-want* [1669] and *self-taste* [1880]
severalittle [1939], from *-little*
sexaholic [1994], from *-(a)holic*
she-being [1881], after *she-man* [1640]
ship-napping [1988], from *-napping*
shockaholic [1970s], from *-(a)holic*
shockumentary [1970], from *-umentary*
shockvertising [2008], after *shockumentary* [1970]
shopaholic [1984], from *-(a)holic*
shopercise [2008], after *sexercise* [1942]
shopgasm [2008], after *wargasm* [2004]
shore-based [1927], from *-based*
show-woman [1820], after *showman* [1742]
shrimpfurter [n.d.], after *Frankfurter* [1877]
simplexity [1849], after *complexity* [1734]
Singlish [1972/1984], after *Spanglish* [1954]
sister-in-love [1939], after *sister-in-law* [c1440]
sitter-napping [2007], from *-napping*
skyscape [1817], from *-scape*
skytel [n.d.], after *motel* [1925]
sleep-in [1965], after *sit-in* [1937]
sloggering [1876], from *sl-* /sl/
slow food [1974], after *fast food* [1954]
slumpflation [1974], after *stagflation* [1965]
snarkaholic [2000s], from *-(a)holic*
snowfari [n.d.], after *safari* [1859]
snubbee [2000], after *snubber* [1861]
soapumentary [n.d.], from *-umentary*
soccerati [n.d.], from *-erati*
sociolect [1963], from *-lect*
SOD [2011], after *OCD* [1977]
softcore [1966], after *hardcore* [1936]

software [1960], after *hardware* [1947] (see -*ware*)
song-fowl [1877], after *song-bird* [1774] or *sweet-fowl* [1877]
sonny [1850], after *sissy* [1846]
sordid [1597] ← *sordor* [1823], after *squalid–squalor*
spacespeak [1963], from -*speak*
spattee [1926], after *puttee* [1882]
speako [2001], after *typo* [1892]
spendaholic [1982], from -(*a*)*holic*
Spexit [2015], after *Brexit* [2012] and *Grexit* [2012]
spin-dry [1927], after *kiln-dry* [c1540] and *sun-dry* [1695]
spinnar [n.d.], after *quasar* [1964]
splendorific [2008], from -*rific*
spokesman [1519], after *craftsman* [1362]
sport-o-tainment [2012], from -*tainment*
sportsaholic [1990s], from -(*a*)*holic*
sportspeak [1968], from -*speak*
Sprung Rhythm [1877], after Running Rhythm [a1887], uncertain
spyware [1983], from -*ware*
squillionaire [1979], after *zillionaire* [1946]
star-eyed [1646], after *star-wise* [1608]
stateful [1989], after *stateless* [1987]
stateswoman [1611], after *statesman* [1592]
STI [1991], after *STD* [1974]
strawberry-breasted [1878], after *strawberry-coloured* [1688] and *strawberry-like* [1862]
straw pool [1995], after *straw-man* [1594]
striporama [1954], from -(*o*)*rama*
strippergram [1983], from -*gram*
Stupid [2010], after *Brics* [2010]
sugarholic [1955], from -(*a*)*holic*
suicide [1732], after *autocide* [1635]
superbulous [2008], after *fantabulous* [1959]
Sweetie-licious [2012], from -*licious*
sweetmannered [1887], after *good-mannered* [1715]
swimathon [n.d.], from -(*a*)*thon*
Swirllgasm [2008], after *wargasm* [2004]
tablet potato [2010], after *mouse potato* [1994]
talkaholic [1980s], from -(*a*)*holic*

talkie [1913], after *movie* [1909]
tanarexia [2008], from -*orexia*
tangry [2013], after *slungry* [2011]
TARFUN [2004], after *SNAFU* [1942]
tauntless [c1879], after *dauntless* [a1616]
taxflation [1976], after *stagflation* [1965]
telecast [1940], after *broadcast* [1921]
ternary [1860], after *binary* [1796]
textercise [2008], after *sexercise* [1942]
tilf [2003], after *Milf* [1992]
tiratini [2008], after *vodkatini* [1955]
tobaccoholic [1954], from -(*a*)*holic*
to eBay [2004] ← *eBay* [1995], after *to Google–Google*, *to Skype–Skype*, etc.
to email [1983] ← *email* [1979], after *to mail–mail*
top-down [1969], after *bottom-up* [1954]
to pen [1904] ← *pen* [c1325], after *to pine–pine*
to Skype [2003] ← *Skype* [2003], after *to Google–Google*
to wait-list [1960] ← *wait-list* [1897], after *to list–list*
townscape [1867], from -*scape*
travelogue [1903], after *dialogue* [c1450]
tree-sitter [1989], from -*sitter*
treeware [1993], from -*ware*
trialogue [1532], after *dialogue* [c1450]
trikini [1967], after *bikini* [1947]
trit [2008], after *bit* [1948]
tRNA [1962], after *RNA* [1942]
try-hard [1922], after *die-hard* [1844]
ttys [2004], after *ttyl* [2002]
turkeyfurter [n.d.], after *Frankfurter* [1877]
turkeywich [1943], after *sandwich* [1762]
tween [1946], after *teen* [1818]
Twetiquette [2011], after *netiquette* [1982]
twiceaday out [1939], after *onceaday in* [1939]
Twitterati [n.d.], from -*erati*
Twitterverse [2013], after *nulliverse* [1847] and *multiverse* [1895]
Twittizen [2010], after *netizen* [1984]
two-phase [1909], after *three-phase* [1892]
typeless [2004], after *speechless* [a1000]
ultimogeniture [1882], after *primogeniture* [a1500]

umbrance [1939], after *substance* [c1330] and *semblance* [a1325]
unary [1931], after *binary* [1796]
underkill [1964], after *overkill* [1957]
underloaded [1898], after *overloaded* [1671]
underwhelm [1956], after *overwhelm* [?a1400]
unmarsed [1964], after *unearthed* [1513]
upcycle [1994], after *recycle* [1925]
urbanscape [1958], from *-scape*
usie [2014], after *selfie* [2002]
uxpiration [1939], after *muertification* [1939]
van-tastic [1975], from *-tastic*
vapourware [1993], from *-ware*
vauntless [c1879], after *dauntless* [a1616]
VBL [2010], after *VPL* [1977]
VBS [2010], after *VBL* [2010]
vegeburger [1945], from *-burger*
viticulture [1872], from *-culture*
VJ–veejay [1982], after *DJ–deejay* [1946]
vlog [2005], after *blog* [1999]
vlogger [2013], after *vlog* [2005]
VOCD [2009], after *OCD* [1977]
vodkaholic [1960s], from *-(a)holic*
VPOTUS [2008], after *POTUS* [1895]
VTD [2008], after *STD* [1974]
wake-and-bake [2008], after *shake-and-bake* [1981]
walkie-lookie [1946], after *walkie-talkie* [1939]
walk-in [1943], after *drive-in* [1930]
Walsingham Way [c1878], after *Milky Way* [c1450]
WAN [1983], after *LAN* [1981]
warm-down [1951], after *warm-up* [1915]
†*waste-time* [1609], after *pastime* [1490]
water-quake [1577], after *earthquake* [c1325]
waterscape [1826], from *-scape*
wealth [a1300], after *health* [c1000]
weavealicious [2007], from *-licious*
Webinar [1997], from *Web*
Webliography [1995], from *Web*
Webmaster [1993], from *Web*
Webmistress [1994], from *Web*
Webzine [1994], from *Web*
weeknight [1782], after *weekday* [OE]
whinealittle [1939], from *-little*
whipping-stock [1615], after *laughing stock* [?1518]
whiteboard [1883], after *blackboard* [1739]
white coffee [1873], after *black coffee* [1818]
whitelist [1842], after *blacklist* [1624]
whitemail [1861], after *blackmail* [1852]
white market [1943], after *black market* [1727]
white money [2012], after *black money* [1939]
Whitewatergate [1993], from *-gate*
whomp [1926], from *-ump* /ʌmp/
whoompf [1958], from *-ump* /ʌmp/
whump [1915], from *-ump* /ʌmp/
wi-fi [1999], after *hi-fi* [1935]
wilf [2003], after *Milf* [1992]
wipealittle [1939], from *-little*
womanity [1836], after *humanity* [a1425]
wonderific [2011], from *-rific*
Woodenhenge [1927], after *Stonehenge* [1297]
woopie [1986], after *yuppie* [1984]
work-hard [1922], after *die-hard* [1844]
workitis [n.d.], from *-itis*
wristlet [1851], after *bracelet* [1438]
writeo [2008], after *typo* [1892]
writerly [1957], after *painterly* [a1586]
wumph [1913], from *-ump* /ʌmp/
yester-afternoon [1806], from *yester-*
yesterclass [2008], from *yester-*
yestereve [1604], from *yester-*
yestermorning [1654–5], from *yester-*
yester-tempest [1888], from *yester-*
yester-week [1839], from *yester-*
yester-year [1870], from *yester-*
yettie [2000], after *yuppie* [1984]
YIMBY [1988], after *NIMBY* [1980]
Yuffers [2006], after *Yuppies* [1984]
yummy [2014], after *yuppie* [1984]
ZIFT [1986], after *GIFT* [1984]
Z-list [1979], after *A-list* [1890]

Subject index

A

Acceptability 11, 13, 16, 20, 21, 111, 193–212, 217
– Average Degree of Acceptability in Context (ADAC) 11, 201, 206–211
– Average Degree of Acceptability in Isolation (ADAI) 11, 201–206, 208–211
Acronym (formation) 7, 8, 18, 39, 59, 65, 82, 84, 99, 100, 114, 121–123, 132, 136, 142–144, 146, 152, 155, 157–159, 161–163, 165, 167, 198, 199, 202, 205, 213
Actual word 7–9, 12, 15, 21, 53, 64, 104, 129, 133
Analogical compound 5, 15, 34, 136, 180
Analogical extension 5, 14, 37
Analogical levelling 14, 17, 37
Analogical Modeling (AM) 2, 3, 15, 16
Analogy
– anaphoric 11, 13, 21, 29, 94, 96, 119, 120, 123, 127, 130, 142–144, 147, 152, 160, 165, 168, 169, 175, 178, 184, 186, 191, 197, 198, 208–210, 217–219
– cataphoric 11, 13, 21, 29, 94–96, 120, 123, 127, 130, 142, 143, 147, 152, 161, 165, 168, 169, 176, 178, 184, 189, 191, 197, 198, 208, 211, 217–219
– endophoric 11, 94, 123, 142, 143, 152, 154, 169, 191, 192, 197, 200, 219
– exophoric 11, 121, 127, 128, 130, 144, 152, 170, 177, 186, 191, 192, 197, 200, 208, 211, 218, 219
– false 61
– four-part 17, 37
– journalistic 11, 19, 24, 57, 111, 154–170, 172, 195, 211, 218, 219
– juvenile 18, 19, 32, 111, 132–153, 170, 172, 211, 218
– literary/poetic 19–21, 33, 111, 171–192, 211, 218, 219
– local (vs. extended) 3, 5, 6, 16, 48, 64
– orthographic 67, 83, 88, 144, 164, 167, 218
– pure surface 12, 17, 64, 65, 113, 133, 155, 156, 191, 194, 214
– specialised 18, 21, 24, 32, 82, 92, 111–131, 141, 163, 170, 172, 211, 218
– sporadic 17, 21, 62
– surface 5–9, 11–13, 15, 16, 18, 20, 25, 27, 41, 44, 48, 49, 51, 52, 56–58, 64–68, 73, 74, 100, 101, 103, 104, 113–115, 128, 134, 169, 173, 175, 177, 180, 181, 184, 187, 190, 193, 194, 197, 199, 200, 202, 203, 205, 209, 210, 215, 217
– surface (with enlargement) 11, 65, 144
– surface (with no Invariable Part) 13, 65, 66
– surface (with reduction) 65, 87
– surface (with rule) 7, 12, 66–68, 115, 128, 133, 136, 152, 155, 173, 181, 190, 191, 214
– via schema 6, 9, 12, 13, 16, 41, 44, 55, 58, 68–73, 106, 116, 128, 137, 139, 152, 158, 169, 174, 182, 190, 191, 194, 197, 199, 205, 215, 218
Anomaly 86, 165, 172, 180, 183, 191, 219
Association 9, 11, 13, 15, 57, 59, 66, 85, 90, 93, 104–106, 113, 141–143, 145, 170, 198, 200, 204, 205, 208, 211, 215, 217
Audacity 183, 189, 191, 192, 219
Availability 53, 54, 190, 215

B

Back-formation 8, 14, 47, 49, 63, 64, 79, 86, 90, 213
Blend(ing) 4, 7, 8, 11, 14–16, 19, 20, 27, 33, 34, 39, 40, 45, 46, 48–51, 54–59, 64, 66, 67, 70–74, 82, 84, 87, 98, 109, 110, 117, 132, 134–136, 141, 154, 157, 161, 167, 169, 173, 183, 184, 188, 192, 194, 198, 213, 214, 216

C

Calque 99
Clipping 27, 39, 59, 60, 66, 82, 90, 98–100, 136, 157, 162, 167, 213

Subject index

Combining form 8, 16, 27, 38–47, 49–51, 59, 61, 62, 65, 68–71, 73, 74, 79, 81, 82, 84, 89, 90, 93, 97, 112, 114, 117, 119, 120, 122, 128, 131, 133, 134, 138, 139, 141, 146, 151, 152, 154–156, 158, 164, 167, 169, 174, 186, 187, 190, 194, 200, 202–204, 213, 214, 216, 218
– abbreviated 39, 97, 138, 146, 151, 153
– neoclassical 68, 81, 84, 97, 120, 153, 186
– secreted 10, 39, 72, 97, 138, 146, 151, 153, 216
Compound(ing) 4, 5, 7–9, 12, 15, 20, 23, 28, 29, 33, 34, 36, 38–40, 46, 48, 49, 51, 55, 58–60, 63, 66, 67, 69, 71, 73, 79–84, 89, 91, 93, 97–102, 104, 106–110, 115, 116, 121, 136, 137, 139, 146, 151, 152, 156, 160, 162, 164, 171–175, 177–180, 182–184, 186, 188, 190–192, 194, 213, 214, 216, 219
– creative 29, 49
– family 83, 106–109, 178
– loose 33, 34, 60, 194, 202, 213
– poetic 19, 26, 30, 171
– strict 33
Conjunct phrase 99
Constraint 2, 21, 22, 53, 86
Construction Morphology 5, 6
Contamination 14, 20, 109, 110
Conversion 97, 103, 156, 181, 203
Creativity 4, 8, 14, 15, 17, 28, 47–51, 111, 144, 151, 172, 189, 218
– rule-creating 50

D

Derivation 3, 4, 8, 9, 12, 15, 20, 24, 30, 36, 37, 40, 46, 49, 54, 59, 60, 67, 71, 72, 79–81, 83, 84, 89, 96, 100, 104, 115, 118, 146, 151, 152, 156, 167, 169, 172, 173, 175, 180–182, 188–192, 194, 202, 213, 214, 218, 219

E

Establishment 11, 16, 18, 24, 28, 46, 126, 133, 146, 180, 190, 218

F

Family Size effect 28, 55, 108
First language acquisition (L1) 3, 15, 18, 19, 37, 90, 100–104, 152
Folk-etymology 15, 47, 62–64, 181
Frequency 21, 28, 31, 42–47, 50, 54, 55, 69, 72, 75, 78, 107, 113, 122, 123, 126, 129, 146, 147, 165
– normalised 45, 74, 122, 123, 151
– token 18, 30, 45, 54, 55, 74, 122, 123, 151
– type 18, 54, 55, 108

G

Generalisation 5, 18, 21, 37, 40, 46, 70, 94, 101, 212, 219
– over- 3, 16, 103
Generalized Context Model 2
Generative (Grammar/Theory) 1, 2, 5, 14, 17, 52
Grammaticalisation 38

I

Inflection 1, 3–5, 8, 15, 17, 36, 38, 58, 64, 68, 100, 101, 173, 183
Initialism 11, 65, 82, 85, 99, 113, 119, 121–123, 136, 139, 142, 146, 152, 162, 167, 213
Institutionalisation 11, 18, 24, 25, 27, 28, 213, 216
Invariable Part (IP) 10, 13, 21, 48, 59, 60, 65, 66, 87–89, 93, 135, 152, 190, 200, 204, 210, 214, 215, 217

L

Language change 3, 12, 14, 17, 36–47, 105
Language learning 3, 4, 11, 101
Language prediction 2, 7, 12, 16, 18
Lexical expansion 12, 14, 26, 73, 74
Lexical innovation 12, 17, 153
Lexicalisation 11, 16, 24, 38, 39

M

Memory-based Language Processing (MBLP) 3, 55
Model (word) 2, 3, 6–13, 16, 18, 19, 21, 24, 27, 31, 32, 34, 37, 39–41, 44, 47–

49, 52–61, 63–70, 74, 78–132, 134–137, 140–145, 147–149, 152–154, 156–171, 173–193, 197–200, 203–215, 217–219
– complex-word 62, 80–83, 136
– concrete (vs. abstract) 52, 56, 64–68, 74, 103, 214
– extra-grammatical 80, 82, 83, 162
– grammatical 21, 80, 81
– marginal 81, 82
– simplex-word 61, 79, 80
Monoreferentiality 18, 120, 130
Morphological change 14, 17, 21, 36, 39, 45, 61
Morphological grammar
  see Morphology, grammatical
Morphological regularisation 18, 20, 37
Morphology 4–6, 14, 16, 36, 37, 52, 101
– derivational 3, 9
– expressive 50
– extra-grammatical 7, 10, 12, 60, 74, 113, 136, 169, 213
– grammatical 7, 12, 60, 74, 169, 213
– inflectional 3–5, 15, 36, 58, 68, 100
– marginal 8, 10, 12, 46, 60, 71, 74, 81, 84, 213
– paradigmatic 14, 36, 214
– ungrammatical 12, 169, 213
Morphosyntactic change 14, 38
Multi-lexical word 33, 34

N
Natural Morphology 7, 15, 16, 46
Neighbourhood
– phonological 61, 197, 200, 204, 210, 217
  see also Similarity, phonological
– semantic 197, 200, 203, 210, 217
  see also Similarity, semantic
Neologism 5, 9, 11, 16–19, 21, 23–28, 30, 33–35, 52, 69, 74, 90, 108, 113, 126, 129, 132, 133, 145, 152, 154, 155, 162, 163, 171, 172, 174, 178–180, 182, 188–191, 213, 218, 219
– past 26, 27, 35
– present-day 27, 35
– recent 26, 27, 35, 129, 133, 155

Neosemanticism 18, 104, 133
New word 5–12, 16, 18–21, 23–35, 40–42, 49, 54, 58, 59, 64, 68, 69, 74, 79, 92, 100–102, 104–106, 112, 113, 123–127, 132, 133, 139, 145–149, 151, 152, 158, 165–167, 172, 173, 177, 190, 193, 197, 199, 200, 210–213, 215, 216, 218
New word-formation criteria 17, 28, 29
Nonce word/formation 11, 19, 20, 23–28, 30, 35, 47, 50, 62, 69–71, 79, 85, 92, 97, 132, 134, 144, 145, 152, 153, 155, 157–159, 162, 164, 167, 172, 173, 176, 179, 180, 182–184, 186, 189–191, 213, 218, 219

O
Occasionalism 5, 11, 16, 17, 20, 21, 24–27, 29, 33, 35, 55, 83, 111, 133, 149, 152–155, 162, 163, 167, 169, 171, 172, 178, 180, 182, 183, 185, 187–191, 213, 219
Optimality Theory 7, 53

P
Paradigm 3, 5, 17, 28, 36, 37, 58, 173, 183
Phonaestheme 84, 85, 87, 134, 181, 182, 213
Poetic licence 19, 26, 182
Potential/Possible word 21, 53, 59, 197
Predictability 6, 36, 41, 51, 111, 118, 182, 215, 216
Prefix 38, 59, 62, 65, 79, 80, 84, 88, 89, 92, 96, 109, 116, 164, 175, 176, 214
Productivity 4, 8, 9, 14–16, 28, 40, 41, 45, 47–51, 54, 64, 71, 73, 74, 136, 153, 158, 216
– full 17
– partial 17
Profitability 40, 41, 47, 54, 55, 190
Proportion 1–3, 7, 8, 10, 13, 14, 17, 37, 41, 47–49, 56–58, 61–63, 65, 66, 100, 103, 214, 215
Psycholinguistic experiments/studies 2, 3, 15, 18, 37, 100–111

R
Reanalysis 14, 16, 23, 47, 61–64, 79–81, 88, 103, 114, 133, 136, 155, 164, 170,

181, 193, 194, 199, 202, 205, 207, 213, 214
Recoverability (model's) 9, 12, 47, 48, 54–56, 59, 61, 119, 130, 152, 162, 169, 175, 186, 192, 200, 204, 208–210, 214, 215, 217
Reduplication/Reduplicative 20, 84, 134, 136, 146, 181, 189, 192, 213
Reinterpretation 61, 79, 82, 86, 136, 164, 181
    see also Reanalysis
Resegmentation 61, 164, 214
Root(-)creation/Root coinage 24
Rule 1–17, 21, 25, 28, 36, 47–54, 65–68, 71, 73, 74, 83, 85, 100–103, 115, 118, 128, 132, 133, 151, 155, 172, 175, 182, 190, 191, 193, 194, 197, 199, 213, 214, 216, 217

S

Schema 4–6, 8, 9, 12, 15–18, 27, 28, 32, 41, 44–46, 49, 55, 58, 68, 71, 74, 87, 97, 106, 112, 116, 117, 120, 128, 130, 133, 134, 137, 139, 141, 143, 152, 154, 155, 158, 161, 169, 174, 182, 190, 191, 193, 194, 197, 199, 200, 202–205, 209–211, 214–219
    see also Analogy via schema
Second language acquisition (L2) 4
Secreted affix 40, 46, 69, 74, 216
Series 8, 12, 13, 27, 40, 41, 47, 49, 58, 68–74, 81, 87, 97, 100, 112, 113, 118, 120, 123, 132, 137, 141, 153, 158, 161, 164, 170, 174, 179, 182, 191, 193, 197, 203, 204, 208, 210, 212, 214–217, 219
Similarity 2, 9, 13, 18, 36, 37, 46, 47, 56, 58–61, 64, 66, 83, 86, 93, 118, 129, 135, 163, 165, 174, 197, 209, 215
– morpho(syn)tactic 9, 13, 40, 48, 58, 65, 66, 86, 87, 89, 90, 93, 120, 121, 134, 141, 143–145, 161, 176, 184–186, 215
– phonological 4, 9, 13, 40, 48, 56, 83, 86–89, 93, 120, 121, 134, 137, 141, 143, 145, 176, 183, 185, 204, 205, 210, 215, 217

– semantic 4, 9, 13, 40, 65, 66, 80, 86, 90–94, 120, 134, 137, 184–186, 204, 205, 210, 215, 217
Slang(uage) 4, 9, 19, 21, 24, 30, 31, 34, 41, 65, 69, 73, 82, 87, 89, 91, 96, 99, 107, 110, 117, 132–134, 136, 137, 139, 140, 142–146, 152, 183, 188, 191, 195, 214, 216
Speech errors 3, 4, 15, 17, 18, 37, 100, 109–111
Splinter 8, 16, 34, 45, 46, 48, 49, 51, 55, 59, 71–74, 82, 87, 98, 117, 119, 128, 135–138, 151, 152, 158, 167, 169, 194, 198, 200, 204, 208, 214, 216, 218
Substitution 1, 23, 29, 41, 63, 65, 70, 79, 111, 134, 161, 181, 189, 190, 215
– paradigmatic 1, 14, 68, 214
Suffix 8, 12, 28, 38, 40, 46, 53, 54, 56, 57, 59, 63, 64, 66, 67, 69, 71–74, 80, 82, 83, 85, 86, 88–90, 92, 93, 96, 98, 99, 101, 102, 109, 116, 118, 120, 129, 140, 157, 167, 172, 173, 176, 181–183, 185, 188, 190, 203, 204, 214, 216, 218

T

Target (word) 9–14, 16, 18, 19, 21, 27, 32, 37, 39, 40, 45, 54–61, 63–66, 68, 69, 74, 81, 83–94, 96–100, 105, 106, 108, 112, 113, 115–122, 128, 130–132, 136, 137, 140–145, 152, 154, 157–164, 168, 170, 171, 174–178, 183–187, 192, 195, 197–211, 213–215, 217–219
– extra-grammatical 84, 85, 169, 193, 194, 197, 202, 207, 210, 217
– grammatical 83, 84, 193, 194, 197, 202, 209, 210, 217
– marginal 84, 197
– ungrammatical 21, 85, 86, 140, 169, 193, 194, 197, 202, 203, 207, 209–211, 217
Tilburg Memory Based Learner (TiMBL) 2

V

Variable Part (VP) 1, 10, 13, 32, 59, 60, 65, 68, 79, 87–93, 105, 106, 143, 152, 190, 200, 203, 204, 210, 214, 215, 217

Virtual word   21, 53
Vocabulary expansion
   see Lexical expansion

W
Word creation   49
Word family   12, 13, 28, 55, 68, 70, 74, 83, 100, 106, 109, 175, 178, 179, 182, 190, 191, 193, 197, 210, 212, 217
Word-formation (Theory)   4–12, 14–19, 21, 22, 28, 29, 32, 34–111, 116, 118, 120, 128, 129, 132, 134, 141, 151, 152, 155, 156, 169, 170, 172, 173, 175, 191, 213–215, 217–219
Word play/Pun   17, 47, 63, 111, 145, 154, 187

Z
Zero-derivation
   see Conversion

www.ingramcontent.com/pod-product-compliance
Lightning Source LLC
Chambersburg PA
CBHW030618230426
43661CB00053B/2042